Islands and Empires: Western Impact

on the Pacific and East Asia

Europe and the World
in the Age of Expansion

edited by Boyd C. Shafer

ISLANDS
AND
EMPIRES
Western Impact
on the Pacific and
East Asia

by
Ernest S. Dodge

UNIVERSITY OF MINNESOTA PRESS □ MINNEAPOLIS

Library of Congress Catalog Card Number 75-46179

ISBN 0-8166-0788-5

086236   MY 1 8 '82

Europe and the World
in the Age of Expansion

SPONSORS

Department of History of the
University of Minnesota

James Ford Bell Library of the
University of Minnesota Library

SUPPORTING FOUNDATIONS

Northwest Area Foundation
(formerly Louis W. and Maud Hill
Family Foundation), St. Paul

James Ford Bell Foundation,
Minneapolis

ADVISORY COUNCIL

EDITORS

FOR BETSY

Editor's Foreword

The expansion of Europe since the thirteenth century has had profound influences on peoples throughout the world. Encircling the globe, the expansion changed men's lives and goals and became one of the decisive movements in the history of mankind.

This series of ten volumes explores the nature and impact of the expansion. It attempts not so much to go over once more the familiar themes of "Gold, Glory, and the Gospel," as to describe, on the basis of new questions and interpretations, what appears to have happened insofar as modern historical scholarship can determine.

No work or works on so large a topic can include everything that happened or be definitive. This series, as it proceeds, emphasizes the discoveries, the explorations, and the territorial expansion of Europeans, the relationships between the colonized and the colonizers, the effects of the expansion on Asians, Africans, Americans, Indians, and the various "islanders," the emergence into nationhood and world history of many peoples that Europeans had known little or nothing about, and, to a lesser extent, the effects of the expansion on Europe.

The use of the word *discoveries*, of course, reveals European (and American) provincialism. The "new" lands were undiscovered only in the sense that they were unknown to Europeans. Peoples with developed cultures and civilizations already had long inhabited most of the huge areas to which Europeans sailed and over which they came to exercise their power and influence. Nevertheless, the political, economic, and social expansion that came with and after the discoveries affected the daily lives, the modes of producing and sharing, the ways of governing, the customs, and the values of peoples everywhere. Whatever their state of development, the expansion also brought, as is well known, tensions, conflicts, and much injustice. Perhaps most important in our own times, it led throughout the developing world to the rise of nationalism, to reform and revolt, and to demands (now largely realized) for national self-determination.

The early volumes in the series, naturally, stress the discoveries and explorations. The later emphasize the growing commercial and political involvements, the founding of new or different societies in the "new" worlds, the emergence of different varieties of nations and states in the often old and established societies of Asia, Africa, and the Americas, and the changes in the governmental structures and responsibilities of the European imperial nations.

The practices, ideas, and values the Europeans introduced continue, in differing ways and differing environments, not only to exist but to have consequences. But in the territorial sense the age of European expansion is over. Therefore the sponsors of this undertaking believe this is a propitious time to prepare and publish this multivolumed study. The era now appears in new perspective and new and more objective statements can be made about it. At the same time, its realities are still with us and we may now be able to understand intangibles that in the future could be overlooked.

The works in process, even though they number ten, cover only what the authors (and editors) consider to be important aspects of the expansion. Each of the authors had to confront vast masses of material and make choices in what he should include. Inevitably, subjects and details are omitted that some readers will think should have been covered. Inevitably, too, readers will note some duplication. This arises in large part because each author has been free, within the general themes of the series, to write his own book on the geographical area and chronological period allotted to him. Each author, as might be expected, has believed it necessary to give attention to the background of his topic and has also looked a bit ahead; hence he has touched upon the time periods of the immediately preceding and following volumes. This means that each of the studies can be read independently, without constant reference to the others. The books are being published as they are completed and will not appear in their originally planned order.

The authors have generally followed a pattern for spelling, capitalization, and other details of style set by the University of Minnesota Press in the interests of consistency and clarity. In accordance with the wishes of the Press and current usage, and after prolonged discussion, we have used the word *black* instead of *Negro* (except in quotations). For the most part American usages in spelling have been observed. The last is sometimes difficult for historians who must be concerned with the different spellings, especially of place names and proper nouns, at different times and in different languages. To help readers the authors have, in consequence, at times added the original (or the present) spelling of a name when identification might otherwise be difficult.

The discussions that led to this series began in 1964 during meetings of the Advisory Committee of the James Ford Bell Library at the University of Minnesota, a library particularly interested in exploration and discovery. Members of the university's Department of History and the University of Minnesota Press, and others, including the present editor, joined in the discussions. Then, after the promise of generous subsidies from the Bell Foundation of Minneapolis and the Northwest Area Foundation (formerly the Hill Family Foundation) of St. Paul, the project began to take form under the editorship of the distinguished historian Herbert Heaton. An Advisory Council of six scholars was appointed as the work began. Professor Heaton, who had agreed to serve as editor for three years, did most of the early planning and selected three authors. Professor Boyd C. Shafer of Macalester College (now at the University of Arizona) succeeded him in 1967. He selected eight authors and did further planning. He has been in constant touch with all the authors, doing preliminary editing in consultation with them, reading their drafts, and making suggestions. The Press editors, as is usual at the University of Minnesota Press, have made valuable contributions at all stages. Between Professor Shafer and the authors—from England, Canada, New Zealand, and the United States—there have been voluminous and amicable as well as critical exchanges. But it must be repeated, each author has been free to write his own work within the general scope of the series.

Ernest Dodge, the author of this book, volume VII in the series, is Director of the Peabody Museum in Salem, Massachusetts, and has been with that noted marine museum since 1931. For many years he has been primarily interested in historical and ethnological studies of the Pacific and its peoples. Pursuing this interest he has traveled and studied widely, in North America, western Europe, New Zealand, Hong Kong, Macao, the Soviet Union, and many island groups of the Pacific such as the Fiji and Hawaiian. Since 1943 he has published six books, including *New England and the South Seas* (1965) and *Beyond the Capes: Pacific Explorations from Captain Cook to the* Challenger, *1776-1887* (1971).

The present book, in his words, "is an attempt to assess the effect of Western impact on the peoples of the Pacific islands and East Asia. The effect on the two areas was very different because, on the one hand, contact was with uncivilized peoples in a neolithic stage of culture, while on the other hand, Westerners came up against sophisticated civilizations more ancient and mature than their own. The lesser reverse influence of Pacific and Asiatic culture is also touched upon. This is the first time this subject has ever been considered combining the Pacific and Eastern Asia."

Boyd C. Shafer

University of Arizona

Preface

The subject of this volume almost automatically divided itself into two parts, the Pacific islands and East Asia, presenting very different problems. Europeans had been unaware of the Pacific island natives until they first entered the Pacific Ocean and made contact with the Stone Age civilization. However, Europeans had been aware of the East Asian mainland at least since Roman times and probably earlier; when the first European visitors trudged overland the long, Asiatic miles to reach Pacific shores, they found not Stone Age man but the courts of great civilizations in all their oriental splendor. In the Pacific the impact was cataclysmic; in East Asia it was cushioned and subtle, absorbed with hardly the blink of an eye.

This is an account of the massive impact of occidental civilization upon the Pacific islands and the Far East (principally China and Japan) and its effect upon the island peoples and the Eastern civilizations. Whereas for the Pacific it was necessary to do a brief historical survey of the area from the time of discovery to the present, this was not necessary nor desirable for the Far East, where European impact was but one aspect of Chinese and Japanese history.

To cover this enormous sweep in one volume it was necessary to simplify and condense, eschewing many tantalizing byways and details. Nevertheless I have tried to mention all the important aspects and to present a well-rounded and meaningful picture. More detail on European activities in India, Southeast Asia, and Indonesia might seem desirable, but these areas are covered by other volumes in this series.

The literature on the Pacific is enormous and it would be tedious to list every book and article referred to. I have confined references, in both the chapter notes and Bibliography, to those works (primarily books) found most useful. Only a few articles of exceptional usefulness are mentioned. Many of the books, particularly the recent ones, contain extensive bibliographies which will lead the reader to many details of the European effect on the South Seas that were impossible to dwell on here. Although the literature on the Far East is equally extensive, I referred only to those works that concerned European-Asiatic contacts and mutual influences.

The writing of this book was made easier by the assistance of many friends. Without the quiet retreats provided by Pen (Francis Lee) and Catharine Higginson, Andrew and Ruth Oliver, Dwight and Mary Robinson, and Walter Muir and Jane Whitehill, the task would have been far more difficult. It would have been difficult, too, without the helpful library staffs of the Peabody Museum of Salem and the Boston Athenaeum, especially the Peabody's Barbara Edkins, librarian, Jean Mills, assistant librarian, and Markham W. Sexton, photographer. Francis B. Lothrup read much of the manuscript and gave me excellent advice. My secretaries Page Welch and Jane Key expertly typed the manuscript and provided much good editorial service. Throughout, Boyd Shafer, the editor of the series, kept the goad in so deep that there was rarely a moment when I was not writing that I did not have a guilty conscience. The long days of research and writing were made a joy by my dear wife Betsy who gave me constant encouragement and comfort and maintained the serene surroundings so necessary for bringing a work of this kind to its fruition. One would like to say that others are responsible for any errors or misinterpretations, but alas, that cannot be — the responsibility rests here and here alone.

Ernest S. Dodge

Salem, Massachusetts
March 18, 1976

Contents

Illustrations Follow page 144

List of Maps

Part I

The Pacific Islands

CHAPTER 1

The Great New Ocean

The day was November 28, 1520, when Ferdinand Magellan emerged from the narrow strait near the tip of South America that now bears his name. Ever since Columbus discovered that it was not plain open-water sailing all the way from Spain to Cathay, European mariners had probed the American continent to find a passage to Far Eastern riches. Now a passage was found, and in front of Magellan stretched the limitless Great South Sea that Balboa had seen from the Panama Isthmus seven years before. Provisions were short. The largest ship, the *Santo Antonio*, had deserted in the strait; but for Magellan there was no turning back—Spain lay far behind. He had no idea of the vastness of the new ocean. Blue leagues beckoned him, the Humboldt Current helped him north along the western Patagonian shore, fair trade winds sped him westerly when he set his course for the Spice Islands.

Magellan did not know, had no way of knowing, how many islands dotted that enormous ocean. He knew the location of the Moluccas—the Spice Islands—and by setting a northwesterly course for them he missed all of the major island groups where his scurvy-sick crew could have been cured with fresh fruits and vegetables, and supplies could have been replenished. For three months the trade winds pushed the four ships westward. Only two uninhabited atolls, called by Magellan the Unfortunate Islands, interrupted the constant blue of sky and water. The weather was fair and the ocean got its new name—the Pacific. But the men were starving. The moldy bread, the sawdust, the ship's rats, the very leather from the yards had been consumed before Guam and Rota in the Marianas were sighted and the scurvy-ridden crew rejoiced.

Magellan stayed at Guam three days. Long enough to get fresh supplies and time enough for the first encounter between Europeans and Pacific islanders. Antonio Pigafetta, chronicler of the expedition, relates what happened:

the captain-general wished to approach the largest of these three islands to replenish his provisions. But it was not possible, for the people of those islands entered the ships and robbed us so that we could not protect ourselves from them. And when we wished to strike and take in the sails so as to land, they stole very quickly the small boat called a skiff which was fastened to the poop of the captain's ship. At which he being very angry, went ashore with forty armed men. And burning some forty or fifty houses with several boats and killing seven men of the said island, they recovered their skiff.[1]

This was the first, but regrettably not the last, case of European overreaction in the Pacific world. Looking back from our late twentieth century viewpoint, one questions, Who were the people who behaved like savages? Was it the Chamorros or the Europeans? When preparations were being made to go ashore on this punitive expedition, sailors "begged us, if we killed man or woman, to bring them their entrails. For immediately they would be healed. And know that whenever we wounded any of those people with a shaft which entered their body, they looked at it and then marvelously drew it out and so soon died forthwith."

As Magellan sailed away the islanders gave a skillful demonstration of their seamanship, sailing their swift outrigger canoes around the ships, offering fresh fish for trade, and throwing stones to vent their frustrated wrath. The Spaniards marveled at these canoes in which "there is no difference between the stern and the bow [and] which are like dolphins jumping from wave to wave."[2] But they were apparently less understanding of grief-stricken passengers in the canoes, for "we saw some of those women weeping and tearing their hair, and I believe it was for love of those whom we had killed."[3]

Pigafetta left a brief description of the life and manners of the people of Guam and concluded that "they worship nothing."

Magellan named these islands the Ladrones—the Islands of Thieves—and, supplied with fresh fruit, vegetables, and water, sailed, on March 9, 1521, for the Philippines.

A week later he arrived off Samar in the southern Philipines, but anchored at the uninhabited island of Suluan for safety, water, and rest. On the eighteenth he had visitors who brought him fruit, fish, and palm wine and to whom he gave red caps and trinkets in return. After over a week's recuperation, during which their new friends returned, Magellan sailed about among the islands.

At Limasawa, off the southern tip of Leyte, he was visited by a "king" named Raia [Raja] Siaiu with two long boats. Friendly pleasantries were exchanged between the Malays and Spaniards. Through him Magellan met the king's brother Raia Calambu—king of part of eastern Mindanao—a handsome man wearing large gold earrings and a gold-handled dagger and who dined from golden vessels. The Spaniards were impressed.

The two kings were equally impressed by Easter Sunday mass and sent a gift of two dead pigs for the solemn occasion. They also kissed the cross and imitated the Spaniards throughout the ceremony, which pleased Magellan very much. The mass was followed by entertainment and expressions of mutual friendliness. Magellan gave the kings a large cross, which he set up on the top of the highest mountain, and assured them it would prevent their being harmed by any tempest. He also unwisely offered to avenge the kings on any of their enemies, but the Malays said that while there were two islands inhabited by enemies the season was wrong for a punitive expedition.

Magellan continued exploring the maze of islands, visited Limasawa, and sailed on to Cebu. Once reassured that the artillery salute did him honor, the raja of Cebu demanded tribute which he said he always collected from the Chinese. Magellan refused. After the raja had consulted with his council, he peacefully agreed to exchange presents and he and Magellan were made blood brothers. When the king sent a delegation to the ship with peace offerings, Magellan received them seated in a red velvet chair and, after delivering some gratuitous instruction in Christianity, offered to have his priest baptize anyone who wished to become a Christian. He pointed out that those who became Christians would receive preferential treatment from him. Thereupon the men of the delegation all cried out together that they wished to be Christians of their own free will. This was fine until they were told they could no longer have intercourse with their women, who were still heathen. They demurred, saying they would have to think that one over, and all hands settled down to a collation. Magellan distributed presents and sent a yellow and violet Turkish robe, a red cap, pieces of glass, a silver dish, and gilt cups to the king.

Pigafetta was one of the party that carried the presents to the raja. The short, fat, betel-chewing monarch was found seated on a mat in front of his palace comfortably dressed in a loincloth and making a meal of turtle eggs and four jars of palm wine. The Spaniards dressed him in the robe and cap and kissed the other presents as they were presented. The raja, pleased, shared his turtle eggs and wine, presented his four musical daughters, and insisted that the visitors dance with three comely naked girls to the music of Chinese brass tambourines. The visitors needed little urging.

After two days' trading of iron for gold and other goods, Magellan set up a platform in the village square. On Sunday, April 14, 1521, the raja and the captain (who was clad in white) sat in red and violet velvet chairs on the platform while the raja was converted (certainly superficially) to Christianity. When the raja said that some of his men objected to becoming Christians, Magellan summoned the reluctant ones and simply told them that if they did not become Christians they would be killed and their possessions confiscated for their chief. There was not a single holdout. A cross was erected in the village square, and Magellan bestowed Spanish names on all the converts. After mass and dinner the queen and forty ladies were baptized. Thereafter business became brisk and eight hundred more men, women, and children became Christians before the day was out. During the next week mass was said on shore daily and the entire island was baptized, except for one village which was burned flat because the people refused to obey. Magellan wrapped up his religious victory by having the raja swear fealty to the king of Spain and ordering all of the idols on the island destroyed.

On April 26 it was learned that the raja of the nearby island of Mactan, though a subject of the raja of Cebu, refused to do homage to the king of Spain. Magellan, refusing help from the raja of Cebu, left at midnight with sixty heavily armed men, arrived at Mactan three hours before daylight, and sent word to the rebel raja that if he agreed to pay tribute and obey the king of Spain all would be well. He refused. At daybreak Magellan, with forty-nine men, waded some distance to shore through shallow, coral-strewn water and attacked a force of over a thousand. The ensuing fight became more furious when the Spaniards began burning houses. Magellan, after receiving a poison arrow through his leg, ordered his men to retreat. During the next hour of fierce fighting he was pierced by lances and killed, and, writes Pigafetta, thus "they slew our mirror, our light, our comfort, and our true guide." The Spaniards were unable to retrieve Magellan's body. On May 1, back at Cebu, twenty-four men sent ashore to receive presents from the Christian raja were all massacred. The Spaniards then sailed away, leaving one poor devil crying for rescue on the beach.

After Magellan's death on April 27, 1521, the expedition disintegrated, but one of his ships, the *Victoria*, arrived at Seville on September 8, 1522, completing the first circumnavigation of the world.

With Magellan's Pacific crossing, one of the world's greatest navigational feats, the true extent of that ocean was realized. But something else had happened. The first contact with Pacific islanders had taken place. Furthermore most of the features of contact between Europeans and island populations during the next three centuries of discovery and exploration were evident in Magellan's visits to Guam and the Philippines. The initial trade for necessities was followed by insensitivity to killing people and burning their houses (forms of brutality long practiced by Europeans upon each other). Then came the mixing into local politics, and the conversion to Christianity—first by persuasion and afterward by force. As had happened elsewhere in the world, Europeans in the name of their monarchs took possession of lands already possessed by contented people. The stealing (by European standards) of property brought death to islanders for whom the foreigners' belongings were fair game. The sight of gold evoked avaricious gleams in Spanish eyes. The first outriggers were seen; the first spears collected; the first blood shed. The long impact of European civilization upon the Pacific that has continued for over four hundred years began on March 2, 1521, at Guam.

The people of Guam were the earliest of many islanders to see the white-sailed Western ships approach their shores. The location of other Pacific islands and their inhabitants was not yet known. It would be revealed slowly over the next three centuries.

Pacific Geography

But there was now some notion of Pacific distances. The size of the greatest geographical feature of the world is awesome to contemplate. The Pacific world is different from any other oceanic area. It is bigger, with an area of over 68,000,000 square miles. It is more homogeneous, more diverse; the water bluer, the swells longer, the trade winds steadier, the typhoons more monstrous. The Pacific extends 9,000 miles from South America to the Moluccas, and even farther from Bering Strait to the Antarctic Circle. No other sea can match its ocean deeps of more than six miles. Some of the world's greatest mountain ranges lie beneath its surface. Its borders and many of its islands are restless. Most of the world's active volcanoes ring its shores and mark its islands. Islands appear. Islands vanish. It is the most unstable third of the earth's surface.

The geography of the Pacific—the number and variety of the islands, the great distances, the variations of climate—all had a profound effect on the indigenous peoples. They also affected the kind of European contact that these peoples experienced.

Magellan saw only three or four of the thousands of islands that stretch from Indonesia across the western and central Pacific to lonely Easter Island, lying over 2,000 miles from the South American coast. These islands, depending on their origins, are of four geological types. There are barren islands, reefs awash, islands of surpassing loveliness—and loneliness. The islands of Melanesia, from New Guinea to the Fijis, are, like the great islands of Indonesia, continental. This means they are distinguished by rock formations, together with volcanic intrusions, characteristic of continental geological construction. It does not necessarily mean that islands of this type were once part of a continent; although this is indeed the case with the large Indonesian islands. Australia and New Zealand are independently continental lands.

In contrast the origin of all the large islands of the well-known groups of the central Pacific is volcanic. In Hawaii, Samoa, and Tonga the volcanoes are still or recently active. In others, the Marquesas and the Society Islands, for example, the long dead cones thrust eroded peaks thousands of feet above the ocean, while their bases rest hundreds of fathoms below the surface. The ancient mountains are weathered into jagged peaks. Their waterfalls drop hundreds of feet down green cliffs. Lush valleys reaching into the interior and mountain-enclosed harbors combine to produce some of the loveliest and most spectacular landscapes in the world.

But it is the low, palm-fringed, coral atolls that are the most numerous of all the island types. They owe their existence to the work of Madraporaria polyps over hundreds of thousands of years. Coral atolls are confined to shallow tropical waters, for the polyps cannot live in waters colder than 68° Fahrenheit or deeper than twenty-four fathoms. Thus, in warm shallow water the polyps have precipitated their lime skeletons on the tops of old volcanic cones or land ridges until they reach the surface and form lovely rings of white coral surrounding lagoons that are the traditional romantic isles of the South Seas.

Rarest of all the types of Oceanic lands are the raised coral islands. These are former coral atolls that have been thrust hundreds of feet into the air by some cataclysmic event or by a series of uplifts in the geological past. The largest island of this kind is Niue. Others are Ocean, Nauru, and Makatéa, whose forbidding, pockmarked cliffs rise three hundred feet above the water. The ancient lagoon of raised islands forms a rough depressed center, difficult to traverse, covered with rough dry coral heads and unsuspected pits overgrown with sparse but concealing vegetation—a wonderful and primeval landscape. Beyond the narrow shelf that surrounds a raised island at the cliff's foot, the shores drop precipitously to unfathomable depths.

Ecology of the Islands

Each of the four types of islands found in the Pacific varies from the others in the quality of its soil and the variety of its plant life. Hence there is a wide range in the ability to support a human population. Some islands have a dense population, for food grows easily and in quantity. Other islands, owing to lack of water, scarcity of food plants, or exposure to hurricanes, are unfit for human occupation. These same variables also influence the kind, quantity, and quality of island products for European export. This, in turn, influenced the amount and involvement of European contact.

Continental islands have the greatest topographical variety. Their richer soil contains more minerals than the volcanic or coral soils. Heavy forests, grasslands, and swamps flourish. The flora is more varied and luxuriant; frequently but not always, depending on other factors, it supports a larger and more diversified fauna. Ample food, rich resources for home use and surplus for export, ensure continental islands as capable of supporting large populations.

Volcanic islands, too, have good soil capable of growing nearly all kinds of plants. But the earth, formed by erosion from the ancient mountains, lacks minerals. Nevertheless, important food plants such as bananas, plantains, and other fruits, coconuts, breadfruit, taro, and sweet potatoes grow easily and abundantly. There are dry and wet lands, streams, and wide variation in rainfall. Most volcanic islands (the Marquesas are a notable exception) are surrounded by fringing reefs lying close inshore or barrier reefs at varying distances offshore. Sometimes there are combinations of both kinds of reefs. The lagoons, sheltered by the barriers, and the reefs themselves are a copious source of fish and other sea life that enriches the food supply.

Coral islands are blessed with the same abundant sea life but, compared to the high islands, their soil is poor. Vegetation is more limited in variety and is usually poorer in quality. Some coral islands are meager in soil and destitute of water. Seabirds and land crabs may be their only inhabitants. So low are some in the hurricane belt that they have been totally inundated by these fierce tropical storms. Occasional atolls are lush and rich, and the breadfruit and coconuts, the bananas and taro, grow with an abandon that produces a South Sea Eden.

Raised coral islands are equally poor in vegetation and, lacking reefs, do not have the seafood supplies of the others. Though poor in resources and, except for Niue, skimpy in inhabitants, raised coral islands, because of the millions of tons of phosphate produced, have, in recent historic times, had an economic importance far beyond their size, number, and population.

In general, throughout the Pacific, food plants grow with little effort except on the poorer coral atolls. Combined with fish, an ample and balanced food supply supported large populations and produced surpluses on most of the high islands at the time of discovery. The larder was further increased by pigs, dogs, and chickens. Some fortunate islands had all three creatures, others only one or two.

Pacific Peoples

When Magellan crossed the Pacific nearly every one of the hundreds of Oceanic islands capable of supporting a human population was inhabited. Following his meeting with Pacific islanders at Guam, nearly every island in the Pacific was to have its European visitors by the end of the next three hundred years.

Who were these people soon to feel the impact of European civilization—soon to trade, to be killed, to be exploited, to be converted, and, perhaps, to be assimilated. The earlier explorers usually referred to them as "Indians." Later, scientists divided them into three convenient geographical groups called Melanesians, Micronesians, and Polynesians. This familiar grouping is still a convenience, but, as Oliver quite correctly points out, it is no longer "possible to draw sharp boundaries among the Pacific Island populations."[4]

The Pacific is bounded on the east by the solid barrier of the Americas. To the north it is closed where Alaska and Siberia nearly meet at Bering Strait. South lies the Antarctic ice. The western boundary is fragmented. From the Kamchatka Peninsula, series of islands—the Kuriles, Japan, Taiwan, the Philippines, and Indonesia—form the western boundary south to Australia. The island worlds which concern us lie in the western and central Pacific. In general, below the equator, the islands tend to get smaller and farther apart from west to east. North of the equator they are all small except for Hawaii.

The large continental islands that stretch from New Guinea to the Fijis (including the Bismarck Archipelago, Solomons, Santa Cruz Islands, New Hebrides, New Caledonia, and lesser groups) are inhabited largely by Malayo-Polynesian-speaking, Oceanic negroid Melanesians. Their many languages are not mutually understandable. In the interior of New Guinea and some of the nearby larger islands dwell frizzle-haired Papuans, speaking many languages not even belonging to the same family and as distinct from each other as they are from all other languages. At the eastern end of Melanesia a Polynesian influence from Samoa and Tonga is strong, and Polynesians inhabit many so-called small island "outliers" within Melanesia, including Rennell, Bellona, Tikopia, and Ontong Java, to mention some of the best known.

Other small islands on the northern Melanesian fringe have Micronesian inhabitants.

There is little uniformity in Melanesian culture, although pigs, dogs, and chickens are common to all of these islands and agriculture is substantially universal. The Melanesian coast dwellers are expert sailors and fishermen. Their excellent, large outrigger canoes and skilled seamanship enable them, in some areas, to carry on regular trades where the specialties of different islands are exchanged. Melanesians range in color from dark brown to black, the bow and arrow is the common weapon to all, and the polished stone adz the universal tool. Otherwise language and customs vary widely.

Mostly north of the equator, roughly parallel with Melanesia, lie the Micronesian islands. They cover an almost equal number of degrees of longitude but, compared with their neighbors to the south, their land area is infinitesimal. The principal groups are the Palau Islands in the extreme west, the Carolines, the Marianas (formerly called the Ladrones) to the north, the Marshalls (divided into the Radak and Ralik chains), and the Gilberts reaching south of the equator toward central Polynesia. Most of the islands of Micronesia are coral atolls, but Guam and others in the Marianas, as well as Yap, Truk, Ponape, and Kusaie in the Carolines are high islands.

The light brown people of Micronesia are culturally more uniform than Melanesians. Their languages, too, belong to the Malayo-Polynesian family. Farming is frugal. Skilled seamanship is evident in the handling of swift-sailing outrigger canoes. In the absence of basalt, coral stone is used for adzes and poi pounders. Copra made from the ubiquitous coconut and phosphate from Ocean Island are the principal export products. But the far-flung islands provide an infinite number of lagoons and sheltered anchorages where whalers could lie in safety and find the supplies and refreshment so constantly needed in that hazardous and monotonous occupation.

Closely related to the Micronesians are the Polynesians inhabiting the vast so-called triangle of the central Pacific. The late Sir Peter H. Buck first bestowed this term upon the geographical area of Polynesia.[5] He described it as a triangle with its three apexes at the Hawaiian Islands, New Zealand, and Easter Island. This is still a convenient and well-established concept in the literature, but it can be misleading. It is too cut and dried, too neat, too pat. However, there is no question that within this area all are Polynesians dwelling on the South Sea islands of romance. The principal island groups of Polynesia are the Hawaiian, Marquesas, Society, Tuamotu, Cook, Austral, Samoa, Tonga, and Ellice islands.

The cultural and linguistic homogeneity of Polynesia is greater than that of either of the other two island areas. Dialectical differences only distinguish the language among island groups. The people range from light to dark brown in color, have handsome features, large stature, and wavy black hair. Pottery was lacking at the time of discovery but has been found archaeologically in Tonga, Samoa, and the Marquesas. The common containers were wooden bowls and gourds. The bow and arrow were lacking for warfare—clubs and spears being the universal weapons throughout the area, although in some islands slings were used. Theirs was a Neolithic, polished stone culture, sophisticated in religion, splendid in seamanship, and with a rich unwritten literature. The islands of Polynesia, with their salubrious climate, amiable people, and absence of malaria, were the first to receive massive European impact. They became the home of beachcombers and expatriates, the source of anthropological controversy, the subject of hundreds of novels and travel books. They have been more industriously studied by scholars over a longer period of time than any other Pacific islands.

The completion of the circumnavigation by the *Victoria* showed to the European world that there was a watery third of the earth's surface still unknown. A region of infinite island worlds now awaited Western discovery. But it was a region already discovered and inhabited almost to its physical limits by several racially mixed peoples. Throughout the island world the ocean was a highway, the outrigger or double canoe the means of settlement and trade. In one sense it was a stable population; in another sense a fluid one. Climate, geography, and food resources dictated a culture as specialized in its most extreme aspects on coral islands, if not as rigorous, as that of the Eskimo. On high rich islands life was easy.

Following Magellan into this island world of enormous oceanic distances came the discoverers and explorers of the European maritime nations, and in their wake came traders, missionaries, naval expeditions, and settlers. It is the sustained impact of the constantly accelerating European contact with and effect on Pacific cultures that concerns us here.

CHAPTER 2

The Claw of the Devil

The age of primary Pacific discovery, from Magellan to Cook, was an age of wonder for the Western discoverers; it also opened a world of wonder for island dwellers whose cultures and life-styles, once matured, had remained unchanged for many centuries. The towering masts and white sails, the pale, often cruel, people, the cannon's thunder, had the same effect on the simple fishermen and agriculturists of isolated Pacific islands that an invasion of heroic gods might have had descending from Mount Olympus into Grecian vineyards and olive groves. It was a traumatic experience—an experience to which various islanders reacted in different ways.

Spaniards, Melanesians, and Marquesans

Four major Pacific island groups were exposed to the Christian arrogance of the Spaniards before another European nationality entered the Pacific. Three of these—the Solomons, New Hebrides, and Santa Cruz Islands—were Melanesian; the Marquesas Islands were Polynesian.

Alvaro de Mendaña sailed with two ships from Callao, Peru, on November 19, 1567, to find the islands that, according to the Incas, produced silver and gold and lay in the ocean to the west. The Spaniards correlated this tale with *Terra Australis Incognita*—the Great Southern Continent. Rather amazingly, Mendaña crossed the entire central Pacific and sighted only one small coral atoll in the Ellice group, where people "who were naked and mulattoes" came out in canoes but kept a safe distance from the ships. Later he was nearly wrecked on a reef near Ontong Java, and finally, on February 7, he sighted Santa Isabel Island in the central Solomons.

13

Almost at once the ships, working their way with difficulty through the coral heads, were surrounded by graceful canoes "shaped like a crescent moon." The Solomon Islanders were allowed on board and took everything not nailed down. Once safely anchored at Estrella Bay, as they named it, the Spaniards landed, erected a cross, and prayed while the Franciscan priests accompanying the expedition raised their voices in a hymn. That same afternoon timber was felled to build a small brigantine for coastal exploration. The Spaniards were not wasting time.

But the adventurers needed food and this was promised by Bilebanara, the local chief, who came aboard the next day—a splendidly painted figure in plumed headdress, shell bracelets, and boar's tusk necklace. Bilebanara, however, could not actually spare enough food to feed the hungry sailors and stalled for time. Besides, he had his own problems. He was at war with a neighboring chief named Meta, and as always the headhunting canoes of other islands were ranging and raiding the coast.

The Spaniards remained in the Solomons for over six months, and during that time many of the features of Magellan's contacts at Guam and the Philippines appeared all over again. The priests counseled Mendaña against using force to obtain food, but the commander's subordinates were not so restrained. Bilebanara, probably unable to supply the amount of food required, retired into the interior for two days. Mendaña, his supplies getting lower by the day, sent a party under Pedro Sarmiento, an able but unattractive, cruel, and remorseless man, into the interior to scale the range of hills and see what lay beyond. The Spaniards reached the foothills, but after a wet, uncomfortable, sleepless night spent firing harquebuses to frighten off the Melanesians, the party returned to the beach guided by Bilebanara and his uncle Havi. Pressed by increasing numbers of Solomon Islanders, Sarmiento seized the chiefs as hostages. Bilebanara escaped. In the scuffle several natives were wounded and Havi was presented to an irritated Mendaña, who released him. His people, overjoyed at this as well as at the return of some of their liberated property, at last brought much needed food.

In early March a second attempt was made to scale Santa Isabel's interior range. This time the camp master, Pedro Ortega, was sent with sixty men. After an easy march through the country of Bilebanara's momentarily friendly tribe, Ortega found himself among hostile inland people. High in the hills he seized a chief as hostage. The natives fled and the Spaniards spent the night in their village. The next day they reached the top of the range and with disappointment saw the ocean on the other side of the island, rather than the interior reaches of a rich continent on which they had hoped to gaze. The hos-

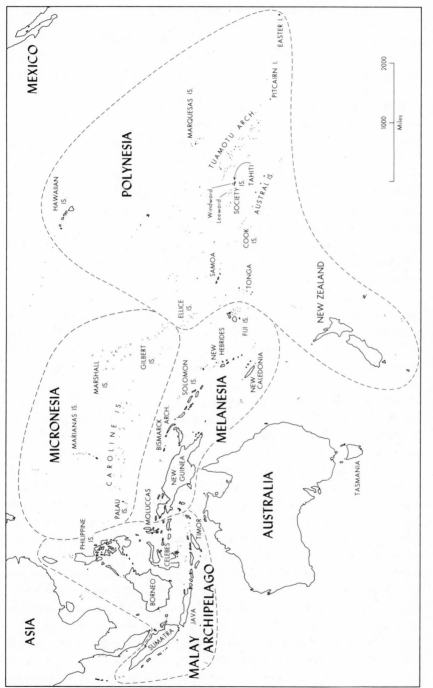

Islands of the Pacific

tage, after drawing a map in the sand confirming the insularity of the land, escaped the following night. On return march the party was heavily attacked. Villages were burned on the way; one native was killed and two soldiers were wounded.

A friendship offering was made a few days later when a fleet of war canoes swept into the bay and the horrified Spaniards were offered the quarter of a boy surrounded by taro. Much to the disgust of the islanders, the strange visitors buried the human fragment. The uncomprehending natives withdrew to a small island to enjoy a cannibal feast. Later Bilebanara and Mendaña successfully exchanged hostages and the Spanish captain offered to aid the chief against his enemy Meta. When the time came the Spanish went alone and captured Meta's son and three others. Bilebanara, although disappointed that Mendaña would not turn the prisoners over to him, was nevertheless pleased with the result. He gave Mendaña some of his fine ornaments and promised to become a subject of the king of Spain.

Completion of the little brigantine, named the *Santiago*, gave the Spaniards the means to explore the shallow, coral-strewn island coasts. They sighted Malaita and at Guadalcanal, which was annexed for Spain, they killed two of a party of stone-throwing natives. As they returned to the ships, they circumnavigated Isabel and obtained some pigs in ransom for captured canoes.

Mendaña moved his ships on May 12 to the good anchorage of Puerto de la Cruz discovered at Guadalcanal. In raising a cross on a high hill two more natives (one a chief) were killed. Coconuts and chickens were obtained and a party sent inland to look for gold, of which not a trace was found. Food was still short, though the land was under cultivation and dotted with villages. The headhunting people of Guadalcanal were understandably unfriendly. They were also interested in the strangers whose deadly weapons and incessant demands for food made them by turns curious, fearful, and hostile. A foraging shore party, led by Sarmiento, stripped a village of its food, but narrowly escaped massacre. A watering party on Ascension Day was not so lucky and nine of its ten men were killed. Mendaña, upon going ashore, was greeted by natives waving his companions' dismembered limbs. Once again Sarmiento was turned loose and burned every village he could reach. A canoe load of natives bringing a pig, probably as a peace offering, were slaughtered by the Spaniards and their quartered bodies laid about at the scene of the massacre of the watering party. So violence begat violence and retribution.

The brigantine, commanded by Hernando Henriquez, a more humane man than most of his fellow officers, continued explorations along the coast of

Guadalcanal, alwa‚s seeking more food. Crossing over to Malaita, the Spaniards were momentarily delighted by golden club heads, only to discover that they were made of iron pyrites. At the island of Ulawa the natives, at first friendly, sang the night away with the Spaniards and then pursued them to their boat. As a result twelve men and women were killed and several canoes were taken. Finally at San Cristobal fever stopped all exploration and Henriquez returned to the ships.

Mendaña, now preparing for his return voyage, took his ships over to San Cristobal for careening to clean their bottoms. There initially friendly relations with the inhabitants became hostile after the Spaniards took by force enough food to fill one of their vessels and burned the village. Cleaning the ships was carried on from a shore camp under the constant surveillance of a ring of Solomon Islanders who killed the only Spaniard who attempted to pass through their lines. After filling water casks and capturing four Solomon Islanders (in addition to two already held) to exhibit in Peru, the ships got under way. Head winds held them near the islands for several days, but on August 17 they finally lost sight of land. From that moment not another European laid eyes on the Solomon Islands for two hundred years. Mendaña, after a difficult voyage, returned safely to Peru on September 11, 1569. Three of the six Solomon Islanders died shortly after their arrival at Lima.

Mendaña's stay of more than six months in the Solomons exhibits much the same pattern, on a more extended scale, as Magellan's. No mass conversion of the tough Melanesians was made, for brief peaceful relations were interrupted by extended hostility resulting in deaths, burned villages, and overreaction. Apparently no attempts were made to understand the native point of view—this would probably have been impossible for Spaniards of that day and age. One chief promised allegiance to the king of Spain, but it is doubtful that he knew what he was doing. The islands were annexed, crosses were set up on hilltops. But there was no gold and no conversions—the two Spanish criteria for a successful expedition.

After his return to Peru Mendaña hankered to plant a colony in his newly discovered Solomons, but he was unable to make the attempt until over a quarter of a century later. At the age of fifty-three he sailed again from Callao on April 9, 1595, with four ships, but did not actually get away from the South American coast until mid-June. He was accompanied by his family and 378 soldiers and sailors with their women and children, equipped to set up a colony of three fortified cities in the Solomons. His chief pilot was Pedro Fernandez de Quiros.

When Fatu Hiva, the first of several islands, was sighted on July 21, Mendaña, even worse in his reckoning of longitude than most mariners in those days, decided that he was back in the Solomons. He soon perceived otherwise, however, and realizing he had made a new discovery named the beautiful, lofty, heavily populated group Las Marquesas de Mendoza for the viceroy of Peru.

Mendaña's discovery of the Marquesas Islands was even more disastrous for the Polynesians than his discovery of the Solomon Islands had been for their Melanesian brothers. The Spaniards stayed there only until August 5. During this two-week period they raised three crosses and replenished their water supply. They also, according to Quiros's estimate, killed two hundred Marquesans. When the ships first approached Fatu Hiva, many outrigger canoes came out from the shore with some four hundred natives clinging to the sides and swimming with them. The Marquesans were a stunning people—tall, graceful, well built, and completely naked, with elaborate blue tattooing taking the place of clothing. They brought refreshing presents of coconuts and plantains, and water in joints of bamboo. Forty of their number came on board the flagship, but when they exhibited a natural, but to the Spaniards an undue, curiosity a gun was fired and they leaped terror-striken into the sea, where they milled around until seven or eight were killed by gunfire.

At Tahuata next day the Spaniards opened fire on the surrounding canoes for no reason at all. To prove himself a good marksman one soldier killed both a Marquesan and the child in his arms with one shot as the man desperately swam for safety. Another day and the persistent Marquesans again attempted to be friendly by bringing fruit and water, but again they were shot down when they attempted to take four Spanish water jars. Magnanimously the Spaniards allowed the Marquesans to stand around and watch while mass was celebrated. Mendaña took possession of the islands for Spain and, while the Marquesans shouted defiance from the hills, the Spaniards occupied their village and loaded wood and water. Occasionally some of the bolder Polynesians brought food to the soldiers, but when they attempted to take two canoe loads of strings of coconuts to the ships half the unarmed natives were killed and three of the bodies hung in the rigging in grim warning. The Spaniards were not only killing under orders, they were killing for target practice. As one soldier said, it was his "diligence to kill, because he liked to kill."

The ships' anchorage in Madre de Dios Harbor at Tahuata was superb and there Quiros admired the Marquesans at their finest—the magnificant men, the beautiful women, the great dugout canoes with thirty or forty paddlers sending them swiftly across the blue bay. But the murder went on until the ships sailed on August 5.

A month later, on September 7, one ship, called the *Almiranta*, disappeared in a thick fog and was never seen again. When the fog lifted a dark, wooded, lovely land lay to port and in the west a flaming volcano rose out of the sea. Its top blew off a few days later and the ships, ten leagues away, shook with the blast and their rigging rattled. Again the Spaniards were met by a fleet of canoes—fifty outriggers led by a big sailing war canoe. The people were black Melanesians with woven garments, dyed hair, and red teeth from chewing betel nut. They wore mother-of-pearl plate ornaments and beads of teeth and bone. Bows and arrows and clubs were much in evidence and their language was incomprehensible—Mendaña's few words of Solomonese got him nowhere.

The natives were different from the Marquesans, but the Spaniards' behavior was the same. Garrulously paddling about the ships, the Melanesians shot some arrows high in the sails and rigging. In return for this harmless volley the Spaniards immediately fired their harquebuses indiscriminately into the canoes, killing and wounding many and sending the frightened paddlers straining in terror for the shore. But the avenging Spaniards pursued them in a boat, chasing them up the beach and into the trees.

The frigate returned from an unsuccessful search for the *Almiranta* and the three remaining vessels found an inadequate anchorage. In searching for a better one they were driven off from one harbor by arrow-shooting natives. Eventually they found a well-sheltered harbor where they anchored the ships near a river mouth in fifteen fathoms of water. All night long music and drumming came from the nearby villages. The next day, Quiros wrote, "many natives came to see the ships and our people. Most of them had red flowers in their hair and in their nostrils, and some of them were persuaded by our people to come on board the ships, leaving their arms in the canoes. Among them there came a man of fine presence and tawny-coloured skin, with plumes on his head of blue, yellow, and red, and in his hand a bow, with arrows pointed with carved bone."[1]

The man of fine presence turned out to be a chief named Malope with whom Mendaña exchanged names. For four days friendly trade went on, the natives coming and going between shore and ships—bringing food and getting feathers, beads, cloth, playing cards, and mirrors in return. Fifty canoes, hanging around the ships, fled when the soldiers reached for their harquebuses and a large crowd on the beach received the visitors joyfully. The soldiers, itching to start shooting, were disgusted by these peaceful signs. They soon had their wishes fulfilled.

The natives abandoned their houses near the shore and carried their belongings to Malope's village. That night great fires flamed high across the bay and canoes darted from one village to another. Next morning a boat's crew taking water at a stream was attacked and three men wounded. The natives were repulsed and revenge followed. "The wounded were attended to," Quiros wrote, "and the Adelantado [the leader] at once ordered the Camp Master to land with thirty men, and to do all the harm they could with fire and sword. The natives stood their ground, when five were killed, and the rest fled. Our people retreated, and, embarking, came back to the ships, having cut down palm trees and burnt some huts and canoes. They brought away three pigs, which they killed."[2]

The following day the camp master was sent with forty soldiers to further chastise the inhabitants. Surrounding a group of houses where there were only seven men, they killed six and badly wounded the other. The party returned to the ship with seven wounded of their own and five dead pigs. That afternoon Malope appeared on the beach, complaining loudly that Mendaña had burned his houses and canoes although those who had attacked the watering party came from another tribe. Eventually friendship was restored.

Mendaña now moved his ships to a better harbor where the inhabitants made the night noisy and assembled, five hundred strong, on the beach next morning. They were aroused and belligerent, offering a good excuse to send a boatload of soldiers to shoot into them. The natives retreated from the beach into the woods, bearing their dead and wounded and leaving a trail of blood on the sand.

Meantime Mendaña decided to establish his settlement at this harbor, which he named Graciosa Bay, where there were bountiful food supplies and good water. The island itself he called Santa Cruz (now Ndeni in the Santa Cruz group). Mendaña was a weak and indecisive man, and throughout the expedition he was unable to control the interminable rows and disagreements between the various elements of his people and his officers. Soldiers, sailors, and settlers argued with each other. One discordant element was Doña Isabel, Mendaña's wife, who emerged as an arrogant, powerful, bitchy woman of particularly unfeeling ruthlessness.

A church was built, but the colony was not happy. Finally the soldiers petitioned Mendaña to take them away from the place. When he refused, the soldiers attempted to induce the natives to attack the settlement by killing two of them. Many wanted to return to Peru. The soldiers were insubordinate and near mutiny. Quiros made an unsuccessful attempt to calm them. The squabbling went on, with the troublesome camp master as the ringleader among the soldiers. When the camp master came on board ship to talk with Mendaña, Doña Isabel urged her husband to kill him while he could, but the commander abstained.

In the midst of these disputes Malope arrived to make peace and arranged to have food delivered to the Spaniards. A great heap of plantains, sugarcane, coconuts, almonds, taro, and other comestibles was assembled. Fourteen pigs were given by the villagers and Malope said he would get more. But the soldiers were not satisfied and said that "they would take, burn, and kill; that the natives were dogs, and that they did not come from Peru to be satisfied with nothing."[3] Quiros attempted to dissuade them and pointed out that the natives had been very generous. On going ashore Mendaña saw thirty soldiers whom the camp master had sent to Malope's village for more food. Mendaña warned them not to kill or harm Malope, who was a good friend, but the soldiers merely laughed as they went off. Mendaña then went with four trusted followers to the camp master who, sitting unarmed, was having breakfast. As the camp master came from his tent he was killed, as was another soldier, and the two heads were set up on posts near the camp.

That same afternoon the foraging party returned and it was reported that while Malope was entertaining them one of the soldiers had killed him. All this was too much for Mendaña. Sick with worry, he died on October 18, 1595, leaving his wife Doña Isabel as governess and his brother-in-law, Don Lorenzo, as captain general.

Sickness now descended on the Spaniards—punishment from heaven, some thought--and men began dying every day. The natives became bolder and attacked three times on the same day. Don Lorenzo died on November 2 and command fell on Quiros. With food scarce, sickness rampant, and natives hostile, the expedition sailed from Graciosa Bay on November 18 and left Santa Cruz "in the claws of the devil."

After much suffering Quiros brought the survivors to Manila on February 11, 1596. Mendaña was buried and Doña Isabel married Don Fernando de Castro, a relative of Mendaña's. One of the ships, the *San Jeronimo*, was repaired and refitted and Quiros sailed in her on August 10, 1596, reaching Acapulco on December 11. The first attempt to establish a European settlement on a Pacific island was a complete and bloody failure.

The Spaniards made one more attempt at settlement. Quiros, whose heart bled at the thought of all the heathen souls in Santa Cruz and the Solomons going to perdition, received permission to return to Santa Cruz in the service of God and spread the holy Catholic faith. He sailed December 21, 1605, with three ships and Luis Vaez de Torres as second in command. Sighting various small islands in the Tuamotus, the expedition made a water stop at an island which they called Peregrina or Gente Hermosa—the Island of Beautiful People (Rakahanga in the northern Cooks). Their stopover followed the familiar bloody Spanish pattern, with people killed and water jars lost.

Just as Mendaña had sought the Solomons and found Santa Cruz, so now Quiros sought Santa Cruz and discovered the New Hebrides when on May 1 he sailed into the great bay which he named St. Philip and St. James at the northern end of the island that he called Austrialia del Espiritu Santo. Quiros, sick and overcome with fanatical religious fervor, acted strangely. Although no settlement was made, he appointed all sorts of city officials for his New Jerusalem. A church was built and religious festivals celebrated with long services and processions. But the Spaniards remained only a little more than a month. Quiros sailed June 8, planned to return, but was blown offshore. His ships were separated; Torres went on to sail to Manila via Torres Strait while Quiros returned to Acapulco, where the voyage came to an end on November 23, 1606.

Thus ended the first European attempts at expansion in the South Seas. No lands were added to the Spanish realm. The Spaniards' navigation was unable to take them back to islands once discovered. But the people of the Marquesas, the Solomon Islands, and Santa Cruz must have remembered with wonder and fear the visits of these white, bearded strangers—their floating fortresses with towering masts and sails, their insatiable desire for food, their crosses and processions, and, above all, their death-dealing war sticks and merciless destruction of houses, canoes, and life. But the unpleasant memory faded, for none of these islands again saw the white strangers for two hundred years.

The Dutch Commercial Folly

The islands discovered by the Spaniards had not been found again when two Dutch explorers, Willem Schouten and Jakob Le Maire, set out in 1615. Their voyage was a commercial attempt to circumvent the Dutch East India Company's monopoly by finding a new way into the Pacific via the Strait of Le Maire and Cape Horn. They made contact with the Polynesians of the northern Tuamotus. The natives, armed with spears pointed with swordfish swords, came from the woods on Takapoto to investigate a boat landing and were shot and killed. Again, in the northern outliers of the Tonga group, a visit by a chief bringing a pig as a present ended when the Dutch fired muskets loaded with flesh-tearing old nails into the canoes. But at Futuna and Alofi (the Hoorn Islands) the situation was more relaxed. Here the Dutch obtained fresh water and coconuts as well as green herbs to combat scurvy. The Hoorn Islanders presented feather crowns while the Dutch blew trumpets for their amusement. After watching traditional kava-making the Dutch opted out of the kava-drinking rite. Continuing west, among outliers of the Fiji and Samoa groups they thought they had rediscovered the Solomons of Quiros. Later, as they skirmished with Melanesians along the coast of New Ireland, they mistook it for New Guinea. Arriving at Batavia they were placed under arrest by officials of the East India Company, who did not believe they had come there by a new route.

Abel Janszoon Tasman, entering the Pacific from the west in 1642, sailed south of Australia and discovered Tasmania, which he named Anthony Van Diemen's Land after the Dutch governor at Batavia. A shore party, landing for water, heard human sounds and something like a gong, but not a Tasmanian was seen. The inhabitants, Tasman thought, must be giants. Among the shiest and most furtive of people, they had probably watched the pale strangers from the undergrowth.

Leaving Van Diemen's Land the Dutch sailed east across the Tasman Sea—the first Europeans to do so—and on December 13 raised the inhospitable shores of New Zealand's South Island. Tasman coasted north and on the seventeenth sighted smoke in several places, indicating the land was inhabited. The next day he sent boats to reconnoiter for an anchorage. They were successful. The expedition's two ships were snugged down by sunset and an hour later in the twilight there were lights on the shore and two canoes paddled toward them. Maoris and Dutch hallooed and serenaded each other until darkness fell. Next morning a fast double canoe circled the ships with apparently friendly Maoris who ignored the Dutch invitation to come aboard. Seven more canoes joined the first and a boat manned by a quartermaster and six men was sent from one ship to the other to warn against letting too many Maoris come on board at one time. As the boat returned from its errand a large canoe bore down swiftly and rammed it. Four sailors were clubbed to death, and the quartermaster and the two others swam to the nearest ship and were rescued. This unfortunate incident reversed the pattern of previous Eu-

ropean—South Sea islander encounters. Tasman sailed without water or refreshments and named the place Murderer's Bay. Once under way, he attempted the usual revenge when his ships met twenty-two canoes crowded
with people. Half of them approached the ships and when they were within
gunshot the Dutch fired canister into them, but only one man was hit. The
entire episode was the first reversal between attacked and attackers in the
usual bloody encounters so far typical of European-islander relations.

After poking into Cook Strait Tasman sailed northward and made a general chart of the west coast of New Zealand's North Island, naming its north-
ernmost tip Cape Maria Van Diemen for the governor's wife. He anchored at
nearby Three Kings Island where he attempted to water. Good streams could
be seen coursing down the mountainside, but surf, current, and high wind
prevented a landing. Also discouraging were more than thirty big men (Tasman called them giants) armed with clubs and shouting on the hillside.

On his return voyage to Batavia, Tasman discovered the Tonga Islands and
spent from January 19 to February 1 sailing from one to another. Here relations were friendly. Beads, nails, and mirrors were exchanged for hogs,
fowls, yams, coconuts, and fruit. The water casks were filled. He sighted various islands and a few more natives on his voyage to Java, where he arrived at
Batavia on June 14.

The last Dutch attempt at discovery in the Central Pacific came nearly
eighty years later with the voyage of Jacob Roggeveen, who sailed with three
ships on August 21, 1721. He did not find the Great Southern Continent as
he hoped. But Easter Island was discovered on Easter Day April 5, 1722, and
even the death of a number of thievish Easter Islanders could not discourage
the natives' friendliness. The Dutch were impressed by the colossal statues before which the natives lit fires and squatted with bowed heads. And they were
amused by the long earlobes with ornamental plugs slatting the shoulders.
"When these Indians go about any job which might set their earplugs wag-
gling, and bid fair to do them hurt," Roggeveen wrote, "they take them out
and hitch the rim of the lobe up over the top of the ear, which gives them a
quaint and laughable appearance."[4]

Leaving the Easter Islanders, Roggeveen continued his westerly course and
cruised through the northern fringe of the Tuamotus. At Takapoto (the same
atoll where Schouten and Le Maire had killed the men coming to greet the
boat landing a little over a hundred years before) five sailors deserted. These
seamen became the first of many European beachcombers who would ever

afterward be a marginal part of the South Sea Islands population—one of the dubious fringe benefits bestowed by probing Westerners upon bewildered islanders. At this same island one of the three ships was wrecked and her crew divided between the other two. On June 2 Roggeveen landed at Makatéa, no easy task on this coral upthrust island with cliffs three hundred feet high and only a narrow bit of land at the shore. His ships must have stood off and on as it is impossible to anchor there. In order to clear the beach for his boat to land, he opened fire into a crowd of peaceful and unarmed people and afterward gave appeasing presents to the survivors. However, these islanders were not so easily reconciled, for the next day, using their women as bait, they lured the Dutch into an ambush, stoned ten of them to death, and wounded many others. With his depleted, scurvy-stricken, and troublesome crew, Roggeveen sailed straight for Batavia.

With the exception of Tasman's apparently peaceful island-hopping among the Tongas, the initial Dutch encounters brought no more joy to the islanders than had the contacts with the Spanish. Usually it was the trigger-happy white men who overreacted at their first meetings.

The English and the Tahitians

When Captain Samuel Wallis in H.M.S. *Dolphin* cleared the Strait of Magellan on Saturday, April 11, 1767, he headed into the Pacific with the intention of finding the Great Southern Continent. He did not find it.

Passing through the Tuamotus he successfully collected coconuts, purslane, and scurvy grass, and replenished his water at Pinaki and Nukutavake. The nervous, armed Polynesians at the landing were subdued by gifts of nails and hatchets. Captain Wallis ordered that they remain unmolested. However, before sailing, he nailed a Union Jack to a pole and left a carved sign saying that the islands, which he called Whitsunday and Queen Charlotte, were now the property of His Britannic Majesty.

Other islands of this wide scattered archipelago were passed, sighted, and named as Wallis pushed on westward. The last of the group, Mehetia, he named Osnaburgh. Here he sent his second lieutenant, Tobias Furneaux, to traffic with the islanders. Furneaux never landed. Putting down a grapple astern, he tossed the unarmed natives a line and they held him steady while he traded a hatchet and some trinkets for plantains, coconuts, and a pig—all he brought back to the ship. An enterprising diver attempted to steal the grapple but was frightened away by a shot in the air when he surfaced.

Wallis saw land at daybreak on June 19, 1767, but as he came close to it the fog closed down at eight o'clock. When it lifted he found himself, to his surprise, surrounded by hundreds of canoes of all sizes. Over eight hundred Tahitians gazed at the ship in astonishment—the first of its kind they had ever seen. They indicated their friendship by waving a branch of a plantain tree.

Tahiti was Wallis's most important discovery and the first notable English discovery in the South Seas. It is perhaps symbolic that one of the first Tahitians on board, while standing on the quarterdeck, was butted in the haunches by a ship's goat. Better than bullets, but still persuasive, for the terrified man dived into the sea. Returning after some coaxing, he was introduced to sheep (another new animal) and to hogs and poultry with which he was already acquainted.

European relations, even with the Tahitians, the friendliest of all Pacific peoples, were not established without bloodshed. One was killed and another wounded when they attacked Wallis's cutter as it approached the shore. For the first time, but not the last, Europeans saw naked, wanton Tahitian girls beckoning them with unmistakable gestures. For the first (and perhaps the only) time the sailors resisted temptation.

After searching about for four days Wallis found the island's only adequate anchorage at Matavai Bay, overlooked by One Tree Hill,—an anchorage that almost every Pacific explorer would use during the next century.

The island was thickly populated, trade was brisk, there was excellent water in the river that emptied into the head of the bay, and food was abundant. On June 24 the *Dolphin* was surrounded by over three hundred canoes with more than two thousand men who attempted to take the ship by bombarding her with rocks. There were injuries; cannon were fired. The Tahitians were not easily discouraged until a ball cut in two the canoe of a chief. Several Tahitians were killed and the fleet dispersed.

Wallis, who was sick, sent Furneaux ashore on June 25 at what was later called Point Venus, where he turned a turf, raised the flag, and took possession of Tahiti, naming it King George the Third's Island. The Tahitians threatened another attack, both from the woods and from canoes, on a watering party who were forced to abandon their casks and return to the ship. Wallis dispersed both the canoes and the men in the woods by a few well-directed cannonballs and some grapeshot and then sent men ashore to destroy about fifty beached canoes, including three double canoes over sixty feet long. Following this, to the Tahitians, disastrous episode the natives sued for peace by setting green boughs in the sand at the water's edge. Peace restored, the casks were filled, presents exchanged, speeches made, and the sick sent on shore. A demonstration of duck shooting persuaded the natives to fear the deadly weapons and ended all hostile demonstrations. The mere pointing of a gun turned them into fleeing sheep.

The young women soon discovered the value of their favors and demanded large nails which the sailors finally could only obtain by drawing them out of the ship. Wallis observed that the ship was in danger of being pulled to pieces for the nails and iron that held her together. As fathers and brothers presented the girls, they recognized the relative value of their product, and "the size of the nail that was demanded for the enjoyment of the lady, was always in proportion to her charms."[5] With unscrupulous ingenuity the sailors soon began to trade imitation nails cut out of lead. This useless base currency was in turn brought back to the ship by Tahitians who, in their simplicity, tried unsuccessfully to swap it for iron.

On July 11 the queen of the island, a tall regal woman of about forty-five, visited the ship, expressed concern about Wallis's illness, and invited him to visit her on shore to recuperate. He did so the next day and found her with many relatives and retainers in a house 327 feet long by 42 feet wide—a handsome structure. The queen ordered that Wallis and his first lieutenant, who was also sick, be given the *lome-lome* treatment—a native massage by women which made them feel better almost at once. It was not the only lesson in medicine given to the English. When the ship's surgeon failed in an attempt to extract a large splinter from a sailor's foot, the local specialist operated successfully with a shell, broken to a point with his teeth, and applied a tree gum that healed the wound in two days. The surgeon was so impressed that he collected some of the gum and used it later in the voyage "as a vulnerary balsam with great success."[6]

An expedition, accompanied most of the way by good-humored Tahitians who cleared paths and assisted the seamen up the hillsides, was sent about six miles up a valley. They found rich soil, a lovely prospect with numerous houses scattered amidst luxuriant verdure, fresh springs, and wooded hillsides. Sugarcane and ginger were growing wild. Tree ferns excited their wonder.

The queen again visited the ship and pleaded with Wallis to remain another ten days. He regretted that he could not, but as a consolation presented her with a full-length blue cloak. Filling the last few water casks and leaving a great and friendly crowd on the beach, Wallis made sail on July 27 and left the lovely island and Oberea or Purea, its queen, weeping in inconsolable sorrow on the bow of her double canoe.

On his passage to Tinian Wallis discovered several other small islands including that now called Wallis Island. He went on to Batavia and thence home around the Cape of Good Hope, arriving May 20, 1768.

The English thus departed from the Tahitians on a friendly basis. The islanders' first contact with Europeans had left them with a respectful knowledge of firearms and probably an infection of syphilis.

The French in Eden

Before Captain Wallis anchored in The Downs, Louis Antoine de Bougainville, after a diplomatic errand with the British and Spanish in the Falkland Islands, had entered the Pacific with two ships, the *Boudeuse* and *Etoile*, for a crossing to the East Indies. On March 22, 1768, he saw Vahitahi, the first of eight of the Tuamotus which he sighted in the next four days. Like the English he found no anchorage among these low, palm-clad atolls. Appropriately he called them the Dangerous Archipelago and speculated that their tawny inhabitants might be European castaways.

On April 2 Bougainville sighted Mehetia (Osnaburgh), and then the blue mountains of Tahiti loomed ahead. As night came on, the French rejoiced to see fires all along the coast, for their supplies were low and men were getting sick with scurvy. Bougainville found an anchorage inside the reef at Hitiaa on the easterly side of the island. As with the English his ships were surrounded by a great fleet of canoes filled with excited Tahitians. The fair, naked women whom the Tahitians urged on their visitors distracted the delighted sailors and Bougainville had his difficulties keeping four hundred young Frenchmen, who had not seen a woman for six months, at their work. The captain and his officers were entertained by a chief named Ereti. The sailors' pockets were picked, water casks were filled, and abundant supplies of hogs, fowls, and fruit gave relief from scurvy and comforted stomachs which had long tolerated only salt provisions.

Relations between the French and Tahitians were notably good. Islanders boarded the ships with confidence. Skyrockets and music entertained them. The French were tolerant of the islanders' petty thieving. The sick were landed. The sailors wandered about the island unarmed, and they seemed to enjoy the women without having to take the ships apart—an indication of superior French salesmanship.

Bougainville was no less enthusiastic about the island than Wallis. He thought he was transported to the Garden of Eden and, with more romance and less nationalism, he named it New Cythère. He walked the island admiring its plentiful fruits and vegetables, its rich soil, its cool streams, the joy of its amiable and happy people. Visits were exchanged with chiefs and the two peoples entertained each other. Only the shooting of one Tahitian and the brutal bayoneting of three others, apparently by four soldiers who were immediately put in irons, marred Bougainville's visit. Even this did not sever the friendly relations.

Bougainville had intended to stay at Tahiti about eighteen days, but foul weather endangered his ships and forced him to leave on April 14 after the loss of four anchors. Before departing, he too took possession of the island for his country by inscribing the claim on an oak board and burying it with a well-corked bottle containing the names of all the officers. As he prepared to sail, weeping women arrived in a canoe and the Tahitians brought parting gifts of food and other presents. Ereti, the chief who had been so friendly and cooperative, persuaded Bougainville to take his brother, Aotouru, who wished to see the world, with him to France.

"Thus," writes Bougainville, "we quitted this good people; and I was no less surprised at the sorrow they testified on our departure, than at their affectionate confidence on our arrival."[7]

After leaving Tahiti Bougainville discovered the Samoa group, naming it the Archipelago of Navigators after the Samoans who skillfully sailed large canoes around his ships while they were running at seven or eight knots. In Melanesia he passed between Espiritu Santo and Malekula, the first European to see the New Hebrides since Quiros. Turning back from the Great Barrier Reef he worked his way with appalling hardship around the eastern end of New Guinea, naming the Louisiade Gulf. He then named Choiseul, passed the island now named for him, and named Bouka. He had sailed through the Solomons of Mendaña, been shot at with arrows by the inhabitants, and still doubted the existence of these islands that Mendaña had discovered. He stopped for water and repairs at New Britain before sailing his foul ships and starving, scurvy-ridden crew to Batavia. Here they were stricken by fevers and Aotourou called the place *enoua mate*—the land that kills. But the Tahitian survived and got his first European view when the *Boudeuse* entered Saint-Malo on March 16, 1769.

White Man's Legacy

With Bougainville's voyage four of the five leading European maritime powers (Portugal never entered the Pacific) had made their earliest notable contacts with the islands. The common denominator was blood on the sand. But the bloodshed diminished from the Spanish to the French; and from the sixteenth to the eighteenth century. Neither English nor French indulged in the slaughter for pleasure that characterized the sixteenth-century soldiery.

Less traumatic, but more lasting, was the introduction of syphilis into Tahiti and hence into Polynesia. The French and English blamed each other. It has been argued that the disease was possibly endemic, for its symptoms are closely related to yaws. In any case Cook found it already established in Tahiti when he arrived there on his first voyage in 1769. Sailors being what they are, probably both the English and French had it to introduce and did.

European nationalism was, of course, something unknown and incomprehensible to South Sea islanders. But each European claimed and recorded his discovery for his king. It made no difference to Polynesians and Melanesians at that time. Many years later, when European powers were carving up the world in the heyday of nineteenth-century colonialism, claims, treaties, and warships determined which white nation cast its thin shadow of culture over which islands. But with these first contacts something not really comprehended by white man or brown was taking place: the swell of European expansion that would crest in the early twentieth century had begun. A phenomenon that had already long since reached the shores of America and Asia had finally arrived at the remote ocean distances of the world's greatest geographical feature. And by the close of the eighteenth century the Pacific was also making its first impact on Europe.

CHAPTER 3

Paradise Found

The late eighteenth century voyages of Wallis and Bougainville were preliminary, scene-setting acts on the stage that shortly introduced the giant figure of the great Captain James Cook. Cook looms larger, stands taller, and sailed farther than any of his predecessors, contemporaries, or successors in that Pacific world he made his own. He also discovered more islands, met more people, surveyed more coasts, mastered more diverse sailing conditions, and brought his crews home in better health than any explorer before his time. In a century of great men Cook, by his deeds, his level-headedness, his firmness combined with humanity, his intelligence, and his tenacity, is a commanding figure among his peers.

Cook's voyages and his discoveries are well known. From the publication of the *Endeavour* expedition onward, the stories of his voyages appeared in innumerable editions, culminating in the magnificent definitive work of the late J. C. Beaglehole published by the Hakluyt Society. The bicentennial celebrations of his achievements brought forth a spate of biographical books, picture books, catalogues of exhibitions, and articles. There is no need to follow in detail his tracks around the Pacific again, but neither can his work be ignored.

The publication of Cook's *Voyages*, especially the first, edited by John Hawkesworth, as well as that of Bougainville, with its idyllic descriptions of Tahiti, created a picture in the mind's eye of Europe that diminished only slowly and, indeed, still colors our mental image of the South Seas. The accounts of Cook's second and third voyages built on the conceptions created by the first, but at the same time introduced a more scientific and objective

31

approach to the study of South Sea islanders and their customs. The sketches and paintings of his artists, interpreted by sometimes imaginative engravers, added visual impressions to the printed work. A good story lost nothing in its constant retelling. It is doubtful if anything has stirred the imagination of European man more than the exploration of the Pacific world in the late eighteenth century. Indeed, uninterrupted European expansion in the Pacific begins with Cook.

Cook's First Tahitian Visit

On his first voyage Cook anchored the *Endeavour* in Matavai (which he called Royal) Bay on April 13, 1769, and, as in previous circumstances, his ship was immediately surrounded by scores of canoes. Cook allowed Owhaa—an elderly man who was recognized by some of his officers who had been there the previous year with Wallis in the *Dolphin*—and a few others to come aboard. In fact it was difficult to keep the Tahitians out of the ship, and the captain remarked that they climbed like monkeys and tried expertly to steal everything within reach. Anticipating a lengthy stay to make his observations on the transit of Venus, the primary purpose of the expedition, and knowing the difficulties that had arisen in past contacts between ships' crews and natives, Cook wisely laid down strict rules of trade and behavior for his men. His first rule, reflecting the nature of the man, was "To endeavour by every fair means to cultivate a friendship with the Natives and to treat them with all imaginable humanity."[1] All trade must be conducted through a trade master. Lost arms or tools would be charged against the pay of the man responsible, with further punishment if the nature of the offense deserved it. The same penalties held true if any part of the ship's stores was embezzled for illicit trade. Cook did not intend to have his ship fall apart from having her iron fastenings taken. He strengthened this with his final rule that no sort of iron, anything made of iron, or any kind of cloth or other useful article was to be exchanged for anything but provisions. Sailors were reduced to peddling their own charms for the girls' favors.

After getting snugged down, Cook, botanist Joseph Banks, and other gentlemen of the expedition went ashore and walked near the *Dolphin*'s watering place and through the woods. Lieutenant John Gore, and others who had been there with Wallis, noticed the changes that had taken place in one year. A local war had raged and the inhabitants were greatly reduced in numbers. Most of the houses, including the magnificent residence of the queen, had been razed. Where hogs and fowls had been plentiful, not a one was now to be seen. But the good clear water of the river still flowed and the high silver threads of waterfalls still dropped down the precipitous sides of the dark green mountains.

When it was discovered that a large heavy quadrant had been stolen from the observatory, Cook detained all of the large canoes in the bay and also considered seizing several chiefs and prominent people as hostages until the important instrument was returned. Banks and astronomer Charles Green went off in pursuit of the quadrant and returned with the instrument later in the day. Cook's restraint under these trying irritations is commendable. He did not smash the great canoes that took so long to build; he did not burn houses and shoot people. He got the quadrant back and preserved good relations with the Tahitians—in fact, enhanced the respect in which he was held. He showed infinite patience but restrained firmness in his dealings; he reciprocated in gift exchanges; and he sat through long ceremonial visits and speeches. He was entertained with drums, flutes, and singing. He received visits from Oberea, the queen, and, as he said, did everything in his power to oblige them.

As Joseph Banks, the attractive young naturalist and sponsor of the expedition, was trading on May 12, he was approached by two young women followed by a servant who gave the scientist some plantains and spread several sheets of tapa upon the ground. Then the women stood on the tapa, dropped their clothing, and slowly turned around displaying their tattooed buttocks. Donning their garments once more, the girls embraced the astonished young man and departed as quietly as they had arrived. As plantains (mountain bananas) are phallic symbols, this was probably a fertility ceremony combined with an invitation.

Banks's popularity with Tahitian women extended all the way to Queen Oberea, who asked him to spend the night with her. Taking advantage of the royal invitation he found in the morning that his clothes had vanished—an incident written up in detail by Hawkesworth. The London satirists also made the most of this episode.

Most of the crew did not need special invitations, it seems. According to Cook, thirty-three sailors and marines contracted venereal disease at Tahiti, for the ship's surgeon had said there was not a single case aboard before arriving at the island. For years a controversy raged over whether Wallis's or Bougainville's men introduced veneral disease to Tahiti. They might have developed yaws with its superficial resemblance to syphilis.[2] More likely members of both crews introduced gonorrhea which was later transferred to Cook's men.

The Tahitians still had no idea of personal property as understood by Europeans. The contrasting points of view were incompatible and mutually incomprehensible. A musket, pistols, a sword, and a water cask disappeared and, on June 14, a rake was stolen. The English called it thieving, but to the South Sea islanders it was good clean fun. Cook seized twenty-two canoes which he threatened to burn although he wrote that he would not actually have done so. Banks questioned the wisdom of this procedure, since the canoes did not belong to the thieves, and thought his captain's bluff might be called.[3] However, the rake was returned.

Cook, having completed his observations, left Tahiti on July 13 and sailed west through the Leeward group, which he named the Society Islands. On August 10 he took his departure from Raiatea and turned south.

The Antipodes

From October 6, 1769, to the end of March 1770 Cook made his remarkable survey of New Zealand, beginning at Poverty Bay on the North Island. He saw his first Maoris on the eighth. The first landing came the next day and the Maoris proved to be a tougher race than the Tahitians. Almost immediately a man was killed to prevent a boat from being cut off and stolen. Shortly thereafter about a hundred armed warriors did a war dance, and one was killed and three wounded while attempting to steal arms. Tupia, a Tahitian with Cook, talked with the Maoris, but it did not improve relations. The next day when Cook attempted to scare two canoe loads of warriors by firing over their heads, they attacked fiercely and were only discouraged after two or three were killed and one wounded. Cook reproached himself for the incident and Banks bitterly reflected, "thus ended the most disagreeable day My life has yet seen black be the mark for it & heaven send that such may never return to embitter future reflection."[4] Three youthful survivors of the canoes were taken on board the *Endeavour* and landed the next day, but they refused to join their people. Another encounter was avoided when, faced by some two hundred armed warriors, Cook decided to withdraw his wooding party aboard ship to avoid bloodshed.

In the course of his circumnavigation and survey of New Zealand Cook was in constant contact with the Maoris. Beads and nails were good currency for fish and sweet potatoes, but curiously enough large sheets of tapa obtained earlier at Tahiti were the best trade articles and were valued more highly by the New Zealanders than anything else the English could offer. Thus began the first inter-island trade in native products by white men in the Pacific. The bold warlike Maoris were often frightened off by cannon fire, which Cook always placed wide of the mark. But frequently a musket ball through a canoe or a blast of small shot merely provoked them to shake their paddles and clubs angrily. Occasionally a bolder chief or group could be enticed on board ship. An unfortunate incident occurred on November 10 when Lieutenant Gore shot a Maori who took a piece of cloth and would not return it. Cook strongly disapproved. The warlike character of the inhabitants was emphasized by a visit two days later to a large fortified village or *pa* near what is now called Buffalo Beach. Obviously a fort so strongly built and so formidable indicated the nature of intertribal relations.

On November 15 Cook, at Mercury Bay, took formal possession of the land in the name of His Majesty. He was working his way up the east coast of the North Island, naming geographical features, including the spacious Bay of Islands, and rounded the North Cape on December 19. Proof that the natives were cannibals came on January 18, 1770, when Cook was offered an arm bone and shown how it was eaten.

The last day of January Cook, having already taken possession of the North Island, proceeded to do the same for the South. He set up the Union Jack at Queen Charlotte Sound and, after taking formal possession of the land for His Majesty, drank the queen's health, handing the empty wine bottle to an old man who was highly pleased with the gift.

Before departing from New Zealand Cook remarked on the excellent timber abounding in the islands and recommended either the River Thames or the Bay of Islands as most suitable, because of good harbors, for colonial settlement. He took his departure from Cape Farewell on April 1, 1770, and, crossing the Tasman Sea, raised the eastern coast of Australia on the nineteenth. Working his way up through the dangerous waters inside the Great Barrier Reef, where he nearly lost his ship at Endeavour Bay, he again added enormous tracts to the realm. Cook, after crediting the Dutch with discovering the western New Holland coast, writes of the eastern:

this place I am confident was never seen or viseted by any European before us, and Notwithstand[ing] I had in the Name of His Majesty taken posession of several places upon this coast, I now once more hoisted English Coulers and in the Name of His Majesty King George the Third took posession of the whole Eastern Coast from the above Latitude [38° South] down to this place by the name of *New South Wales*, together with all Bays, Harbours Rivers and Islands situate upon the said coast, after which we fired three Volleys of small Arms which were Answered by the like number from the Ship.[5]

Finally extricating himself from the Barrier Reef, Cook worked his way through Torres Strait, touched at Timor, made a stop at Batavia where many of his men died of fever, and continued home via the Cape of Good Hope, anchoring in The Downs on July 13, 1771.

A Continent Lost and Islands Gained

Cook's second voyage began when he sailed from Plymouth July 13, 1772, exactly one year to the day after his arrival from the first. During that year he had been promoted to commander. It had also been a busy social year. His company was sought by the learned and the great. The social, the literary, the philosophical—all wanted to meet the famous circumnavigator.

After the near disaster to the *Endeavour* on the coast of New South Wales, Cook realized the importance of having two ships. Therefore the *Resolution* and *Adventure*, both Whitby collier types, were acquired and outfitted. Lieutenant Tobias Furneaux, a veteran of Wallis's circumnavigation in the *Dolphin*, was chosen to command the *Adventure*.

The first object of this voyage was to establish the existence or nonexistence of the Great Southern Continent. Cook, in three long sweeps around the world into the high southern latitudes, eliminated this geographical fantasy from the map. On the last day of January 1774 he reached 71° 10' South—a record that lasted until James Clark Ross's famous expedition of 1839 to 1843.

But he also did much more. During the winter seasons, after refreshing his crews at Queen Charlotte Sound, New Zealand, and Matavai Bay, Tahiti, he cruised about the South Seas visiting Easter Island, the Marquesas (the first visitor since Mendaña), Tonga (the first visitor since Tasman), and the New Hebrides, where he recognized the very Bay of St. Philip and St. James where the starry-eyed Quiros endured his tribulations. He discovered the large island of New Caledonia, inhabited by good-natured cannibals, and the Isle of Pines off its southern tip. In short, by his survey and discoveries he fixed some of the most important islands and groups on the map as they had not appeared before. In his visits among the islands Tongan red feathers and carved clubs were introduced in Tahiti and trading was never quite the same there again.

Cook's second voyage had lasted three years and eighteen days when he arrived off Spithead July 29, 1775. Furneaux, whose ship had been separated from the *Resolution* in a storm, returned about a year earlier, bringing with him Omai, a native of Huahine in the Society Islands. Thus Cook's second voyage not only made known several new or long-lost island groups to Europeans, but actually brought a live South Sea islander to a London already titillated by the accounts of the first voyage.

The scientific results of this voyage were enormous. Besides Cook's account of his work, the Forsters, the distinguished naturalists on the voyage, made large collections and published voluminously.

The Hawaiians

Cook's final contribution to European knowledge of the Pacific came with his third voyage. The man needed a rest, but he did not get it. There was still one important geographical problem to be solved—the existence of the Northwest Passage, sought for centuries from its eastern end. Cook was conned into volunteering to try to find its western opening and at the same time to return Omai to the Society Islands. Sailing in the *Resolution* and *Discovery* from Plymouth Sound July 12, 1776, he again entered the Pacific via the Cape of Good Hope. He stopped at Tasmania for the first time and spent a fortnight at Queen Charlotte Sound.

Cook left New Zealand with two young Maoris aboard whom Omai requested as servants. After discovering several islands of the Cook group, he tried to make Tahiti, but contrary winds forced him off and he decided to refresh at Tonga. Here the expedition rested for two and a half months. There was ample time for observing native life. Gifts were exchanged and the crews feasted on quantities of fresh pork and chickens, coconuts, yams, plantains, breadfruit, and other fruits and vegetables. Valuable gifts of red feathers, sometimes made into gorgeous headdresses, were received. Livestock and iron hatchets were given in return. The Tongans entertained their visitors with boxing and wrestling matches, with music and dancing. Cook reciprocated with the sloppy drilling of marines and overwhelmed his hosts with firework displays. The usual thefts went on but were controlled by taking hostages. Paulaho, king of all Tonga, acquired a taste for wine.

Cook left Tonga on July 17 with his people rested, their health good, and his stores replenished, and less than a month later, on August 12, he arrived at Tahiti, where Omai was at last among his own friendly people. Matavai Bay again became the headquarters. From his many friends Cook learned of an unsuccessful Spanish attempt to establish a mission. A garden was planted and the remainder of the livestock landed. The Tahitians were delighted with the Tongan red feathers which became the most valuable articles in trade, reducing nails to near worthlessness. Most astonishing to the Tahitians were the first horses they had seen and the officers' equestrian demonstrations. The Tahitians were at war with the island of Moorea (as they had been on Cook's second voyage) but he wisely declined to help them, although he witnessed a human sacrifice made to obtain the good graces of a god in the conflict.

On September 29 Cook left Matavai Bay for the last time. He sailed to Moorea, where a goat was stolen and Cook ordered houses and canoes destroyed in reprisal. A change was taking place in Cook—he was tired and more irritable. The infinite patience of his first voyage had worn precariously thin. The long years of responsibility, hardship, and sea rations were taking their toll.

Going on to Huahine, where Omai decided to settle, the Tahitian traveler was landed, a house was built for him, and he was installed with his quantities of gifts and supplies, along with the two young Maoris. Here, when a sextant was stolen, Cook had the offender's ears cut off. Cook then went on to Raiatea where he spent a month and left the Societies on December 7.

In his peregrinations around the Central Pacific, Cook seemed to dawdle, almost not wanting to leave his beloved tropical islands to sail northward into cold ice-filled seas. Late in 1777 he headed north and celebrated Christmas at a newly discovered atoll which he named Christmas Island. Proceeding on his voyage he wrote:

We continued to see birds every day, of the sorts last mentioned, sometimes in greater numbers than at others: and between the latitude of 10 and a 11 we saw several turtle. All these are looked upon as signs of the vecinity of land; we however saw none till day break in the Morning of the 18th when an island was descovered bearing NEBE and soon after we saw more land bearing North and intirely ditatched from the first; both had the appearence of being high land.[6]

Thus Cook recorded his first sight of the Hawaiian Islands—his greatest geographical discovery.

He coasted the island of Kauai as a parade of canoes came from the shore laden with pigs and sweet potatoes which were purchased with nails. Anchoring at Waimea Bay he stepped ashore, and to his astonishment the natives prostrated themselves on the ground. They loaded him with pigs and other gifts for which they would take no payment. Cook described the place with great satisfaction and noted the *heiau* or temple (which he called by the Tahitian word *morai*) with its hideous carved wooden figures. After getting yams and salt at Niihau, where the *Resolution* was blown, Cook did not linger to investigate his discovery, for it was the season to make his first attempt to find the western end of the Northwest Passage. He stood to the northward on February 2.

Cook spent the next seven months exploring the Northwest Coast and Alaska and reached 69° north through Bering Strait before being stopped by the ice. His original plans had called for a winter layover in Kamchatka, but he quickly decided that his newly discovered islands in a tropical climate, where the people spoke a language he understood, would be far more agreeable and desirable. On October 26 he turned his ships south for the Sandwich Islands, named for his friend the Earl and First Lord of the Admiralty. Exactly a month later he raised the island of Maui and in another four days the big island of Hawaii. Sailing around the rocky northern and eastern coasts of the island in bad weather, he at last found an anchorage on the western side at Kealakekua Bay.

Never at any of the many islands previously visited had the navigator received a welcome so impressive as the one that now took place. A chief came aboard and covered him with red tapa; hogs and coconuts were presented. Cook went ashore and was taken in procession to a heiau where lines of skulls and great grinning images looked at him with nonseeing eyes. Men threw themselves face down on the ground before him. Well-chewed pork and other food was put into his mouth. Kava was presented to him. He was named Orono (Lono). He was pleased but mystified, for he was receiving the welcome of a god. And, indeed, to the Hawaiians he was. To them the arrival of Cook was the return of Lono, god of the *makahiki* season—that time beginning in October when war was taboo and the people devoted themselves to sports and religious festivities. Lono had left the country ages before, prophesying that he would return in a great ship bringing gifts.

There seemed no question that the sails of the *Resolution* were the white banners of the returning Lono—the gifts were bountiful; the season was right; the god was white. Food in plentiful quantities flowed to the ships. The natives adored this returned god. On January 24 the king, Kalaniopuu (Cook's Terreeobo), arrived alongside the *Resolution* with three canoes. He was surrounded by chiefs all dressed in red and golden feather cloaks and helmets shining in the sunlight. Cook was decked in a magnificent cloak and helmet and a treasure of feather capes and cloaks was heaped at his feet. He distributed presents in return. Throughout this ceremonial visit not a sign of life was seen around the bay. No canoe was about; no fisherman disturbed the water. All the people ashore lay prostrate on the ground or remained indoors during the solemn occasion.

As the stay lengthened, supplies in the country began to run short. The chiefs cautiously inquired when the ships might be sailing. As all available firewood was used up the priests gave their wooden fences and the very idols from the temples. The overstayed visit of a god can bring hardship on a people. When Cook decided to leave, an unprecedented quantity of pigs and vegetables was given as the people stripped themselves to make one final sumptuous parting gift. As the vessels sailed on February 4, they were followed by a long parade of canoes and further gifts from the king.

The Hawaiians had entertained a god and acquitted themselves well. They were relieved and satisfied. So was the god whose ships sailed bountifully laden. Neither foresaw the unfortunate accident that was to change everything.

Shortly after sailing a gale arose. In the screaming wind sails split and the *Resolution's* foremast was sprung. Cook could not find another harbor and he could not continue with the damaged mast. Caught in a dilemma, therefore, he returned on February 11 to his old anchorage at Kealakekua Bay. The silence was ominous; the priests were friendly, but the king had gone away. All was peaceful for two days while the mast was taken on shore and repairs begun. The king returned and seemed irritated. Thefts began. The natives became increasingly hostile. Indeed, had they not stripped themselves that a god might be fittingly sent on his way? And now here he was for more.

Finally, on the night of the thirteenth, *Discovery's* cutter was stolen and Cook, the next morning, went ashore with an armed party of marines, resolved to take the king himself as a hostage and force the return of the boat. Cook marched to the village, where Kalaniopuu received him with respect. The king could not have cared less about the cutter and volunteered to go with two of his sons with Cook aboard the *Resolution*. But a large crowd gathered and would not allow it. Then a messenger arrived with news that the English had fired on a canoe across the bay and a great chief had been killed. Cook did not know this. The Hawaiians were aroused at what they considered open and unprovoked warfare. They began throwing rocks. A man threatened Cook with a stone and Cook replied with birdshot. Stones now rained on the marines, who fired their muskets. Cook discharged another barrel and killed a man. The scuffle became general and the English retreated to the beach. As

Cook reached the water's edge and turned to wave the boats in, he was stabbed in the back. The god lay face down in the water as the howling Hawaiians rushed over him, raining blows with clubs and daggers. The god was dead—the great navigator was dead. The attempt to retrieve his body failed, for he was being given a chief's burial. The flesh was stripped from his bones and burned and the bones were wrapped in tapa—some were delivered aboard the ship.

The stunned expedition had to go on. Captain Charles Clerke, now in command, got the foremast back aboard, fired a village, and then made peace with Kalaniopuu, for the tragedy was not premeditated. English and Hawaiians alike mourned the death of their commander and their god. On February 22 the expedition went on its way.

England, indeed all of Europe, was stunned by Cook's death. It was the classic death of a hero just as he completed his labors. The scientific results of this voyage of over four years were enormous. But its impact was more than that. A play entitled *The Death of Captain Cook* ran for months in London, throughout the British Isles, and in Paris. Half a dozen artists tried their hand at painting the last dramatic scene of the tragedy. Commemorative poems were written. Cook acquired legendary proportions—the "first navigator." He also acquired legendary proportions in Tahiti, New Zealand, Tonga, and Hawaii, where his memory lasted for years. In Tahiti his portrait, painted by John Webber, artist on Cook's third voyage, was brought out to each navigator touching there for years afterward to be autographed and then carefully returned to hiding. In Hawaii it is said that the possession of a similar portrait caused a civil war. But Cook's greatest memorial is the substantially modern map of the Pacific which he left behind.

The impact of the South Seas on the European imagination in the late eighteenth century, made principally by the Cook voyages, was further heightened by several native visitors from those distant islands.

Tourists from the Islands

Since the beginning of the European age of exploration commanders of expeditions had been bringing home people from the newfound lands. Frobisher brought Eskimos to London, as did many later Arctic explorers. Cartier introduced Huron Indians to the inhabitants of Saint-Malo, the Spanish carried hundreds of terrified Caribs into Iberian slavery, and Champlain showed off Algonkians in Paris. Iroquois kings were presented to George III. It will be remembered that Quiros transported Melanesians to Peru—the first South Sea travelers. But the most famous tourists from the South Seas returned with the circumnavigators and traders. Let us consider four of the most celebrated. Two were Tahitians, one a Hawaiian, and one a Micronesian from Palau.

Aotouru, a Duchess's Favorite

When Bougainville sailed from his New Cythère, he carried with him an enthusiastic young man about thirty years old who wanted to see for himself the wonders of the land whence came the white strangers with all their marvelous possessions and their gigantic sailing canoes. Aotouru was the brother of the chief Ereti, and the son of a Tahitian chief and a captive woman from Raiatea.

In the course of the voyage home Aotouru was a willing informant. A natural impediment in his speech did not prevent his telling Bougainville about Wallis's visit and discovery of the island some eight months before. He identified fruits, vegetables, and other plants for M. de Commerçon, the expedition's botanist. He helped Bougainville complete a useful Tahitian vocabulary. He knew the Tahitian names of all the principal stars and shortly after leaving Tahiti he told Bougainville that if he steered by the bright star in Orion's shoulder it would bring him to an island where there was plenty of food of all kinds and complacent women. The Frenchman passed up this opportunity, although he would probably have discovered the Leeward group of the Society Islands had he not done so. The captain questioned Aotouru about his native religion without much success. The ship's clerk, Louis de St. Germain thought that taking Aotouru was all a mistake; that he would regret it; that he would never get back home; and that he only wanted to marry a white woman for a while. Perhaps this was on his mind—in any case he was one of those who developed venereal disease after the ships left Tahiti. Actually, however, almost all the information about Tahiti in Bougainville's book must have come from Aotouru, for the Frenchman's stay at the island was brief.

Aotouru was a sensation in Paris. Here were no pressed plants, no boxes of rocks, no preserved fish, birds, or corals. Here was a real live South Sea islander, uncorrupted by civilization, in his basic goodness, from Tahiti—that most perfect and desirable of all the islands so far known. The recently published theories of Jean Jacques Rousseau and his followers were popular. The Tahitian was an example of that happy simple society where nobility of mind combined with the simple virtues of an uninhibited happy people.

Aotouru's welcome was not only sensational, it was warm. He was the living example of the philosophers' theories on the unspoiled way of life. He stayed eleven months in Paris, where his benefactor spared neither time nor money on him. People traveled for miles, indeed from all over western Europe, to see the personification of the "noble savage." He was a curiosity to be viewed with wonder. He never learned more than a few words of French, which may in part have been due to his natural speech impediment as Bougainville implies. Or it may have been due to stupidity as John Reinhold Forster, the acerbic naturalist of Cook's second expedition who translated Bougainville's voyage into English, maintained (on the authority of some Englishmen who had met the Tahitian, but whose opinions may have been motivated by national jealousy).

In any case Aotouru managed to explore all Paris by himself. He never got lost. He shopped without getting cheated. He loved dancing and the opera was his delight. He was not only a curiosity, he was popular—especially with the ladies who cared not that a few gawking Englishmen thought him stupid. There was a deep mutual attachment between Aotouru and the Duchess of Choiseul, "who has loaded him with favours, and especially shewed marks of concern and friendship for him, to which he was infinitely more sensible than to presents. Therefore, he would, of his own accord, go to visit this generous benefactress as often as he heard that she was come to town."[7]

Taking the Tahitian to Paris turned out to be an expensive proposition for Bougainville, who began to have doubts "for having profited of the good will of Aotourou, and taken him on a voyage, which he certainly did not expect to be of such a length."[8] He had originally thought that the young man would be useful as an interpreter when he stopped at other islands and that he could be sent back to Tahiti after a sojourn in Paris, well treated and enriched by useful knowledge.

The problem of getting Aotouru back to Tahiti preyed on Bougainville's conscience and he dug deep into his own pocket to achieve that desirable end. Aotouru left Paris in March 1770 and Bougainville made arrangements for him to sail to the French colony of Mauritius, from where he could be returned to his home. Bougainville also sent instructions to the governor of Mauritius to charter and equip a vessel for the trip to Tahiti and spent a third of his fortune, some thirty-six thousand livres, for this purpose. The Duchess of Choiseul also came to the help of her protégé and spent a considerable sum of money for the seeds of useful plants, cattle and other livestock, and tools for Aotouru to take back to his people. The king of Spain granted permission for the ship to touch at the Philippines for refreshment on the voyage.

Alas, all this expense and planning came to nothing. Aotouru, who enjoyed his stay in Paris and appreciated all the French had done for him (he now called himself Poutavery), was looking forward to returning to Tahiti. When he arrived at Mauritius the able governor, Pierre Poivre, took a keen interest in sending him home. Marion Du Fresne, a naval officer settled in Mauritius, had long hankered to be an explorer and volunteered to command the expedition. He made a plan to combine the return of Aotouru with a voyage of exploration, which Poivre accepted, and furthermore he put up some money towards the expense.

Aotouru hung around Mauritius for ten months while Marion outfitted the two ships. Following Tahitian custom he again changed his name to Mayoa after his new benefactor. But his health began to deteriorate and a smallpox epidemic was raging when Marion, worried about his decline, hurried him aboard ship and set sail on October 18. Marion sailed to Madagascar where, off Fort Dauphin, Aotouru died on November 4, 1771. The exploring expedition continued anyway. It was a disaster and Marion met his own death months later at the hands of New Zealand Maoris. Had Aotouru been along he might have saved the gallant Marion's life.

Omai, the Lion of London

In 1773, during Cook's second voyage, the *Resolution* and *Adventure* lay at Huahine in the Leewards for five days. When they sailed on September 7 the chief, Oree, with whom Cook had excellent relations, requested that several of his people, about to sail away in the *Adventure*, be returned. He was mistaken, for there was only one. A youth, twenty-one or twenty-two years old, named Omai had come on board the *Adventure* the moment she dropped anchor and never left her. He became particularly fond of the ship's surgeon and armorer and he assured the Tahitians that he intended to sail with the visitors. Captain Tobias Furneaux of the *Adventure* wanted to take him and Cook granted the request.

Omai was born on Raiatea, but his father had been killed by raiding warriors from Bora-Bora and he had fled to Tahiti. During Wallis's visit there in 1767 he was wounded by an English musket ball at One Tree Hill. He was also scarred by spear wounds acquired in native wars. Following Wallis's visit he studied to be a native priest and this is what he was doing when Cook arrived at Tahiti two years later during his first voyage. After Cook's departure Omai went to Huahine where he had lived since. Daniel Carl Solander, a botanist on the first expedition, described him as a very brown, well-built but not handsome young man. In fact he opines that one reason Omai wanted to leave was because his people laughed at his unusually wide nostrils. He hoped that when he returned the tales of his travels would make people forget his poor looks.

Like Aotouru, Omai imparted a good deal of information about Tahitian customs, including human sacrifice. He was often a not particularly accurate informant, for apparently with him a tale lost nothing in the telling. At first, when the ships got to sea, Omai was seasick, but he soon got his sea legs, his normal high spirits returned, and his appetite was a source of comment. He had never sailed the open ocean before, and when the ship rolled and pitched the limit in a furious gale with mountainous seas the young man was terrified. By December 19, however, Furneaux entered the young Tahitian on the books of the *Adventure*, under the name Tetuby Homy, as an able seaman.

Cook did not have a very high opinion of Omai. He considered Odiddy, who sailed on the *Resolution* for some time but who was left in the islands, a much better specimen of the Tahitian race. He seemed to rather regret that such a poor example should be brought to England, for he wrote: "Indeed he [Odiddy] would have been a good specimen of the Nation in every respect which the man [Omai] on board the *Adventure* is not, he is dark, ugly and a downright blackguard."[9] ("Blackguard" at this time meant someone of low social position, not a criminal.) David Samwell, a surgeon on the ship that later returned Omai to Tahiti, was of somewhat the same opinion. Writing to a friend, he remarked, "If Master Omiah's Countrywomen are not handsomer than him I shall bring many of my Nails back." But, he contined, "Omiah is a droll Animal & causes a good deal of Merriment on Board."[10]

When Omai arrived in England on July 14, 1774, he was soon taken to see Joseph Banks, the botanist of Cook's first voyage, and recognized him instantly. He also recognized Solander by the sound of his voice, but could not believe it was the same man he had met in Tahiti, as the Swedish botanist had gotten so fat. Both naturalists remembered their Tahitian friend and had no difficulty talking with Omai.

Omai lived at Banks's house for some months and during that time his friends very sensibly had him inoculated for smallpox. Accompanied by Banks, Solander, Andrews (the surgeon of the *Adventure*) and others, he was taken to Baron Dimsdale's in Hertford for the medication. They all stayed with the Tahitian during his confinement. Boredom was relieved by the officers of the Horse Guards, who were stationed at Hertford at the time.

Omai was popular and gracious. He spent a week at the country home of Lord and Lady Sandwich and was the star of a reception held to honor the officers of Cook's two ships. Solander wrote: "He is well behaved, easy in his

Manners, and remarkably complaisant to the Ladies. I will onely mention one thing as a proof of his good breeding. We dined with him at the Duke of Gloucesters, at going away the Dutchess gave him her pocket handkerchief, which he properly recieved with thanks, and observing her Name marked upon it, he took an opportunity when she looked at him to Kiss it."[11]

Omai stayed in England nearly two years, until the sailing of Cook's third expedition in July 1776. During that time his fame increased, along with his invitations and his self-confidence. He became a dinner-party favorite—a social lion of London. The bluestocking hostesses vied for him. Lady Carew, Lady Townsend, the Duchess of Devonshire, Mrs. Thrale, and Fanny Burney were all charmed and delighted. They marveled at his tattooed hands and the tortoise-shell comb in his hair. For his part Omai greatly admired the big English hogs (as he called horses and cows) that carried people on their backs and gave coconut milk. He had a perfectly wonderful two years. Articles detailing his activities appeared in all the popular magazines. His portrait was painted by Sir Joshua Reynolds and Nathaniel Dance. He was lively, witty, and openhearted. He was welcomed by King George, who presented him with a sword which he received and wore with easy grace.

Cook must have been astonished that this Polynesian, whom he thought little of, should become the drawing-room favorite, the sought-after dinner companion, for, as Beaglehole says: "Never was savage more patronized and petted by the nobility and gentry, talked over by the polite and learned, entertained at the best tables . . ."[12] He quickly learned to dress in the latest fashion; he learned some English but was never fluent; he skated, but he never mastered riding. At first he lost his way in London but soon he was going all over town. He had his own living quarters in Warwick Street and like Aotouru enjoyed the opera. The king gave him an allowance to live on.

Omai added the final fillip to the impact of Cook's voyages on English society. Already writers and verse satirists were turning out satirical pamphlets and using the voyages, natural life in Tahiti, Oberea the queen, Banks, and Omai to make their japes at English society. Playwrights adapted the topics to the stage, and William Hodges, the artist of the second voyage, began introducing South Sea backgrounds into Italian landscapes. Here was a real Tahitian to add to the cast and they made the most of it.

But at the end of two years both the king and the Earl of Sandwich, First Lord of the Admiralty, said Omai must go home. Cook thought Omai would want to return to his homeland even though he was told that if he did not like it there, having become accustomed to English life, he would be allowed to come back to England. Cook was going to make sure he did not, for as James Boswell confided to his journal "the Captain would take care to leave the coast before Omai had time to be dissatisfied at home."[13]

And so on Monday, June 24, 1776, Cook and Omai set out from London at six o'clock in the morning. Omai left with mixed emotions. When he thought of leaving his English friends his eyes filled with tears, but as soon as he and Cook began to talk about seeing Tahiti again they sparkled with joy. Some of the English did not approve of the high life Omai had led while in London. They thought it shameful that he had not been taught a trade, although just what trade and what good it would have done him is not clear. The Fundamentalists thought the time should have been given to Christian moral instruction.

Anyway he boarded the *Resolution* loaded with presents. The king himself had given Omai everything he thought his countrymen might need to improve their lot. Lord Sandwich, Joseph Banks, and many others whose hospitality he had enjoyed were generous with their gifts on his departure. Everything he wanted he had, no matter how frivolous. Although there were many useful household things, he cherished most his hand organ, suit of armor, muskets and gunpowder, a mechanical Punch and Judy, toy soldiers, a globe of the world, and a supply of port wine.

The *Resolution* on this voyage was a floating barnyard. The first object, to return Omai, presented the opportunity of introducing livestock to the islands. Cattle, horses, sheep, goats, hogs, and poultry for New Zealand, Tahiti, and Tonga crowded the vessel. Omai joyfully gave up his cabin to the horses.

Omai was useful on the outward voyage, especially as an interpreter at the Cook Islands and Tonga. After the Tonga visit, he had many red and yellow feathers of enormous local value which he mostly squandered foolishly in Tahiti. In fact Otu, the chief, gave ten large hogs for one Tonga red-feather headdress. Omai requested and, surprisingly, was allowed to take two young Maoris with him from New Zealand.

Leaving Tahiti, Omai was finally settled at Huahine, where he had relatives and where he had been embarked over three years before. He was left livestock, and all kinds of fruits, including grapes, melons, and pineapples, were planted in his garden. Omai soon discovered that most of his kitchen utensils were useless. A hog baked in the ground tasted better than a boiled one. He traded his dishes to the sailors for hatchets and other more useful things. He was eventually taken advantage of, as anyone with large possessions unusual to his society would be. He was left a horse and mare, a goat big with kid, a boar and two sows. Cook built him a house twenty-four feet long, eighteen feet wide, and ten feet high, over which Omai later built a larger native house enclosing the European one within it. After the departure of Cook, Omai was exploited, robbed, and lived only a couple of years.

His influence on the Tahitians quickly subsided, but his impact in England lingered and Omai continued to be a subject for writers and philosophers. Over six years after he left England, a musical comedy called *Omiah, Or, With Captain Cook Around the World* was the hit of London.

Lee Boo, the Prince of Palau

In August 1783 Captain Henry Wilson in the East India Company's packet *Antelope* was shipwrecked in the Palau Islands of Micronesia. In a remarkably short time he and his men built a small schooner named the *Oroolong* (for their temporary island home) in which they embarked for China.

During their stay in the Palaus they were fortunate in having a man who spoke Malay and in finding a Palauan who also spoke Malay, so communication was easy. Wilson became close friends of the king, Abba Thulle, and joined him on an expedition against his enemies. Abba Thulle was so impressed with his unexpected visitors that on their departure he told Captain Wilson that he intended to send his second son, Lee Boo, with him to learn what he could in England and return with knowledge that would be of great benefit to Palau. Wilson replied that he was singularly honored and that he would look after the young prince with the same care and affection he would have given his own son.

Lee Boo, who turned out to be about nineteen or twenty years old, was a sensible, amiable, gentle, and sensitive young man. Abba Thulle, in further conversation with Wilson about his son, said he wished him to make him an Englishman. He also realized that the boy would be exposed to foreign diseases and if he was sick he was convinced that Wilson would do all he could for him. If he died the king would not hold the captain to blame. On November 12 Wilson and his crew bade farewell to their enforced home and accompanied by a fleet of canoes got the *Oroolong* over the reef and squared away for China.

For the first few days at sea, Lee Boo, like Omai, was seasick, but he soon recovered and dined on flying fish and yams. By the last day of the month they were at Macao. Here Lee Boo was known as the "New Man"; he was made much of and in turn was overwhelmed with admiration for all he saw. The foreigners in Macao equally admired his native polish, good manners, and amiable disposition. Taken to Canton, he gave an expert exhibition of spear throwing and marveled at all he saw in that great city. He was particularly fascinated by flat ceilings and could not comprehend what held them up.

Finally in December, Captain Wilson took passage ? England for himself and his young charge. Lee Boo was a bright boy and expressed a desire to learn to read while on the voyage. At Saint Helena he was taken to see a new school and, unlike Omai, he had no difficulty staying on a horse even at a gallop. Wilson and Lee Boo arrived safely at Portsmouth on July 14, 1784. The young Micronesian lived at Wilson's house during his stay. Although Lee Boo was in England only five months he was, in a far more limited way, nearly as popular as Omai. He was taken to dine and introduced to the directors of the East India Company. Wilson intended to have the youth inoculated for smallpox, but regrettably he delayed too long, deciding to wait until the Micronesian knew the language better so that he could explain the purpose of inoculation. To hasten this end he was sent every day to an academy at Rotherhithe for instruction in reading and writing. He became an intimate member of the family, calling Mrs. Wilson "Mother," and a close friend of their son. Quickly adapting to English ways he was a favorite dinner companion for Wilson's friends. Lee Boo picked up table manners quickly, was deeply concerned when a lady fainted, took particular pleasure in riding in a coach, and was extremely fond of going to church. His portrait was drawn by Miss Keate (daughter of George Keate who wrote his story).

Just as he was mastering English and Wilson was about to have him inoculated, he caught smallpox on December 16 and died on the twenty-seventh. He was buried in Rotherhithe churchyard and a great crowd of people, including all the academy students, attended his funeral. The East India Company ordered a tomb erected ever his grave "as a testimony of the esteem for the humane and kind treatment afforded by his father to the crew of their ship the Antelope." The inscription closed with the words:

> "Stop, Reader, stop!—let Nature claim a Tear—
> A Prince of *Mine*, Lee Boo, lies bury'd here."[14]

Prince Lee Boo never moved in the high circles that were open to Omai (although had he lived longer he might well have, since Captain Wilson restricted his movements for fear of the very disease that killed him); but he was no less generally admired. The story of this amiable Micronesian, as told by George Keate in his account of Wilson's shipwreck and subsequent events, went through several editions and in a popular cheap version ran through twenty editions—a consistent best seller of the turn of the century. As a final tribute, a Northwest Coast fur-trading vessel was named for him.

Kaiana, the Wonder of Canton

In 1787 Captain John Meares, returning to China from a fur-trading voyage to the Pacific Northwest Coast, stopped at Kauai in the Sandwich Islands for refreshment. Kaiana, younger brother of the king of Kauai, wanted to go to England and Meares took him aboard. China was as far as he got.

In Canton the well-known resident English merchant, John Henry Cox, took a liking to the Hawaiian chief and did all he could for his happiness. Kaiana was a striking man about thirty years old. Six feet two or five (depending on which contemporary account you read) inches tall, he was well built and muscular—even Herculean. He was also handsome and haughty as befitted an *allii*—one of noble Hawaiian birth. He had brought with him his handsome feather cloak, his Grecian-style feather helmet which added at least another eight inches to his height, and his long, barbed *toa*-wood spear.

He carried himself with the great dignity of one who was aware of his superior rank. Like the other Pacific islanders he was graceful, quickly adopted European manners, and wore European clothes, once used to them, with ease. He delighted in the striking portrait painted of him and it was his most treasured possession.

During his stay of several months in Macao and Canton, Kaiana gloried in decking himself in his dazzling cloak and helmet and, barbed spear in hand, striding through the streets like a tower of fire, terrifying the smaller Chinese whom he held in scorn. As a Polynesian he was particularly vexed at the Chinese custom of keeping their women secluded from strangers. He also became excessively prejudiced against their customs in general and their very appearance revolted him. He developed such an intense hatred for the race that on one occasion he was barely prevented from throwing a Chinese pilot overboard for some trivial offense. Thus he strode about through awestruck crowds who opened a way for him like the parting of the waters of the Red Sea.

In spite of his dislike he had great concern for the afflictions of the poor and hungry.

A Captain Tasker, of the Milford, from Bombay, gave a sumptuous entertainment to a number of English gentlemen, and of course Tyaana [Kaiana] was among the rest. After dinner, being upon deck, a number of poor Tartars, in small sampans, were about the ship asking alms, as is customary there on such occasions of entertainment and festivity. Tyaana immediately enquired what they wanted, and being told that they were beggars who came to supplicate the refuse of the table, he expressed great concern, saying that he was very sorry to see any persons in want of food, and that it was quite a new scene to him; for that they had no people of that description at Atoui [Kauai] ; he seemed to be under great impatience to procure them relief, and became a very importunate soliciter on their behalf. The captain's generous disposition readily co-operated with his importunities, and he ordered all the broken victuals, being a large quantity, to be brought upon deck, and Tyaana had the distribution of it among the poor Tartars, which he did, observing the most equal, impartial division he was able to make of it; and his pleasure and satisfaction in the performance of that task were not less visible in his countenance than his actions.[15]

He greatly enjoyed attending religious services and stood, knelt, and conformed to all procedures of the congregation. He never understood the use of coins and tried to make his purchases with nails and bits of iron, much to the disgust of the Chinese vendors.

It had been the original desire and intention of Kaiana to go on to England and, indeed, arrangements had already been made for his passage. But upon reflection Cox and the other English merchants at Macao and Canton decided that if he went to England he would probably never be able to return to his own islands. Therefore they raised a sum of money to furnish him with livestock, plants, tools—in fact anything that they could conceive might be useful to him on the island of Kauai.

Arrangements were made with Captain Meares, who was sailing on another Northwest Coast voyage, for the return of Kaiana, as well as three other Hawaiians who had been brought to China on other ships, and a Northwest Coast Indian. Meares sailed with two ships on January 22, 1788, on his combination errand of mercy and commercial venture.

Kaiana made the voyage to the Northwest Coast before reaching the Hawaiian Islands in December. There he found a civil war raging and, not daring to return to Kauai, had his possessions unloaded and himself disembarked at the island of Hawaii, where he allied himself with the great Kamehameha who gave him a large tract of land. He played an important part in the king's wars of conquest and became a very prominent chief in the islands. Had he gone to England he would probably have outshone Omai in his reception.

While he never reached England, the engraved portraits and descriptions of him in the popular accounts of Portlock and Meares again helped to build up the favorable image of the amiable, uninhibited, noble South Sea islander in England.

Europeans were not sufficiently experienced at this time to realize that in entertaining Polynesian and Micronesian visitors they could hardly go wrong. Eskimos, Tartars, and assorted American Indians were all viewed as curiosities, but they were difficult to entertain. To Londoners and Parisians they were unattractive. They did not assimilate upper-class European ways easily. They wore barbaric clothes. They picked their noses. They often retreated into an aloof arrogance. They were bored. On the other hand the South Sea islanders by nature were cheerful, gay, considerate. They were all shocked by the poverty in Europe, for they could not imagine people not having enough to eat. They appreciated pageantry. The church and the opera house were their favorite spectacles. Furthermore South Sea islanders are natural mimics and actors. They have panache. Their sensitivity in pleasing other people is undiminished even today. The result, and it could not have been otherwise, was that these visitors to Europe and English residents in China all helped to solidify the attractive South Sea image in the European mind. And Omai was the star of them all.

End of an Era

European penetration of the Pacific in the late eighteenth century was not politically imperialistic. Rather it was a combination of an increasing desire to discover more new lands, to study the natives of the newly found islands, and finally to exploit the natural resources that might benefit trade and commerce. All this was accompanied by an increasing religious disapproval, especially in England, of native massacres of sailors—whether or not provoked—cannibalism, infanticide, and what they presumed to be sexual licentiousness.

Nearly all of the expeditions carried naturalists. But with the increasing studies of plants and animals there came an awareness that man himself was not being studied scientifically at all. The notable exception to this was the Forsters on Cook's second expedition, who are only now being recognized as pioneers in the scientific study of man in the Pacific. The opening of the Pacific, with its hundreds of inhabited islands uncontaminated by European civilization and cultures, provided the ideal laboratory for the study of man himself. The romantic view of the South Sea islander as the "noble savage," the child of nature—a view never wholly forgotten—was, nevertheless, being replaced by a more pragmatic curiosity. This was one of the more fruitful seeds from which the science of anthropology (and especially ethnology) would sprout and grow luxuriously a century later.

The thirst for scientific knowledge about man was stimulated rather than quenched by the published accounts of voyages (perhaps at least as much by the lavish plates of engravings as by the text), by the collections of artifacts eagerly acquired by every virtuoso and proprietor of the increasingly popular private museums—both those run for gain by quasi-dealers and collectors such as Sir Ashton Lever, George Humphrey, and William Bullock, and the cabinets of nobility and royalty like the Duchess of Portland, the dukes of Florence, the great Duke of Gotha, and the Hapsburgs in Vienna. Interest was constantly increased by the accounts of navigators, scientists, and artists returning from expeditions. The waterfront bubbled with the tales of sailors and their adventures. Perhaps it was these tales of sailors—by word of mouth--as much as the popular books of their commanders, that got back to the little villages. They also came to the ears of the prudish, ill-educated, Fundamentalist, growing lower middle class. These reasonably prosperous quasi-fanatics became inspired with a zeal to enlighten and clothe the benighted inhabitants of this morally troublesome island world. With tenacious determination they set out to do something about it. This desire began with the publications of Hawkesworth's account of Wallis's discovery of Tahiti and Cook's first voyage and culminated with the founding of the London Missionary Society.

Almost simultaneously the same sources that inspired scientist and missionary also inspired adventurer and entrepreneur to consider the profits that might be gained from the resources of Pacific waters and islands. Sailors on Cook's third voyage had sold sea otter skins obtained for a few nails on the Pacific's Northwest Coast for fabulous prices in China. What other desirable products of this little known island world might be turned to handsome profits? The dreamers always hoped to find gold. More practical eyes saw the tall stands of forest and the whales in their migratory cruises and connived at ways to get their gold at second or third hand. Established traders were wary, but there were those willing to risk a small inheritance for lifelong riches. And there was always the con man.

Governments continued to mount exploring expeditions for another hundred years after Cook met his violent death at the hands of frustrated savages on the shores of Hawaii's lovely Kealakekua Bay. But his death marked a turning point in the European attitude toward the Pacific islands. It was no longer completely romantic. The immediate European expansion into the Pacific was economic and religious. Romantic tales lured the adventurous and helped to fill out the crew lists; avarice provided the ships and supplies; glowing, righteous, religious intolerance established bewildered lower middle class Englishmen on palm-shaded coral beachheads.

South Sea islanders did not know it, but their world of easy living, restricting taboos, sacrificial ceremonies, singing, dancing, and loving was about to undergo traumatic change. They thought the tall white sails brought the return of Lono. Instead they brought his destruction. He and Tane, and Tangaroa, and all the other gods went the way of the *menehune*—the little people. Islanders soon learned that the great white-bannered canoes carried not divinities but disease, rum, firearms, the need of money, the Word of God. Many of the islanders enjoyed every minute of it, but for others it was a disaster, and demoralization was followed by a loss of the will to live.

CHAPTER 4

Island Harvests

The three expeditions of Cook opened up the island world. Before his voyages, the vast Pacific basin was virtually unknown. To be sure, Spanish settlements fringed the western Central and South American coastline and their annual galleons crossed the ocean, nonstop except for Guam, to the Philippines. But neither the discoveries of Mendaña and Quiros nor the galleons' voyages ever led to occupation or commercial activity. On the western fringe the Portuguese and Dutch were busy exploiting the Spice Islands and the English had reached China, where the East India Company held a monopoly.

Curiously enough it was the Hawaiian Islands, the last major islands of the Pacific to be discovered, that were the first to be opened to exploitation. The reason was simple. On Cook's third voyage, during the survey up the Northwest Coast, his sailors traded nails, beads, and other knickknacks for a few pelts of the sea otter—an animal they had never seen before and which abounded in those waters. To their astonishment and pleasure, when the *Resolution* and *Discovery* arrived at Macao, the skins sold for enormous prices—as high as $120 each for the finest. Any product that sold well in the China market was a desirable commodity. Cook's ships returned to England in October 1780. In 1783 John Ledyard, an American, published a book on the voyages in which he urged the establishment of a trade in sea otter skins.[1] The following year Captain James King, who wrote the third volume of the official account of Cook's explorations, laid out a plan for a fur trading voyage and recommended two small vessels sailing in company.[2]

Only a year later the first fur trading voyage was sent to the Northwest Coast. A little sixty-ton brig, appropriately named *Sea Otter* and commanded by James Hanna, sailed from Macao on April 15, 1785, and by early August was trading off Nootka Sound. Then this pioneer fur trader returned to China, though whether he called at the Hawaiian Islands is not known. In any case the trade so begun lasted until 1825, and it is doubtful if it could have been carried on profitably at all, especially in its early days, without the existence of the Hawaiian Islands.

For the first three years the trade was entirely British, with vessels arriving on the Pacific Coast from India, China, and London. In 1788, however, the *Columbia Rediviva* and the *Lady Washington*, sent out by a group of Boston merchants under Captains Robert Gray and John Kendrick, arrived, and from that time on the trade became increasingly an American one. The French, who made three voyages in the 1790s, were forced out by the Napoleonic Wars and they attempted only one trip afterward, in 1717-18. The British collapse in the trade was also due in part to the almost constant European wars from 1793 to 1815, but even more to the conflict between the two great English monopolies in the Pacific—the aggressive East India Company and the moribund South Sea Company. From Stuart times no British subject could trade east of the Cape of Good Hope without a license from the East India Company. The South Sea Company, on the other hand, controlled the entire western coast of the Americas from Cape Horn to Bering Strait for three hundred leagues out into the Pacific Ocean.

Thus it was necessary for British traders, in order to operate legally, to obtain licenses from both of the two great companies. The voyage of Portlock and Dixon in 1786-87, described below, so operated. But it was difficult to get permission from both companies and it was also expensive. Various dodges were tried to get around this dilemma. Some traders obtained a license from the East India Company only, figuring that the South Sea Company could not enforce its monopoly anyway. Others obtained only the South Sea Company's license and took their furs to England, where they were transshipped to China. More, however, like Captain John Meares, who flew the Portuguese flag on his second trading venture, simply sailed under foreign colors. Other captains flew the flags of Austria and Sweden, sometimes temporarily changing the names of their vessels while in the Pacific.

But such subterfuges did not end the matter, for once having taken their furs to Canton, the British could only sell them there legally through the East India Company agent. Having thus disposed of the furs, traders could only get cargoes of tea and silk from the company for the homeward voyage. In short, the English independent traders were reduced to common carriers, and it was almost impossible for them to participate in the high profits being made in both China and Europe.

The Americans, on the other hand, their country only recently independent, were not subject to strangling restrictions nor hampered in any way by ancient monopolies. And the fur trade solved another problem for the Yankees. There was nothing in the United States of any value for trading in China except ginseng, which soon gave out. Unless other products were found, Yankees were forced to buy their cargoes in Canton with Spanish silver dollars—the standard international currency in China. Not only did this greatly reduce the possible profits but specie was scarce in America. Sea otter skins, bartered from the Northwest Indians, were an answer to the problem. For these reasons the American trade increased and the British trade disappeared after 1801.

Another adjunct of the American trade was Spain's long and largely unprotected western coastline from Chile to California. On the way to the fur coast it was not unusual for unscrupulous Yankee captains, under the pretext of needing supplies, water, or repairs, to smuggle manufactured goods into the Spanish ports. The Spaniards, finding their humanity imposed upon, clamped down, but the Yankees often fought it out with the *guardacostas* in illicit warfare and went on to the next port.

The Fur Trade Opens the Islands

Nootka Sound and its vicinity, while providing furs in abundance, did not supply fresh provisions and other necessities. Another difficulty was that except for a few of the earliest voyages vessels could not get a full cargo of furs in one season on the coast. Early on it was discovered that the Hawaiian Islands, so ideally located, so richly endowed, provided not only a suitable stopping place to break a voyage to China, but also the ideal place to winter before returning to the Northwest Coast for a second season. Here in a mild climate ships could obtain hogs, coconuts, plantains, sweet potatoes, yams, and taro in abundance. The Hawaiians also made salt from seawater and the native rope was excellent replacement for worn-out hemp. Crews were rested and refreshed in the mild climate, and increasing numbers of Hawaiian men filled out the crew lists. More and more Polynesian sailors were voyaging between China and the Northwest Coast.

The first vessels to visit the Hawaiian Islands, eight years after Cook's death, were the *King George* and *Queen Charlotte*, commanded by Captains

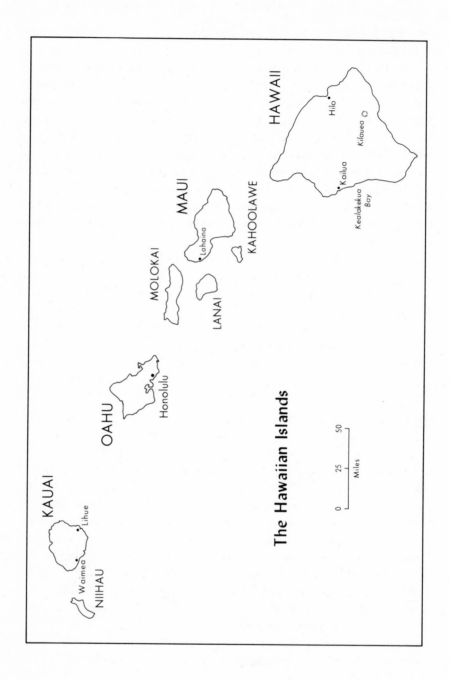

The Hawaiian Islands

Nathaniel Portlock and George Dixon on their fur trading voyage. Both men had been there with Cook. Arriving at Kealakekua Bay in May 1786, they found that old King Kalaniopuu had died and been succeeded by Kamehameha. Provisions, including fresh fruits, were ample. So was salt. Water was obtained at Oahu. Women were allowed to spend the nights on board and on going ashore in the morning exhibited to their delighted husbands the beads, buttons, and pieces of iron which the appreciative sailors had given them. Yams were most plentiful at "Yam Bay," Niihau. Portlock and Dixon sailed in June from Kauai and, after spending the summer trading for sea otter skins on the coast, returned to the islands for wintering.

While these were the first ships at the islands since Cook, they established a pattern that lasted throughout the commercial fur trade. Almost at once Hawaiian labor became slanted toward this lucrative business. The different islands commenced specializing in products the ships needed. Already the plentiful yams at Niihau required a visit to that island. Kauai had no yams and little breadfruit, but abundant supplies of taro and sugarcane. Native sennit and rope were found to be excellent for replacing frayed rigging. Dixon bought coils of rush and grass rope for rounding cables and bast rope for running rigging. Soon the Hawaiians were manufacturing rope for the visiting ships. Sheets of tapa (kapa in Hawaii) were found to be excellent protection for ships' bottoms under the copper sheathing. Trade in artifacts for souvenirs was also brisk as sailors bought tapa, clubs, adzes, feather work, calabashes, wooden bowls, tapa beaters, fishhooks, and other material cultural products of the islands, particularly if they were decorative, to take home to their wondering families. And there were always the women.

The effect of the fur trade on Hawaiians was considerable. South Sea islanders were not strangers to trading. Islands that produced better adzes, shell work, feathers, carvings, or whatever carried on local commerce for necessities or specialities from elsewhere. But with the profits made by raising vegetable products commercially for the fur trading vessels, they could obtain desirable manufactured goods. These luxuries soon became necessities.

The demand for sailors—and the Hawaiians were admirable sailors—carried them to America and the Orient and they returned to the islands with an enlarged perspective of the world.

The lucrative sea otter trade began to dwindle in 1805, although it did not end until 1825. Vessels were no longer able to obtain a full cargo of skins in two seasons, let alone a single season as had occasionally been possible in the early years of the enterprise. By this time, too, the trade was entirely American, for the Union Jack disappeared after 1801. Up until 1794 thirty-five British and fifteen American vessels took part. From 1795 to 1804 there were sixty-eight American vessels and only nine British. Wintering in the islands disappeared by 1804 in favor of wintering on the coast. With the depletion of sea otters other skins came to be in demand. Fortuitously another product was found in the islands that was almost equally desirable in the China market, for ships from the West Coast still called there on their Pacific crossings.

The Scented Wood

Clinging to the steep and rocky mountainsides or growing in the scrub of rolling hills on the dry sides of certain Pacific islands, sandalwood abounded. The tree is unusual in being a root parasite that can therefore grow only in the company of other trees. The aromatic oil in the light brown wood was used by Polynesians to scent the coconut oil with which they rubbed their bodies long before any European voyager ventured among their far-flung islands.

Across the Pacific in China the same fragrant aroma rose from the Buddhist temples where sweet joss sticks burned continually upon golden altars. Thin papers, soaked in the distilled oil of sandalwood, were burned about homes to purify the air and cleanse houses of disease. The highly placed and affluent members of the Celestial Empire owned sandalwood furniture that perfumed the room. Carved sandalwood fans stirred the humid air and wafted their scent above blue-robed merchants while they conducted affairs of commerce over their teacups. An enormous tonnage was required to fill the insatiable Chinese desire for sandalwood. For centuries this need had been supplied from the Malabar Coast of India and the islands of Malaysia.

With the opening of the Pacific, traders soon found the valuable wood as they threaded uncharted waters to land on coral beaches. About nineteen species of *Santalum* grow on various high islands of the Pacific. Not all species hold their fragrance for long. But some do, and commercially exportable wood was early discovered in the Fijis, Hawaii, and the Marquesas, and later in New Caledonia, the New Hebrides, and lesser Melanesian islands.

The first impact of sandalwooding was felt from about 1790 to 1820 in the Polynesian islands and Fiji. In Hawaii the trade was conducted almost entirely by Americans, while in Fiji and Central Polynesia the Yankees shared it with English traders sailing out of Indian ports under an East India Company license to Malaysia and China. Marquesan wood was cleaned out in only three years, beginning in 1814, but sandalwooding in Hawaii and Fiji spanned a decade or two and had a profound effect on the people of those islands. The western Melanesian trade (considered in Chapter 11) did not develop until about 1840 and was almost entirely out of Australia and Hobart.

As early as 1790 captains had found that sandalwood grew in the Hawaiian Islands and might be a means of increasing Canton profits. Not until 1804, however, was a cargo of Hawaiian wood taken to China, though not as part of a fur voyage. By about 1810 Hawaiian sandalwood became a standardized way of completing a cargo begun with sea otter skins. Between 1810 and 1820 the sandalwood trade rose to such importance that ships devoted themselves to it exclusively. Although Hawaiian wood was inferior to that of India's Malabar Coast or Timor in Malaysia, it was still sufficiently valuable for American traders to take to Canton. Almost sixteen thousand piculs (one picul equals 133 1/3 pounds) were sold there by Americans in 1817-18. In 1821, the peak year of the Hawaiian sandalwood trade, thirty thousand piculs were sent to China.

King Kamehameha I soon saw that the fragrant wood was the answer to fulfilling his ambition to build up a Hawaiian navy. From 1815 he and his son, Liholiho, bought no fewer than six vessels with sandalwood. They were swindled unmercifully, for the prices were exorbitant and the vessels frequently nearly unseaworthy. Six more vessels were sold for wood between 1820 and 1825. Some of these vessels were built expecially to be sold in the islands, others were sold to get rid of them or, like the famous Crowninshield yacht *Cleopatra's Barge* of Salem, because they particularly took the fancy of a monarch.

Sandalwood was a monopoly of Kamehameha on all the islands excepting Kauai, where a chief named Kaumualii remained unconquered. The impact of the trade on the ordinary Hawaiian was substantial. The gangs of men sent to the mountains to cut wood suffered from exposure and left their fields uncultivated. The women worked nearly as hard as the men, winding their way in long lines by night, carrying the wood from the mountains to the sea.

Kamehameha made one unsuccessful attempt to become a merchant himself and sent a cargo of wood directly to Canton without any American middleman. The voyage failed, but from the experience he learned about port charges and immediately instituted them in Honolulu, appointing a pilot and charging forty or sixty dollars for each ship.

With the death of Kamehameha I in 1819 and the accession of Liholiho as Kamehameha II, the tight regulations on sandalwood cutting were relaxed. The new king proceeded to exploit the most important natural resource of the islands. He gave permission to favored chiefs to deal directly in sandal-wood. To supply themselves with rum, firearms, vessels, and all kinds of frivo-lous luxuries, the chiefs ran up enormous debts—so large that they could no longer supply enough wood to buy new vessels. The debt-ridden chiefs then lost interest in the trade. More significantly, as in the case of sea otters, by 1823 the wood became so depleted that it was impossible to secure a full car-go and as the supply diminished, the quality also deteriorated. A brief revival occurred in 1827 when each Hawaiian working for the local government was allowed to cut on shares one-half picul for himself. Prices of wood began to fluctuate in Canton due to heavy imports from other islands and from India. Simultaneously, Hawaiian wood was increasingly of poor quality, being small, crooked, and inferior—suitable only for burning in the joss houses. By the end of 1831 Hawaiian wood was worthless in the Canton market; only a dollar and a half a picul—down from thirteen dollars four years before.

The chiefs' indebtedness had brought howls of anguish from the American traders and they appealed to the United States government to intervene in their behalf. This resulted in a series of visits by American warships—four of them between 1826 and 1836—whose commanders all appealed to the chiefs to liquidate their debts (estimated at some fifty-thousand dollars) to the trad-ers. By the 1830's most of the chiefs who had incurred the debts were dead and the new generation couldn't have cared less about the obligations of their ancestors. The Hawaiian government eventually took over the debts.

The Hawaiian sandalwood trade laid the foundation of American influ-uence and interest in the islands. It also introduced the native aristocracy to luxuries and comforts for which they acquired an insatiable fondness—fine clothes and carriages, yachts and billiard tables, frame houses furnished with imported furniture, silver, and Canton export china. For the common people it meant neglected taro beds, unharvested breadfruit, and physical exhaustion which left them open to respiratory and other diseases.

The Fijian sandalwood trade was almost contemporaneous with the Ha-waiian. Shortly after 1800 (the exact date is disputed) a schooner named the *Argo* left China with supplies for the Australian penal colonies at Port Jack-son (as Sydney was then called) and Norfolk Island. The ship was blown far off her course and wrecked on what is still called Argo Reef, eleven miles east of Lakeba Island in the Fiji Islands. The crew was dispersed and most of them eventually died in native wars. A sailor named Oliver Slater survived, however, and lived for over two years at Bua Bay on Vanua Levu. Here a wandering ship from Port Jackson found the castaway and took him to China. Slater spread the word that sandalwood grew abundantly at Bua Bay. Within months vessels were lying off the Sandalwood Coast, as the southern shore of Vanua Levu came to be called. Bua Bay soon became Sandalwood Bay. In 1804, the same year that the first load of sandalwood left the Hawaiian Islands, two vessels, the *Fair American* and the *Marcia*, sailed from Fiji with full cargoes of wood.

At first small vessels from Port Jackson pioneered the trade, but they were soon joined by larger East Indiamen from Calcutta and brigs and ships from Salem and other New England ports. Rivalry was intense and when the American ship *Jenny* was forced off by two ships from Australia she moved along the coast to Wailea Bay, on the advice of a local chief. There she loaded a full cargo of 250 tons of wood, worth about £20,000 in China, for which the captain spent only £50 worth of trade goods. Profits like this brought ships by the dozen, with trade reaching its peak in 1808 and 1809. By 1816 sandalwood in the Fijis was commercially gone and the boom was over.

To procure the wood, traders negotiated with chiefs who not only sold it to them but also supplied the labor. As in Hawaii, gangs were sent into the mountains with axes, crosscut saws, draw shaves, and digging tools. The large butt of the tree was the most valuable, but not a scrap was wasted. When the trunk had been sawed into four-foot lengths, the bark and sap wood were shaved off. All branches and twigs down to a quarter of an inch in diameter were saved and the very roots (which brought some 20 percent less) were dug out of the ground and tied into bundles. The wood was sorted into three or four different grades, called chops by the Chinese, for which the prices varied accordingly.

The Fijians lacked the sophistication of their Hawaiian counterparts, although the chief at Bua had a framed house built in payment for a load of wood, but they had their own ideas of what constituted wealth. Whale's teeth, believed to possess magical properties and worn as ornaments, were especially desirable. So were razors, knives, axes, and hoop iron to make into chisels. Nails, beads, and knickknacks were not scorned. East Indiamen brought elephant tusks from which large fake whale's teeth were made. The chiefs were avid for the manufactured teeth and produced enormous quantities of sandalwood to possess them. Some are still treasured heirlooms in Fijian families. To acquire these desirable possessions chiefs vied with each other for control of groves of sandalwood trees. But the amount of wood was limited. As thickets were cut out, there was ever more intense competition between rival ship captains to get a cargo and between rival chiefs to control the wood for sale.

The first vessels to load at Sandalwood Bay were well received. Wood was plentiful and the Fijians, by nature a hospitable people, welcomed the Europeans. But Fijians are also warlike and they were increasingly exploited by the traders. To obtain cargoes captains promised to aid chiefs against their enemies. Once the wood was on board sailors armed with muskets helped their Fijian allies burn villages and massacre the inhabitants. Then they turned their backs on the cannibal feasts which followed. This pattern became standardized toward the end of the sandalwood period, and it upset the political balance among the chiefs.

In 1808 Captain E. H. Corey in the American brig *Eliza* arrived in the Fijis for sandalwood after picking up two stranded sailors at Tonga. One of the sailors was Charles Savage who, during the next five years, became notorious in the islands. Before Captain Corey reached Vanua Levu for wood the *Eliza* piled up on a reef and became a total wreck. She was carrying a large quantity of firearms and forty thousand Spanish dollars. Most of the money, nautical instruments, arms, and clothing was loaded into the longboat. No sooner had the Americans landed on an island and finished burying the money, however, than Fijians arrived and stripped the crew of all their possessions. Eventually the captain and most of the sailors made their way to Sandalwood Bay, where they were taken aboard other ships. But the tale of buried treasure spread like wildfire among the crews of sandalwood vessels. Sailors deserted by the score, taking up the beachcomber life and serving the chiefs as mercenaries.

Of all these men Charles Savage was the worst. Salvaging a large supply of muskets and ammunition from the wreck and collecting a force of twenty ruffians around him, he allied himself with Tanoa, the chief at the island of Mbau. In a series of bloody campaigns Savage and his armed mercenaries helped Mbau defeat all its enemies and laid the foundation for Mbau's paramount political power in the Fijis. After about five years of terror, Savage met his fate when he was captured by warriors of Wailea, drowned, butchered, cooked, and eaten, and his bones made into sail needles. But the damage had been done. The Fijians now had muskets and waged bloody warfare among themselves, burning villages and massacring people by the hundreds. Cannibalism increased from a ritual feast to a form of gourmandism. A taste for rum was acquired. On top of all this, disease, introduced from the ships, decimated the people. As early as the wreck of the *Argo* an unknown epidemic, perhaps cholera, raged throughout the islands. With the traders came tuberculosis and pneumonia; measles, influenza, and whooping cough; dysentery and dengue fever; gonorrhea and syphilis. The increased consumption of cheap rum still further lowered the resistence of the people to the ravages of diseases against which they had no immunity.

The Succulent Sea Slug

By 1825 Fijian sandalwood was gone; the traders had departed; the islands were in turmoil. Inflamed by rum and armed with muskets, warriors terrified each others' villages. Raiding was constant, particularly between the powerful chiefs of Mbau and Rewa. Villages were burned, widows were strangled, people were slaughtered, and the great stone ovens never cooled for the lack of "long pig." But men will enter any environment, no matter how dangerous or unpleasant, if the profits are high enough.

Nowhere in the Pacific do *Holothuria*, or sea cucumbers, abound in greater numbers and variety than in the shallow warm waters of the Fijian reefs. For centuries Malay fishermen combed the seas in their swift praus from the Gulf of Siam to Australia and the islands of the Indian Ocean to collect these creatures, which they called trepang, for the Chinese market. Cured and sold at good prices at either Manila or Canton, they were made into soup which was enjoyed by the mandarins and other prosperous Chinese. Trepang was one of the few dependable trade staples in a market where only a few imported articles could be sold.

About 1828 Captain Benjamin Vanderford in the Salem ship *Clay* found Malays curing trepang at the island of Amboina and learned the process. He went on to the Fijis for sandalwood. The wood was gone, but finding the waters abounding with trepang he, with his mate William Driver, gathered the first cargo of bêche-de-mer (as the sea cucumbers became known in the Pacific trade) ever cured by white men. The next year two more Salem vessels and one from Tahiti were in Fiji, and the trade increased over the next ten years. Salem vessels dominated the bêche-de-mer trade for more than a decade.

The method of collecting, curing, and packing bêche-de-mer for market required a large labor force which could only be obtained from the Fijian chiefs. Bêche-de-mer exists in a number of species and for trade purposes six varieties were recognized. Much of it could be collected at ebb tide in two to three feet of water, but the larger kinds which brought the highest prices in the market could only be obtained by diving in one to three fathoms of water. During the collecting process the fish, as they were called, had to be kept in the shade or they would turn into a glutinous mass. As the canoes brought in their catches, the bêche-de-mer were weighed or counted and then dumped into large casks filled with sea water, or pools dug in the sand with channels open to the sea at high tide. Here the slime was removed and the fish were slit open and cleaned. This had to be done quickly and carefully to prevent spoilage by the sun. Next came the boiling process. Each ship carried several large iron kettles—smaller than a whaler's try-pots and actually identical with Vermont sugar boilers and made by the same company. One can still occasionally see sugar boilers on a beach or lawn in the Fijis. These kettles were set up on shore and the bêche-de-mer were parboiled twice in salt water, for about ten minutes each time.

In the meantime a smokehouse had been erected—a large, thatched, watertight building, sometimes over a hundred feet long, fifteen to thirty feet wide and about as high at the ridgepole, but with eaves only approximately five feet from the ground. There were doors at each end and in the middle of one side. Running the entire length of the building was a double row of staging (called batters), twelve to fifteen feet wide covered with reeds. The split bêche-de-mer were laid upon the reeds to smoke. In a long trench underneath the batters a constant slow fire was kept going by Fijians working under the direction of one of the ship's officers. Earth from the trench calked the lower part of the house, making it as nearly airtight as possible. Green wood was used for the fires, and the smoke and heat cured the slit fish, which were spread out with short sticks to prevent their curling. During the several days required for the smoking process the fish were turned at least once. At the end of the curing process they were as hard as shoe leather and rattled as they were bagged and stowed aboard ship.

The greatest danger during the whole procedure was the possibility of the drying shed catching fire. After a few days of use it was like tinder and many a shed filled with bêche-de-mer was lost either through accidental fire or the intentional maliciousness of the natives. Once a ship was loaded the smokehouses were purposely burned. The entire equipment for the bêche-de-mer industry was simple and inexpensive, though the actual curing process was a rather delicate operation that took a good deal of experience.

But if the equipment was simple, the industry required a large labor force. To get sufficient labor a procedure was worked out between Yankee captains and Fijian chiefs. Arriving off a good bêche-de-mer fishing area, the captain first sought a safe anchorage with a village nearby. Once securely moored the captain, accompanied by an interpreter if one was necessary, took a large whale tooth, landed, and was met by the chief. Together they walked through a crowd of several hundred yelling Fijians and settled themselves on the mat-covered floor in the spirit house—a sort of combination church and town hall. Here, face to face, with lesser people standing around, the captain produced his prize whale's tooth and handed it to the chief, who made a short speech of welcome and friendship. A large wooden bowl of kava was brought in and the coconut-shell cup passed around for each to drink the necessary pledge of friendship.

Captain and chief haggled over arrangements for hiring the gangs to work the reefs and split and dry the sea slugs. The chief was paid in muskets, powder, knives, and hatchets. Neither side, however, entirely trusted the other even after these amiable formalities. Frequently the interpreter or a mate was left as hostage on shore, and a chief or his son taken on board the vessel where he was given sleeping quarters below deck and watched day and night. While the sugar boilers were being sent ashore, canoes arrived loaded with yams, coconuts, clubs, and spears for sale. Often boarding nets were rigged on a ship to prevent a surprise attack. In spite of all precautions, skirmishes were common and if a vessel ran on a reef it was certain to be looted by the Fijians; the crew's clothes were stolen, but their lives were usually spared.

Certain captains did business with particular chiefs on voyage after voyage and an atmosphere of natural, if somewhat watchful, confidence developed between them. But always ships and drying areas had to be guarded against treachery or raids by unfriendly neighboring tribes.

While the bulk cargo of bêche-de-mer was being cured, an enterprising captain always sought as much tortoise shell and pearl shell as he could buy. Both these articles brought high prices in the Canton market and thirty pounds of tortoise shell worth several hundred dollars could be purchased for a couple of muskets that cost about $1.25 each. At the islands where traders called regularly, South Sea islanders accumulated tortoise shell for trade.

Collecting nacre or mother-of-pearl involved hiring divers at a friendly island and then proceeding to and anchoring at a known pearl bank. The divers quickly reached the bottom with the aid of ten to twenty pounds of stone ballast in their collecting baskets, which were attached by ropes to the ship. As the oysters were collected the stones were removed. When a diver's basket was filled or his wind was exhausted, he jerked on the rope and was hauled to the surface. Competition was keen among the divers to stay under water as long as possible and they were often hauled up with eyes bulging and blood oozing from mouth, nose, and ears.

After the oysters were cleaned they were placed in the hot sun and searched for pearls. The shells were then dried and packed in casks or baskets and stowed in the hold. At the termination of the agreed time the divers were returned to their island and paid off either individually or through their chief.

When it was no longer feasible to obtain a full cargo of furs, sandalwood, or béche-de-mer for the Manila and Canton markets, traders became mixed shoppers. Cruising around the islands, perhaps after getting as many sealskins as possible on the remote uninhabited islands skirting Antarctica, southern South America, or Juan Fernández, some béche-de-mer would be gotten at one place, pearl shell and tortoise shell at another. At still other places sailors, rowing along the shore, could knock edible birds' nests from the rocks with a hook on a pole, and could gather marine moss from the coral reefs. Both these products, like béche-de-mer, were favorite soup ingredients of the wealthy Chinese.

Probably most of the captains played the game fairly with the island chiefs. After all, their lives as well as their success often depended on it. But the best possible bargains were driven. Charity toward the native was not part of the trader's nature and it is doubtful that he worried much if a diver's health was ruined or if his crew left behind a disease that debilitated or even eliminated a village. Neither did he consider it his concern if warriors, inflamed by the rum and armed with the muskets he traded, wiped another village from the face of the earth.

CHAPTER 5

Whalers Ashore

While traders dickered for pearl shell and sandalwood, for tortoise shell and bêche-de-mer, another set of men were sailing the Pacific from north to south. Whalers, English, French, and American, but mostly the latter, were crimsoning the blue water wherever they could make their kills. The demand for whale oil was on the increase when the first hunters entered the Pacific in the late 1700s and it continued to grow for about another fifty years. The best oil came from the sperm whale or cachalot, and sperm (although distributed around the world) were more abundant in the Pacific than elsewhere.

The *Amelia*, owned by the aggressive London firm of Enderby and Sons, was the first whaler to enter the Pacific. Although of English registry, as with so many English and French whaleships her captain and many of her officers and crew were American. In fact a Nantucketer in her crew was the first white man to kill a sperm whale in the Pacific. The *Amelia's* sailing from London in 1787 and her return from the South Seas in 1790 with a full cargo of oil had a catalytic effect in whaling circles. The following year one New Bedford and six Nantucket whalers sailed for the Pacific and in 1792 three vessels from the American-manned fleet based at Dunkirk, France, returned with full cargoes. By the 1840s the American fleet numbered 675 vessels, totaling over 200,000 tons, and the majority of them cruised the Pacific.[1]

We are not concerned, however, with the history of the whale fishery in the Pacific, but rather with the contacts and effects of that fishery and its personnel upon the islands and their inhabitants. Nothing in Atlantic whaling compared with hunting in the Pacific islands. These widely scattered natural bases were a new experience for the whalers and the whalers were a new experience for the South Sea islanders.

While there was hardly an island of the Pacific that was not visited by a whaler at one time or another, certain islands and groups were favored far above others and certain ports became regular entrepôts for supplies and refitting. In Melanesia, for example, aside from Fiji, the natives were too unfriendly and malaria too prevalent to encourage a whaleship's visit except in an emergency. One notable exception was the little island of Buka in the Solomons, where the local canoe paddles were eagerly sought by whalemen. These carved paddles, decorated with anthropomorphic figures in red and black on a white ground (often still found in old New England whaling ports), were said to be the quietest obtainable and were therefore the most suitable of any for approaching a sperm whale sleeping on the surface. Thus, this island had the rare distinction of offering a locally manufactured, useful product for trade—something other than the usual fresh food, water, and recreation.

As the Japan whaling grounds came to be exploited, the islands of Micronesia (where Ponape became the most active port) saw their share of whalers. But it was the Central Pacific, where the Marquesas early felt the impact, centering on the popular Tahitian port of Papeete, that soon became the focal point. Later whalers congregated at the Bay of Islands in New Zealand, and finally at Lahaina and Honolulu in the Hawaiian Islands; supplies were plentiful, rum flowed freely, and miscegenation flourished. The Polynesians of these ports soon acquired great sophistication in dealing with the whalers, in contrast to islands less frequently visited where the danger was often as great to one side as to the other. Historians of the whaling industry, however, have seldom had any understanding whatsoever of the South Sea islanders' side of the story. Starbuck, the dean of writers on the subject, for example, said:

The natives of many of the numerous groups of islands, with which the Pacific is so thickly studded, were more relentless than the waves, more treacherous than the reefs, and after the first emotions of surprise and awe the firing of a gun caused among them were over, woe to the ill-fated crew which fell into their clutches. It must be acknowledged that, in far too many cases, their barbarities were perpetrated in revenge for injuries received at the hands of some preceding ship's crew, but they were not punctillious as to whether the actual culprit was punished or one of his kind—they warred against the race and not individuals. Many vessels carried with them the various gewgaws which would please the savage eye for the purpose of trading among the islands, and these, in cases where the natives were not sadly over-reached, served to excite their cupidity and invite attack.[2]

Life on a whaler was generally so wretched, the food so poor, the work so hard, that captains often found it difficult to keep a full crew once the men got a taste of life on a South Sea island. Desertions were frequent. Islanders, called Kanakas by the whalemen, were enticed on board and carried off or otherwise engaged to fill out the thin crews. Seldom were they returned to their own islands, but instead dumped wherever it was handiest when the ship was full and bound home. Thousands of sailors who had deserted or been discharged settled upon various Pacific islands. "Some of them," Starbuck noted, "scoundrels under any circumstances, became leaders of the natives in their attacks upon trading and whaling vessels; some of them became influential men upon the islands."[3]

Sailors discharged in the islands did not always want to remain there. Sometimes these men were troublemakers, but unscrupulous captains also used flimsy charges to cut down crews, thereby avoiding paying them on returning home. Charles Wilkes, commander of an official U.S. exploring expedition in the South Seas, took on board several of these unfortunate men.[4]

Two men who settled in the Fijis represent the extremes of behavior. Charles Savage, the shipwrecked sailor mentioned earlier, was one of the greatest villains who ever walked. David Whippey, on the other hand, who deserted from a Nantucket whaler, settled in Fiji and lived there for over thirty years; he raised a family and became the most influential man and greatest stabilizing influence in the islands.

The Port of Papeete

Papeete, the pearl of the Central Pacific, was early on a favorite port of call for whalers. Ample fresh provisions, good water, friendly people, a salubrious climate—all made the place a sailor's paradise. While whalers called briefly at the Marquesas, Tonga, Fiji, and, in fact, every island of the South Seas where there was anchorage, the stays at Tahiti, for obvious reasons, were more extended, although the place never rivaled the Bay of Islands or the Hawaiian ports of Lahaina and Honolulu in the number of ships calling there.

Announcements of ship arrivals in New England newspapers clearly indicate the extent that Papeete was used as a port of refreshment for whalers—most of them American. For instance the ship *Alliance* of Newport, Rhode Island, arrived from Tahiti with 2,300 barrels of sperm oil on June 9, 1828.

The New Bedford ship *Maria Theresa* returned to New Bedford July 17, 1831, after a voyage of 109 days from Tahiti.

The *Oregon* of Fairhaven was wrecked while working out of Papeete Harbor on May 4, 1837, but all of her officers, crew, and cargo of oil were saved. Five days later the bark *Osprey* was declared unfit for use at Papeete and her 800 barrels of oil sold. In July of the same year, the ship *Victory* of New Bedford was likewise condemned and her oil sent home in the ships *Congress* and *Atlantic*.

The *Timoleon* was abandoned by her officers and crew at Tahiti after her captain was killed in a fall from aloft, and she was brought back to Boston by men from the U.S. brig *Perry*. In mid-February 1845 the ship *Averick* of New Bedford was blown ashore in a gale at Raiatea and sank in three hours. Her crew and cargo were saved and landed at Tahiti. Another severe gale the next year damaged the *Sarah* of New York to such an extent that she was condemned and sold at Tahiti and her 3,000 barrels of oil shipped home. The fully loaded ship *Factor* of New Bedford was also similarly condemned in 1847. Of the nineteen whaleships calling at Papeete that year (1847) all but two (one French, one English) were American. In 1852 twenty-three whaleships were fishing in the vicinity of Tahiti. This is but a sampling of the whaling activity around the Society Islands.

There were better natural harbors in the Central Pacific than Papeete (at Nuku Hiva and Fiji, for instance), but none so well equipped to handle the business. The missionaries of the London Missionary Society, who first arrived in 1797, were well established and successful. Government and society were stable and the port continued to develop under the French, who took over the Society Islands in 1842. A regular government harbor pilot guided ships in and out of the tricky harbor, but the pilotage was apparently not always of the best, for Captain Luce of New Bedford, writing home on February 14, 1853, complained:

> On the 9th the ship James Edward, under my command, took her anchor at 6 AM to proceed to sea with the land breeze in the first place the pilot ran me on the outer buoy, and took off some of my copper. The ship then stood on the wind, but fell off at the mouth of the passage. We let go both anchors, with 45 fathoms of chain on one, and 30 fathoms on the other, but the ship struck her stern on the reef, dragged to about amid-ships, and then rolled and struck heavily where she lay about 25 minutes.
>
> With the assistance of boats of the whaleships and Men-of-War, who hauled her off, but we could not keep her clear with 5 pumps. We got her into the wharf, where she now lies full of water. I am making every exersion [sic] to roll her, to save the ship and cargo.[5]

Captain Luce sent his oil home in another vessel, got his ship repaired, and sailed on July 6 for New Bedford with a cargo of whalebone.

Another important facility of the port was the government-owned marine railway, the only one in the Central Pacific. Captain Green of the brig *Emeline* wrote home to Boston that his vessel was badly damaged in a squall near Flint Island on January 21, 1853—a difficult year for whaleships in that area. Putting into Papeete four days later with the pilot on board, the *Emeline* was further damaged by running on the point of the weather reef at the harbor entrance. She was making six knots when she struck forward of the main rigging, injuring her bottom and increasing her leak. Her cargo was discharged at the government yard, but "while the government officials were hauling her upon the railway she fell off the cradle, and remained a wreck, hogged six inches."[6] There she stuck and Captain Green abandoned her to the French government, claiming sixteen thousand dollars for the vessel, cargo, and expenses. Everything in Tahiti still works the same way.

With ships constantly entering and clearing, vessels being abandoned, sailors deserting, there were problems for the authorities even in this reasonably stable port. The Eden-like land and its amiable people were so popular after the long harsh months at sea with atrocious food and grueling, dangerous work under harsh taskmasters, that serious situations often developed. When the *Mohawk* of Nantucket, for example, was at Tahiti on April 19, 1851, her captain, Swain, reported that "a plan to set fire to the ship or murder the captain and officers had been discovered in season to put a stop to it. The second mate, carpenter and two or three others were engaged in the scheme. The two men were in prison at Tahiti, and the second mate, Mr. Clark, had been discharged, but was at large."[7] When a mutiny actually got started on the American ship *Auckland* in 1854 the sailors began looting the ship looking for liquor. "The captain sent for the police, who after some difficulty, took all the mutineers, imprisoned them, and gave the captain peaceable possession of his vessel. He afterwards took the mutineers on board."[8] A few days in the Calabooza Beretane, as the local jail (where Herman Melville served some time in 1842) was called, apparently cooled them off or sobered them up even though confinement there, like most things in Tahiti, was rather casual; so long as the sailors showed up to sleep, few restrictions were placed on them during the day.

The majority of the deserters and discharged seamen eventually shipped over on other vessels; but many, fed up with life at sea, became beachcombers or settled down with a local girl and raised a family. Not always did such a life work out ideally. When the ship *Warren* arrived at her home port in Rhode Island her captain, Mahew, brought distressing news:

Capt. Charles Spooner, of the ship Erie, of Newport, whose extraordinary marriage to Miss Kingatarn Oruruth, a native of Otaheite [Tahiti] Island, has been lately noticed in most of the papers of this country, was deprived of his bride soon after his marriage, under the following painful circumstances: She had gone into the water to amuse her husband with an exhibition of her extraordinary feats of swimming, when she was attacked by a large shark. The shark first seized her by a limb, but releasing his hold he made another attack and with one effort of his powerful jaws, severed her body in two. The unhappy husband was a spectator of this awful scene, but could render no assistance.[9]

Whenever the carousing, drunken, disease-carrying, irrepressible whalers came ashore they were the despair of the missionaries, a nuisance to the authorities, and often the ruination of the Tahitians. In 1841 the *Don Quixotte* introduced a smallpox epidemic that swept the island.

One missionary who had a good deal to say about the American whalers at Tahiti was the Reverend Daniel Wheeler, an English Quaker, who visited there in 1835. One English and six American ships lay in the harbor. Wheeler was at first encouraged that so many of the American officers were Quakers and that their vessels were called "temperance ships." He held Friends' meetings on board the vessels, distributed tracts to the crews, and noted: "We have met with great civility and willingness to lend a helping hand in many of the American captains."[10] His satisfaction, however, turned to disillusionment, for he soon found,

with horror and surprise, that the word temperance applies only to the ships, and not to their crews, none probably of which are members of a Temperance Society, but are merely bound by articles that the voyage shall be performed without any spirits being on board, except as medicine, if needed, and that their sobriety only exists because they cannot get the liquor; when on shore, and unbound by these articles, they are lamentably, in many instances, notorious for drinking to excess; and their immoral conduct, at this place, makes me shudder for the awful and woeful consequences, both as regards themselves, and the daughters of Tahiti. Although great exertion is made and promoted by the missionaries here to stop this overwhelming torrent of iniquity, yet all their measures are abortive, and can never be successful, unless co-operated with on the part of the masters of the shipping. Notwithstanding the disuse of spiritious liquors is rigidly enforced at Tahiti, and no person is allowed to have the article in his house, or if the breath of any of the natives smell of it, a severe fine is imposed; yet this bane of the human race is still to be purchased on shore, and the supply is kept up by the American ships; it is clandestinely landed at times, amongst the supposed empty casks which are sent on shore for water . . .[11]

Wheeler further observed:

We find that the voyages of the whaling-vessels are much longer than formerly, their success being more precarious and uncertain, owing to the increased number of ships engaged in that employ, which constantly disturb a great breadth of ocean, by looking over several hundred square miles of its surface every day . . .[12]

And he went on:

Rum, muskets, and gunpowder, are articles brought in great abundance, particularly by the American ships, many of which are styled "Temperance ships." It is an absolute fact, incontrovertible, that vessels of this description have landed larger quantities of spirits on some islands than any other class of ships. On almost every island the population decreases, and the dreadful ravages made by disease is much aggravated by the use of spirits.[13]

The Bay of Islands

While Papeete was popular, the most active place in the Pacific for "wooding and watering," as the sailors called it, was the Bay of Islands. This was true from the time whaling became common until 1840, when the British established sovereignty over New Zealand. There were some whaling contacts elsewhere on the New Zealand coast, especially around the South Island as Robert McNab recounted in *The Old Whaling Days*, but compared with the Bay of Islands it was infinitesimal and its impact on the country slight.

The bay was fingered with protected anchorages where ships could lie safely in deep water close to shore. Another advantage was its proximity to the whaling ground between New Zealand and Australia. Timber for masts, spars, and firewood was plentiful. Pure water, fruits, and vegetables were abundant. In 1793 British governor Phillip Gidley King of New South Wales introduced hogs to the area and so pork, too, was in good supply. The next year King gave potatoes and other seeds to two Maoris visiting Norfolk Island; they took them back to the Bay of Islands where the vegetables flourished. Four rivers flowing into the bay provided an abundance of fresh water. As early as 1801 six English whalers were fishing off the northern end of New Zealand. By 1805 the Maoris had many acres of land under cultivation and were doing a thriving business with whalers and traders; and Governor King,

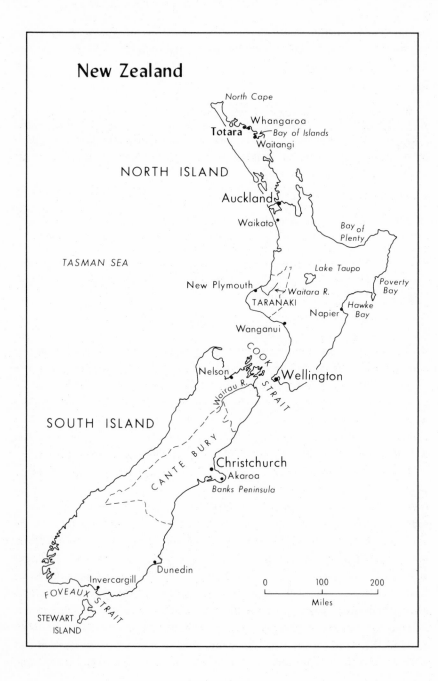

New Zealand

North Cape

Whangaroa

Totara ⚓ *Bay of Islands*

Waitangi

NORTH ISLAND

Auckland

Waikato ● *Bay of Plenty*

TASMAN SEA

Lake Taupo

New Plymouth ● ↙ *Waitara R.* *Poverty Bay*

TARANAKI

Napier ● *Hawke Bay*

Wanganui ●

COOK

Nelson ● STRAIT ● Wellington

Wairau R.

SOUTH ISLAND

CANTEBURY

Christchurch

● Akaroa

Banks Peninsula

Dunedin ●

Invercargill ●

FOVEAUX STRAIT

STEWART
ISLAND

| 0 | 100 | 200 |

Miles

writing to the Earl of Camden that year, said: "The many vessels that have put into the Bay of Islands and other parts of that coast have never, as far as I have learn'd, had any altercation with the natives, but have received every kind office and assistance in procuring their wood and water, &., at a very cheap rate in barter . . ."[14] He further pointed out that the native flax made an excellent rope which the leakage of oil would not damage but on the contrary strengthen, and that he was continuing to send sows and other livestock by whalers from Norfolk Island to the most powerful chiefs at the Bay of Islands.

So many whalers with Polynesians on board were appearing at Sydney from New Zealand and the islands that a government order was issued on May 26, 1805, in an attempt to protect these innocent people from exploitation:

Whereas a number [of] Otaheitans [Tahitians] and Sandwich Islanders have been brought from Otaheite by the Harrington, letter of marque, and two Spanish prizes she took out of the Ports of Coquimbo and Caldera, for the purpose of manning them, and several New Zealanders being brought here and left by South Sea whalers from the east coast of that island; and it being intended by the persons who have hitherto been allowed to frequent the islands in Bass's Straits to send some of these credulous people to that place where their treatment and return are very suspicious and doubtful; and it being of the utmost consequence to the interest and safety of Europeans frequenting those seas, and more particularly the South Sea whalers, that these people should suffer no illtreatment, but, on the contrary, experience every kindness until they can return to their native country;—it is, therefore, hereby strictly forbid sending any Otaheitan, Sandwich Islander, or New Zealander from this settlement to any island or other part of this coast on any sealing or other voyage, or to any place to the eastward of Cape Horn. . . .

During their stay here, those whose service they are employed in are not to beat or illuse them; but if their employers, or those who brought them to this Colony, are not able to maintain and employ them, they are to report it to the Governor, who will take measures for their employment and maintenance until they can be sent home.

And it is to be clearly understood that all such Otaheitans, &c., are protected in their properties, claims for wages, and the same redress as any of His Majesty's subjects.[15]

There was no formal settlement of white men at the Bay of Islands until 1814. Previously an occasional sailor jumped ship and lived among the Maoris. After sending an advance party from New South Wales in June 1814 to scout the lay of the land, the Reverend Samuel Marsden of the Church Missionary Society of London arrived from Sydney in December and on Christmas Day preached to the Maoris from the text, "Behold I bring you good tidings of great joy." Here at Rangihihoua the Anglicans settled on two hundred acres which the Church Missionary Society purchased from the Maoris for twelve axes. Converts were few at first, but trade for timber, flax, and food products was brisk. A Wesleyan arrived in 1822. The Roman Catholics established a chapel across the bay at Kororarika in 1838, which was the residence of the bishop of the South Sea Catholic Mission at the time of Wilkes's visit in 1840.

With the increase in shipping, more white residents became scattered through the Maori villages. Deserters disappeared into the back country until their ships had sailed. Whaling captains often lived ashore while their ships were refitting. Runaway sailors were joined by escaped convicts from New South Wales. Local chiefs became expert at catching deserting sailors and returning them to their ships for a reward of rum or ammunition. Robert Coffin, a sailor on the whaleship *Logan* at the Bay of Islands in the fifties, wrote: "Several of the boys tried to run away, but the Maoris caught them, tied their feet and hands together, slung them on poles, and brought them back after a reward was offered."[16]

As trade increased the Maoris became more sophisticated in their demands. Liquor, firearms, and ammunition no longer satisfied them. They also wanted cotton goods and blankets, metal tools of all kinds, and fishhooks. In addition to their potatoes, *kumura* (sweet potatoes), pork, and dressed flax, a macabre trade in tattooed heads was offered. A captain might order a head on the hoof, so to say. If he expressed a desire for a particularly fine bit of tattooing he saw wandering around, arrangements could be made to have the head collected, cured, and waiting for him when he returned on his next voyage.

By 1840 Commodore Wilkes of the U.S. exploring expedition could write:

The trade in native curiosities is not quite so great as it used to be, particularly in tattooed heads. So great at one time was the traffic in the latter article, between New Zealand and Sydney, that, in 1831, it was prohibited by law. In Governor Darling's administration of the colony, the chief Shougi is supposed to have made large sums by it, and there are some persons who, in part, impute his wars to his desire of gain; for, having been in England, he became acquainted with the value set upon them, and the demand for them. It is generally thought that many of the heads thus sold have been prepared by the white runaway convicts, who have learnt the mode of doing this from the natives. They are still to be obtained, though great precaution is used in disposing of them. A missionary brig, lying at the Bay of Islands, had many curiosities on board, in the possession of the steward; and after the buying of mats, &c., had been finished, he invited our officers to step down to his little store-room, under the forecastle, where he had a curiosity which could not be brought out. After this mysterious enunciation, they followed him to the bottom of the ladder; he then told them he was about to put his fate into their hands, believing that they were too much men of honour to betray him. He then proceeded to inform them that he had two preserved heads of New Zealand chiefs, which he would sell for ten pounds. He could not venture, he said, to produce them on board the brig, but if they would appoint a place, he would bring them. The penalty for selling them was fifty guineas, and he conjured them to the most perfect secrecy. These proved to be beautiful specimens, and now form a part of our collections. So effectually has the fine prevented this traffic, that it is an extremely difficult matter to obtain a head; they are as rare now as they have been common heretofore; and the last place in which it could have been expected to find them, would have been on board a missionary vessel.[17]

There was also a lucrative business in supplying the captains—more fastidious than their crews—with temporary wives. All of this activity was carried on with no local regulations, laws, or government. The only semblance of law and order was administered by a self-constituted settlers' association—a rough and ready sort of justice. The Bay of Islands was a frontier beyond the pale, and it continued so for twenty-six years after Marsden's first settlement. Across the water from the Anglican mission was Kororarika, where the action was. Wilkes said of it in 1840: "Kororarika is still the principal settlement [on the bay], and contains about twenty houses, scarcely deserving the name, and many shanties, besides tents. It is chiefly inhabited by the lowest order of vagabonds, mostly runaway sailors and convicts, and is appropriately named 'Blackguard Beach.'"[18]

John B. Williams, the second American consul at the Bay of Islands (1842-44), noted the effect of all this on the Maoris. He remarked in his journal: "European diseases have been introduced and the natives are easy victims. They have begun to depopulate and degenerate very fast. From 1818 to 1839 it is estimated that more than one half of some tribes have died of disease."[19] When a ship arrived, he continued, it became "a floating castle of prostitution. How can it be otherwise when the Master and Officers set the example . . . Mischief and misery have been reduced to a system and trade."[20]

Wilkes also noted that measles, whooping cough, influenza, and other epidemics had been introduced from foreign vessels and that unchecked venereal disease was rapidly reducing the numbers of natives.

Commodore Wilkes was preceded by a few months at the Bay of Islands by Captain William Hobson, R.N., who had been appointed lieutenant governor by the British Colonial Office, which, in its wisdom, had finally decided that the chaotic conditions could not continue indefinitely. British whaleship owners had expressed the hope in 1823 that a stable colonial settlement would be established and again in 1826, with many others, they memorialized the Colonial Office, pointing out the products and advantages of New Zealand, the increasing trade, the availability of local manpower (twelve Maoris serving on one whale ship), and the chaotic conditions, and requesting a settlement backed by military force to keep order. Hobson arrived in January 1840 and read a royal proclamation establishing sovereignty over New Zealand as part of New South Wales.[21]

Law and order had arrived and the port never needed anything more. The next week Hobson began negotiations with the Maori chiefs which resulted in the Treaty of Waitangi. The effect on American interests was immediate and final. Port charges, tonnage duties, duties from 10 to 500 percent on trade articles, charges for transshipment of oil, and the exclusive right of the crown to timber drove the business away. No longer did sleek, brown, muscular men sell their women to the highest bidder; no longer was there the surreptitious bartering for magnificent tattooed heads; no longer did deserting sailors lurch into the bush to shack up until their ships had sailed; no longer were they returned for ransom strung on a pole like game; no longer were the oil casks stored for transshipment. The American vessels had vanished—gone to more benevolent ports, to Hobart, Tasmania, and especially to the Hawaiian Islands.

Lahaina and Honolulu

Whalers had frequented the Hawaiian Islands for twenty years before Governor Hobson took over at the Bay of Islands, but after 1840 the numbers soared and for the next twenty years they dominated other economic interests. The first whaler in the islands touched at Kealakekua Bay in 1819, the same year that the Reverend Hiram Bingham and the first party of missionaries sailed from Boston; coincidentally, the whale ship *Mary* (*Maro?*) of Nantucket arrived at Honolulu in 1820, the same year that Bingham's party descended on the island. Lahaina on the island of Maui was favored by whalers in the early years, but that port is an open roadstead and gradually Honolulu with its sheltered harbor became the principal anchorage. It was the best Pacific base for vessels working the Japan whaling ground and through Bering Strait. Lesser ports were all used as the captains shopped around, and in the later whaling days Hilo developed into one of the favorite stops. But even as late as 1844, 326 whalers called at Lahaina and 160 at Honolulu. In 1846 the number had increased to 596 for both ports. By the following decade Honolulu was booming, the peak coming in the early 1850s at the height of Arctic whaling. Between 1851 and 1860 almost 4,500 ships, according to the marine register, visited that port and the majority of them were whalers. "It has been said, and probably with a very great degree of truth," observed a historian of the industry, "that the 'whaling-fleet made Honolulu,' and when one considers for how many years large fleets of whalemen . . . rendezvoused there, the known prodigality of the sailor, and the increasingly heavy bills for refitting, of all of which Honolulu reaped the benefit, it is easy to believe the statement."[22]

No longer did many of the whale ships make the long voyage home around the Horn. Oil and whalebone (over 17,500,000 gallons and 14,000,000 pounds during the decade of the fifties) were transshipped from Honolulu in merchant vessels. Owners were registering their ships, destined to cruise the Japan gounds and the Arctic, in Honolulu, which itself became a whaling port. Whalers joined missionaries in making the growing town a New England outpost. Not all Hawaiian whalers operated under absentee ownership. People living in the islands, aware of the profitable industry operating on their doorstep, bought and even, occasionally, built ships.

The merchandise required to service the hundreds of ships was enormous. Each whaler required some 650 different items in its supplies. Besides necessities sixteen different trade articles for the Eskimos were carried by ships going to the Arctic. The cooper, the carpenter, the sailmaker needed the wherewithal of his craft. Forty different articles could be purchased by sailors from the slop chest. All these things required renewing every year or two. Responding to the needs of shipping and the increase of commerce, port facilities improved, wharves and a shipyard were built. Native tapa cloth, made from the inner bark of the paper mulberry tree, was purchased from the chiefs by the thousands of yards after it was found to be the ideal material to cover the bottoms of ships as a base for copper sheathing. Hotels, boardinghouses, grog shops, and brothels thrived along the waterfront, and money began to take the place of barter. The activity was at the town, but the economic effects were felt in the remote parts of the kingdom where vegetables, cattle, hogs, and chickens were raised and firewood gathered to take to market at the ports. Young people too, attracted by the bright lights, drifted to the growing towns.

Of the thousands of sailors given leave, numbers disappeared to the outer islands or remote areas. Crews were filled out with Hawaiians to replace the deserters. So prevalent did this practice become that the monarchy passed a law requiring captains to post bonds guaranteeing the return of islanders at the end of a voyage, but nevertheless many never saw their homes again. As early as 1826 Captain Thomas Ap Catesby Jones gave some stability to the port when he visited Honolulu in the United States sloop of war *Peacock* to round up American runaway sailors and help the traders press their claims for debts against the Hawaiian king.

Inevitably conflicts between whalers and missionaries were constantly erupting. The sailors as usual spent their money on rum, women, and occasionally souvenirs—they wanted a wide-open town. "The traders find profit in vice," said one observer, "and they stand constantly opposed to the efforts of the missionary to check an evil which threatens the very existence of the people. In a low hole I saw a man acting as fiddler and master of ceremonies to a dancing squad of half-drunken sailors. Once he considered himself a gentleman, and had sailed master of a large East Indiaman."[23] The missionaries interrupted the sailors' carousing by instigating blue laws, preaching against their activities, trying to persuade the women not to go aboard the ships, and generally discouraging Jack's fun and games. This cavorting, however occurred for only about two or three months in the spring (when ships were fitting out for Bering Strait and the Arctic) and again in the fall (when vessels prepared for sperm whaling in the tropics), for whaling operations were seasonal. But during those two periods the rabble sought their unrefined pleasures, enjoyed brawls and street fights with each other and with the native constabulary, and occasionally incited riots.

When the London whale ship *Daniel* arrived at Lahaina early in October 1825, the sailors took exception to the new Hawaiian vice law prohibiting Hawaiian women from going aboard ships. They threatened to massacre the Reverend William Richards and his family if he did not use his influence to have the law repealed. After threatening him for four days, they entered his yard armed with knives and pistols and were only prevented from carrying out their threat by Richards's native parishioners, who came to his rescue and guarded his house until the *Daniel* departed. Later the crews of other whale ships made similar threats, but in the end only demolished his house, looted the town, and sailed off to Oahu when the native women fled to the hills. In January 1826 Lieutenant John "Mad Jack" Percival, arriving at Honolulu in the U.S.S. *Dolphin*, did himself and his country no credit when he forced the repeal of the vice law in Honolulu by threatening to fire on the town. As late as 1852 a mob of sailors burned down the police station and took over Honolulu for twenty-four hours.

Hawaiians (whom the sailors consistently called Kanakas) were popular crew members. As the sailors could not pronounce the island names, the natives were called "Spun-yarn," "Maintop," "Jack of Maui," "Jack of Oahu," and similar nicknames.[24] During the dog watches a Hawaiian bard, accompanied by his comrades, sometimes sat on the bowsprit bitts entertaining his fellow crew members with the soft songs and chants of the islands—songs of Kamehameha the Great, of Pele the fire goddess, of Maui fishing the islands from the sea.[25]

No sooner had a whaler dropped anchor in a Hawiian port than she was surrounded by outrigger canoes piled with bananas, breadfruit, pineapples, coconuts, sugarcane, shells, and souvenirs to trade for hoop iron, knives, needles, fishhooks, and tobacco. If Hawaiians could get a shirt or a coat for their products it was a banner day, for they could never get enough of *haole* (white men's) garments.

The visiting whalers, during the mid-decades of the century, brought great prosperity to the Honolulu merchants and received favored treatment in port charges and import duties from the kingdom. There was an increasing demand for Irish and sweet potatoes, fresh beef, and pork. Both the social and economic effects of whaling on Honolulu, Lahaina, and Hilo were extensive and there were resulting changes in the population. Spreading disease probably retarded the birthrate, and young men by the thousands sailed away on vessels—many never to return. There was a drift towards urbanization.

Because of the domination of Pacific whaling by American ships, the whalers' impact on the area was largely American. Almost uniformly eyewitness accounts of the whaling rendezvous, whether by traders, captains, sailors, or missionaries (not always the most objective informants), describe the ports as lawless, frontier-type towns (except for Papeete under the French regime). The swindlers and prostitutes, the rum, the deserters and escaped convicts, the degraded natives and corrupted chiefs, indicate a society centered on drunkenness and fornication and also on enormous and completely uncontrolled profits.

The impact of whaling on the Pacific islands was great and lasting. The practice of shipping islanders as crew members and leaving them wherever convenient mixed the populations. Although it would be difficult to prove, whalers almost certainly contributed more white blood to the population than did any other Caucasian group. But perhaps the greatest effect was speeding up urbanization in the Hawaiian Islands and to a lesser extent in Tahiti, and on agricultural development in those islands as well as New Zealand.

The Bay of Islands was the worst, but the waterfronts of the other towns were little better. In spite of the reactions of observers, it is doubtful if these wide-open seaport towns of the Pacific were any better or any worse than similar sailors' red light districts elsewhere in the world during the first half of the nineteenth century. Missionaries and traders daubed with piety for appearance' sake are not the most unbiased chroniclers of a town's history.

The differences between Papeete, Bay of Islands, and the Hawaiian ports and similar towns in more civilized countries lay in the effect on the Polynesians. In the Pacific there was no background of a resilient population long exposed and therefore partially immunized to the rampant disease, the immorality, and the human degradation associated with a busy port. In civilized countries such an atmosphere was confined to a restricted area; most of the population were no more than slightly aware of the rough and ready life of the waterfront. The main population was neither corrupted nor diminished.

Not so with the impingement of this kind of life upon the South Sea islander. Decimated by uncontrolled diseases, corrupted by some of the worst elements produced by Western civilization, increasingly desirous of metal tools, cloth, liquor, and firearms, the populations of New Zealand, Tahiti, and Hawaii were dramatically affected.

But a counter influence was working to restore the dignity of the native even if it did nothing immediately to halt the reduction in his numbers. The missionaries had moved in about the same time as the whalers, and South Sea islanders found themselves exposed to another extreme and far more incomprehensible facet of Western civilization.

CHAPTER 6

Save Thy Brother

The first two mission attempts in the Pacific, following the haphazard experiments on the voyages of Mendaña and Quiros, were Spanish and Roman Catholic. One was successful; the other abortive.

It is not surprising that Guam, the port of call for refreshment for the Manila galleons, became the one Pacific island to receive Spanish missionaries at an early date. A Franciscan padre made the first attempt as early as 1596, but not until 1668, when the Jesuit Diego Luis de Sanvitores landed, was a permanent mission established. The missionaries were at first well received. However, conflicts with native mores caused disputes and friction. When Sanvitores and eleven of his colleagues were killed in 1672, war between the natives and Spaniards erupted and lasted for thirty years. The Jesuits, suppressed by royal Spanish edict in 1769, were replaced in Guam by the Augustinians. The work of converting the Chamorros continued successfully and the population of Guam is mostly Roman Catholic to the present day. The missionaries taught the Chamorros the use of garden tools, introduced various American plants, especially maize, tobacco, and cocoa, and brought in cattle and horses.

Except for Guam the Spaniards made no attempt to carry the word of God to the Pacific islanders for about a century and a half after the return of Quiros. But English voyages to the Pacific (an ocean the Spaniards considered their private domain) and the discovery of Tahiti prompted the viceroy of Peru to send Domingo de Boenechea, who sailed in 1772 in command of the frigate *Aguila*, to find that island and investigate what was going on. Two padres were included in the ship's company with special instructions expressing their sovereign's chief wishes in reference to Tahiti: in addition to "the rescue of the Indians there . . . from their wretched Idolatry, and winning over of them by discreet and gentle methods to a knowledge of the true God and the profession of our catholic religion, besides securing, by means of an effective occupation, that no other nation shall possess itself of the said island, His Majesty resolutely wishes to form a settlement there with a prudent officer in command. . . . Your Reverences have accordingly been selected for the fulfillment of this holy mission."[1]

Instructions to the contrary, no attempt was made to establish a settlement on this voyage. But Boenechea returned in 1774-75, bringing two missionary friars, Fathers Geronima Clota and Narciso Gonzalez, together with an interpreter named Maximo Rodríguez and a sailor to act as cook and gardener. It was a small but well-equipped party. They had 34 casks of cereals, 2 barrels of sugar, 7 barrels of corn, 150 pounds of table oil, honey, wine, brandy, wheat, salt, and 4 barrels of lard and bacon. All this for four men on an island noted for its abundance of food. They were also supplied complete outfits of tools of all kinds, weapons, trade axes, and household utensils. Nor were the accouterments of their profession neglected. There were new missals, wine vessels, crystal goblets, an altar bell, a gross of rosaries, half a gross each of medallions and crosses, phials of holy oil, and a crucifix. A portable altar, draped with violet-flowered crimson satin, with all its fittings was provided, together with brilliant vestments and robes for all occasions. The afflictions of the body could be treated from a well-equipped medicine chest.[2]

The Tahitians helped the ship's carpenter build a house and the *Aguila* then made a trip to Raiatea in the Leewards. During the few days of the frigate's absence it became obvious that two more ill-suited, craven bigots could not have been selected for attempting to persuade the Tahitians to abandon their own ancient, intricate religion for Christianity. The friars could not endure the petty thieving, the gawking curious crowds, the noise and chatter and howling that went on day and night. They had no idea how to gain the goodwill of the exuberant population and exhibited narrow-minded, cranky, illiberal attitudes on all occasions which did not work toward their benefit.

Boenechea died in January 1775 after his return from the Leeward Islands and was buried with all solemnity and honors. Two days later the *Aguila* set sail for Lima.

Not only did the padres not get on with the Tahitians, they were not congenial with the interpreter, Rodríguez, whom they accused of drinking kava, sleeping with girls, and dallying around. They tried their best to make him into a menial, without success. Actually he was dealing with the chiefs without whose consent or approbation nothing could get done, not even the kitchen garden fenced. The good fathers also fought with everyone and ill-treated their seaman-cook. Besides all the rowing the air was punctuated by Padre Narciso's flatulence, with which he was continually afflicted. The mission was short-lived. Nine months later, on October 30, 1775, the *Aguila* returned. During that time the two padres had cared for injured Tahitians, but they were bedeviled by thefts and terrified by the human sacrifices made at the morai—they could not wait to leave and they were aboard the frigate when it sailed for Peru on November 12.[3]

In the end these notably unsuccessful men had refused to stay on unless a guard of soldiers was provided for them. The viceroy wrote to the Secretary of State for the Indies: "the two missionary Padres and the other lad who was with them as a menial gave, it seems, ample cause for drawing upon themselves the disaffection, not to say odium, of those unbelievers, in consequence of which our nation missed the laurels it should have gained through four of its subjects living for the space of nine months in an unknown country peopled by barbarians and infidels."[4]

More extensive and lasting than the Spanish efforts were the late eighteenth-century English evangelical endeavors to be now considered and the nineteenth-century American mission discussed in Chapter 8.

The English Tahitian Mission

In the first half of the eighteenth century both established and nonconformist religion in England had deteriorated in influence and existed as a form of dull respectability. By the end of the century it had shaken off its spiritual torpor. An evangelical movement shook the Church of England, the Methodist societies displayed enormous vigor, and other nonconformist groups were stimulated into activity.

One of the manifestations of this revival was the formation of the missionary societies. The first was organized by the Baptists in 1792. The formation of the London Missionary Society by an evangelical group in 1795 soon followed, with the sole object of spreading the knowledge of Christ among the heathen and other unenlightened nations.

One of the prime targets for the word of God, selected because of shocking accounts of morality in the recently published voyages and because of a lack of stable governments capable of repelling outsiders, was the South Sea islands. No time was lost. On September 25, 1796, thirty missionaries, some with families, watched Lands End fade over the horizon. Captain James Wilson, who had volunteered his services, was taking the ship *Duff* on the first leg of her 14,000-mile voyage to Tahiti.

A safe quick passage brought the *Duff* off Tahiti on March 4, 1797, and at seven the next morning—a Sunday—she closed the land. Seventy-five canoes, loaded to the gunwales, surrounded her and in minutes, ignoring English protests, a hundred or so Tahitians were scampering around the deck. The missionaries were bug-eyed. Nothing in their simple backgrounds had prepared them for a sight like this. The laughing, yelling, disorderly crowd, the stench of coconut oil, the wanton actions of the *arioi* (a fraternity of young, aristocratic performers who traveled about the islands) appalled them, but the islanders' good nature soon removed their momentary prejudices. It was a favorable beginning.

Of the thirty missionaries, only four were ordained ministers. The others were carpenters, weavers, bricklayers, shoemakers, and other craftsmen. Generally speaking, it was a simple, ill-educated group—poorly endowed and unsympathetic. On the voyage it had been decided among them which islands to settle. Eighteen, including all the married men, chose Tahiti; ten decided to go to Tongatabu; and two chose the Marquesas. Morale was high, the land was beautiful, light would chase the darkness from the islands.

Pomare, son of the chief of Captain Cook's day, had consolidated his rule over all of Tahiti and Moorea. A couple of Swedish beachcombers, who turned out to be useful interpreters, roamed the island. Lodging was solved by taking over a large house, 108 feet long by 48 feet wide, built by Pomare.

Getting the group settled at Tahiti by March 26, Captain Wilson went on to Tonga and anchored at Tongatabu April 10. Here he was greeted by two more beachcombers who also served as interpreters. Settling the missionaries under the protection of the most powerful chief on the island, the *Duff* sailed off for the Marquesas. One look at these wild islanders took the courage out of one missionary, who refused to stay, leaving the other in precarious loneliness.

Returning to Matavai Bay in Tahiti, Wilson found that in his absence the missionaries had had their first encounter with ceremonial infanticide by a chief and his wife. Unsuccessfully they called down the wrath of God upon the offending couple. They were further shocked upon discovering that

Pomare and his wife no longer cohabited, each preferring the favors of others. The missionary mind was beginning to boggle at island customs.

The *Duff* sailed for home August 4, 1797, taking two of the missionaries along, and the little colony did not see another ship until a year later when the *Nautilus* arrived. When the missionaries attempted to help the ship's captain by persuading Pomare to return two deserters, four of them were stripped of their clothing and beaten up by the Tahitians. They were so discouraged by this treatment that when the *Nautilus* sailed for Australia, eleven of the missionaries went with her, leaving only seven on the island. The party was further weakened when Thomas Lewis, one of the ministers, decided to marry a Tahitian. After a pious discussion by his peers he was excommunicated and ostracized. A few months later he died and his late comrades buried him. By this time the survivors were discovering that the language must be mastered before there was any hope of getting on with their chosen calling.

Erosion of the Tahitian party continued; John Harris, the man who had refused to stay at the Marquesas, elected to go to Tongatabu on a passing ship. There was some encouragement in January 1800 when William Henry, a carpenter who had fled to Australia, returned with his wife. But this was offset when Benjamin Broomhall, who contributed the unlikely craft of harness making to the party, renounced the gospel and, like Lewis, took a native wife. Near the end of 1800 a passing whaler brought the further unhappy news of the capture of the *Duff* by the French on her second voyage out with reinforcements. And still the language had not been sufficiently mastered to preach to the Tahitians.

Meantime the mission group at Tongatabu fared even less well. Caught in the middle of a local civil war in which eight runaway sailors took part, one missionary went native, three were massacred, and the remainder fled the island in January 1800. William Crook, the lone missionary left at the Marquesas, after less than two years there, returned to England on a whaler. The thirty original members of the mission had shrunk to five workers of remarkable tenaciousness on Tahiti.

Diligently and unsuccessfully the five attempted to show that rapidly spreading venereal disease, resulting from women prostituting themselves to the sailors of the increasing number of ships, was wreaking havoc with the race. Matavai Bay, the favorite anchorage, was almost depopulated by disease during the first four years the missionaries were in residence.

But better times were coming. In July 1801, nearly four years after the

Duff's departure, the *Royal Admiral* arrived with letters from home, fresh supplies, and, most welcome of all, nine new helpers. When the ship departed three weeks later, she carried off three runaway disturbers of the peace who had been a continual nuisance. The mission had turned the corner. The next twenty-five years would see unbelievably complete success.

The work began to advance quickly with the mastery of the language. Henry Nott, one of the ablest and most steadfast of the original group, preached the first sermon in Tahitian in February 1802 and followed that important event by making a preaching tour of the entire island with a colleague. A brief civil war interrupted the work but by October two more of the brethren were touring the island preaching in the vernacular before large enthusiastic audiences.

The old chief, Pomare I, who was affectionate toward the English but unsympathetic to the missionaries' religion, died, presumably of a heart attack, while paddling his canoe out to visit a brig off Matavai. His son, sympathetic to the new religious teaching, now became King Pomare II.

The year 1805 was devoted to perfecting knowledge of the language and reducing it to a written form. The missionaries began teaching the chiefs to write and in this skill Pomare excelled. The mission suffered a serious loss in September 1807 with the death of John Jefferson, one of the ordained ministers who came out in the *Duff* and who had acted as secretary and, indeed, informal leader of the group through its most trying times. If his death had happened earlier it is doubtful that the mission could have survived. But people were now coming and going; the group was larger and flourishing; the language had been mastered. Shortly after Jefferson's death, Nott expanded his evangelistic tours to the Leeward Islands, visiting Huahine, Raiatea, and Bora-Bora.

The mission reached its lowest ebb late in 1808 when a civil war broke out and Pomare II was defeated. The married missionaries fled to Huahine and the four bachelors, headed by Nott, were forced to move to Moorea, whither Pomare had fled. This seeming disaster turned out to be a fortuitous circumstance, for it threw Nott and Pomare together and the ardent missionary made the most of it. The king had been defeated and perhaps the old gods, to whom he had been faithful, were not so effective after all. But old beliefs die slowly. Not until four years later did Pomare request Nott to baptize him.

On a quick trip back to Tahiti (where Pomare had gone to mend political fences) Nott discovered that a group of Tahitians, led by two of their former servants, were holding prayer meetings in a banana grove. He persuaded them to come to Moorea, where they formed the nucleus of a group of about forty converts. In January 1815 the regular congregation numbered three hundred, but none had been baptized since Pomare wanted to be the first and the missionaries hesitated to christen him because of his heavy drinking.

By 1815 Nott was back in Tahiti preaching to large congregations. The results of spreading literacy showed strongly in 1815 and 1816. Important priests burned their idols, several morai were torn down, prominent chiefs violated the food taboos and asked blessings before meals. The collapse of traditional religious beliefs came even more quickly after the death of the chief who led them in a battle against Christians. The missionaries' triumph now arrived with surprising swiftness. Tahiti and Moorea were nominally completely Christian and the Leeward Islands soon followed.

Further strength was received in 1817 when eight more missionaries arrived, including William Ellis with a printing press which he set up at Moorea, and John Williams, the most energetic of them all. Now Tahitian spelling books, catechisms, the Gospel of Luke, and hymnals poured by the thousands from the little press. When the missionaries built themselves the brig *Haweis* to facilitate their moving easily among the islands their effectiveness further increased.

The climax came in 1819 on the anniversary of the mission's founding. Pomare had built an enormous royal mission chapel, 712 feet long and 54 feet wide, supported by 36 massive breadfruit tree pillars and surrounded by 280 more. There were 29 doors and 133 windows with sliding shutters. Three pulpits graced the interior and from them three different sermons were delivered simultaneously to the congregation of five to six thousand that crowded the huge room on June 10. On Sunday the sixteenth Pomare was at last baptized before an assembled multitude. Conversion now went rapidly ahead. By 1825 nearly all the inhabitants of Moorea had been baptized. Christian churches were established. Nott was translating the Bible into Tahitian. Meanwhile Pomare II had sunk completely into alcholism, gluttony, and homosexuality; he developed elephantiasis and died on December 7, 1821. Although he tended to antinomian notions, the missionaries lost in him a good friend and supporter. He was succeeded by his young son Pomare III.

A deputation sent out by the home office of the society in London, consisting of the Reverend Daniel Tyerman and George Bennet, arrived at Tahiti on September 25, 1821, on a whaler. They stayed in the Pacific for nearly three years during which time they visited the Hawaiian Islands as well. Their overall purpose was to visit each of the society's missions, encourage the missionaries, advise on such aspects of the work as seemed desirable, and report to headquarters on their return. The task took them eight years and Tyerman died in Madagascar on the trip. Their report, published in two volumes, was extensive and their observations on the Tahiti Mission favorable. So favorable, indeed, that they thought it should be self-supporting:

When it is considered what vast sums of money have been expended upon these islands, by the Society, in supporting this Mission for nearly thirty years, it will be admitted as highly reasonable that now, having embraced the gospel, the people should do all in their power, if not to reimburse the Society, at least to meet the present expenses of the Mission, that its funds may be devoted to the support of the gospel in other parts of the heathen world.[5]

But genuine satisfaction was also fully expressed:

While we see, with great satisfaction, all these islands living under just and humane laws, and blessed with all the institutions of the gospel, in full operation, we rejoice in beholding the progress which civilization has made in islands so lately in the depths of barbarism and the grossest superstition. That, in so short a period since the downfall of idolatry, so many of the people should have become acquainted with the arts of reading, writing, and arithmetic—so many excellent places of divine worship and numerous comfortable dwelling-houses built, and articles of furniture made—such a complete change effected in the manners of the people, from gross sensuality to the greatest decency and good behaviour—a people degraded by crime below any other people upon the face of the earth, but now the most generally, and most consistent, professors of Christianity of any nation under heaven:—these are to us facts so singular that we are at a loss for words to express our gratitude to God, while we would encourage you, dear brethren, to proceed in your noble career with zeal and delight, aiming at still greater things—the entire extirpation of every remaining evil, and advancing your flocks to a still higher elevation on the scale of moral character, and in the ranks of civilized society.[6]

In spite of all this goodly work the rising port of Papeete remained, and indeed still remains, a center of relaxed living, and even the most successful missionary achievements have had difficulty coping with the Tahitians' easy sexual morality and taste for liquor.

The Islands Beyond

The first quarter century of the Tahitian Mission had been dominated and its work consolidated by the steadfast perseverance and, one suspects, the linguistic ability of Henry Nott. The second generation, one of rapid expansion, began with the arrival of John Williams, the young, restless, bold, innovative, reformed ironmonger who would be the inspiring leader until his martyrdom.

Williams landed at Moorea on November 17, 1817. He was just over twenty-one years old. Less than a year later, with Lancelot Edward Threlkeld, he moved to Raiatea, the center of the worship of the Tahitian religion not only for the Society Islands but for all the islands within a five-hundred-mile radius.

Raiatea is not a large island and John Williams fretted for bigger pastures. The Lord smiled on him March 8, 1821, when a canoe load of some forty castaways arrived from the island of Rurutu in the Australs. The newcomers were enthralled by the new religion and Williams lost no time giving them a crash course in Christianity. They were returned, accompanied by two Tahitian deacons, to their own island by an English brig in July. Within a week of their arrival the entire island of Rurutu was converted, all of the principal morai demolished, and their carved gods shipped to Williams on Raiatea. This remarkable result to his hurried endeavors made a deep impression on Williams's mind.

Near the close of 1821 Williams and his wife went to Sydney for their health. On the way he expanded the range of his mission by leaving two Tahitian preachers on Aitutaki in the Cook Islands; here he was excited to hear of a mysterious unknown island somewhere nearby called Rarotonga.

At Sydney Williams lost no time in purchasing the sound little schooner *Endeavour* for mission work around the islands. He also envisioned a profitable trade in tobacco and sugarcane (soon foiled by an exorbitant New South Wales duty on tobacco) between Raiatea and the Australian colony. Williams returned to his base at Raiatea by way of Rurutu. The two Tahitian deacons had things well in hand; he was met by all the women wearing bonnets and all the men in hats. The Rurutuans were reading the Gospels and preparing coconut oil and arrowroot for sale. Williams left them with five hundred catechisms and the same number of spelling books and then went on to Raiatea.

Word now came to Williams from his teachers on Aitutaki that the people there were ready for the word of God and that Rarotongans were on the island. Choosing six more Tahitian teachers, he set out in the *Endeavour* in July 1823 on a remarkable three-month voyage. The conversion of Aitutaki was completed, the idols burned, and again the morai destroyed. Traveling to other islands in the Cooks, Williams was rebuffed at Mangaia, but salvation carried the day on Mauke and Mitiaro, and Atiu soon followed. Guided by natives, Williams searched for Rarotonga; he was nearly ready to give up when a cloud bank dispersed and there were the island's towering heights shining in the sun. Papeiha, the most successful deacon, was left on the island at his own request and within a year's time the island was converted.

Polynesian religion was intricately tied in with the government. As each island was converted the missionaries found that it was necessary to devise some form of civil laws to replace the old taboos. Codes of law were therefore drawn up in consultation with the chiefs in each island, with Tahiti, the first, serving as a model for all the others. After the chiefs agreed, the king of each island formally proclaimed the new code before a public assembly. Polygamy was one of the most difficult practices to resolve and was usually dealt with by having a chief select one of his wives and uniting the couple in a Christian marriage, while assuring his support of the others as well.

Williams revisited Rarotonga in 1827 and was detained there for some time, unable to return to Raiatea. Here in three months, with no experience in shipbuilding whatsoever, he built the *Messenger of Peace*, a sixty-foot vessel. The mission at Rarotonga was now placed under the direction of Aaron Buzacott, a blacksmith missionary, who arrived with his wife and a quantity of iron from Sydney. The iron was put to immediate use strengthening the *Messenger of Peace*, in which Williams sailed for Tahiti. On April 16, 1828, one year after his departure, he was back at Raiatea.

Williams, who could never be confined within one coral reef, probed even farther afield in his little vessel. The Society, Austral, and Cook islands were now well consolidated and he looked farther west. Niue was visited, and the Tongas, where he found the Wesleyans established. A quick agreement was made with the Wesleyans, who would henceforth concentrate on Tonga and Fiji while the London Society sent missionaries to Samoa. Williams now went there, taking along a Samoan chief and his wife who had been visiting in Tonga. Eight Polynesian teachers were landed on the island of Savaii and left under the protection of King Malietoa and his brother.

The ever-energetic Williams built another vessel called the *Olive Branch* in which George Pritchard and a Mr. Simpson attempted to establish a mission at the Marquesas in 1829. The effort failed when they were scared off by the warlike and cannibalistic inhabitants. On December 18, 1835, Henry Nott, the bricklayer who mastered the language, completed his great lifework: the translation of the Bible into Tahitian.

After the 1840s, when the French took over Tahiti and established a protectorate, the Protestant missionaries, though invited to continue, formally ceased direct activities with the natives. Their schools, chapels, and premises were registered as national property for the use of Protestants. No longer was their advice put into law. There was backsliding. By 1848 licensed houses of prostitution were established. The mission received a blow in March 1852, when the French passed a law depriving the churches of the right to elect their own pastors and handed that power over to the district subject to legislative confirmation.

During the last half of the century the Tahitian Mission was subjected to more control by the French Government. The resident missionary presided over the bethel for English-speaking whites and advised the native clergy who ran the other chapels. By agreement the Paris Evangelical Mission Society took over the Protestant work and in 1886 the directors of the London Missionary Society decided to relinquish their Tahiti Mission. A historian of the society summed up its accomplishments:

This decision closed a chapter in the society's history which must ever remain among its most cherished possessions. Nothing exactly like it is to be found in any other portion of the century's story. The wonderful burst of enthusiasm out of which the mission sprang, the courageous perseverance with which those who remained faithful laboured through "the night of toil," the marvellous and dramatic conversion of the island, the way in which it became "a city set on a hill" to the whole of Polynesia, the many lessons learned there in the hard school of experience, and turned to good account in many other portions of the great harvest field of the world—all give Tahiti an abiding place in the affection and the memory.[7]

A treaty made between Great Britain and France in 1847, guaranteeing the independence of the Leeward Islands, was abrogated in 1888 and the entire Society group became part of the French protectorate. The London Missionary Society withdrew from the Societies in 1890 and handed the mission over to the French Protestants, who also soon took over the Austral Islands.

John Williams had gone back to England in 1835 to raise money for a larger missionary ship—a project dear to his heart—and to see a Rarotongan New Testament through the press. While there he published in 1837 *A Narrative of Missionary Enterprises in the South Sea Islands* which was enthusiastically received and aided his efforts. In April the following year he sailed again for Polynesia in the *Camden*, his new vessel, with a band of young neophyte missionaries and five thousand copies of the new Rarotongan Testament.

With the abandonment to France of the Society Islands, the core of the London missionary effort became Rarotonga, where Aaron Buzacott was in charge and where a training college for native teachers was set up. Between 1839 and 1893, 490 native teachers trained there took the Gospel to Samoa, the Loyalty Islands, the New Hebrides, and, in 1872, to southeastern New Guinea. Melanesia was a hazardous place to work. Between 1872 and 1891 fifty-two couples were sent to New Guinea, of whom seventeen men and twenty-three women died of fever, four men and three women were killed, and three couples returned home in discouragement.

The first six permanent English missionaries sent out to the Samoa group arrived there in June 1836. Reinforcements came later with Williams in the *Camden*. In contrast to the Society Islands it was native warfare rather than organized native religion that was the greatest hindrance to progress, but in general conversion of Samoa was efficient, rapid, complete, and without major incident. The Bible was translated into Samoan and educational emphasis was constantly stressed. The activities of the London Society, expanded and made easier by a series of missionary vessels (all after the *Camden* named *John Williams*) continued to push westward.

In 1839, with great courage but appalling naivety, John Williams and a Mr. Harris, with several teachers, sailed in the *Camden* for the New Hebrides. After leaving three Polynesian preachers at Tanna, they went on to Erromanga. They found the language incomprehensible, and Williams's attempts to distribute presents to four natives in a passing canoe was scorned. Nevertheless, Williams and Harris were rowed in to shore while natives on the beach gestured them to go away. They did not. As they waded into the surf the natives made a swift attack and clubbed the two missionaries to death under the eyes of the helpless boat's crew. It was later learned that the attack was provoked by a previous visit of sandalwood traders who had killed the chief's son and committed other atrocities. Perhaps Williams, the most tireless and energetic of all the missionaries, ended his life as he would have liked—a martyr in the service of the Lord.

The killings discouraged missionary efforts in the New Hebrides for only two years. In 1841 the *Camden* again visited these islands with the Reverend A. W. Murray in charge. Samoan missionaries were landed and hung on until 1848, when the mission was turned over to the Reverend John Geddie of the Presbyterian Church of Nova Scotia. Other missionaries from Scotland settled on Tanna. Smallpox left by a vessel devastated the islands. In 1860 the Reverend and Mrs. G. N. Gordon from Nova Scotia were murdered on Erromanga because the natives blamed them for a previous deadly epidemic of measles. Several of the native teachers were killed on other islands. Meanwhile the northern New Hebrides, along with the Banks, Solomon, and Santa Cruz groups, were being missionized from New Zealand, where Bishop George A. Selwyn established the Melanesian Mission. John C. Patterson became the first bishop of Melanesia in 1861.

Polynesians, especially Samoans and Rarotongans, carried much of the workload of the expanding missions. Work began in the Loyalty Islands in 1841 but activities were finally curtailed in 1869 by the French Government which also refused to allow the Protestants to expand into New Caledonia.

A station on Niue was established in 1846 and in the Tokelau group in 1861. That same year a canoe load of Christian castaways from the Cooks was thrown upon Nukulaelae in the Ellice Islands. A native teacher among the shipwrecked people began work immediately and, after being rescued, returned with other teachers. The Gilbert Islands were added to the Samoan mission in 1870.

The most difficult and discouraging of missions (and the last London Missionary Society expansion effort) began in New Guinea in 1871 and was strengthened after the annexation of Papua by the British in 1888. Numbers of stations were founded on the southeastern peninsula of New Guinea, the most important at Port Moresby. Polynesian teachers died like flies from fever and native spears, but the work went on slowly and was never abandoned. Work in Melanesia, however, with its fragmented peoples, multiplicity of languages, and difficult climate could not go forward with the facility developed in the highly structured Polynesian societies under strong chiefs with a common language in a healthful climate.

The Wesleyans in Fiji

The *Duff* missionaries at Tonga, appalled by the strangling of wives and sons at a chief's death, the cannibalism, and the almost constant warfare, had left the area in its native state after 1800. Three were killed and the others did not stay long enough to learn the language or make any converts.

An attempt to fill this vacuum was first made in 1822 by the Reverend Walter Lawry, a Wesleyan, with a small group of companions. He was beginning to earn the respect of the natives when his wife's illness forced him to leave after little more than a year's work. The permanent mission of the Wesleyan Missionary Society began in 1826 with the arrival of the Reverend John Thomas. Within six years he had six thousand converts, and when he departed the Tonga group in 1850 only a handful of the unconverted remained. Conversion in the group was greatly aided by the chief Taufaahau, whom the missionaries called King George Tubou and who eventually became king of all Tonga.

With the constant canoe voyages between Tonga and Fiji, it was only natural that the Wesleyans should move into the latter group of islands, only two hundred and fifty miles away. The only previous attempt in Fiji had come in 1830 when two Tahitians, teachers of the London Missionary Society, were sent to Lakemba and later moved to the small island of Oneata. By 1835 the constant intercourse between Tonga and the Lau group in the eastern Fijis had spread the word about Christianity to some extent and helped to prepare the way for William Cross and David Cargill, two ministers who arrived at Lakemba with a message of recommendation to the Lakemba chief from King George Tubou.

Most of the first converts were Tongans living in the Fijis. For three years the missionaries nearly starved. After relief arrived in 1838, Cross attempted to establish a mission at Mbau, but was told by its king, Thakombau, that his safety could not be guaranteed. He then moved to Rewa (Mbau's great rival) on the main island of Viti Levu, where he nearly died of fever. His convalescence was helped by the arrival of John Hunt. Cross may have set back Christianity in the Fijis some years by not settling at Mbau, for Thakombau, the most powerful chief in the islands, was personally friendly to the missionaries but lost face when they chose to settle among his greatest rivals.

Meanwhile James Calvert and others from England joined Cargill at Lakemba. The mission took on a hazardous permanency as the ferocious local warfare continued and the great stone ovens smoked with victims for the cannibal feasts. No apparent progress was made on Viti Levu for years, but the missionaries and their families clung doggedly to their discouraging, dangerous task. Ono was the first of several of the small outer islands to become totally converted in 1842.

In the 1840s the missionaries became onlookers at a long, cruel war between Rewa and Mbau, but were unmolested by the generally friendly chiefs. A mission opened at Somosomo in 1839 was abandoned in 1847. Other missions were established at Vanua Levu in 1847, at Levuka in 1851, and finally at Mbau in 1854. A breakthrough came on April 30, 1854, when King Thakombau of Mbau openly professed Christianity. Early in 1857 he gave up all but one of his wives, to whom he was married in a Christian ceremony. Both were baptized, with Thakombau taking the name of Ebenezer. From that time on, the persecution of Christians ceased at Mbau and conversion went forward rapidly.

It has been pointed out that at every mission station in the Fijis white missionaries were preceded by courageous native teachers or preachers who paved the way. These men took greater risks than the whites, for they lacked prestige. Nevertheless, the English missionaries and their heroic wives were often in danger. Many of them barely escaped being clubbed, although Thomas Baker (in 1867) was the only white missionary killed in the Fijis. This is the more surprising as both the missionaries and their wives, time after time, fearlessly exposed themselves by constantly and strenuously objecting to cannibalism, warfare, and the custom of strangling widows. Although they were helpless to do anything about these established customs, their protests put the missionaries in constant peril.

In 1844 French Catholic Marists established a mission at Lakemba, but abandoned it eleven years later. With it, however, began a continuing feud between Wesleyans and Catholics, exhibiting a bitterness and narrow-mindedness on both sides which was only confusing to the Fijians.

When Christianity became general, it did so quickly. It is true that the chiefs were conservative and the new religion was opposed to everything the chiefs cherished. The missionaries, for example, urged their converts not to engage in warfare and this irritated the chiefs when they were trying to raise a war party. But once a chief became converted, it was usual for his entire tribe to follow, and when Fijians adopted Christianity they took their new religion seriously. The chiefs became aware that many of their customs were abhorrent not only to the missionaries but to the other Europeans who arrived in the increasing numbers of ships. The captains of warships made it clear that they did not look with favor on constant warfare and pillage. Chiefs became ashamed of their customs and surreptitious in eating their fellow men and strangling their widows.

Missions swept across the Pacific from Tahiti to New Guinea during the nineteenth century. As the century progressed other groups sent their missionaries into the Pacific. Various Catholic orders entered the field and in New Caledonia they had no competition. The Seventh-Day Adventists proselyted almost everywhere. Mormons sent out their young college men in pairs for two years' service in the vineyard. Other missionaries came from Australia, North America, and elsewhere. The Church of England's mission in Melanesia happened because of a clerk's error in defining boundaries when the Anglican diocese of New Zealand was established. George A. Selwyn, the diocese's first bishop, was thus inadvertently given jurisdiction over a wide area of the Pacific. Selwyn, not one to shirk his responsibilities, welcomed the error which gave him an opportunity to enter the mission field. He visited Melanesia first in 1849 and organized the Melanesian Mission, which domi-- nated the field in the Solomons, northern New Hebrides, Santa Cruz, and adjacent islands. The Anglicans depended more on an annual visit to each island by a missionary vessel and bringing natives back to New Zealand for instruction rather than on workers in the field. Those in the field, however, included some eminent men, among them Robert H. Codrington, the great authority on Melanesians and their languages. But it was the early missions in the field that fought the primary fight with heathenism.

Some anthropologists would feel better if the South Sea islanders and their cultures had never been disturbed. But European impact was inevitable, and the missionaries were an important part of that impact.

Narrow-minded and inflexible as they were, on balance the missionaries did more good than harm at least from a Western point of view. Their greatest contributions were in the fields of literacy and education. Invariably it was the missionary who produced dictionaries, grammars, spelling books, and translations to further spread Christianity. But they also gave the various islanders written languages enabling schools to be established. Missionary effect on agriculture was profound. Many new and useful plants were introduced, and more effective agricultural methods taught. In general, populations became less scattered and while the missionaries did not dramatically influence the urban trend as did the whalers, and indeed deplored the vices of the waterfront urban centers, they tended to attract the population into small village groups clustered around chapels.

What happened in Rarotonga, for instance, between 1828 and 1857 is typical, with individual variations, of many of the changes that took place on other islands under missionary influence. European clothing replaced the breechcloth, nudity, tattooing, and coconut oil. Cement was manufactured and stone cottages of block coral for individual families replaced thatched houses and communal dwellings. European-type furniture became popular. The introduction of cattle, better breeds of pigs, and several kinds of poultry, as well as citrus fruits, vegetables, pineapples, maize, arrowroot, rice, and tapioca, improved and diversified the diet. Horses were also introduced, and cotton and indigo cultivated. The language was reduced to writing. Schoolbooks and slates were widely distributed. Schools were founded. By 1857 the whole population of Rarotonga could read and most could write and do simple arithmetic.[8] Codified laws and port regulations were introduced in most islands. All of these changes took place in addition to the religious priorities, including the keeping of the Sabbath.

Regardless of occasional questionable methods, the missionaries were always on the side of the native and against his exploitation. It must have been refreshing to islanders to see that paradox of the South Seas—white men who did not want their food and their women. Local warfare was reduced and often eliminated. This gave more time for cultivation of the land and for group activities, which were encouraged.

Of all the diverse invaders of the Pacific, the missionaries were almost certainly the greatest single influence in the nineteenth century. In their westward push, however, they would have had a far more difficult time without naval backing—especially French and English. Chieftains soon learned that if missionaries were harmed, a day of reckoning, though perhaps long delayed, would arrive in the form of a warship.

CHAPTER 7

Ceremonies and Conflicts

The exploitation of the Pacific coasts and islands that began almost immediately after the publication of Cook's third voyage in 1784 was at first an economic one. New products for the China market lured traders who crisscrossed the Pacific from Antarctica to Alaska and from Peru to Australia. The abundance of whales and the demand for oil pushed hundreds of whale ships into this new bonanza. Reeking tryworks smudged the blue horizons of all the vast whaling grounds. Soon the first invaders for other than economic reasons appeared; black-frocked missionaries, bringing the word of God and the promise of eternal salvation, sweated out their dour convictions, worked and died, but always progressed.

The process was inevitable but the times would have been more difficult, even more dangerous, and exploitation and conversion probably slower, though nonetheless certain, were it not for the expeditions and warships that continued to be sent to the Pacific regularly by the great seafaring powers. Exploration was the primary purpose at first. Nobody knew how many more islands there were to discover. Many of those already known, as well as thousands of miles of coastline, still remained to be surveyed. Studies of the fauna and flora had scarcely begun. And strange people with exotic customs, religions, and pastimes excited the imagination.

To complete Cook's work the governments of Great Britain, France, Russia, and the United States sent well-equipped scientific naval expeditions into the Pacific until as late as the 1870s. Gradually the purposes of the naval cruises changed. When it became evident that there were no more lands of consequence to discover, emphasis shifted to surveying and exploring lands already known. As the traders and whalers increased in the Pacific, their complaints were heard in the halls of state. They wanted protection. They wanted insurance on their investments. It was almost standard practice to have the search for new whaling grounds included in the instructions to a warship or expedition bound for the Pacific. Debts owed by chiefs for sandalwood or the chastising of a village for burning a bêche-de-mer drying shed or, even more serious, the death of a trader or missionary became standard reasons for shows of force, which ranged all the way from a display of fireworks and a few cannon shots to the razing of a village or the execution of a supposed culprit.

Naval commanders excelled at entertaining South Sea aristocrats at dinner on board ship, with plenty of wine followed by brandy. The ship's band played and the marines drilled for the edification of crowds of delighted islanders. They in return produced sham battles, wrestling, spear-throwing contests, and dancing girls. Polynesians, especially, love ceremony as much as naval officers.

While for convenience and clarity traders, whalers, missionaries, and expeditions are treated topically in this volume, it should be kept in mind that all these things were going on simultaneously during the first half of the nineteenth century and that usually not all white men on a particular island were helping each other. More frequently, if not bitter enemies they were at best rivals. Traders and whalers opposed missionaries who tried at least to keep the activities of the former within some kind of bounds. Protestants and Catholics bitterly opposed each other. National rivalries, particularly between the French and English, broke out consistently. All this bickering was not lost on Pacific islanders who were past masters of village or family feuds, betrayals, ceremonial warfare, ambush, surprise, political double-dealing and double-cross. This was all good innocuous fun.

How did these naval commanders conduct themselves—what impact did they make? Let us consider a few of their contacts during some of the best-known expeditions as examples of the many that took place.

The French answer to Captain James Cook's great voyages was an ambitious expedition commanded by Jean François de La Pérouse, a highly regarded career naval officer of proven competence, in the two ships *Boussole* and *Astrolabe*. Thoroughly equipped, bountifully supplied, and manned by a selected company of officers, men, and scientists, it was anticipated that the expedition's results would be worth the preparations and funds that had gone into it.

La Pérouse's official instructions were voluminous, covering far more than a single expedition could ever accomplish. They were to take him north and south, east and west, across the Pacific and to some of the islands. It would have been impossible to do all the things he was charged with even had he survived, which he did not. La Pérouse sailed from Brest August 1, 1785. Three years later, on March 11, 1788, the *Boussole* and *Astrolabe* sailed into oblivion from Botany Bay, New South Wales, and their wrecks were not found until nearly forty years later. Before his disappearance, however, La Pérouse managed to visit some of the Pacific islands.

He called at remote Easter Island for one day on April 9, 1786. In that brief time he examined the interior of the island and left seeds of useful plants along with sheep, goats, and pigs. In return for the livestock and potential improvements to local agriculture, the Easter Islanders relieved the ships of as many small items as they could and offered the Frenchmen their women. La Pérouse is noncommittal about the offer. Perhaps it influenced his tact and humaneness in dealing with the thievery.

Sailing north to carry out orders in the North Pacific, La Pérouse made only a short stay, but surprisingly complete observations, at the Hawaiian Islands. He then went on to the Northwest Coast, where he lost six officers and fifteen men when two boats swamped in the breakers. He crossed the Pacific to Manila, visited Formosa and Macao, and arrived at Kamchatka September 6, 1787, from where he sent a copy of his journal and dispatches overland to Paris.

Samoa, which he reached on December 6, was his next South Sea island group. He cruised slowly through the lovely islands, trading red cloth and beads for fruit, pigs, and delicious edible dogs. Tutuila seemed a paradise and the abundance of food was overwhelming. In a couple of days the expedition got five hundred hogs, dozens of chickens and pigeons, and bushels of fruit. Clear fresh water filled the stale casks. The sailors bought hundreds of wood pigeons, turtledoves, and parrots tamed by the Samoans.

But, as so often happened in early South Sea contacts, the idyllic quickly changed to the tragic. Taking on two last boatloads of water casks, De Langle, one of the officers, waited for the tide to give him water enough to pass over the reef. A crowd of twelve hundred Samoans assembled and began throwing stones. A musket was discharged; the clubs came out; and fighting became general. In five minutes twelve Frenchmen, including De Langle and a naturalist, were killed and twenty others badly wounded. Forgetting the pleasant first days, La Pérouse named the place Massacre Island and sailed off to Tonga still so shaken that he never anchored there—merely passing through the group and on to Botany Bay. La Pérouse's score was two friendly and one hostile contact with the islanders.

Captain William Bligh's voyage in search of breadfruit plants has always been dominated by the dramatic story of the mutiny and Bligh's four-thousand-mile voyage to Timor in the cutter. But its contribution to the knowledge of Tahiti should not be shortchanged. Sailing from England in late 1787, Bligh arrived in Tahiti October 27, 1788, and spent twenty-three idyllic weeks there. He spoke the language. He loved the island. The book he subsequently wrote contributes more to our ethnological knowledge of the Tahitians at this period than any other writings save Cook's own.

Bligh especially remarked on the changes that had taken place, due to European contact, since his earlier visit there with Cook in 1777. Stone tools had been abandoned in the eleven-year period. Not only that, the Tahitians no longer wanted iron blades made in the shape of their stone ones; they wanted European tools to which they were now accustomed, blades that would cut and shorten the making of a dugout canoe by weeks if not months. The native breeds of pigs and dogs had given way to European varieties. A war between Tahiti and Moorea had shifted the balance of power. All the great Tahitian houses of Cook's day had been destroyed. Only two or three of the mighty seagoing canoes were left. The livestock which Cook had hoped would be a lasting benefit to the people had all been slaughtered.

On the other hand the dress had not changed and the young people still went surfing on their canoe paddles, danced, and made love. Bligh poignantly wrote that Tahiti and Moorea were "certainly the Paradise of the World and if happiness could result from situation and convenience, here it is to be found in the highest perfection. I have seen many parts of the World, but Otaheite [Tahiti] is capable of being preferable to them all, and certainly is so considering it in its natural State."[1]

The principal chief of Tahiti at the time of Bligh's visit was Tu (Pomare I), who arrived on board the *Bounty* the same day she anchored in Matavai Bay. He was accompanied by numerous attendants. The chief introduced Bligh to his wife and the two men rubbed noses in the customary greeting of the country. Tu (whom Bligh had met on his earlier visit with Cook) informed him that his name was now Tinah.

The name of Tinah's wife [Bligh wrote] was Iddeah: with her was a woman, dressed with a large quantity of cloth, in the form of a hoop, which was taken off and presented to me, with a large hog, and some bread-fruit. I then took my visitors into the cabin, and after a short time produced my presents in return. The present I made to Tinah (by which name I shall hereafter call him) consisted of hatchets, small adzes, files, gimblets, saws, looking-glasses, red feathers, and two shirts. To Iddeah I gave ear-rings, necklaces, and beads; but she expressed a desire also for iron, and therefore I made the same assortment for her as I had for her husband. Much conversation took place among them on the value of the articles, and they appeared extremely satisfied; so that they determined to spend the day with me, and requested I would shew them all over the ship, and particularly the cabin where I slept. This, though I was not fond of doing, I indulged them in; and the consequence was, as I had apprehended, that they took a fancy to so many things, that they got from me nearly as much more as I had before given them. Afterwards, Tinah desired me to fire some of the great guns: this I likewise complied with, and, as the shot fell into the sea at a great distance, all the natives expressed their surprize by loud shouts and acclamations.

I had a large company at dinner; for, besides Tinah and his wife, there was Otow, the father of Tinah, Oreepyah, and Whydooah, two of his brothers, Poeeno, and several other chiefs. Tinah is a very large man, much above the common stature, being not less than six feet four inches in height, and proportionably stout: his age about thirty-five. His wife (Iddeah) I judged to be about twenty-four years of age: she is likewise much above the common size of the women at Otaheite, and has a very animated and intelligent countenance. Whydooah, the younger brother of Tinah, was highly spoken of as a warrior, but had the character of being the greatest drunkard in the country; and indeed, to judge from the withered appearance of his skin, he must have used the pernicious drink called Ava, to great excess. Tinah was fed by one of his attendants, who sat by him for that purpose, this being a particular custom among some of the superior chiefs; and I must do him the justice to say, he kept his attendant constantly employed: there was indeed little reason to complain of want of appetite in any of my guests. As the women are not allowed to eat in presence of the men, Iddeah dined with some of her companions, about an hour afterwards, in private except that her husband Tinah favoured them with his company, and seemed to have entirely forgotten that he had already dined.[2]

Bligh returned Tinah's visit the next day and was invited to appear at his brother Oreepyah's house near the beach.

At this place [Bligh observed] I found a great number of people collected, who, on my appearance, immediately made way for me to sit down by Tinah. The croud being ordered to draw back, a piece of cloth, about two yards wide and forty-one yards in length, was spread on the ground; and another piece of cloth was brought by Oreepyah, which he put over my shoulders, and round my waist, in the manner the chiefs are clothed. Two large hogs, weighing each above two hundred pounds, and a quantity of baked bread-fruit and cocoa-nuts, were then laid before me, as a present, and I was desired to walk from one end of the cloth spread on the ground to the other, in the course of which, Tyo and Ehoah [expressions of friendship] were repeated with loud acclamations. This ceremony being ended, Tinah desired I would send the things on board, which completely loaded the boat; we, therefore, waited till she came back, and then I took them on board with me; for I knew they expected some return.—The present which I made on this occasion, was equal to any that I had made before; but I discovered that Tinah was not the sole proprietor of what he had given to me, for the present I gave was divided among those who, I guessed, had contributed to support his dignity; among whom were Moannah, Poeenah, and Oreepyah; Tinah, however, kept the greatest part of what I had given, and every one seemed satisfied with the proportion he allotted them.[3]

Captain Bligh arrived back in England from his dramatic voyage in March 1790. That same year one of the greatest eighteenth-century Royal Navy surveying expeditions departed. Captain George Vancouver sailed from Deptford in December in H.M.S. *Discovery* (shortly joined by the *Chatham*) to complete the survey of the Northwest Coast. On the voyage out Vancouver discovered the island of Rapa, and Captain William R. Broughton discovered the Chatham Islands, naming them for his ship. After Broughton's first cheerful meeting with the Moriois (as the Chatham Islanders are called), in which the natives expressed surprise and seemed to ask if the visitors had come from the sun, relations deteriorated. Spears and clubs were brandished and in the skirmish one Moriori was shot and killed. As he left the Chathams, Broughton lamented "the hostility of its inhabitants that rendered the melancholy fate that attended one of them unavoidable, and prevented our researches extending further than the beach, and the immediate entrance of the adjoining wood."[4]

The ships, which had been separated, rendezvoused at Tahiti in December 1791 and stayed there three weeks. As soon as Vancouver dropped anchor he sent a messenger to inform the local king of his arrival. Vancouver reported: "The messenger that had been dispatched to inform *Otoo* [the king, Pomare I] of our landing and proposed visit, returned with a pig, and a plantain leaf, as a peace-offering to me; accompanied by a speech of congratu-

lation on our arrival, and offers of whatever refreshments the country afforded."[5] After this short ceremony had been completed, Vancouver was
greeted on the beach by the king's son.

> We found *Otoo* [the son] to be a boy of about nine or ten years of age. He
> was carried on the shoulders of a man, and was clothed in a piece of English
> red cloth, with ornaments of pigeon's feathers hanging over his shoulders.
> When we had approached within about eight paces, we were desired to stop:
> the present we had brought was exhibited; and although its magnitude, and
> the value of the articles it contained, excited the admiration of the by-
> standers in the highest degree, it was regarded by this young monarch with an
> apparently stern and cool indifference. It was not immediately to be pre-
> sented; a certain previous ceremony was necessary . . . A ratification of peace
> and mutual friendship being acknowledged on both sides, and these cere-
> monies concluded, which took up fifteen or twenty minutes, the different
> European articles composing the present, were, with some little form, pre-
> sented to *Otoo*; and on his shaking hands with us, which he did very heartily,
> his countenance became immediately altered, and he received us with the
> greatest cheerfulness and cordiality.[6]

Vancouver entertained King Pomare and the Tahitian chiefs lavishly. After
one dinner where the wine flowed freely, Pomare drank an entire bottle of
brandy and went into convulsions. Four strong men gave him the native massage treatment. He then passed out, slept soundly, and awoke sober with a
new respect for "ava Britarne," as he called rum or brandy. For the rest of
Vancouver's stay he restricted his drinking to a few glasses of wine.

> We had a very large party [Vancouver wrote] of royalty and of the dif-
> ferent chiefs to dinner at the marquee; after which it was proposed, that the
> "*Heava no Britarne*," that is, the English entertainments, were to commence.
> *Pomurrey* requested that some guns from the ships should be fired as a pre-
> lude; that the marines on shore should go through their exercise, and fire; and
> that the efforts of the field pieces should be exhibited. From the latter were
> fired both round and cannister shot, which the surrounding multitude beheld
> with surprize, admiration, and terror, manifested by their expressions, partic-
> ularly on observing the distance to which the small three pounders threw the
> round shot; and the execution that evidently could be done by the cannister,
> which was fired at a rock in the sea, lying at a convenient distance. On firing
> with some dispatch, three rounds from the field pieces, the fear of *Pomurrey*
> completely overcame his curiosity, and he exclaimed "*Ateerara*;" signifying
> he was perfectly satisfied. . . . A numerous crowd were assembled on the oc-
> casion, who expressed as much astonishment and admiration, as if these had
> been the first exhibited in the island. I endeavoured to prevail on *Pomurrey*
> to assist in the performance. He once took the port fire in his hand, but his

heart failed, and calling his youngest wife *Fier re te*, desired I would instruct her. She was by no means so alarmed as her husband; and, with a little of my assistance, she fired several rockets, a catharine wheel, some flower pots, and balloons. Having displayed an assortment of these, together with some water rockets, &c. the exhibition was closed; and the natives retired in the most perfectly good order to their respective habitations, excessively well pleased with their entertainment; although it was evident, that the major part had been as much affected by terror, as admiration.[7]

Pomare appropriately reciprocated Vancouver's hospitality. Large hogs, chickens, vegetables, fruit, and tapa cloth arrived at the ships in abundance. Vancouver was even presented with not one but three of the rare mourning costumes—the most lavish gift Tahiti produced.

Like Bligh, Vancouver commented on the changes that had taken place in Tahitian life since his visit with Cook in 1777:

So important are the various European implements, and other commodities, now become to the happiness and comfort of these islanders, that I cannot avoid reflecting with Captain Cook on the very deplorable condition to which these people on a certainty must be reduced, should their communication with Europeans be ever at an end. The knowledge they have now acquired of the superiority and the supply with which they have been furnished of more useful implements, have rendered these, and other European commodities, not only essentially necessary to their common comforts, but have made them regardless of their former tools and manufactures, which are now growing fast out of use, and, I may add, equally out of remembrance. Of this we had convincing proof . . .[8]

Vancouver arrived at the Hawaiian Islands on March 1, 1792, and spent only eighteen days there, mostly shopping around for supplies, before going on to the Northwest Coast. During his great Northwest Coast explorations, however, Vancouver returned to the islands each season and made the earliest thorough survey of the group.

For his first island wintering, Vancouver left the coast in January 1793. On the island of Hawaii he landed cattle, the first to be introduced to the islands. The people were greatly impressed with these creatures and the king placed them under a taboo so strict that they increased unmolested for years and became a nuisance. At Hawaii also he met Kamehameha, obviously the most powerful chief of the island, on the threshold of his rise to paramount power of all the Hawaiian Islands. Vancouver gave Kamehameha presents to distribute to all his people and for himself, "a scarlet cloak, that reached from his neck to the ground, adorned with tinsel lace, trimmed with various coloured gartering tape, with blue ribbons to tie it down the front. The look-ing glasses being placed opposite to each other displayed at once the whole of his royal person; this filled him with rapture, and so delighted him that the cabin could scarcely contain him."[9] Kamehameha reciprocated handsomely:

before the ship was well secured, eleven large canoes put off from the shore with great order, and formed two equal sides of an obtuse triangle. The largest canoe being in the angular point, was rowed by eighteen paddles on each side; in this was his Owhyhean majesty, dressed in a printed linen gown, that Captain Cook had given to *Terreoboo* [Kalaniopuu] ; and the most ele-gant feathered cloak I had yet seen, composed principally of beautiful bright yellow feathers, and reaching from his shoulders to the ground on which it trailed. On his head he wore a very handsome helmet, and made altogether a very magnificent appearance. His canoe was advanced a little forward in the procession, to the actions of which the other ten strictly attended, keeping the most exact and regular time with their paddles, and inclining to the right or left agreeably to the directions of the king, who conducted the whole busi-ness with a degree of adroitness and uniformity, that manifested a knowledge of such movements and manoeuvre far beyond what could reasonably have been expected. In this manner he paraded round the vessels, with a slow and solemn motion. This not only added a great dignity to the procession, but gave time to the crowd of canoes alongside to get out of the way. He now ordered the ten canoes to draw up in a line under our stern, whilst, with the utmost exertions of his paddlers, he rowed up along the starboard side of the ship; and though the canoe was going at a very great rate, she was in an in-stant stopped, with that part of the canoe where his majesty was standing im-mediately opposite the gangway. [Following this impressive arrival,] he then presented me with four very handsome feathered helmets, and ordered the ten large canoes that were under the stern to come on the starboard side. Each of these contained nine very large hogs, whilst a fleet of smaller canoes, containing a profusion of vegetables, were ordered by him to deliver their car-goes on the opposite side. This supply was more than we could possibly dis-pose of; some of the latter he was prevailed upon to reserve, but although our decks, as well as those of the *Chatham*, were already encumbered with their good things, he would not suffer one hog to be returned to the shore.[10]

Vancouver and Kamehameha got on well together and the king aided the captain in surveying and refitting while the latter approved the monarch's politics. Before Vancouver left in March to continue his Northwest Coast sur-vey there were mutual entertainments and feasting. Vancouver set off a splendid display of fireworks and Kamehameha brought on some of his best warriors to stage a sham battle. The Hawaiians' dexterity in parrying the flying spears astounded the English. As a final present the king gave Vancouver "the superb cloak that he had worn on his formal visit at [Vancouver's] arrival. This cloak was very neatly made of yellow feathers; after he had displayed its beauty, and had shewn me the two holes made in different parts of it by the enemy's spears the first day he wore it, in his last battle for the sovereignty of this island, he very carefully folded it up, and desired, that on my arrival in England, I would present it in his name to His Majesty, King George."[11]

Vancouver returned to the islands again for wintering in 1794. This time he concentrated on completing the survey of the islands, but there was another important duty to perform. King Kamehameha had expressed a desire to cede Hawaii to the king of Great Britain, so Vancouver brought him, the queen, and the principal chiefs on board the *Discovery* for formally ceding the island to George III. Everyone made speeches and some of the officers went on shore, displayed the British colors, and took possession "in conformity to the inclinations and desire of Tamaahmaah [Kamehameha] and his subjects." Vancouver wondered if this addition to the realm would ever be of any use to Britain or bring any happiness to the Hawaiians. But, having accomplished it, Vancouver spent one last season on the Northwest Coast and then returned to England, where he arrived in the fall of 1795.

A new national flag was seen in the central Pacific when the Russian ships *Nadeshda* and *Neva* arrived at Nuku Hiva in the Marquesas Islands on May 5, 1804. Captain A. J. von Krusenstern had sailed from Kronshtadt the previous August, primarily to take a diplomatic delegation to Japan. That errand was unsuccessful, but he became the first Russian navigator to sail around the world.

Soon after Krusenstern dropped anchor at Nuku Hiva, two beachcombers, an Englishman named Roberts and a Frenchman named Cabri, made themselves known. Because of these two men, who were fluent in the local language, the reports of the Krusenstern expedition are unusually rich in their accounts of the life and customs of the people.

Krusenstern, having in mind the highly structured political systems of Tahiti and Hawaii, treated the first chief he met as a king when he and his suite came on board.

He was a very strong, well made man, with a thick and extremely fat neck, from forty to forty-five years of age. His body was tattooed with a dark colour approaching to black, so completely, that it even extended to spots on his head from which the hair had been cut away. He was in no wise to be distinguished from the lowest of his subjects . . . I led him to my cabin, and gave him a knife and a piece of red cloth about twenty ells long, which he immediately bound round his loins. To his suite, consisting chiefly of his relations, I also made some presents, although Roberts advised me not to be so generous, telling me that not one of them, not even the king, would ever make me any return for them. I did not fail to draw the king's attention to the size of our ship and the number of our guns, assuring him, at the same time, that I had no wish to employ them against his subjects; but that he must recommend to them, in the strongest terms, not to drive us to violent measures. At this time I imagined that the king's authority here was equal to that of the sovereigns of the Sandwich and Society islands; but I was soon convinced of the contrary. When he returned upon deck he was struck with the appearance of some small Brazil parrots, at which he expressed his pleasure and astonishment in no very moderate terms, sitting himself down, and considering them for some minutes. I conceived that I should ensure his friendship by making him a present of one . . .[12]

When Krusenstern, accompanied by the two beachcombers, landed to examine the countryside and find a suitable place to fill his water casks, he was greeted by a multitude of people and told that the king awaited him at a house not far from the beach.

About five hundred paces from this house, the king's uncle . . . came to meet us. He was an old man of seventy-five years of age, yet seemed to enjoy perfect health. . . . He was one of the greatest warriors of his time, and was now suffering from a wound on his eye, over which he wore a bandage. In his hand he held a long staff, with which he endeavoured, but in vain, to keep back the crowd that followed close upon us. He took me by the hand, and led me to a long narrow building, in which the king's mother, and all his relations of her sex, were seated in a row, and appeared to be expecting us; and we had scarcely entered the precincts of this building, when the king likewise came to meet us, and welcomed us with much familiarity and friendship. The people here stood still, and separated in two bodies, the king's dwelling being tahbu. I was forced to sit down in the middle of the royal ladies, who all examined me with a great deal of curiosity, holding my hand by turns clasped within their's, and only dropping it to examine my clothes, the embroidery of my uniform, my hat, &c. There appeared so much frankness in all their countenances, that I was in the highest degree prepossessed in their favour, and presented them with some buttons, knives, scissors, and other trifles, which I had brought with me; but they did not appear to derive that pleasure from them which I had expected, and they seemed much more occupied with us than with our presents.[13]

The expedition left Nuku Hiva on May 17, 1804, and except for a brief visit to the Hawaiian Islands this was their only contact with the Pacific islanders, but it was an important one. The Russian visitors, unlike many Europeans, got on well with the Marquesans.

Another great Russian navigator, Otto von Kotzebue, spent considerable time in the Hawaiian Islands. He arrived at Kealakekua Bay late in 1816 where King Kamehameha, always the generous host, entertained him lavishly and furthermore directed that all the Russian sailors be treated the same way. On this fabulous occasion the sailors were seated and given the same attention as the officers. Behind each man stood a Hawaiian with a fly whisk, flicking away insects, while an abundance of taro, bananas, roast pig, chickens, and fish were served. After the banquet Kotzebue accompanied the king to a *heiau* (temple) and, while his majesty went inside, stood outside admiring the colossal wooden sculptures. Nor was this all. Kamehameha gave the Russian all the wood he wanted, forty-three hogs, and fowls, geese, fruit, and vegetables in great quantity. When Kotzebue went to Oahu and arrived off Honolulu Harbor, he was met by eight double canoes. The straining backs of sixteen to twenty glistening paddlers in each craft towed his ship majestically into the harbor. Here he was again entertained with the music, songs, and hula dances. The Russians were enraptured by the beating of the hollow gourd, the rattling of the dog-tooth anklets, the skillful body movements, and the plaintive songs. Kotzebue became a confirmed lover of the South Seas then and there, and when he later began his explorations around Micronesia it was with regret that he was torn away.

Following La Pérouse, a number of well-equipped French government expeditions cruised the Pacific during the first half of the nineteenth century. Exploration, the search for La Pérouse, the locating of new whaling grounds, and simply showing the flag were all among their various purposes. There was scarcely a major island group that commanders such as Baudin, de Freycinet, Duperrey, Dumont d'Urville, Dupetit-Thouars, Laplace, and others did not touch. Not least among the unstated purposes, perhaps, was advancing claims to islands as the competition for colonial possessions began to be felt in European halls of state. But this aspect, particularly Dupetit-Thouars's takeover of Tahiti, will be discussed in Chapter 12.

As islanders became more accustomed to the increasing numbers of ships, as they recognized the superior power of muskets and cannon, and especially as the ruling chiefs became more dependent on foreign imports and even luxuries, relations became generally more amicable. In 1819 de Freycinet, who was not impressed by the Hawaiian court, was met at the beach by Liholiho

(Kamehameha II) dressed in the full naval uniform of an English captain and surrounded by splendid chiefs in red and golden feather cloaks and helmets. It was an impressive ceremonial beginning to a two-hour reception during which enough rum, brandy, and wine was consumed to supply any large yacht club's annual cruise. At the end of the party the king requested two last bottles of brandy from de Freycinet to taper off with and cheer the French commander on his way.

The most celebrated Pacific explorer after Cook was Captain J. S. C. Dumont d'Urville who, in the course of two extended cruises from 1826 to 1829 and 1836 to 1839, visited and surveyed hundreds of miles of island shores. He was at heart a frustrated anthropologist, long before the profession had been invented, and had a high regard and great concern for the natives. He was particularly interested in the Maoris of New Zealand and during his cruises along those shores often had two or three of them on board his ship, the *Astrolabe*.

New Zealand is a large land compared with the Oceanic islands. There were a number of powerful chiefs who controlled certain districts, but no all-powerful native ruler of either the North or South Island. The regional chiefs were comparable to those of the Marquesas rather than to the kings of Tahiti or Hawaii. D'Urville's eighteenth-century compatriots in New Zealand, de Surville and Marion Du Fresne, had acted with great brutality toward the Maoris. As a result, in fact, Marion was killed there. But these were other times. The warlike Maoris were now used to dealing with Europeans and Dumont d'Urville was a compassionate and humane man.

The air was calm with only a slight wind as d'Urville left Tolaga Bay on February 6, 1827. About mid-afternoon, he spotted a great Maori war canoe approaching swiftly, its grotesquely carved figurehead with extended tongue bobbing toward him, its high carved stern streaming feathers and rising on each swell. D'Urville welcomed the gracious chief Oroua and invited him to dine on board.

We talked at length of the different chiefs of the Bay of Islands, and he appeared to be well acquainted with the wars which divide the peoples of the north. After the meal, he asked me, indeed begged me, to anchor at least twenty-four hours in his waters. To persuade me to do so he went so far as to offer me two fine pigs free of charge. I thanked him politely and saw that they were paid for out of the ship's account. His canoe held more than twenty of these animals; but as we had just bought as many as we could carry from the Houa-Houa natives, no one came forward to buy them. However,

Oroua's companions were so anxious to dispose of them, so as not to have to take them back again, that in the end they gave them in exchange for knives. [14]

This was typical of d'Urville's relationships with the chiefs. Two days later he was approached by three canoes. In the third was

a chief of fine physique and wearing a woollen blanket [who] drew alongside the corvette without any hesitation and came on board. Having immediately inquired who was the *rangatira rahi*, he saluted me with a certain ease, explaining at once that he was Shaki, the son of Pomare, and chief of Wai-Tepori, and that he had brought pigs to barter for guns and powder. I told him that he was welcome, that he should have some powder, but not any guns, as we needed them for self-defence. This seemed to annoy him, but he made up his mind at once and lively bargaining soon began. Several new cloaks were bought. M. Sainson got five beauties for an old shooting gun, and M. Bertrand secured one for a pistol, or rather the remains of a pistol. I bought six pigs, two medium and four tiny ones, for three pounds of powder. Here the wish of the natives to obtain wool coverlets (which they call *para-iket*, a corruption of the English blanket) in exchange for their goods was much more clearly expressed than anywhere else; unfortunately, no one had a supply of things of this kind. [15]

Wherever d'Urville went, whether to Tonga, Fiji, Guam, or Melanesia, he was equally civil, cautious, alert, and fair in all his dealings with the native peoples.

The official American contribution to the Pacific caldron, bubbling merrily, was the United States Exploring Expedition, a fleet of six ships, under the command of Commodore Charles Wilkes in the U.S.S. *Vincennes*, which sailed from Hampton Roads on August 18, 1838, and returned to New York in 1842.

Wilkes, in his cruising through the islands, did an enormous amount of charting and surveying of the greatest importance, particularly of the Samoan and Fiji groups. He also aggressively showed the flag in support of American traders. He tried a Samoan on board the *Vincennes* for the murder of an American sailor. As noted earlier, he surreptitiously obtained two tattooed Maori heads (the fine was fifty guineas for trading in them) from a missionary brig at the Bay of Islands. He captured Vendovi, the Fijian chief who had led the massacre of the crew of the American merchantman *Charles Doggett* eight years before. He hobnobbed with chiefs and island kings. He witnessed cannibal feasts. He watched exhibitions of native dances. Although relations with the Fijians were friendly, he did not hesitate, after the theft of a launch, to order a village burned to the ground.

Shortly thereafter an episode at the island of Malolo in the Fijis showed Wilkes at his worst. Two of his officers (one his own nephew) were killed while trading for food. There were two villages, Sualib and Arro, on the island of Malolo, and Wilkes determined to take swift and awful revenge for the deaths of his two men. All canoes on the island were destroyed to prevent anyone's escape. The party dispatched to attack Sualib had orders to spare only women and children, and as they advanced they destroyed all the plantations. Wilkes himself led the attack on Arro, which he found deserted. He burned it to the ground and then turned to join the attack in Sualib. Rockets soon set fire to the fortified town and "the moment the flames were found to be spreading, a scene of confusion ensued that baffles description. The shouts of men were intermingled with the cries and shrieks of the women and children, the roaring of the fire, the bursting of the bamboos, and an occasional volley of musketry."[16]

Besides burning the two towns flat, fifty-seven of the best warriors of Malolo were killed and all the surviving men of the island forced to crawl on their hands and knees to meet their conquerors. The Fijians petitioned for mercy and Wilkes decreed his peace terms and landed his whole force.

Towards four o'clock, the sound of distant wailings was heard, which gradually drew nearer and nearer. At the same time, the natives were seen passing over the hills towards us, giving an effect to the whole scene which will be long borne in my memory. They at length reached the foot of the hill, but would come no farther, until assured that their petition would be received. On receiving this assurance, they wound upward, and in a short time, about forty men appeared, crouching on their hands and knees, and occasionally stopping to utter piteous moans and wailings. When within thirty feet of us, they stopped, and an old man, their leader, in the most piteous manner, begged pardon, supplicating forgiveness, and pledging that they would never do the like again to a white man. He said, that they acknowledged themselves conquered, and that the island belonged to us; that they were our slaves, and would do whatever I desired; that they had lost every thing; that the two great chiefs of the island, and all their best warriors had been killed, all their provisions destroyed, and their houses burned.[17]

In the mid-nineteenth century seldom did any European power inflict such unrestrained revenge on a non-European people. In his own eyes Wilkes felt justified in committing barbaric actions more typical of the days of Mendaña and Quiros then of his own. "The blow I inflicted," he piously proclaimed, "not only required to be done promptly and effectually, as a punishment for the murder of my officers, but was richly deserved for other outrages. It could not have fallen upon any place where it would have produced as much effect, in impressing the whole group with a full sense of our power and determination to punish such aggressions."[18] As he further protested, "The blood of the slain imperatively called for retribution, and the honour of our flag demanded that the outrage upon it should not remain unpunished."[19]

The naval expeditions of the first half of the nineteenth century did not have the same strong impact on island cultures as that of the traders, whalers, or missionaries. Their increasing frequency, however, tended to increase the respect of all turbulent elements for law and order. Chiefs soon learned that if a trader or missionary was harmed sooner or later a warship would appear and some retribution was certain. Gradually, too, the expeditions' objectives changed from exploration and surveying to power politics and colonialism.

CHAPTER 8

They Came to Do Good

As we have seen, the London Missionary Society began its mission in Tahiti and, after establishing a secure foothold, moved westward to ever more remote islands. Beginning somewhat later, but in imitation of the London group and operating parallel with them north of the equator, the American Board of Commissioners for Foreign Missions established their base in the Hawaiian Islands and eventually pushed west through Micronesia.

The American Board was founded in Boston in 1810. In 1817, stimulated by a young Hawaiian named Obookiah, it established the Foreign Mission School at Cornwall, Connecticut, specifically to train young men from foreign lands in Christianity with the hope that they would return to their homes as missionaries—a scheme similar to that of the later Melanesian Mission operating out of New Zealand. Five of the first ten pupils at the Cornwall School were Hawaiians. The twenty-six-year-old Obookiah died in February 1818, "with a heavenly smile on his countenance and glory in his soul," as his tombstone tells us, before he could return to the islands. But his brief biography, published the following year, stimulated exceptional interest in the Pacific as a prime area for missionary endeavors.

Two young men, Hiram Bingham and Asa Thurston, students at Andover Theological Seminary, were immediately inspired and volunteered their services as missionaries to the Hawaiian Islands. By the autumn of 1819 the two were ordained ministers. They were joined by two schoolteachers, a physician, a printer, a farmer, and three of the young Hawaiians who had attended the Cornwall school—the first missionary group of New England Calvinists to go to the Hawaiian Islands. On a fine October Sunday morning over five hundred people assembled at the Park Street Church in Boston for a special service at which Thomas Hopu, one of the Hawaiians, appropriately delivered the sermon. On the following Saturday, October 23, a great crowd bade the missionaries farewell as they sailed with their wives in the brig *Thaddeus*, chartered by the board for the voyage. During the next thirty-five years the Boston group sent twelve other contingents to Hawaii—a constant stream of needed reinforcements. Bingham and his companions arrived at Kailua on the island of Hawaii on March 30, 1820.

Two events of the utmost importance occurred about the same time. The first whalers arrived in the islands the same year, and the Hawaiians repudiated their ancient religion shortly before the Congregationalists arrived.

The missionaries came to Hawaii determined to convert the entire population of the islands where their fellow New Englanders had been trading for over a quarter of a century. They brought all of the conservative Congregational beliefs from a New England where waves of both political and religious liberalism were already making more than a ripple on the stern Puritan sea. The Sabbath must be strictly kept; the Scriptures were sufficient unto themselves; the doctrine of original sin was axiomatic; moral codes were to be rigidly applied; the values of hard work and education were fundamental. Surely these beliefs, industriously applied, would raise the entire Hawaiian nation from murky, licentious heathenism to an elevated civilized Christian enlightenment. The islands would become dotted with happy New England villages, their inhabitants leading industrious, morally impeccable, tiresome lives. The missionaries could not have selected a more propitious time to launch their endeavors.

King Kamehameha I had consolidated his rule over the islands before he died in 1819 at the age of eighty-two. He was a tough old pagan who enforced all the rigid, elaborate taboos which controlled the native Hawaiian society. As long as he lived the old deities were worshiped and all the ancient religious customs were strictly observed in spite of the fact that many of the leading chiefs, and even some of the priests, had ceased to believe in the powers of their gods. For years their skepticism had increased as they watched the foreigners living among them ignore the taboos with no ill effect. The women found the taboo system particularly objectionable and with the death of the old king they became more active and aggressive on the subject.

Liholiho, a handsome but irresolute prince, succeeded his father as Kamehameha II and found himself with a feminist movement on his hands, led by his mother Keopuolani and another of his father's widows, Kaahumanu. The two queens proposed that the taboos be disregarded, that women no longer eat inferior food and that they eat with the men. Liholiho hesitated, remembering the last injunction of his father not to forsake the old religion on any account. But the queens were insistent and in August 1819 the king and several of the leading chiefs sat down to eat at the same table with the women, who enjoyed the better food hitherto reserved for the men. It was a public feast with a multitude of the common people as spectators. When no harm came to the aristocracy the crowd cheered, the taboos were broken, the pagan religion collapsed. A conservative element attempted to rally the people to the defense of the old gods, but they were defeated by the king's forces on December 20, 1819. After the battle Liholiho ordered all the wooden figures on the heiaus (temples) burned and the sacred enclosures destroyed. In only a few isolated places did some of the old beliefs and practices hang on. Thus Hawaii was a religious vacuum when Hiram Bingham and his companions, entirely unaware of these events, landed the following March. They were astonished to hear that Kamehameha I was dead and that the religion had been repudiated.

In spite of these fortuitous events Kamehameha II was reluctant to allow the missionaries to settle in the islands. His British advisers indicated that the pioneer missionaries might become commercially powerful, interfere with local politics, and perhaps even plot to bring the islands under American control—actually a quite prophetic vision if applied to the next generation. The younger Kamehameha did not want to offend the British government and he was afraid of American aggression. Finally, albeit reluctantly, he gave his permission for the missionaries to remain one year and allowed Bingham and his party to go on to Honolulu while Asa Thurston, with Dr. Thomas Holman and their wives and two of the Hawaiians who had come out with them, remained at Kailua on Hawaii. The third returning Hawaiian was George Kaumualii, son of the leading chief of Kauai. He persuaded the two teachers, Samuel Whitney and Samuel Ruggles, to accompany him on a visit to his father. Kaumualii welcomed them so warmly that the two Americans established a third mission station at Waimea.

The abandonment of their ancient religion by the Hawaiians was an exceedingly lucky break for the missionaries, but, nevertheless, their first two years were discouraging. Honolulu almost immediately developed into the paramount mission post. Centrally located at the most important port and under the leadership of Hiram Bingham, the unofficial but generally recognized spokesman, the Honolulu missionaries traveled more extensively than the others, met more foreigners, and were more familiar with what was going on throughout the islands. Bingham dominated the enterprise with his forceful character. He was stubborn, courageous, opinionated, devoted, an articulate speaker and a skillful debater.

Like their brethren in Tahiti, the American missionaries soon realized that a knowledge of the language was essential if real progress was to be made. Their first regular public Sunday services were in English and drew a few foreigners as well as curious Hawaiians. Undoubtedly the Cornwall-trained Hawaiians were helpful as interpreters and in aiding the missionaries to learn the language, which they soon set about doing. While foreigners and Hawaiians were equally indifferent to the religious endeavors, the missionaries' relations with both groups were good at this time, and officers of visiting vessels subscribed over three hundred dollars toward the building of the first church at Honolulu, which was dedicated September 15, 1821.

As good New Englanders the missionaries firmly believed that religion could best be spread through education. In May 1820 a school with instruction in English, presided over by Mrs. Bingham, was opened. Of necessity most of the students were foreigners and half-castes. The school was popular with visitors and local foreign residents; but, because it was accomplishing little toward the conversion of the Hawaiians, it was discontinued after a year —a move unpopular with the resident American population.

The missions at Honolulu and Waimea soon became the two stable stations. The Thurstons at Kailua on Hawaii were fortunate at first in numbering Kamehameha, his queen, and other aristocracy among their pupils. The king valiantly attempted to learn the alphabet and begin reading English, but he soon became bored and sent a couple of deputies to study in his place. One of these was John Ii, an excellent student, who eventually became one of the most influential men in the government of the monarchy. The king was fond of the Thurstons and when he decided to transfer his capital from Kailua, Hawaii, to Honolulu the missionaries were invited (which amounted to an order) to move also. Kailua was abandoned with regret and the personnel joined their companions in Honolulu.

As early as 1821 religious services in Honolulu began drawing several hundred Hawaiians, but the missionaries were cautious in admitting them to church membership. It was early decided that there would be no solid progress until the Hawaiian language was reduced to writing. A simple and arbitrary alphabet was devised in 1821 and in January 1822 Elisha Loomis, the mission printer, ran off on his press a simple speller and reader—the first printing in the Hawaiian language. Kamehameha was so impressed that he insisted that he be the first to receive instruction in reading and writing his own language. Although often an indolent student, he set an example for the chiefs who in turn, by their studies, set the example for the common people.

Lack of textbooks and personnel kept instruction of the eager Hawaiians to a modest pace. Inadequately trained native teachers endeavored to be helpful, but instruction continued to be slow and poor. Despite the low quality, the establishment of schools on Oahu and Kauai nevertheless provided a nucleus of stability to the endeavors. The situation was somewhat alleviated in 1823 by the arrival of more missionaries, and others continued to arrive at intervals. The mission was also aided by the Reverend William Ellis, an Englishman, who came up from the London Society's mission in Tahiti to lend his assistance.

With the arrival of reinforcements, plans were made to establish a mission at the bustling whaling port of Lahaina on the island of Mauai. Lahaina was the residence of the king's mother, Queen Keopuolani, who was friendly and sympathetic toward the missionaries. Charles S. Stewart and William Richards were assigned to the new station. Queen Keopuolani became one of their most devoted pupils and before she died in 1823 she requested baptism. She was the first Hawaiian convert received into the church.

In the summer of 1823 a mission was reestablished at Kailua on Hawaii and an additional one at Hilo. A year later it was obvious that the mission was firmly established. The king and most of the leading chiefs were friendly, wanted to become literate, and occasionally attended divine services. Queen Kaahumanu asked to be baptized. The powerful chieftainess Kapiolani, as a demonstration of her faith, descended into the crater of Kilauea where she sang hymns, ate berries sacred to Pele the volcano goddess, and threw stones into the seething caldron. The goddess so defied did not harm her.

Kamehameha, while friendly, showed no interest in becoming a Christian. He alternately pleased the missionaries by his encouragement of their work and then conducted himself in a licentious manner which exasperated them. To some extent, no doubt, the Polynesian desire to please influenced the chiefs to adopt outward forms of Christianity while having little understanding of its inner tenets.

Late in 1823 Kamehameha II went to England with his queen and an entourage of powerful chiefs. There he and the queen died of measles in July 1824, and his eleven-year-old brother, Kauikeaouli, became king as Kamehameha III under a regency. In 1825 several distinguished converts, including the old Queen Kaahumanu, were admitted to the church. This event influenced thousands of Hawaiians to attend public worship, and in increasing numbers they asked to be taken into church membership. While the missionaries were hesitant to do this until they were certain that their converts were prepared to lead morally upright lives, by the summer of 1832 about six hundred Hawaiians had been admitted into the fold.

After printing began in the Hawaiian language the educational work went forward more rapidly. A second printing press was established at Lahainaluna in 1834 and from it the first Hawaiian language newspaper, *Ka Lama Hawaii*, was issued on February 14. In 1832 the New Testament was completed and by May 10, 1839, the entire Bible had been printed in Hawaiian. The output of the two mission presses was very substantial considering the meager resources.

While the system of education introduced by the missionaries was far from ideal, it was effective. In the first decade of its establishment, grass thatch schoolhouses dotted the islands. Thousands of Hawaiians, both adults and children, clamored to attend. The training of native teachers and the constant improvement in their training could hardly keep up with the need. More than half the adult population could read by 1832, some could write, and a few had mastered simple arithmetic.

The schools had their ups and downs. As the thatched schoolhouses deteriorated, efforts were made to concentrate schools in more permanent buildings near the mission stations. By 1829 at least forty-five thousand Hawaiians were receiving instruction in over seven hundred schools. The first high school, founded in 1831, was followed by several other schools of higher learning. Finally in 1840, as a result of constant missionary pressure, a national system of public schools was established by law and supported by the government.

By 1832 reinforcements had increased the number of adult missionary workers to over fifty men and women from the mere fourteen of 1820. This was still a small number to convert and minister to a population estimated at 130,000. The clergy were slow to admit converts to church membership even though the Hawaiians clamored for it. In missionary eyes each individual's moral character and behavior should harmonize with the stern Calvinistic teachings before he was baptized.

In June 1837 the dam broke and for the next three years Hawaiians were taken into the church in unprecedented numbers. During the Great Revival, as the period was called, the preaching of the gospel drew congregations of thousands. An assembly estimated at ten thousand people attended a service on the west coast of Hawaii in the autumn of 1838. Huge congregations required enormous meetinghouses. One thatched building at Kailua, 180 feet long and 75 feet wide, held over three thousand people. Hiram Bingham preached to congregations of two to three thousand. The Great Revival reached its peak on the island of Hawaii, where the Reverend Titus Coan, a powerful evangelical preacher, inspired thousands. Both he and Lorenzo Lyons, the author of a number of Hawaiian hymns, admitted Hawaiians to the church wholesale at Waimea. New meetinghouses and churches went up all over the islands, and contributions rolled in for their support. By 1840 it could be truly said that the Hawaiian Islands were a Christian nation although, ironically, King Kamehameha III never became a church member.

The Morning Stars to Micronesia

So successful was the work during the next decade that by 1850 it was decided that the mission church itself must turn missionary. In that year the Hawaiian Missionary Society was formed at Honolulu with the purpose of extending the word of God two thousand miles to the southwest. There on hundreds of small Micronesian islands of the Marshall, Gilbert, and Caroline groups thousands of people were living in a state of contented heathenism. The high islands of Kusaie and Ponape in the eastern Carolines were selected for the first stations. On July 15, 1852, two years after the new society was founded, three missionaries and their wives with two Hawaiian assistants boarded the schooner *Caroline* at Honolulu in the midst of a scene reminiscent of that which took place when Hiram Bingham and his party bade farewell to their friends at Long Wharf, Boston, thirty-three years before.

The *Caroline* arrived at Kusaie on August 21. One American and one Hawaiian, with their wives, were welcomed by "Good King George," the local chief. The others were deposited on Ponape a fortnight later. It soon became evident that the mission badly needed a vessel of its own in order to maintain contact with the Micronesian stations and provide supplies and reinforcements regularly.

Swift answer came to a nationwide appeal in 1856, and the first *Morning Star*, financed by American children's ten-cent shares, was launched on November 12 in Chelsea, Massachusetts. She was eventually followed by five other vessels of the same name. By 1857 the first *Morning Star* was cruising in Micronesia, and stations were established at Ebon in the Marshall Islands and at Abaiang in the Gilberts.

Generally, the mission made good progress, expanding from island to island, although there were occasional reverses. On Ponape considerable hostility erupted when smallpox broke out and vaccine received from Honolulu proved worthless. Unscrupulous foreigners circulated the report that the missionaries were spreading the disease. This setback was overcome when a new batch of vaccine was received: the missionaries boldly proceeded with their vaccination program and saved many lives. Foreigners established brothels, but the missionaries established schools and toiled on. The Bible was translated into the Micronesian languages and literacy increased.

With the takeover in 1885 of the Carolines by Spain and the Marshalls by Germany, and the annexation of the Gilberts by Great Britain in 1892, work became restricted. Activity in the three Micronesian groups was carried on, mostly by Hawaiians, until 1900, when the Hawaiian Society closed out its Micronesian Mission.

The only other islands which the Hawaiian Missionary Society attempted to convert were the Marquesas where, at the request of a local chief of Hiva Oa, a mission was established in 1853. Here they were not only entering a land of fierce, warlike, and cannibalistic people, but were also coming into competition with French Roman Catholic missionaries who were already established in some of the islands. The Marquesan mission, staffed entirely by Hawaiians, was never as successful as that in Micronesia and was eventually abandoned.

The Missionary Influence

The original instructions issued by the authorities of the American Board of Commissioners for Foreign Missions cautioned the first group going to the Hawaiian Islands against becoming involved in local politics. To dedicated, industrious men brought up in the New England Puritan ethic, this was an anachronism. It was not enough to teach the Hawaiians to read and write, to convert their souls, to lead them in the ways of righteousness. It was also necessary to ensure these obvious benefits by appropriate legislation. Thinking of this kind guaranteed a collision course with other foreign residents of the islands, who did not share the rigid moral standards that were elemental to the missionaries.

From the days of Kamehameha I, Hawaiian monarchs depended heavily on the advice of Europeans. At first these advisers were almost exclusively English, and, as we have seen, Captain George Vancouver even accepted the cession (never ratified in London) of the island of Hawaii to Britain. The rising American resident population, however, and the increasing number of American ships calling at the islands extended Yankee influence.

When the first missionaries arrived, their relationship with their fellow Americans and other foreigners was generally good. The traders approved of their school and gave at least lip service to, and sometimes attended, their church services. But with the discontinuing of the English-language school and the missionaries' increasing attention to the welfare of the Hawaiians, a mutual suspicion sometimes amounting to antipathy developed. The traders were primarily interested in making money. The missionaries proceeded from encouraging the government in such relatively innocuous laws as prohibiting unnecessary work on Sundays, which caused no especial opposition, to attempting to suppress vice and intemperance among the crews of ships visiting Hawaiian ports, which did. Furthermore any proposal of moral reform made by the missionaries during the regency received sympathetic attention from the two queens who held power during the minority of Kamehameha III. But missionary proposals almost invariably ran contrary to the interests of whalers, who wanted their crews to have a good time and be rested and relaxed for the next arduous six months' cruise.

In 1825, under missionary influence, there were public edicts suppressing vice, intoxication, theft, violations of the Sabbath, gambling, and adultery. These blue laws were viewed by the foreign population with increasing apprehension. While the Hawaiians had a predictably Polynesian skepticism about moral rigidity, devotion, and hard work, they realized that the missionaries genuinely wanted to improve their economic lot as well as to Christianize them.

The nearly tragic conflicts over a vice law between the whaling crews and the Reverend William Richards at Lahaina in 1826 and 1827 have already been noted (Chapter 5). In 1836 Richards resigned his connection with the American mission to become adviser and instructor in government to the king and chiefs. The missionary influence on the government was no longer unofficial.

Richards was responsible, within a year after his appointment, for the first Hawaiian code of laws and bill of rights. In 1840 he wrote a Hawaiian constitution that set up elaborate legislative, judicial, and administrative systems. As ambassador for the Hawaiian government, he toured Europe and the United States from 1842 to 1845 and obtained guarantees of Hawaiian independence from Great Britain, France, and the United States. In 1846 he was made minister of public instruction, a position he held until his death in 1847. He was succeeded in this office by Richard Armstrong, who was also a missionary.

Another missionary with a long and statesmanlike career as the confidant of the monarchy was Dr. Gerrit Parmele Judd. Dr. Judd, a physician, and his wife had arrived with the third company of missionaries in March 1828. His hours were long, medicine was scarce, and his duties arduous. He spent long hours traveling over mountain trails, looking after the sick, and studying local diseases.

When Richards went on his journey as ambassador, Kamehameha III persuaded Dr. Judd to take his place. In addition to assuming Richards's duties Judd was made head of the treasury, empowered to receive taxes and other income of all kinds and to pay the government's debts. For many years he was an efficient and devoted servant to his adopted country.

The missionary impact on the Hawaiians was strong, sustained, and lasting—more durable than that of the whalers, more intense than that of the traders. Much fun has been poked at the missionaries, but they deserve better. Their bigotry, their Mother Hubbards for the girls, their inflexible moral attitudes, are but minor peculiarities compared with their achievements. The anthropologist, for example, may be intrigued by their idiosyncrasies, but he should also admire the courage, perseverance, character, and devotion of these stern ambassadors of Western culture to the island world. In a relatively few years they made an illiterate people literate. And while there is little doubt that there was much superficiality in the conversion of thousands of Hawaiians to Christianity, there was also much sincerity and devotion. The Hawaiians were basically a religious people. Their own religion, except for a few isolated backwaters where surreptitious believers in the old religion lingered (and indeed still linger), had been swept away. Christianity came, not always easily, into that void.

The missionaries soon found that in order to disseminate knowledge of the Scriptures, to open and prepare the Polynesian mind for Christian philosophy, education was not only desirable but necessary. The prodigious task of reducing the language to writing, of printing and distributing textbooks and religious texts, with the inadequate means and personnel available, was enough to discourage any but the most sanguine. They were also notably successful in obtaining the favor (a favor not only gained but always kept) of the chiefs, so that there was no question of their leaving at the end of the probationary year. That they not only succeeded, but succeeded superlatively in a relatively short time, is an enormous tribute to their intellect, tenacity, and industry.

It is interesting to observe that the American missionaries in Hawaii were, in general, a much better educated, probably a more intelligent, group than their English counterparts in Tahiti. Most of them were graduates of good colleges and they had been trained in the tough intellectual atmosphere of New England Puritanism—a totally different background from the evangelical emotionalism of the ill-educated English artisans of the Tahitian mission. Their effect on education was massive and their influence in government critical. It is no accident that while the population of Hawaii today is largely oriental, the mores are a New England-Polynesian blend.

While traders fumed at the Hawaiians' being taught the value of a dollar, and missionaries abhorred the sale of barrels of New England rum marked "paint oil," nevertheless the interests of the two groups gradually merged, making the American position dominant in the islands. Without the influential combination of interest in the islands there might well have been no fiftieth state.

CHAPTER 9

Botany Bay

Not all Europeans in the Pacific in the first half of the nineteenth century came directly from Europe or America. With the growing colony in New South Wales there was not only increasing trade from Sydney to the islands, but the beachcomber population was being augmented by escaped convicts from the penal colonies.

On his first voyage Captain James Cook, after observing the transit of Venus at Tahiti and making his remarkable survey of New Zealand, sailed westward and on April 29, 1770, discovered the eastern coast of Australia. The shores of his first anchorage bloomed with flowers against a background of abundant shrubs, and he named the place Botany Bay.

Although it was the middle of the dry season Cook found the land well watered and he considered the virgin soil suitable for growing fruits, grain, and vegetables and providing feed for infinite herds of cattle. The few aborigines observed around Botany Bay seemed rather unfriendly, and because they were so uniformly dirty Cook had difficulty in ascertaining their color. As he cruised north in the *Endeavour* Cook admired the plains and valleys, the woods and fields, but in general considered New South Wales, as he named the country, a barren rather than a fertile land. Most later explorers agreed with him and found Australia a cheerless, depressing, monotonous country. Cook was forced to discontinue his explorations when the *Endeavour* ran on the Great Barrier Reef near Cape Tribulation and was nearly lost.

Cook's claim to New South Wales as a British possession was soon extended to all of Australia—then, and for a few more years, known as New Holland. But claims without colonization do not ensure possession, and it was nearly twenty years later before the first convict-colonists arrived. Criminal codes in England, and indeed all of Europe, were incredibly severe in the late eighteenth and early nineteenth centuries. Thievery could result in death or life imprisonment. Some countries sent their criminals to slave in mines or on galley benches. Others worked them on government projects, usually in remote areas. England transported them to distant lands under contract to plantation owners. Up until the American Revolution, America, especially Virginia and Maryland, received thousands of criminals. With the independence of the thirteen colonies, transportation to America stopped and a large population of criminals began to fill the prisons and hulks where many of them were kept awaiting exile.

But the British government acted slowly. It was not until August 18, 1786, sixteen years after Cook had annexed New South Wales and a decade after the American Declaration of Independence, that Lord Sydney, the home secretary, directed that a fleet should take 750 convicts to Australia. Six transports and three storeships, escorted by a warship and an armed tender, sailed from Plymouth in May 1787 under the command of Captain Arthur Phillip, R.N., the first governor of the new colony. The reluctant pioneers were well equipped with two years' provisions, ample clothing and necessities for both convicts and marines, and tools for building houses and tilling the land. A stop was made at the Cape of Good Hope for hogs, cattle, and seed corn.

Governor Phillip reached Botany Bay on January 18, 1788, after a good passage and by the twentieth all eleven of his ships had assembled there. After a few days' examination, Phillip concluded that Botany Bay was not a suitable place for a settlement. The roadstead was open. Where there was ample water the land was swampy; where it was dry and high there was no water; where there was both dry land and fresh water it was too shallow for the ships to approach the shore. He soon found the ideal location, however, when he examined Port Jackson, a scant ten miles to the north; as he passed between what would later be called Sydney Heads, one of the great natural harbors of the world opened before him. Here a thousand ships could lie in sheltered safety; here coves with good bold water opened on either hand, suitable places for building wharves where ships could dock close to land. Selecting a cove about half a mile in length and a quarter mile across at its entrance, Governor Phillip named the place Sydney Cove in honor of Lord Sydney and decided this was the spot for his colony.

The whole fleet was ordered around from Botany Bay on the morning of

January 24, but they were interrupted by the arrival of La Pérouse and his French exploring expedition. By the twenty-sixth the vessels were all assembled in Sydney Cove, a flag staff was set up on shore, and the governor with his officers stood around and drank the king's health and success to the new settlement.

Governor Phillip had his problems establishing the new settlement. Certainly no other English-speaking nation ever began under more uninspiring circumstances than did Australia. The combination of large trees and the inertia of convict labor made clearing land and constructing storehouses, dwellings, and other buildings a slow process. At the same time, Phillip was familiarizing himself with the countryside—finding new harbors, looking for fertile land to plant, and tentatively probing inland toward the Blue Mountains. But one of the most useful things he did almost immediately was to send Lieutenant Philip Gidley King, with one of his ships and two hundred of his people, to occupy Norfolk Island, some eight hundred miles to the east. At one point this island seemed so much better a place for a colony that Phillip almost moved the entire settlement there. In spite of all the equipment and the seemingly ample provisions, the colony was soon near starvation and more convicts were sent to Norfolk Island to relieve the distress in Sydney. Meanwhile additional convicted criminals arrived and only too few free settlers.

Phillip and his successors held the little colony together under appalling difficulties and hardships. Although there were some political prisoners, especially Irish ones, most of the convicts were hardened street criminals from the cities. Men and women prisoners were herded together and lived in complete licentiousness. There were riots. Through convict ignorance of farming, the seeds did not sprout. Most of the difficulties of the colony were due to the necessity of depending on convict labor. A more lazy, insubordinate, disorderly, drunken lot of ruffians could not have been chosen to pioneer a settlemen in a new country. Sheep died and cattle wandered off. There were no provisions for the education or religious instruction of the children who began to appear in the most miserable and wretched surroundings. With unmarried harlots for mothers and felons for fathers, they were being dragged down by their own diseased parents. And no help came from England—only more convicts. Out of sight, out of mind seemed to be the home attitude.

Growth of the New South Wales colony was very slow. The first free settlers, eleven of them, arrived in 1792 and more continued to trickle in. Convicts who had served their time, known as emancipists, were encouraged to settle but hardly improved the tone or industry of the colony. As Philip Gidley King, the second governor, grumbled, it was impossible "to make farmers out of pickpockets." Settlement was somewhat encouraged by giving land to soldiers who would serve in the New South Wales Corps. But these troops were not much better than the convicts. There was almost constant friction between the military and the governor. The soldiery, particularly the officers, controlled the stores sent out by the government and sold them at enormous profits to the settlers. Most profitable of all was the liquor traffic. The entire population was composed of the thirstiest of guzzlers and anything could be purchased for rum. If there was not enough arriving on government ships, spirits were distilled in the bush or illegally purchased from American traders.

Slowly, very slowly, despite all the difficulties, the number of free settlers increased. The government was liberal in its land grants. Settlers were given convicts for laborers and servants and while this was poor help it was free. Sheep raising, to become the country's greatest industry, began.

Transportation of criminals to New South Wales lasted until 1840, to Van Diemen's Land (not officially known as Tasmania until January 1, 1856) for another ten years, and to Western Australia from 1850 to 1868. Altogether during that time some 160,000 prisoners were transported to the Australian colonies. Some were exiled for life, others for a period of years. Few ever got back to Britain, for free return passage was not provided when a convict's term was up. Furthermore since no record of sentences was sent out with the prisoners it was largely a matter of guesswork when their terms were served.

Many died of scurvy and other diseases, some ran away into the bush where they usually died, and others stowed away on ships and fled to the Pacific islands to take up the life of beachcombers. Inevitably this colony, perched on the edge of a new and virtually unknown continent, had an adverse effect on the aborigines, the original inhabitants of the land, and influenced history in the Pacific islands.

The Aborigines

When Governor Phillip first landed at Botany Bay in 1788, he was met by a group of armed but naked aborigines. He walked up to them alone and unarmed and they laid their weapons on the ground. The natives seemed pleased with this peaceful meeting and with the beads and red cloth which Phillip gave them as a token of friendship. A meeting with a second group of armed natives at Port Jackson was equally tranquil.

The aborigines of Australia are a totally different race from any of the Pacific islanders. No other people in the world exhibited such a simple technology. They were a survival into modern times of a people living in an Old Stone Age culture. Nomadic hunters and gatherers, they eked out a meager existence in a country not only amply productive for the native, but sufficiently so to leave him time and energy for a very elaborate ritual life. The native Australian had no effect whatsoever upon his environment and he lived in harmony with it. He gathered grubs and the seeds of edible plants. He dug out wombats and speared kangaroos, stalked the emu and caught lizards. His boomerang brought down birds for his limited larder. He took what was there, and that was all. To fill his belly he ranged a wide territory and his habitation was a temporary hut of sticks and twigs or spinifex grass that could hardly be characterized as a dwelling.

The natives lived in considerable numbers around Port Jackson and work parties were constantly meeting them. Governor Phillip began his administration determined to have nothing but friendly relations with these simple people and to treat them always with kindness. His policy was immediately and annoyingly infringed by La Pérouse who, in his stay at Botany Bay, quarreled with and fired on the aborigines. Phillip was further frustrated, and the natives' shyness increased, when it apparently dawned on them that the newcomers were going to stay. The aborigines were also irritated by convicts fleeing to the woods and taking over the best fishing places. In return for treating the natives carelessly and pursuing an aggressive attitude toward them, some convicts were killed and others badly wounded. On a trip to Broken Bay Phillip continued his good relations with them when he met a group of men, women, and children. Although an old man threatened him with a spear there was no serious incident. The governor had the opportunity to better observe many of their ways and customs, simple paraphernalia, and canoes than ever before.

Phillip's policy was put to a test on May 30, 1788, when two convicts, gathering rushes for thatch, stole a canoe at a fishing place and were killed. The governor went out with a dozen men to conciliate the natives. He again met over two hundred alone and unarmed and in great friendliness. There was no way to prove that these were the killers of the rush cutters. It was customary for fishing parties to give a portion of their catch to the natives, but on June 9, probably driven by necessity, about twenty aborigines, backed up by a much larger number with poised spears, forcefully took fish from a fishing party without waiting for the usual handout.

The Southwest Pacific

In the early days the English became quite accustomed to meeting groups of these timid people. The distance and accuracy attained by the natives' spears amazed them. They were amused by the spritsail yard worn by the men through their noses; puzzled by the women's amputated fingers; admiring of the decorative red and white painting on the men's bodies.

In 1789 an epidemic of smallpox raged among these unfortunate people. John Hunter[1] said it was shocking to walk around the shore and find the bodies of men, women, and children in caves, and the sick abandoned by the well with no way of combating the fearful disease.

Attempts were made to establish closer relations with the natives by kidnapping individuals, having them live in the settlement for some time, and then allowing them to return to their own people. This policy seemed to be moderately successful, but while attempting to reestablish relations with two of the returned men, Governor Phillip was speared (not seriously) through the right shoulder by a terrified strange native. Gradually relations between the two peoples improved, largely through the liaison provided by Bannelong, a native whom Phillip had detained and treated with kindness. By 1791 the natives became very familiar, wandered around through the settlement, slept in peoples' houses, and even put on an exhibition of their dancing. The governor gave them hatchets in exchange for their spears and shields, and he also supplied them with bread, rice, and vegetables in return for their surplus fresh fish.

The increased intimacy brought on an increased boldness in the natives. While Governor Phillip gave strict orders concerning the treatment of the aborigines, behavior was difficult to control. Spears were thrown, potatoes and fish stolen, muskets discharged, and men occasionally died on both sides. Convicts got lost in the outback and starved to death or fell victim to natives' spears.

For all of this, during the early years of the settlement, Governor Phillip's humane efforts and earnest labors to give the aborigines fair treatment were reasonably successful. But after Phillip's day, when settlers began pushing farther inland the situation deteriorated. It was not helped by convicts who went native and encouraged the aborigines, with whom they lived, to raid and plunder the settlers. The settlers in turn organized punitive expeditions and shot down natives as they would shoot crows. Whites were seldom punished for their actions, while an aborigine who killed a white was usually hanged. Natives who attempted to defend themselves faired worse than those who fled.

The worst incident was to occur at Myall Creek, New South Wales, where in 1838 a group of armed white men from the cattle stations rounded up and murdered twenty-eight men, women, and children in cold blood. This action did not go unpunished. Seven men were convicted and hanged for the atrocity, protesting to the last that they were not aware that in killing blacks they were violating any law. Other shootings occurred at Port Phillip and one settler is said to have poisoned some natives by giving them arsenic mixed with flour.[2] Today about 40,000 Australian aborigines remain.

If the treatment of the native Australians beyond the line of advancing settlement was harsh, that of their relatives in Tasmania was even more severe. These originally gentle and harmless people were progressively squeezed out of their hunting grounds by the expanding settlements. Outlaws, called bushrangers, who were usually escaped convicts, roamed the island and stole their women. Some were carried away into slavery, many were brutally massacred by the whites. Small wonder that the natives occasionally turned on their oppressors and made fierce raids on scattered settlements.

In 1830 an attempt was made to round up the most troublesome tribes. A so called "Black Line," formed by 4,000 soldiers and settlers, was stretched halfway across the island and moved forward in the hope of driving the natives into the extreme southwest corner of the island. But the bush-wise natives slipped like shadows through the advancing line and only a lone woman and a boy were caught in the tightening noose.

By 1834 all but one Tasmanian family had been rounded up and eventually these remnants of an unfortuante people, numbering under three hundred, were settled on Flinders Island in Bass Strait. There the wretched individuals died of disease and homesickness. By 1847 only forty-four remained and in 1876, with the death of Trucannini, the last woman, the race became extinct.

The Pork Trade

While the interior of Australia was unknown, inhospitable, and inhabited by a nomadic Stone Age people, to the east of the colony lay the Pacific with its lush islands and island inhabitants well known and accessible without hardship. Therefore settlement westward was very slow, but eastward contact with the islands was early and continuous.

In the almost perpetually food-short penal colony of Sydney, one of the standard items rationed to everyone was salt pork, imported largely from Great Britain. But there was a closer supply which Governor Philip King decided to try and exploit. Since the days of Captain Cook the islands of the Pacific had been the source of fresh fruits and vegetables and, especially, hogs. Cook had developed a method of curing pork with salt alone and he was imitated by every explorer and trader who sailed the Pacific. And of all the islands the one with the most dependable and ample supply of pigs was Tahiti.

In 1792 Captain George Vancouver, at the beginning of his great Northwest Coast survey, sent the storeship *Daedalus* to Port Jackson with orders to call at Tahiti and pick up supplies for the convict colony. About a hundred pigs were obtained there and eighty of them were taken alive to the colony—the first shipment of pork from the Pacific. But the trade did not really begin until 1801 when Governor King sent H.M.S. *Porpoise*, equipped to salt pork, to Tahiti with letters to King Pomare and the London Society's missionaries proposing the establishment of a pork trade with the colony. Pomare was agreeable and the missionaries were cooperative. The voyage was a profitable one and the *Porpoise* returned to Sydney with 31,000 pounds of salt pork.

The *Porpoise* made a second voyage in 1802 and King also sent out two other ships under contract. One of them went to Hawaii for salt and picked up five hundred hogs there as well. After 1802 the government gave up the pork trade, which was then carried on by private enterprise mostly out of Sydney.

During the first three years of the trade, pork in quantity could be purchased for nails, axes, hatchets, edged tools of all kinds, red cloth, and garments. As Tahitians became supplied with such things, more and different products were required for barter. But the greatest change in trade items came with the demand for muskets and ammunition to be used in local wars, and these were the principal articles used in buying pork for the next fifteen years.

There was a hiatus in the Tahitian trade between 1803 and 1807. Some 300,000 pounds of pork taken in a year's time had depleted the pig population, which had to be given time to recover. But by 1807 a number of vessels built in New South Wales, mostly small brigs and schooners, were engaged in the trade. From 1810 until about 1825, when the pork trade virtually ended, it was carried on almost entirely by Sydney merchants and shipowners in these small vessels. Helped by the prevailing winds, the voyages took about thirteen weeks of sailing plus two to six months in Tahiti for obtaining a cargo.

Toward the end of the Tahitian civil war period in 1815, when Pomare and the missionaries were living on Moorea, pork could be obtained only in the

Leeward Islands and the supply became greatly depleted. After Pomare's return to power in Tahiti (due in no small part to his continuously obtaining muskets from the pork traders), the supply increased again. With the end of the civil war there was another change in the products bartered—muskets were no longer useful and clothing, calicoes and other prints, and hardware of all kinds came into demand. In the very last days of the trade barter gave way to monetary transactions.

From about 1817 on, the Tahitian missionaries also exported pork, including it among the mixed cargoes of coconut oil, arrowroot, pearl shell, and other products which they shipped to Australia in order to increase their meager resources. Although Tahiti was the main producer of pigs and the center of the Australian pork trade, during its last five years there was competition from New Zealand, Tonga, and Fiji.

While the main source was Tahiti, the principal port was Matavai Bay, considered the best anchorage at the island by all Pacific voyagers from the days of Captain Cook on. Because of this location it was no accident that the Pomare dynasty became the dominant family of high chiefs of the island, despite the fact that two other *arii nui* (aristocratic) families on Tahiti outranked them. Their contact with explorers, missionaries, and above all pork traders, who supplied them with arms and ammunition, established their eventual dominance as the royal family of the Society Islands.

Tahiti was the most important entrepôt for the pork trade not only because trading conditions were more stable at Matavai Bay than elsewhere in the Pacific islands, but also because the island produced better pork. Native pigs of the Pacific islands were small, long-legged, long-snouted animals of the Asiatic kind. In 1774, when Boenechea made his abortive attempt to establish a Spanish foothold on the island, he had left a lot of large European hogs that in a few years greatly improved the Tahitian breed. In fact by the time of Captain Bligh's visit in 1788, the pure native variety had disappeared and the pigs were large, heavy meat producers.

The Sydney merchants were able to conduct the pork trade (as well as the higher risk, but more profitable, sandalwood trade with the Marquesas and Fiji islands and the pearl-shell trade in the Tuamotus) without impinging on the monopoly of the East India Company, because the territorial jurisdiction of the governor of New South Wales included the islands of the South Pacific Ocean between the latitudes of 10° and 45° South. They assumed, without being disputed, that this included Tahiti and the Tuamotus. Even the Marquesas and New Zealand were included although all or partly outside the prescribed latitudes. Although Tahiti was declared to be outside British dominion in 1817, commercial relations with Australia continued unchanged.

The quarter century that the pork trade lasted had important effects on both Australia and Tahiti beyond providing some three million pounds of salt pork for hungry convict bellies. It gave Australians the experience in Pacific shipping which enabled them to dominate the island trade down to modern times. In Tahiti the pork trade was probably the principal factor in the rise to power of the Pomare dynasty. It also provided a product for barter that flooded the island with hardward, textiles, and other European trade goods. For a decade the availability of these goods put Tahitian life, at least by European standards, on a higher, more sophisticated plane than any other Pacific group excepting the Hawaiian Islands.

Convict Beachcombers

Beachcombers took up their scattered residences on Pacific islands as soon as the first European ships sailed the waters of the South Seas. But throughout the period of exploration their numbers were small and their impact on island life insignificant. The golden age of beachcombing came with the beginning of commercial activity in the Pacific and lasted until the mid-nineteenth century. Some beachcombers, as we have seen, were deserters from trading vessels or whalers, tempted by idyllic island life after the rough existence in the forecastle. Seldom were they from men-of-war, where discipline was strict and any shore leave well supervised. Others were castaways, forced by shipwreck to take up an involuntary life in the islands while awaiting rescue or an opportunity to ship on another vessel. Some of the European dregs were those unfortunate troublemakers marooned by exasperated captains, or surplus sailors picked up at some obscure port and later dumped on the most convenient island by unscrupulous ones. The establishment of the convict colony in New South Wales added another and significant source to the growing beachcomber population in the islands.

Beachcombing existed as a way of life on different islands at different times. Hawaii and Tahiti saw the earliest arrivals while the less hospitable and less known Melanesian Islands entertained the latest scattered few. Most of the beachcombers resided in Polynesia or Micronesia. At each island, too, the beachcomber population varied with the local political climate. When civil wars broke out most of the beachcombers drifted to more peaceful scenes. Occasionally, on the contrary, they took part in local wars or joined belligerent chiefs in hectoring missionaries.

There were several ways by which convicts from New South Wales and Norfolk Island reached the islands. Legitimately a local Sydney captain could sign on convicts as crew members with the assurance that they would be returned at the end of the voyage. Many of these men made certain it was a one-way trip and jumped ship in the islands. Groups of convicts often seized boats, and on at least half a dozen occasions fair-sized vessels, and sailed them into the Pacific, often visiting several islands before settling down on one. Americans were responsible for increasing the beachcomber population by assisting convicts to escape. A popular convict trick was to stow away on an American ship. But when as many as eighteen men ostensibly stowed away on one vessel it could obviously be done only with the connivance of the captain, who equally obviously was filling out his crew.

One group of convicts who unsuccessfully tried this stratagem was landed at the Bay of Islands, New Zealand (a favorite and lawless place that attracted the floating dregs of the Pacific), from the American ship *General Gates*, whose captain had taken them on as seamen. They were subsequently rounded up by the master of H.M.S. *Dromedary* and returned to Sydney.[3] More often convicts obtained their freedom in return for serving as sailors.

Tahiti, the Bay of Islands, Hawaii, Fiji, and Tonga were the earliest places to have beachcomber populations that included many escaped convicts. Fiji harbored one of the largest floating populations, and beachcombers there often allied themselves with the more powerful chiefs and took an active mercenary part in the incessant native wars. As we have seen, characters ranged from the responsible David Whippey, who deserted a whaler and eventually became United States vice-consul, to the notorious scoundrel, Charles Savage. Paddy Connel, an escaped convict from Port Jackson, was one of the best-known residents of the Fijis for thirty years. He left a ship at Sandalwood Bay and lived at Rewa for many years where he was a favorite of the chief. His late years were devoted to endeavoring to increase the number of his children from forty-eight to an even fifty.

The role of the convict in a native community, like that of any other beachcomber, was a varied one. Some served as jesters to island monarchs; all were admired for their technological knowledge. A handy beachcomber kept his chief's muskets in repair, cast musket balls, sharpened all the hatchets, axes, and other edged tools, built boats and European-type houses. He sometimes became invaluable as an interpreter and liaison man between chiefs and traders. Some acquired land and became subsistence agriculturalists, trading vegetables to ships for tobacco, spirits, or necessities.

Like the sailor-beachcomber who had most likely deserted from an English or American ship, the convict-beachcomber from Australia was a pioneer, coming from the opposite direction, on a new frontier. He adapted himself to native life and customs, had one or more native wives, raised a large family. By the 1850s there were few left. Some departed the islands on visiting ships; others were killed in native skirmishes; a few became planters or traders.

The establishment of the convict settlement at Sydney began a new white impact on the Pacific that continues, particularly in the southwestern area, to the present day. Almost immediately the deteriorating effect on the Australian aborigines, which was to continue for many years, became apparent. The founding of a convict colony at Van Diemen's Land was the beginning of the end for the unfortunate Tasmanian aborigines, who were extinct before the nineteenth century ended.

Shipping from the colony in New South Wales added to the increasing number of traders in the South Seas. The pork trade, mostly with Tahiti, established regular communication with that island, enriched its economy, and had a decisive influence on Tahitian politics by firmly establishing the Pomare dynasty. The trickle of convicts into the islands added to the beachcomber population. This influx was influential in teaching natives to become expert in the new technological culture to which they were becoming exposed and added significant numbers of white genes to the native population. Their influence as interpreters of native culture, into which they were absorbed, to Europeans, traders, and other visitors, and as explainers of European ways to their island hosts had certainly some effect in cushioning the impact of the one culture upon the other.

Extended to New Zealand, colonial government brought the beginnings of stability to that chaotic land, but did not complete the job before head-on conflicts took place between the English and the country's proud and warlike people.

CHAPTER 10

Pakeha and Maori

Australia and New Zealand are very different countries: different in their dimensions and topography, different in their native inhabitants, different in their origins as English-speaking European nations. They are alike in their isolation until the days of modern air travel, and both owe their first European discovery to the Dutch.

Australia, continental in its dimensions, is, except for narrow coastal belts, largely arid plains and desert. Its long coastline has few good harbors; the plant life is gray; the animals are marsupials; the nomadic aborigines are one of the most primitive people on earth. New Zealand is ruggedly mountainous; the coast is indented with many harbors; the plant life is lush and green; it lacks native mammals save for the rat; the natives, known as Maoris, are a branch of the great Polynesian race that inhabits all the islands of the central Pacific.

As different as their natural settings are their respective native peoples. The proud, bold, warlike, village-dwelling, seafaring Maoris bear little resemblance to the land-bound, nomadic, furtive Australian aborigine fading into the outback.

The first contact between Maori and *pakeha*, as the native called the white man, precipitated an act of violence. In 1642, when Abel Janszoon Tasman discovered New Zealand, three men of a boat's crew were killed by warriors circling his ships in canoes. Over a hundred years later, in 1769, when Captain James Cook landed at Poverty Bay, the Maoris attacked his landing parties on two successive days. Each time they were repulsed and a warrior was shot. The French captain, de Surville, in 1770, found the Maoris more friendly, but when they stole a boat he burned a village and detained a chief. Two years later his compatriot, Marion Du Fresne, along with sixteen companions, was massacred and eaten. Remaining members of the expedition killed many warriors and destroyed their fortified villages in revenge. Captain Tobias Furneaux, on Cook's second voyage, was more restrained when he discovered a large group of Maoris making a cannibal feast on ten men of a boat's crew whom they had slaughtered. He rescued and buried their remains and departed.

Contacts between the two races continued to be sporadically violent after the period of exploration. In the early years of the nineteenth century an increasing number of merchant vessels and whalers called at New Zealand, especially at the Bay of Islands, for fresh water, food, and wood. Sweet potatoes were native to New Zealand and early on Irish potatoes and hogs were introduced and became not only staple foods for the Maoris, but important trade items for them as well. The local kauri pine was superb for masts and spars, and native flax made excellent replacement rope for rigging. These assets encouraged Europeans, mostly English, to settle gradually in this productive and temperate land despite the threat of ambush and cannibalism.

Nor were deserters deterred from leaving the sealers, traders, whalers, or timber ships that touched there. Some runaway sailors were killed and others enslaved by the Maoris. Some took up the same kind of beachcomber life found in the islands—attaching themselves to a chief, adopting native customs, learning the language, raising a family. Often the "pakeha Maori," as they were called, played an important role as interpreters and go-betweens during trading activities. Besides the deserters and escaped convicts, adventurous traders settled down at the Bay of Islands, bought native products (usually for rum or firearms) to sell to ship captains, procured temporary native wives for ships' officers spending a few weeks ashore, and otherwise profited from the ungoverned and chaotic conditions that prevailed until 1840.

The Missionaries

The first stabilizing influence occurred with the arrival at the Bay of Islands, in December 1814, of the fifty-year-old Anglican clergyman Samuel Marsden with a missionary party. Marsden had been active in mission work and public life in New South Wales since 1794. He first became interested in New Zealand through meeting Te Pahi, a high-ranking chief, who was brought to

Sydney about 1803. Conversations about God and religion with this bright Maori, as well as Te Pahi's regular attendance at divine services, made a deep impression on Marsden. Te Pahi returned to New Zealand, but about two years later Ruatara, a young and well-disposed chief, accompanied by several other Maoris, arrived at Sydney aboard a whaler and Marsden had the opportunity of extensive communication with them.

The more I examined into their national character, [he wrote,] the more I felt interested in their temporal and spiritual welfare. Their minds appeared like a rich soil that had never been cultivated, and only wanted the proper means of improvement to render them fit to rank with civilized nations. I knew that they were cannibals—that they were a savage race, full of superstition, and wholly under the power and influence of the Prince of Darkness— and that there was only one remedy which could effectually free them from their cruel spiritual bondage and misery, and that was the Gospel of a Crucified Savior.[1]

So strongly did Marsden feel on the subject that he made a special trip to England as early as 1807 to convince the Church Missionary Society of the desirability of a New Zealand Mission and to obtain recruits for the service. It took fourteen months to convince the society, but its members were more easily persuaded than the clergymen, who unanimously and assiduously refrained from volunteering their services to a country whose population enjoyed an unenviable reputation for barbarity and cannibalism. Not a single ordained man came forward and Marsden settled for two laymen. These men, William Hall, a carpenter and shipwright, and John King, a craftsman who could turn his hand to several useful occupations including cobbling and farming, fitted in well with Marsden's theory that the best way to spread the gospel among the unenlightened was to first teach them useful arts and crafts. Hall and King, later joined in Australia by Thomas Kendall, a schoolteacher, formed the nucleus of the mission.

Marsden returned to Sydney in 1809 but was deterred from proceeding to the Bay of Islands by the shocking news that all but four of the seventy crew members and passengers of the ship *Boyd* had been massacred at Whangaroa. This tragedy inflamed the countryside. Reprisals and retaliation swiftly followed. Marsden's friend Te Pahi, who was innocent of the *Boyd* massacre, was slaughtered by avenging whalers along with every man, woman, and child on his island, which was left desolate.

Unsettled and wild conditions at the Bay of Islands notwithstanding, Marsden, who had purchased the brig *Active* for the purpose, requested official permission to take his mission group there. The governor of New South

Captain James Cook. From a 1784 engraving after the portrait by Nathaniel Dance. Courtesy of the Peabody Museum, Salem.

Captain Henry Wilson, who brought the Palauan Prince Lee Boo to London. From an engraving in George Keate, *An Account of the Pelew Islands . . . ,*. 5th ed. (London, 1803).

Matavai Bay, Tahiti, from One Tree Hill, showing H.M.S. *Endeavour* at anchor. From an engraving in John Hawkesworth, *An account of the Voyages Undertaken by the Order of His Present Majesty . . .*, vol. 2 (London, 1773).

Omai, the Tahitian brought to England by Captain Tobias Furneaux on Cook's second voyage. From a 1780 engraving after the portrait by Sir Joshua Reynolds, published by John Jacob.

Te Rangihaeata, Maori chief who was one of the leaders in the so-called Wairau massacre of 1843. From a c. 1840 watercolor by Charles Heaphy. Courtesy of the Peabody Museum, Salem.

King Thakombau of the Fiji Islands, c. 1870. Courtesy of the Peabody Museum, Salem.

Queen Liliuokalani, last Hawaiian monarch, c. 1885. Courtesy of the Peabody Museum, Salem.

Captain John Hunter's party surprises an Australian mother and child in a beach hut, 1789. From the title page engraving in John Hunter, *An Historical Journal of the Transactions at Port Jackson and Norfolk Island . . .* (London, 1793).

Village on Kusaie, Caroline Islands. From L. J. Duperrey, *Voyage Autour de Monde . . . La Coquille . . . 1822-1825* (Paris, 1826).

King Malietoa and Samoan chiefs listening to the reading of the peace treaty, 1881.
Courtesy of the Peabody Museum, Salem.

Wreck of the German man-of-war *Adler* after the Samoan typhoon of 1889.
Courtesy of the Peabody Museum, Salem.

Recruiting labor at Malekula, New Hebrides, c. 1870. Courtesy of the Peabody Museum, Salem.

Fijian village on the Rewa River, c. 1870. Courtesy of the Peabody Museum, Salem.

An Anga man, Eastern Highlands, Papua New Guinea, 1967. Courtesy of D. Carleton Gajdusek.

Sir George Grey, governor of New Zealand, c. 1885. Courtesy of the Peabody Museum, Salem.

Elevala Island and Port Moresby, New Guinea, c. 1870. Courtesy of the Peabody Museum, Salem.

The great Jesuit missionaries Francis Xavier and Matteo Ricci. From the engraved title page of *De Christiana Expeditio . . . 1615.* Courtesy of the Essex Institute, Salem, Mass.

K'ang hsi, emperor of China. From a nineteenth-century painting on silk by an unidentified artist. Rogers Fund, 1942. Reproduced by permission of the Metropolitan Museum of Art.

Macao, c. 1847. From an oil painting by an unidentified Chinese artist. Courtesy of the Peabody Museum, Salem.

Whampoa Anchorage showing the opium hulks, c. 1850. From an oil painting by an unidentified Chinese artist. Courtesy of the Peabody Museum, Salem.

The Canton factories, c. 1800. From an oil painting on glass by an unidentified Chinese artist. Courtesy of the Peabody Museum, Salem.

Hong Kong, c. 1850. From an oil painting by Youqua. Courtesy of the Peabody Museum, Salem.

Shanghai, showing the Bund and rowing match, c. 1865. From an oil painting by an unidentified artist. Courtesy of the Peabody Museum, Salem.

Houqua, Hong merchant. From a c. 1830 watercolor. Courtesy of the Peabody Museum, Salem.

Commissioner Lin. From a Lithograph in Alexander Murray, *Doings in China* (London, 1843).

彼理五十八歳

Robert Morrison, missionary to China. From an 1824 engraving after a drawing by J. Wildman. Courtesy of the Peabody Museum, Salem.

Commodore Matthew C. Perry. From an 1854 painted scroll by Suetomo Ishibashi. Courtesy of the Peabody Museum, Salem.

Portuguese ship. From a Japanese Namban-byobu seventeenth-century screen. Courtesy of the Museum of Fine Arts, Boston.

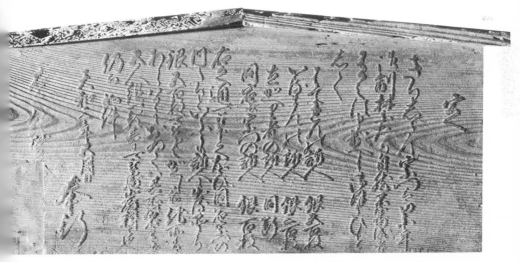

Japanese sign displaying the anti-Christian edict, 1683. Courtesy of the Peabody Museum, Salem.

Dutch factory on De shima Island, Nagasaki. From a c. 1820 watercolor by C. Petersen. Courtesy of the Peabody Museum, Salem.

Commodore Perry "passing the Rubicon" during the opening of Japan, Yedo. From an 1855 colored lithograph by Sarony & Co., N.Y. after the watercolor by W. Heine, published by E. Brown, Jr. Courtesy of the Peabody Museum, Salem.

Wales refused. Hall and Kendall were then sent on a reconnaissance to ascertain conditions at the bay. They returned accompanied by several Maori chiefs, including Ruatara, who had been assiduously preparing the way for the mission, and his uncle Hongi, the most influential chief in the area, and another important chief named Koro Koro. Their report was favorable and the governor gave his consent.

Marsden eventually got under way, accompanied by his lay missionaries, their families, and assorted New Zealanders, Tahitians, and Europeans, including an escaped convict. He also embarked a breeding stock of horses and cattle, along with sheep and poultry.

The *Active* cleared Sydney Heads on November 28, 1814, made a seasickness-plagued passage of the Tasman Sea, and arrived at the bay on December 22. There Marsden, aided especially by Ruatara, lost no time in establishing friendly relations with the Maoris and attempting to pacify warring tribes. He shortly felt sufficiently secure to spend a night ashore among Hongi's people. It was an experience he never forgot.

The night was clear [he wrote evocatively], the stars shone brightly, and the sea in our front was smooth. Around us were numerous spears stuck upright in the ground, and groups of natives lying in all directions like a flock of sheep upon the grass, as there were neither tents nor huts to cover them. I viewed our situation with new sensations and feelings that I cannot express— surrounded by cannibals who had massacred and devoured our countrymen, I wondered much at the mysteries of Providence, and how these things could be. . . . I did not sleep much during the night; my mind was too anxiously occupied by the present scene, and the new and strange ideas it naturally excited.[2]

On Christmas Day 1814 Marsden conducted the first public Christian worship ever performed on New Zealand soil. The congregation included ranks of friendly warriors, their chiefs dressed in regimentals, who stood and sat in imitation of the Europeans. The natives told Ruatara that they did not understand what the preacher meant although they enjoyed the ceremony. He explained the sermon as well as he could and assured his compatriots that they would understand these things better in the future.

Ruatara was invaluable in getting the mission established. Two hundred acres of land were deeded to the Church Missionary Society, north of present-day Auckland. Houses were built and Marsden had the satisfaction of seeing the mission well established when he sailed for Sydney on February 26, 1815. A few days afterward the faithful Ruatara died.

Around the missionaries' small enclave of hope the wars and raiding of the natives swirled for the next twenty years. But throughout this chaotic period the mission was an important conciliatory influence both among quarreling tribes and between the races. Religious progress was another matter, for not a single Maori was converted for ten years.

Hongi, the great chief in the Bay of Islands area, a protector of the missionaries and a friend of the English, who had accompanied Marsden to New Zealand and helped get the mission established, was responsible for much of the disturbance. In 1820 he went with Thomas Kendall, the only missionary who had learned any Maori, to England. As had happened so often before with exotic visiting dignitaries, Hongi was well received and loaded with presents by George IV and others. On his way back home, when the ship put in to Sydney, Hongi exchanged nearly all his gifts for three hundred muskets and plenty of ammunition. Back at the Bay of Islands, with his warriors well armed, Hongi went on the warpath, ignoring the peaceful words of the missionaries as he raided far and wide over the northwestern part of the North Island. Clad in a coat of mail given him by the king of England, he waged fierce warfare against his enemies at Waikato in 1825 and his neighbors at Whangaroa, where the Wesleyan mission (established in 1823) was destroyed. His career of ravage terminated when he was wounded in battle and died in 1828. Curiously enough, while pursuing his cruel and treacherous warfare he remained a protector of the missionaries and other Europeans. In the Cook Strait area, Rauparaha, another warrior chief, raided, devastated, and consolidated his power. While the Maoris continued fighting each other, there was sometimes dissension within the mission ranks, unscrupulous traders bartered for tattooed heads, and cannibal feasting on fallen warriors continued. But the work slowly progressed.

Samuel Marsden more or less commuted for the rest of his life between Australia, where his fat sheep flourished, and New Zealand, where for the first few years his missionaries clung with indifferent success. Altogether he made seven trips to encourage and oversee the work. Between his visits the mission floundered for some years without strong leadership. On his fourth visit, in 1823, however, he brought the Reverend Henry Williams, an ex-naval officer turned clergyman, and the mission prospects improved under his firm guidance. Marsden was also accompanied on this same trip by two Wesleyan ministers who established the mission at Whangaroa, and who became encouraging and cooperative allies of the Anglicans. Three years later Henry was joined by his brother William Williams, who was to become a great authority on Maori customs and language and a bishop. The brothers provided the strong aggressive leadership needed in that turbulent land and the family has continued to be eminent in New Zealand to the present day.

After Marsden's sixth visit in 1830, when he and Henry Williams managed to prevent a general native war after some bloody fighting between two factions supplying girls to a whale ship, he became a strong advocate of the establishment of British authority over the country. It was the beginning of a series of circumstances that resulted in the appointment of a British resident. Marsden died in New South Wales in 1838, the same year the first Roman Catholic mission in New Zealand was established at Totara by Bishop Jean Baptiste François Pompallier.

The seed planted by Marsden was flourishing when Charles Darwin arrived on the famous *Beagle* voyage. The naturalist, a house guest of Henry Williams in December 1835, was astonished at the large gardens producing every English fruit and vegetable, the varied park-like fields, the well-fed livestock, and the busy water mill. "All this is very surprising," Darwin recorded, "when it is considered, that five years ago, nothing but the fern flourished here. Moreover, native workmanship, taught by the missionaries, has effected this change."[3]

Another of Darwin's observations, that the New Zealand missionaries were not as successful in making converts as their brethren in Tahiti, was confirmed five years later by Commodore Charles Wilkes who, in 1840 also met Williams and expressed admiration for the missionaries' agricultural achievements. The American further remarked:

Many reports have been put in circulation by the evil-disposed, in relation to these missions [Episcopal and Wesleyan] ; but as far as my observations went, they seemed exemplary in their duties; they were also occupied in farming, in which native labourers were employed. Mr. Williams having a large family growing up, many of them obtained farms, and are now in the successful occupation of them. There is no doubt the hue and cry against the father, that the mission had obtained all the best land from the natives, arose from this cause. Some circumstances were remarked, from which it was evident that the interests of the natives were looked after by the missionaries, who protected their lands and induced them not to sell to the emigrants, who would otherwise have found them only too ready to part with them.

It is true that the situation of these missionaries of the Church of England is different from that of any we had heretofore seen, and equally so that they do not appear to have succeeded as well in making proselytes as those in the other Polynesian islands; but I am persuaded that they have done and are still endeavouring to do much good.[4]

In 1832 the governor of New South Wales appointed James Busby as resident at the Bay of Islands. Busby had no real authority whatsoever, but working with the missionaries he traveled among the tribes and attempted to reconcile the growing differences between Maori and pakeha. But conditions remained chaotic and increasingly troublesome for the next eight years.

In 1835 a comic-opera character named Baron de Thierry, who had already appeared on the scene in 1822, returned and attempted to set himself up as the sovereign of a Maori kingdom, claiming he had French support. The scheme was as ephemeral as it was quixotic.

By 1838 there were about two thousand European residents in New Zealand, mostly around the Bay of Islands and other harbors of the northern peninsula. The continuing influx of sailors, convicts, and other disorderly types, the growing number of land speculators, the intertribal Maori fighting, the increasing prosperity of the traders and tribes in the Bay of Islands area—all created a situation wherein law and order was desirable. Throughout this period the missionaries were gradually augmenting their influence and becoming an important stabilizing element without formal authority. As chiefs became converted, entire tribes followed them into Christianity. This happened with more frequency as warfare and disease began to take their tolls among the Maoris. Conversion, in turn, decreased the raiding and eliminated cannibalism.

No real effort was made by the British or any other government to establish any sort of control over the lawless situation until 1839 when the Colonial Office was finally spurred to recommend the appointment of a British consul to New Zealand. In that year Edward Gibbon Wakefield, who had already established a colony in South Australia, dispatched a group (organized as the New Zealand Company, but without any official charter) under his brother to found a settlement. William Wakefield arrived at Port Nicholson (now Wellington) in January 1840. Here, in a fast moving series of deals guns and ammunition, sealing wax and Jew's harps, red blankets, fishhooks, combs, handkerchiefs, tobacco, and liquor were given to the Maori chiefs in exchange for the transfer of huge tracts of territory to the New Zealand Company. Millions of acres changed hands in compacts that the Maoris did not understand, for they had no conception of individual land ownership. The acquisitions of the company and other land sharks were the source of friction between the two races for many years to come.

The impervious Colonial Office continued its reluctance to take on any more overseas possessions, but the unscrupulous Australian land speculators, with their preposterous claims to over half the area of the islands at one point, finally pushed the British authorities into action.

The Treaty of Waitangi

On January 29, 1840, Captain William Hobson, who had made a visit to New Zealand in 1837 in H.M.S. *Rattlesnake* to survey the situation, landed at the Bay of Islands with a commission authorizing him to accept the cession of all or part of New Zealand. Hobson lost no time in calling the chiefs together at Waitangi and presenting them with a treaty. The chiefs debated it for a day and on February 6 fifty of them signed the document. Hobson then sent the treaty on a tour of New Zealand and collected some five hundred more signatures, although the chiefs of several important tribes never signed up.

The Treaty of Waitangi consisted of three articles. Under the first the chiefs ceded all their lands to the queen of England forever. By the second article the queen in turn confirmed and guaranteed to the Maoris full possession of their lands, homes, and possessions. The chiefs, however, yielded to the queen the right to oversee the sale of land between consenting parties at an agreed-upon price. Under the third article the queen extended her protection to the Maori people and granted them all the rights and privileges of British subjects.[5] New Zealand became territorially a part of New South Wales and Hobson lieutenant governor under the governor at Sydney. This arrangement did not last long, for on May 3, 1841, New Zealand was made a separate crown colony.

With the treaty signed Hobson was confronted immediately by two serious problems. The exorbitant land claims of the New Zealand Company and others had to be resolved. But as he began turning his attention to these swindles an international affair presented itself. A shipload of fifty-seven French settlers was headed for Akaroa on the Banks Peninsula in July 1840 and a rumor circulated that the French were about to annex the South Island. Nor were these suspicions allayed by the presence of the French frigate *Aube* at the Bay of Islands.

Hobson dispatched two magistrates in H.M.S. *Britonmart* to hold courts wherever they could land. They beat the French to Akaroa by four days and established civil authority there which was not disputed. The French settlers were allowed to occupy the land they had purchased and for many years thereafter the settlement kept its French characteristics.

With the establishment of a government came customs regulations, which almost immediately cleared the whalers and other foreign ships out of the Bay of Islands. Hobson considered the bay as his capital, but settled on Auckland as a better location. Wellington, which finally became the capital in 1865, although larger and more centrally located, was not chosen at the time because of the government's prejudice against Wakefield and the New Zealand Company.

Land Troubles

Nevertheless it was the New Zealand Company that was instrumental in founding, in quick succession, all the principal New Zealand towns. After the first settlement at Wellington came New Plymouth, settled by a Devonshire group in 1840, Nelson in 1841, Dunedin founded by Scottish Presbyterians in 1848, Invercargill in 1857, and Christchurch begun by a Church of England colony in 1850.

The steady influx of settlers amplified the already sensitive land troubles. With his government established, Hobson attempted, without notable success, to make some order out of the excessive land claims. Some were allowed and others not. To establish its settlements the New Zealand Company sold land to prospective settlers in England without any of them having seen it. The land, purchased for a trifle from a Maori chief, or sometimes from a Maori who did not even belong in the district, was not acknowledged by the Maoris as having changed hands, for Maori land was owned by the whole tribe and could only be disposed of by common consent. Maoris did not recognize individual land ownership.

The land problem was further intensified, after the Treaty of Waitangi, by confiscation of large tracts of Maori land—sometimes taken as punishment from rebellious tribes, sometimes taken simply as unoccupied land. More and more the Maoris found themselves in one way or another disposing of millions of their most productive acres.

Hobson worked diligently trying to straighten out the tangle that became daily more confused until he died, a discouraged and worn-out man, on September 10, 1843. He was succeeded by Robert Fitzroy, an ineffective governor under whom native-white relations steadily declined until he was replaced by Captain George Grey in 1845.

The Maori Wars

The first indication of troubled times ahead in the relationship between the two races occurred in 1843 before Fitzroy arrived. The settlers at Nelson discovered that there was not enough land to go around. William Wakefield claimed that the New Zealand Company had purchased the fertile Wairau valley, some seventy miles to the east—a claim that was disputed by the Maoris. The famous chief, Te Rauparaha, and his son-in-law, Te Rangihaeata, insisted that the land had never been sold and wished to have the problem taken before a land claims commissioner. When surveyors were sent to Wairau the Maoris pulled up their stakes and burned their shelters, after first thoughtfully removing the surveyors' personal belongings. In spite of this considerate treatment one of the surveyors went to Nelson and swore out a warrant for the arrest of the two chiefs.

Armed with the warrant as well as with muskets, a party of forty-nine men, headed by Arthur Wakefield, another of the Wakefield brothers, and H.A. Thompson, the police magistrate, went to make the arrest. The party of settlers met the chiefs, who were surrounded by about eighty to a hundred of their armed followers. Te Rauparaha and his son-in-law refused to be arrested. The magistrate unwisely insisted on serving his warrant, an argument ensued, an English musket, accidentally discharged, killed Te Rangihaeata's wife, who was also Te Rauparaha's daughter, and the fight was on. Men began falling as muskets were fired and the English fled before the overwhelming Maori attack. Wakefield and eight others surrendered and all were immediately killed by Te Rangihaeata and his men in revenge for the death of his wife. Altogether twenty-two English and five Maoris were killed in this encounter, called the "Wairau massacre." Twenty-seven English escaped to Nelson and the Maoris settled back to await reprisals, which never came. When the whites did not take revenge, Te Rauparaha, whose warriors were aroused by their success, planned an attack on Wellington, but he was dissuaded by Octavius Hadfield, a missionary, and other calm heads. The land decision was left to the government, and Te Rauparaha, while expressing sorrow, claimed that it was impossible for him to prevent his warriors from following Maori custom and killing their prisoners. The Nelson settlers continued to agitate for revenge, but Governor Fitzroy, sitting in judgement at Nelson in February 1844, while condemning the killings, would not condone revenge on the part of the English, as he believed responsibility for the aggression began with them. This was a right and humane decision but it lowered British prestige in Maori eyes, and it never satisfied the inhabitants of Nelson.

Things had barely quieted down around Cook Strait when trouble erupted in the north, where the lush trade with whalers, cut off four years before by the new customs duties, created severe economic problems. Gone was the market for white and sweet potatoes and hogs, and the Maoris around the Bay of Islands were resentful. On July 8, 1844, Honi Heke, the chief of the principal local tribe and a son-in-law of the famous Hongi, rightly blamed the British for his people's hardship and cut down the flagpole at Kororarika. Honi Heke was fined, the flagpole reerected, and an armed guard posted around it. But again, in 1845, Heke came to Kororarika with eight hundred warriors, overcame the guard, and cut the offensive pole down again. Governor Fitzroy then offered a reward for the capture of Heke, who reciprocated by making a similar offer for the head of the governor. Heke then attacked the town and cut down the pole a third time. The settlers attempted a defense, but the town was plundered, burned to the ground, and abandoned. Losses were considerable on both sides and the whites fled to Auckland. Fortunately the Maoris were not unanimous in this conflict. Many of them condemned Heke's actions and aided the British. Nevertheless there was some panic as news spread that the Maoris were on the warpath and Auckland, Wellington, and other settlements were hastily fortified. Fitzroy's failure to handle this explosive situation resulted in his recall. He was replaced by Captain George Grey, hastily summoned from South Australia, who arrived with soldiers from Sydney in November 1845.

Grey lost no time in ending the Maori War. He forced the wavering chiefs to declare themselves friendly or otherwise and ended the arms trade. Finally he attacked Heke in his *pa*, as the Maori fortifications are called, and, after bitter fighting with heavy losses, forced him to surrender. In two months the fighting was over.

With the north pacified Grey turned his attention to the south, where skirmishing was still going on. Te Rauparaha and his son-in-law were still agitating over disputed land. Grey hastened to Wellington, seized Rauparaha and forced Te Rangihaeata to flee into the forest. The Maoris respected Grey for his strong action and for his understanding. He learned the language, studied their customs, and became an authority on their traditions. Rauparaha was released in 1847, his son-in-law settled down, and Grey achieved peace in both the south and the north. The last incident of the first Maori War occurred near Wanganui, where an English woman and four children were killed in revenge for the accidental killing of a native. Five Maoris were tried and executed for the act.

Grey discontinued the private purchase of Maori lands and forced all land sales to be made through the government. The New Zealand Company was not happy with Grey's decisions, but he was a strong, autocratic individual who kept the disparate elements under his control. The problems of the New Zealand land settlements, however, were long and complicated. When Sir George Grey (he was given the title in 1848) left in 1853 he thought his work was done. It proved otherwise.

A peaceful interlude now lasted until 1860. During that time the settlements at Dunedin and Christchurch were established, small towns grew up along the coasts, communications were greatly improved, and the entire country, from a European point of view, made substantial advancement.

The decade before 1860, although outwardly peaceful, was nevertheless one of unrest. Settlement was steadily progressing; the land pressure on the Maoris was constantly increasing. Feelings ran high, triggered by a land purchase, between the races in the Taranaki district in 1856. But no fighting between Maoris and settlers erupted from this incident, although intertribal skirmishing was constant. A jittery peace prevailed until settlers on the same disputed district around New Plymouth decided that they needed more land. The new governor, Thomas Gore Browne, who arrived in September 1853, upheld the right of the Maoris to their lands, but the colonists contended that such disputes should be settled by the local, elected government—the first Parliament had assembled at Auckland in May 1854—not by the governor.

That same year, a month earlier, about a thousand Maoris, mostly from the Taranaki tribes, held a meeting to discuss their steadily diminishing lands and other problems caused by the settlers. An attempt was made to agree not to sell any more tribal land to the pakeha. This was the beginning of a series of great meetings that led to the rise in Maori nationalism called the "king movement." Again, in 1856, a large assembly of influential Maori chiefs held at Lake Taupo decided to sell no more land to anyone, including the government. The movement culminated in the election of a Maori king in 1858.

The "king movement" was not one of rebellion against the government. At this time the Maoris were in general peaceful but uneasy and concerned. They felt that a single leader or king would have more authority and success in dealing with the pakeha and help reassert the fast-fading *mana* (authority) of the Maoris. Even so, the Maoris were far from completely united on the idea and only with difficulty was agreement reached on who should have the job. Finally an elderly, noncontroversial chief named Potatau Te Wherowhero, who had been a great warrior in his prime, was elected king. The real power, however, rested between a moderate chief named Te Wiremu Tamihana or William Thompson, and an extremist named Rewi. Governor Browne was not particularly sympathetic to the "king movement" but he left it alone.

Trouble began in 1859 when the settlers at Taranaki wanted to buy six hundred acres of land known as the Waitara block. Arrangements were made by the governor to do so, only to have the agreement vetoed by Wiremu Kingi, one of the most important chiefs of the district. The land was bought anyway and government surveyors sent in. Kingi tried to assert his rights. The governor declared martial law and moved onto the Waitara block with 340 men. Wiremu Kingi retaliated by building a *pa* within the same boundary. On March 17, 1860, the English opened fire, the Maoris abandoned the fort, and soldiers moved in the next day. Thus the Taranaki war began and fighting continued intermittently over many parts of the North Island for the next ten years.

Browne, obviously incapable of handling the situation, was recalled and George Grey brought from Capetown to serve a second term as governor in 1861. By a combination of military vigor and conciliatory gestures he endeavored, unsuccessfully, to pacify the country. He wanted to suppress the king movement, now headed by a chief named Tawhiao, who had succeeded Potatau. On the other hand, he admitted Wiremu Kingi's claim to the Waitara block and arranged to have the land given back to him. Still the fighting went on--people were massacred, more soldiers were brought in, *pa*s were taken, the Maoris were aroused by the resumption of their old martial activities.

Another element entered the picture in December 1854 with the proclamation of the Hau Hau movement. The king movement was political; the Hau Hau movement religious. The new religion, named for their war cry, was a composite of old Maori beliefs and Christianity, with the angel Gabriel as the chief deity. Missionaries saw hundreds of their converts go over to the new religion. The white man was to be exterminated; bullets would not harm the Hau Haus; pagan customs, including cannibalism, were revived.

Governor Grey, for all his knowledge of the Maoris, did not have a smooth second administration. He was at constant odds with the military commander, General Duncan A. Cameron; he quarreled bitterly with the ministers of the colonial government; he antagonized the Maoris by suggesting that the government seize rebels' lands as punishment. The imperial government thought him infirm, the colonists considered him tyrannical. He seemed unable to please any of the divergent elements with whom he had to work. His differences with the home government resulted in his recall in 1868—an act that raised his popularity with both Maoris and settlers in New Zealand. He was succeeded by Sir George Bowen in 1868.

The War dragged on to its inevitable conclusion. No matter how bravely the Maoris fought, no matter how many stout *pa*s were successfully defended, no matter how many settlers were massacred, no matter how inept the army officers were, there could be only one result—the defeat of the natives. By the mid-1860s imperial troops were withdrawn and the settlers' defense depended on their own militia and their Maori allies. The Maoris had a temporary resurgence of guerrilla success under an able chief named Te Kooti. But gradually the various Maori chiefs either made peace or were hounded into exile in the interior of the island. By 1870 the long series of Maori wars had drawn to a close.

The effect of defeat on the Maori was catastrophic. They became dispirited, debt-ridden, drunken, and landless. Depopulation followed demoralization. The approximately one hundred thousand Maoris of the 1840s were reduced to less than half that number by the end of the wars. Villages were deserted as the elderly died and few children were born. The white population exceeded the Maori after 1858 and continued to increase. By the last decade of the century, however, the tide began to turn. The Maori king had made his peace, the exiled chiefs were pardoned, the Maoris had a small representation in Parliament, education was improving, and the birthrate began a long rise. The Maoris were on their way back from near oblivion.

CHAPTER 11

Traders and Blackbirders

From the time of discovery the principal island groups of Polynesia were exposed to continual European contact. Exploration ships were quickly followed by traders and whalers; missionaries established their footholds; beachcombers and other stray settlers began to leaven the population. Thus the commercial, religious, and political impact, from the late eighteenth century onward, was constant and increasingly complex. By the mid-nineteenth century, therefore, the islands of the Central Pacific had long since been drawn into a western European and American orbit whose diverse influences were reaching out along the commercial trade routes of the world. There were good reasons for this. The islands of the far-flung Polynesian triangle were ideally located for whalers' refreshment; many of them produced raw materials for an increasingly important China trade; they were free of diseases inimical to white settlement; their climate was agreeable; their people were generally amiable, of one linguistic family, and controlled by strong chiefs with whom agreements could be made and kept.

But none of these circumstances applied to the Melanesian islands of the Southwest Pacific—most of which were discovered no later than those of Polynesia. Europeans soon learned that death lurked near those shores where verdant mountains rose high above mangrove swamps and yellow sands. In the crescent of large islands stretching like a far-off bow around northeastern Australia, from New Guinea to New Caledonia, the people were fiercer; the chiefs weaker; the languages extraordinarily numerous, diverse, and difficult; the women less attractive and less generous. Malaria infested all the coasts excepting New Caledonia and the nearby Loyalty Islands. Occasional explorers sailed along their shores but seldom lingered to make extended surveys. Except in emergencies whalers and traders alike avoided these little-known islands of ill repute. No beachcombers settled, and pioneer missionary efforts were unsuccessful. Melanesia, except for Fiji, lingered in undisturbed isolation.

Not until the fourth decade of the nineteenth century did economic circumstances provide an impetus for the first wave of cultural impact, an impact which more salubrious islands had known for seventy-five years. Not only was this a late phenomenon; it was different. Although no less white and European, it was not the direct contact from the British Isles and New England that so dominated the rest of the Pacific in the early 1800s. Rather it was a backwash of colonial English influence from Australia.

We have already seen in Chapter 4 the importance of Polynesian and Fijian sandalwood to the China trade of the late eighteenth and the first quarter of the nineteenth centuries—a trade dominated by New England Yankees with a scattering of independent English traders from India. In the 1840s the old question still remained of what the Chinese wanted in exchange for their tea and silk—and they wanted very little. The English, dominated by the monopoly of the East India Company, purchased their goods with silver specie until they solved the exchange problem with Indian cotton and above all opium; but the Australians, like their American cousins, were short of cash. Both had to scrounge around for trade goods; and for the colonists in Australia, occupied with establishing themselves during the first fifty years of settlement, the trade was later, smaller, and more confined. Nevertheless, the economic demands of this trade created a new Pacific frontier.

To satisfy the universal and insatiable tea-drinking habit of the Australians, a custom brought with them from England, the currency resources of the country were strained for some years. In addition direct trading from Sydney to Canton by colonial vessels was prohibited by the monopoly of the East India Company. Until this was abolished in 1834, merchants in Sydney operated under an almost insuperable handicap. Occasional American ships were chartered to carry sandalwood or bêche-de-mer to Canton, but this was illegal, and heavy duties on exports increased the New South Wales trading difficulties.

Melanesian Sandalwood

Captain Peter Dillon (famous for discovering the fate of La Pérouse) found sandalwood growing abundantly in Erromanga as early as 1825, but he also found the natives impossible to do business with. Unlike the Polynesians they had at that time no desire for trade goods. They were oblivious to anything dangled before them in an attempt to get them to cut wood. Hard labor to little purpose was not for them.

Four years later a Captain Samuel P. Henry imported a labor force of Tongans to Dillon's Bay and succeeded, between fights with the Erromangans, in obtaining two cargoes of wood. One cargo, reaching Honolulu for transshipment, inspired in Boki, governor of Oahu and a famous Hawaiian chief, a brief flurry of imperialism. Sandalwood was gone from Hawaii by this time, but the knowledge of its value lingered on. With two vessels, the *Kamehameha* and the *Becket*, Boki departed for the New Hebrides by way of Rotuma, from where the ships sailed separately. Boki in the *Kamehameha* was never heard from again. The *Becket* made a disastrous voyage to Erromanga and arrived back at Honolulu on August 3, 1830. Only twelve Hawaiians and eight foreigners survived the expedition. Harvesting New Hebrides sandalwood was simply too difficult and dangerous at this time.

Substantially, the colonial sandalwood trade in Melanesia began in 1841 and continued to 1865, petering out toward the end. After the London Missionary Society's brig *Camden* deposited missionaries on various Melanesian islands in 1841, she went to Sydney, where one of her crew members peddled the information that he had seen sandalwood growing at the Isle of Pines. An attempt to keep the information secret was unsuccessful, and within a year a couple of dozen vessels were searching the islands for the fragrant wood.

The swarm of vessels engaged in the competetive business successfully cleared the sandalwood from the Isle of Pines in about a year. It was the same pattern the Americans had followed in Polynesia a quarter century earlier. Exploitation of trees growing in New Caledonia, the Loyalty Islands, and the New Hebrides soon followed. Dorothy Shineberg, in her thorough study of the sandalwood trade from 1830 to 1865, provides us with great detail about the merchants, captains, ships, and methods of this profitable but hazardous enterprise.[1]

Obviously the trade was profitable, but the risks were high. Charts of the waters were nonexistent and navigation was uncertain. Truculent Melanesians made more than one meal off woodcutters following the frequent skirmishes. Firearms traded for wood introduced a more deadly intertribal warfare. Missionaries and traders were light-years apart in their approach to the natives. The incessant unruliness of the crews, their lust for the women, their drunkenness, their incivility and loutish actions, were all a constant source of embarrassment to missionaries attempting to plant the seeds of Christianity in about as infertile a soil as any of God's gardeners ever tried to cultivate. The trade, the life, the men were rough. The traders dealt with a variety of people who were their match on all counts. And yet, the cruel and vindictive individuals among them were probably the exception. Once Melanesians learned the value of trade goods, especially iron, once trade goods became necessities to them rather than luxuries, honesty was the best policy for the trader. And this happened very quickly. Iron fishhooks replaced the laboriously made shell hooks of the islands. Brightly colored beads soon were favorite ornaments. But most of all hoop iron, tomahawks, axes, adzes, scissors, and knives soon made stone and shell cutting tools no more than a memory. The use of tobacco and pipes, once introduced, quickly became universal and furthermore tobacco supplies required constant replenishment. Bolts of red and blue cloth and scarlet caps were eagerly acquired in exchange for wood and labor. Firearms made hunting more efficient and warfare more deadly.

There was a progression in the introduction and popularity of most trade goods which reflected the increasing technological sophistication of the Melanesians, although fishhooks and beads were always in demand. Hoop iron was replaced by cheap tomahawks, which in turn were replaced by good ones. Firearms were expensive and late. Certain articles favored in one location were useless for trade in another. The demand for pigs, tortoise shell, and other island products by certain tribes increased the complexity of trading in Melanesia as captains shopped around to get the best product to trade for sandalwood in a particular place.

Two entrepreneurs, James Paddon and Robert Towns, implacable competitors, dominated the Melanesian sandalwood trade for twenty years from the mid-forties. Paddon, who settled at Aneityum in the New Hebrides, where he introduced cattle in 1844, began there the more efficient system of stations that replaced ship-to-shore operations. The stations were settlements where trade goods were dispensed and sandalwood collected and accumulated to await shipment. Robert Towns emulated Paddon in establishing his first station at the Isle of Pines in 1849. The two men, who occasionally did business with each other, were very different personalities. Paddon lived in the islands all his life, set up housekeeping with a Melanesian woman, and raised a family; Towns became a Sydney merchant, sending his ships to the islands and China. As the supplies of sandalwood dwindled in the fifties, both men endeavored to fill out their cargoes with other island products—pearl shell, tortoise shell, bêche-de-mer, and coconut oil. The wood was cleaned out of the Isle of Pines, Efate, and the Loyalty Islands, and greatly depleted in New Caledonia, by 1853, but that same year it was discovered growing bountifully in Espiritu Santo, which gave the trade another spurt. But because of dwindling supplies and high costs the Melanesian sandalwooding was over by 1865.

Until the late forties the wooders were almost the only European contacts for the Melanesians. Earlier missionary efforts were unsuccessful and sometimes tragic. In 1848, however, Bishop George Selwyn of New Zealand visited the Melanesian part of his diocese for the first of many times. That same year the Reverend John Geddie settled at Paddon's station on Aneityum. The trader and the missionary were at first friendly, but relations between them later deteriorated until Geddie became Paddon's bête noire. Gradually more missionaries—Anglicans, Wesleyans, Roman Catholics (French Marists in New Caledonia), and others—infiltrated the islands. As missionary activity increased, visits by French and British naval vessels became more common, although they were never as frequent as the traders would have liked.

From all the Europeans, but especially through the traders, Melanesians encountered what other Pacific islanders had come up against long before— technological revolution; epidemics of measles, influenza, smallpox, and other diseases; disruption of their social and religious lives. The ancient pattern of their days was broken forever. The trade, too, brought about another change in islanders' lives as whites and blacks became increasingly familiar with each other. After the station system became established, Melanesians more and more provided the labor for cutting and transporting wood, manning boats, and serving as sailors on the ships. In the later days of the trade, crews were often over three-quarters natives who, like their Polynesian cousins, made good sailors and liked to travel.

The Blackbirders

If the cultural impact of sandalwooding, wherever the wood occurred, was considerable, that of the labor traffic which followed was traumatic. To be sure, it was the later sandalwooders who first persuaded Melanesians to work in gangs for trade goods. They were often moved to other islands than their own to cut, transport, and load wood. By the time sandalwooding ended in the mid-sixties, iron-edged tools and other trade goods had become necessities. Indentured labor offered a way for the islanders to continue obtaining these essentials, and from the 1860s to the 1880s Fiji and Queensland were the centers of a traffic in human labor.

As early as 1847, Benjamin Boyd had experimented unsuccessfully with taking men from Tanna, New Hebrides, to Australia, where he hoped they would make good shepherds. Curiously enough it was the American Civil War that brought about the systematic labor trade (known as blackbirding in the early days) on a large scale. When the Union embargo prevented cotton exports from the Southern states, European mills began looking for other sources of raw cotton. With this stimulation, the infant cotton industries of Queensland and Fiji blossomed for a few years.

Robert Towns, who had learned how to deal with Melanesian labor in the sandalwood trade and was now investing in Queensland cotton land, brought the first sixty islanders to Australia in his ship *Don Juan* in 1863. By the time the Queensland labor traffic ceased in 1904, and all individuals were repatriated two years later, over sixty thousand island laborers had migrated and far from all of them made it back. Fiji received its first island labor in 1864, and all together about twenty thousand workers were imported before the practice ended in 1911.

The Civil War also doomed shiploads of Polynesians, who were taken from the outlying islands of the eastern and central Pacific to Peru, at first for the cotton fields, and then to work in the guano beds of the Chincha Islands and the silver mines of the mainland, where most of them perished. After about three years, pressure from the great powers put an end to this cruel human exploitation and the sick and emaciated remnants were sent back to the islands, but not necessarily to their own islands. This trade nearly depopulated Easter Island. Laborers were imported from other islands to work in New Caledonia and Samoa, though on a lesser scale than in Fiji and Queensland, where sugarcane plantations, also requiring large amounts of manual labor, soon replaced cotton.

In the early unregulated days of labor recruiting, force was not unusual. Natives were enticed on board ships by every ruse that could be invented. At least one vessel masqueraded as a missionary ship. Canoes were run down or smashed by dropping pig iron on them, and their occupants plucked from the water and stowed below decks. Kidnapping was not unusual. In 1871 the kidnapping of five high-ranking men from Nukapu in the Santa Cruz group by a Fiji labor ship resulted in the murder of Anglican Bishop John Coleridge Patteson. He was killed in reprisal soon after he landed and the natives returned his body, marked with five wounds and with a palm branch tied by five knots laid on his breast, to the missionary vessel.[2] Earlier that same year a dreadful massacre occurred on the brig *Carl*. She was boarded two months later by officers of H.M.S. *Rosario*, who found her empty but unusually clean and with all papers in order. Only after she had returned to Levuka, and a passenger confessed, was it known that eighty kidnapped natives, rioting in her hold, had created panic among the crew. Gunfire was poured into the hold for eight hours. At the end of that time over fifty Melanesians had been killed and another twenty-five wounded. Dead and wounded together were thrown over the side and the hold cleaned and whitewashed.

When recruited men, taken by deceit or violence, were returned home after three years of servitude, their tales often made it impossible for a ship of any kind to stop at the place without being attacked or having crew members ambushed. On the other hand, in areas such as the southern New Hebrides, where the people were long familiar, because of sandalwooding, with white methods and trade goods, the labor ships often had no difficulty getting a cargo of voluntary recruits for the cane fields. It was essential that these people, usually indentured for three years (which they frequently innocently misunderstood to mean three months) be returned to their home islands or localities, for if they were landed elsewhere, as they often were by unscrupulous captains, they were almost certain to be killed. Thus in filling the ships some men were obtained by force and others sold by relatives, some were fleeing enemies, some wanted to see the world or get a gun and ammunition. Coastal chiefs occasionally sold kidnapped bushmen from the interior of their islands.

The ships used in the labor trade were small, fifty to three hundred tons, with those from Queensland averaging somewhat larger than those from Fiji. They were old, run-down, and leaky. But it was a short and fair-weather run to the islands and there was plenty of muscle to keep the pumps going. Long after a ship had gone beyond any usefulness for other purposes, two tiers of bunks were built in her hold, and with ragged sails, rotten rigging, and copper dangling from her bottom she was sent on a recruiting voyage. The rivalry between Fiji and Queensland ships was intense. In general the Queensland recruiters paid better prices, but it was thought that the treatment was sometimes better in Fijian ships.

Many islands contributed to the migrant labor force, but by far the greatest number of recruits came from the New Hebrides and the Solomons. Gilbert and Ellice islanders were taken in numbers early on, but these people were poor workers. Others, from the Bismarcks and the islands around eastern New Guinea succumbed quickly to disease and could not be worked long enough to pay for their taking. Because of the high mortality, recruiting in those islands was prohibited in 1884.

Mortality among the plantation labor was high in any case. Dysentery, always prevalent on labor ships, carried some off before they ever reached Queensland, and many died in quarantine. More died of diseases, especially tuberculosis, to which they had no immunity; others of homesickness; and many were simply worked to death. The death rate was much higher on the sugar plantations, where the work was hard, the punishment often severe, and the food less adequate, than on the sheep stations. Mortality was highest during the first years of labor before the new recruits were hardened to the work. Those who survived were returned home with their boxes of trinkets, their tomahawks, their guns and ammunition, and became the envy of their neighbors.

An attempt by the Queensland government through the Polynesian Labourers Act of 1868 to regulate the labor traffic and supervise employment conditions was a failure. Stimulated, however, by the death of Bishop Patteson and the *Carl* massacre, the British government finally took steps to correct the abuses of the labor traffic. In 1872 Parliament passed the Pacific Islanders Protection Act whereby ships were licensed; kidnapping was outlawed; and for the first time a native could testify, at the discretion of the judge, in court. This measure was adopted with only a few changes by the new colonial Fiji government in 1874. There is some evidence that the act was better enforced by the Fiji crown colony government and that the labor trade was more closely controlled there than in Queensland. Regulations on tonnage, space for passengers, rations, and the length of the voyage varied somewhat between the two places. A naval patrol of five fast schooners was set up to enforce regulations, but this was a difficult business. Abuses, though reduced, continued. Missionaries and colonial officials were critical and the labor trade became increasingly unpopular in Australia.

Beginning in 1870, government agents were placed on labor vessels to see that the regulations of the act were lived up to. They were charged with inspecting the rations, clothing, and sanitation on each ship; and also with making sure that each recruit was obtained legally and that returning laborers were landed at their home villages with all their possessions. The agents' relationship with the ship's captain and the recruiter was obviously a delicate and difficult one. Unless the agent was a man of unusual ability and character, and he seldom was, he was at the mercy of the master, who could make his life intolerable. Agents were in general pretty low-class people. The job was unattractive and most of the seedy individuals who took it could not have found any other employment. Regulations required that when the boats approached the shore only the boat with the agent in it could actually recruit, while a second boat, containing men with guns at the ready, stood a short distance offshore and covered the first. Boats were usually manned by islanders accompanied by armed Europeans. The agent seldom understood what was going on, for negotiations for recruits were not always interpreted correctly. The gifts distributed might be for community consent, to pacify relatives of the men being recruited, or for the sale of a bushman by a coastal chief.

As it was virtually impossible to regulate the recruiting, so too was it almost impossible to supervise the conditions of employment. Corruption and sharp practice were common not only in the trade but among the employers and in the courts. All aspects of the regulatory process were characterized by ineffectiveness, laziness, disinterest, and lack of concern for the Melanesians. Medical care for indentured labor was minimal. It is no wonder that the mortality was high and about one-quarter of the laborers brought to Queensland died there. Under often appalling conditions, revolts sometimes resulted in the death of a taskmaster.

Minimum pay per man prescribed by law was six pounds a year in Queensland and half that in Fiji. However, some laborers preferred Fiji, where the food was said to be better and more adequate although the wages and trade goods were inferior to those in Queensland. The traffic reached its height in the 1880s, when there were over ten thousand imported laborers in Queensland and over five thousand in Fiji. Throughout the labor trade period, half the recruits came from the New Hebrides.

While most of the labor trading was British, some Germans were also recruiting for Samoa and the French for New Caledonia. Most of the vessels sailing out of Nouméa, although they flew French colors, were British owned and manned. Both French and Germans, as well as local planters in the New Hebrides and other islands, did not come under the Fiji and Queensland regulations and were even more unscrupulous and deceitful in kidnapping and dealing with the natives. Their labor traffic was completely unsupervised and their operations often jeopardized the lives of missionaries, traders, and copra makers resident in the islands, as well as the personnel of the next labor ship that might arrive off a village after a violent incident.

After the federation of Australia, the trade came to an end and in 1906 nearly six thousand Melanesians, all that remained in Queensland, were returned to the islands. Not until 1911 did the island labor traffic end in Fiji, although it declined after 1890 when Indian labor, first imported in 1879, was found to be more efficient.

At its worst the labor trade was hardly distinguishable from slavery; at its best it was rewarding to some of the later laborers, who rejoiced in the guns and goods they could buy with their meager three years' wages and the prestige acquired when they returned to their homes. In the early unregulated days it was probably as bad as claimed by the missionaries, its severest critics; certainly it was never as beneficial as claimed by its apologists in the business. One finds it difficult to agree with that old labor trader, Captain William T. Wawn, who wrote: "Notwithstanding all the tales of bloodshed, murder, and kidnapping, in connection with the labour trade, which have been dinned into the ears of the public, for the last few years especially, I conscientiously affirm that it has been, in the main, equally beneficial to the colony and to the islanders themselves."[3]

Removing thousands of young men in the prime of life certainly had an effect on the population of many islands. The cultural evolution of the islands—caused by a changed technology, exposure to new diseases, the introduction of firearms, and begun by the sandalwooders—continued during the labor traffic period at an ever-accelerating rate. Overall it was the greatest single acculturating factor in Melanesia, changing the native way of life forever and providing good reason for the often reluctant political takeover of island groups by European powers.

CHAPTER 12

From Confusion to Colonies

Even as traders bartered for sandalwood and bêche-de-mer, for pearl and tortoise shell; as whalers traded rum and firearms for fresh fruit and vegetables, for girls and a day ashore out of the stinking forecastles—while all this was going on, smart naval vessels were crisscrossing the greatest ocean in the world. The swindling trader, it was thought, had to be protected from the sneaky island con man. The whaler, while dispensing rum and gunpowder, gonorrhea and syphilis, smallpox and measles, must be sheltered from the lascivious grin of a twelve-year-old maiden or the stealing of nails by technologically impecunious sneak thieves. Missionaries must be protected as they Christianized cannibals, and clothed incontinent minds with piety and bodies with calico.

The age of discovery in the Pacific evolved into one of exploration, charting, and surveying; into a search for new whaling grounds; into the protection of traders, missionaries and other nationals; into showing the flag, chastising chiefs, and ultimately into colonialism. The English were followed by French and Americans, by Germans, and eventually by Japanese.

Naval commanders, especially the British, took possession in the name of their sovereign and raised their flags with considerable regularity over many islands the length and breadth of the Pacific. But these precautionary ceremonies were never confirmed by home governments. The British particularly were reluctant to take responsibility for distant territories of questionable use or productivity. Only toward the end of the nineteenth century, after the Franco-Prussian War, under the pressure of international rivalries, including the race for naval bases, did the many islands groups begin to fall quickly into rapidly expanding European empires.

In the meantime, by right of discovery in the third quarter of the eighteenth century the British could have claimed more islands in the Pacific than any other power. Following the spectacular voyages and discoveries of Cook there was an opportunity to make the entire Pacific British. Britain did not avail herself of it. There was no gold, no commercial value—only natives. The English Protestant missionaries could have further solidified British claims had they been made, but raising the Union Jack over an island meant little to the home government. British governmental policy toward the islands was nonexistent and the attitude of Parliament and officials alike almost uniformly one of indifference. But while indifference and anticolonial feeling were negative influences on British territorial activism in the Pacific, there was another very positive obstacle to any settlement in the area. The East India Company consistently insisted that no settlement, and therefore less chance of competition, be allowed within the area of their monopoly. If there was any policy at all, it was one of minimum intervention. Some islands were regarded as sovereign states ruled by native "kings." This convenient attitude coincided with the lack of desire for any political interference in the islands. After the Napoleonic Wars the Royal Navy was paramount in the Pacific as elsewhere, and noninterference suited island traders as well as the home government. Only the missionaries hoped for more formal protection, for they alone seemed to sense a threat from the increasing interest of France and to regard the arrival of Roman Catholic missionaries as forerunners of French imperialism.

The notable exception to this apathetic attitude was the deliberate establishment of the penal settlement in New South Wales in 1786. This step provided the Royal Navy and colonial traders with an excellent base in magnificent Sydney Harbour, from which the islands were easily accessible. From 1826 regular naval visits began to New Zealand and from 1829 on, the Admiralty, under the prodding of the Foreign Office, sent warships on annual visits to New South Wales, Tahiti, Tonga, and other islands.

Growing trade between New South Wales and New Zealand brought increasing pressure from the Australian colony for the establishment of law and order in New Zealand. This pressure, augmented by the appeals of missionaries and traders at the Bay of Islands and finally the colonization efforts of Edward Wakefield, resulted in the Treaty of Waitangi with the Maori chiefs in 1840—the first breakthrough in the British wall of indifference toward the

Pacific. Then came the slow adjustment between Maori and pakeha—the wars and violence. A native land court was set up in 1865, followed two years later by suffrage for Maori men and four seats in Parliament. Politically New Zealand, like Australia, moved from colony to dominion to independent member of the Commonwealth.

French Oceania and New Caledonia

The first move toward taking political possession of any of the Oceanic islands came not from Britain but from France. Indeed, in the same year that British sovereignty was proclaimed over New Zealand, the British had to act quickly to forestall the French from getting a foothold in the South Island.

Louis Phillipe was eager to restore to France the imperial power lost in the Napoleonic Wars. Changes in the economies and politics of Oceanic lands were foreseen and island bases in the Pacific would be essential to any interested power. Nevertheless another war with Britain was to be avoided at all costs. The weak French attempt at colonization in New Zealand in 1840 was therefore more in the nature of a feeler than a serious official effort.

The scene for a serious French attempt was set earlier when two French Roman Catholic missionaries left Valparaiso, Chile, in July 1834 and, after calling at the Gambier Islands (Mangareva), arrived at Tahiti. The entrenched London Society missionaries made strenuous objections to their arrival, and in December 1836 the two Catholic priests were expelled from the island: The French government would not listen to the British suggestion that rival missionary groups stay out of territory already occupied and being converted by others.

The French now deliberately decided to regard the expulsion of the priests as an insult. In 1838 Captain Dupetit-Thouars arrived at Tahiti, after landing two more Catholic missionaries at the Marquesas Islands, and demanded an indemnity of two thousand Spanish dollars from the Tahitian government and an apology from Queen Pomare IV within twenty-four hours; if they were not forthcoming Papeete would be bombarded. The demands were complied with and Dupetit-Thouars then proposed a perpetual peace between Tahiti and France with mutual promises of most-favored-nation treatment.

Queen Pomare as well as the Reverend George Pritchard, leader of the Protestant mission and British consul, endeavored to get the British government to intervene. The queen sent a petition to Queen Victoria requesting a protectorate over the island. Pritchard and the London Missionary Society also requested government action. The Foreign Office's problem, however, was made more difficult by a Tahitian law passed at the same time Pomare's petition was written, stating that the London Missionary Society's brand of Protestant Christianity was the only and official religion in Tahiti. This legislation antagonized the French.

If any island should have been an English colony it was Tahiti, and this was the time to do something about it. Wallis had discovered Tahiti, Cook's voyages publicized it, English missionaries converted it, but the government remained passive. In any case it had its hands full with the situation in New Zealand. The final decision not to accept the sovereignty of Tahiti was made in 1839 and Pritchard was so notified.

The French once more took advantage of British reluctance and the nonintervention policy in 1842 when Dupetit-Thouars again appeared on the scene. Sailing from Valparaiso, he arrived at the Marquesas and took possession of those islands for France, and they have remained French possessions ever since. He then went on to Tahiti, where he demanded another payment of ten thousand Spanish dollars in forty-eight hours—a sum the Tahitian Government could not raise. Under his threat of occupation the Tahitians agreed to whatever terms he laid down. He then declared Tahiti a French protectorate, a move which was ratified the following year by his home government. When Dupetit-Thouars returned to Tahiti a third time, he decided to proclaim full French sovereignty and depose the queen, but this high-handed action his government refused to support. In the meantime Pomare had retired to Raiatea and there was bitter fighting before the queen accepted the protectorate in 1847.

The aggressive French action, however, created a violent popular British reaction, especially in the Australian and New Zealand colonies. Somewhat reluctantly the French agreed to equal treatment and protection of the Protestant missionaries. With these assurances the British government decided not to intervene in spite of an inflamed press and heavy missionary pressure— again the policy was one of nonintervention.

Britain and France signed an agreement in 1847 recognizing each other's sovereignty over New Zealand and the Marquesas respectively, as well as France's protectorate of Tahiti (which did not include the Leeward Islands of the Society group), and preserving the status quo in the Pacific. Britain, rather impractically, hoped to maintain the independence of all the other island groups.

The French consolidation of eastern Polynesia eventually followed when the Marquesas, Tuamotus, Tahiti, and Moorea were made colonies in 1880.

The next year Mangareva in the Gambiers and two islands of the Austral group (Tubuai and Raivavae) along with the island of Rapa were annexed. The Leeward Islands were added in 1888 and the following year the last two of the Australs—Rimatara and Rurutu—became a protectorate. Today all the islands and groups that now comprise French Oceania are an overseas territory of the French Republic, administered from the capital in Papeete.

Great Britain had reacted weakly to the French acquisition of Tahiti, and its policy was even feebler when in 1853 the French annexed New Caledonia, where the English had an equally good claim by right of discovery. Captain Cook had taken possession of the island in the name of George III when he discovered it on his second voyage, but no effort was ever made to establish that claim. Purely by clerical error, New Caledonia, along with much more of Melanesia, was included within the original boundary of the New Zealand colony, but the only British to take advantage of this error were the missionaries who established the Melanesian Mission in 1850. The colonial government of New South Wales subsequently came up with a plan to send a colony from Sydney to New Caledonia, and George Pritchard, the missionary-consul at Tahiti, always suspicious of the French, warned the British government of French ambitions. Captain John Elphinstone Erskine, on the first of a series of official naval cruises around the Southwest Pacific in 1845, recommended that something be done about the island because of its closeness to Australia. But the Foreign Office turned a deaf ear to all suggestions that Britain annex New Caledonia.   •

Meanwhile the French Marist missionaries were well established though living under constant harassment by the natives. In 1847 after a native raid destroyed their mission and killed one of their number, the missionaries retreated from the main island to the Isle of Pines until 1851. After the British and French had eyed each other for a decade the French decided to act. Napoleon III sent secret orders to his naval commanders in the Pacific area to proceed to New Caledonia and annex the island. First on the scene was Rear Admiral Febvrier-Despointes who, after receiving his orders at Lima, sailed immediately to New Caledonia, ascertained that no British action had taken place, and took possession of the island at Balade, the mission headquarters, on September 24, 1853. He then proceeded to the Isle of Pines and, in spite of the presence of a British warship, carried out another annexation ceremony with no objection from the British commander. There is some indication that the French may have anticipated similar action by the British commander by a narrow margin, although there is no evidence that the home government had any such plans. The nearby Loyalty Islands also became a part of the new French possession.

In 1863 France, deciding to emulate the earlier British use of New South Wales, established a penal colony in New Caledonia. The first shipload of convicts arrived the following year and from that time until 1897, when transportation ceased, about forty thousand prisoners served sentences there.

Land problems with the natives of New Caledonia were as severe as in New Zealand. Within three years of annexation the natives retained possession of only one-tenth of the land. By the 1870s, when the great mineral wealth of the island had been ascertained and was being exploited, the influx of colonists and laborers put further pressure on the native Melanesians as more and more land was expropriated. A food shortage and numerous wanton incidents, culminating in the death of a convict and his native wife, inflamed the latent tinder of Melanesian rebellion in June 1878. By the time the revolt was suppressed a year later, over two hundred whites and an uncounted number of natives had been killed and heavy destruction of crops and property had taken place. While subdued, native hostility to the French persisted for many years, with the last outbreak occurring as late as 1917.

The French occupation of New Caledonia caused some flurry in British government offices, but an alliance with France against Russia was considered more important than a little-known South Sea island. Britain's future interests were given more prestige, however, by beefing up the number of consuls in Pacific island towns.

Cannibal Kingdom to Crown Colony

For the first half of the nineteenth century, the Fiji Islands were as wild, violent, and cannibalistic as any place on earth. The native ferocity of the warriors had become intensified by the introduction of firearms, the brutality of equally savage beachcombers, and the avariciousness of sandalwood and bêche-de-mer traders. The slight ameliorating influence of the courageous Wesleyan missionaries was precarious indeed. When the establishment of a colonial government in New Zealand began to have a stabilizing effect on that previously unruly country, much of the disorderly element at the Bay of Islands moved out to less restrictive ports. Fiji was a natural haven for these undesirables.

By the late 1840s the leading figure in Fiji was Thakombau (Cakobau in modern Fijian orthography), the chief of Mbau who had an insatiable desire to become *Tui Viti* or king of all Fiji. Although his father Tanoa, the infirm and tyrannical head chief of Mbau, did not die until 1852, Thakombau was in fact the real ruler. He was a warrior of unusual ability and rapacious ambition who, in a series of aggressions, subdued many lesser villages. In a war that began in 1843 and lasted eleven years he finally conquered his most powerful rival, the village of Rewa.

While the wars with Rewa were going on, two characters arrived in Fiji who were to have great effect on Thakombau's political ambitions and ultimately upon Fiji's becoming a crown colony. In 1846 John Brown Williams of Salem, Massachusetts, became the first U.S. government representative in Fiji, the commercial agent for several American companies, and a trader himself. Two years later Ma'afu, a Tongan chief and relative of King George of Tonga, was banished from his native islands because of his own political ambitions. He settled in the eastern Fijis where he soon became the leader of all the Tongans who lived there and Thakombau's great rival.

On July 4, 1849, Williams fired a patriotic salute from a cannon on his property so successfully that the blazing wadding set fire to his house. As the flames spread to other structures, the exuberant Fijians emptied his house and storage buildings, saving his property from the fire only to disappear with it into the bush. When Williams's threats of revenge were ignored, he brought legal claim for damages against Thakombau and sat back to await the arrival of an American man-of-war.

The claim did not prevent Thakombau, who had admired a schooner in Charles Wilkes's fleet when it visited Fiji in 1840, from ordering through Williams a similar vessel to be paid for with a thousand pounds of bêche-de-mer. In this he was emulating the Kamehamehas in Hawaii, who plunged themsleves into irrevocable debts by promising sandalwood in exchange for American yachts and other vessels.

Thakombau's prestige suffered a serious loss in 1853 when he was accused by European traders of instigating an interior tribe to burn the town of Levuka. Thereupon the whites formed an alliance with his old enemies of Rewa and isolated Mbau with a tight blockade. Finally under advice of the Wesleyan missionaries and of King George of Tonga, the proud old heathen publicly announced his acceptance of Christianity and took the baptismal name of Ebenezer. His influence, however, plunged to a new low because his conversion alienated all the heathen chiefs.

Thakombau was saved by the fortuitous visit of King George of Tonga, who arrived in March 1855 with two thousand warriors in a fleet of thirty canoes. An incident involving the death of a Tongan chief at the hands of Thakombau's enemies resulted in a bloody battle and the defeat of these enemies. King George imposed peace terms and Thakombau then ruled as a quiet and reformed dominant chief. In return for his help King George sailed back to Tonga with Thakombau's unpaid-for American vessel and his largest and finest canoe. His help also left Thakombau with another problem, for the wily, skillful, and ambitious Tongan chief Ma'afu, his prestige enhanced by King George's visit, now became Thakombau's principal rival for the title of *Tui Viti.*

Prestige also brought other responsibilities to Thakombau. Rewa people burned the house of John Williams, and Williams held Thakombau responsible. Nor was Williams (who, incidentally, had not been paid for his earlier claims) the only American who had property destroyed by Fijians. Thus when Commander E. B. Boutwell in the U.S.S. *John Adams* arrived in September 1855, he was beseiged by Williams and other Americans to collect for their losses. Boutwell promptly slapped Thakombau with claims of nearly forty-five thousand dollars. The damages were undoubtedly exaggerated, but Thakombau, under threat, had no choice but to sign a document acknowledging his liability.

Part of the old rascal's problem sprang from the fact that increasing numbers of Europeans were settling in the islands. British, French, and American warships called with increasing frequency. But Thakombau's assumed position as king of Fiji was strengthened when, in June 1857, the United States government negotiated a treaty with him to protect Americans from molestation. In 1858 he signed a similar treaty with the French. That same year the British sent W. T. Pritchard, son of George Pritchard of Tahitian fame, to Fiji as official consul.

Pritchard had hardly arrived on the scene when Commander Sinclair in the U.S.S. *Vandalia* dropped anchor and reviewed the American claims. Sinclair told Thakombau that his debt, as assessed by Boutwell, must be paid within a year. The Fijian chief signed a statement agreeing to do so, although he knew he could not keep his promise. He hastily gave a document to consul Pritchard offering to cede the Fiji Islands to Britain, and to give the crown two hundred thousand acres of land, if the British would liquidate his American debt. A further condition provided that he would hold the title of *Tui Viti* and govern, under British guidance, the Fijian population. Pritchard immediately left for London with the document and returned a year later with the offer still under consideration.

By this time Thakombau was under the threat of attack from Ma'afu, who hoped to assume the title of *Tui Viti* himself. Pritchard, backed up by a British warship, patched up a peace between the old rivals. While the consul, without any real authority to do so, was trying to keep peace in Fiji, the British sent Colonel W. T. Smythe on a mission to examine the situation and report on whether Thakombau's offer should be accepted. The colonel soon perceived that Thakombau did not have the authority to be king of Fiji nor did he possess the two hundred thousand acres of land he promised to give away. Furthermore Smythe thought little of the white population and less of the Fijians. He recommended that the offer not be accepted and this information was conveyed to Thakombau in July 1862. Pritchard, whom Smythe also complained about, was removed from office the following January.

But the white population grew steadily as more speculators arrived to start cotton plantations or produce coconut oil. Some kind of stable government was essential. Attempts by Thakombau, Ma'afu, and other chiefs to form a government were fruitless, but affairs limped along with some European guidance for a few years. At last Ma'afu accepted Thakombau as king of Fiji in 1871. (Meanwhile, the United States, with pachyderm persistence, had sent another warship to collect the debt in 1867.)

The last few years of Thakombau's independent government were held together by a group of white ministers led by John B. Thurston, a planter who had been British consul. Sentiment for annexation was increasing, and in January 1873 Thurston wrote to London asking if the government would consider accepting the cession of the kingdom of Fiji provided this was the desire of the king and the people.

The British government replied, as it had some fifteen years earlier, by sending a commission to investigate the Fiji question and report. On arriving in 1874, the commissioners found that nearly everyone (Europeans, chiefs, Tongans, and Fijians) was in favor of annexation, and they sent back a strongly positive recommendation. Both the Australian and New Zealand colonies also urged that the offer be accepted. With some reluctance the home government agreed and on October 10, 1874, Fiji became a crown colony. Britain had at last acquired her first Oceanic island possession. After ninety-six years as a colony, Fiji became independent on October 10, 1970, and shortly thereafter a member of the British Commonwealth and the United Nations.

The Samoan Affair

The change of Samoa from its native-ruled state to colonial status is complicated indeed compared with Fiji, for not one but three great powers were intimately involved. As with New Zealand and Fiji, a point was reached where the native wars and undisciplined elements needed control if traders, missionaries, and other more orderly people were to be able to conduct their affairs with some degree of stability and safety.

Unlike Hawaii and Fiji, the Samoans had never established anything approaching a permanent centralized native government. Competition and warfare were constant between the leading Samoan families, the two most powerful of which were the Malietoa and Tupua clans, with the latter clan itself split into rival factions. Native politics were complicated, heated, and incessant.

While native wars swirled around them, the missionaries prospered in their conversion efforts. By the early 1860s there were few unchurched Samoans left. About this time another European organization appeared in Samoa and soon made its influence paramount. The aggressive German trading firm of J. C. Godeffroy and Son of Hamburg first entered the Pacific in 1845 and established headquarters at Samoa in 1857. As a result of their activities, the town of Apia developed into the leading trading port of the Central Pacific. The firm, at first interested primarily in coconut oil, established agents throughout the islands who sent oil to Apia for transshipment to Europe. In the late 1860s Theodor Weber, a local manager of the firm, developed a process for making and shipping copra rather than oil—a far more profitable procedure. From coconut oil the enterprising Godeffroys became involved with every aspect of Pacific trading. They set out plantations of coconut, coffee, and cocoa, and became land owners. Still, it was always copra that remained the most important island export.

Through the Godeffroys, the Germans developed a strong interest in Samoa—an interest not matched by Americans until after the Civil War. The British, with their nonintervention policy, hoped to encourage independent native rulers in Samoa and to prevent other foreign powers from acquiring more influence than that possessed by Great Britain, All three nations appointed consuls, who became increasingly involved in Samoan politics and intrigues.

As steam replaced sail for ship propulsion, it became increasingly evident that the possession of fueling stops in the Pacific was not only desirable but essential for both merchant and naval vessels. At the instigation of an American steamship owner, who had his eye on Pago Pago as a coaling station for his service between California and Australia, Commander Richard W. Meade in the U.S.S. *Narragansett* called at that Samoan port and made a treaty with the island's chief for the exclusive privilege of establishing a naval station

there. This involvement by the U.S. Navy led to an increased American interest in Samoan affairs, which developed in conflict with British and particularly German interests. Although Meade's treaty was not ratified by the U.S.
Senate, it was followed by a petition from a group of Samoan chiefs requesting the United States to annex the islands. This resulted in the arrival on the
scene of an extraordinary person named Colonel A.B. Steinberger, who was
sent out from Washington as a special agent of the United States government
to report on the Samoan situation.

Sporadic fighting had been going on between rival factions for the Samoan
kingship and Steinberger helped the three consuls to arrange a peace which established Malietoa Laupepa as king in April 1873. The colorful colonel returned to the United States to make his report but came back to Samoa in
1875, assisted the king in setting up his government, and became his premier.
He then began double-dealing—posing as an American assisting the Samoans
but actually furthering the German interests of Godeffroy on a commission.
The U.S. consul, fed up with Steinberger's chicanery, high-handedly persuaded the British consul to have him deported on a British warship; this
action resulted in the American consul's recall and a reprimand for the Royal
Navy captain.

In 1878 a group of Samoan chiefs visited the United States, which finally
accepted the Pago Pago naval station. Similar treaties were signed with both
Germany and Britain in 1879 and an agreement was made by which the three
foreign consuls governed the town of Apia under a system worked out by Sir
Arthur Gordon, the governor of Fiji. This agreement also made Apia a neutral
territory during native civil wars. The arrangement lasted through twenty
years of native intrigue and consular jealousies.

The combination of the rivalries between the chiefly Samoan families and
among the three great powers made the decade of the eighties one of increasing tension, confusion, intrigue, and bitterness. By 1889 Germany and the
United States were on the verge of war over the Samoan situation. They
agreed that there should be one Samoan king, but they backed rival chiefs for
the honor. As March rolled around six U.S. and German warships were eyeing
each other hostilely and the H.M.S. *Calliope* stood by to watch out for British
interests. Fortunately an act of God averted certain armed conflict.

Of the seven warships that were trapped in Apia Harbor by a hurricane on
March 16, 1889, only the British *Calliope* managed to claw her way out beyond the reef to the open sea. The German and American ships were all

wrecked or beached. The Germans lost ninety-two and the Americans fifty-four men in the disaster. A touching scene occurred as the crew of the doomed U.S.S. *Trenton* lined her rail and cheered the *Calliope* as she cleared the reef in a magnificent exhibition of seamanship.

The loss of the warships took the edge off German and American belligerency. In June 1889 the three powers signed the Berlin Treaty, acknowledging Malietoa Laupepa as king of an independent Samoa, formalizing the control of the three consuls over Apia, and establishing a commission to settle land claims between Samoans and Europeans. The old rivalries cropped up again, however, in 1898 when Malietoa died. Final solution to the Samoan internal trouble did not come until November 1899 when the group of islands was partitioned, Germany annexing Western Samoa and the United States taking over Eastern Samoa as a territory administered by the Navy. At the same time Great Britain renounced all its claims to Samoa in return for Germany's abandoning claims to Tonga and the Solomon Islands excepting Bougainville and Buka.

Germany, because of British preoccupation with the Boer War, came out by far the best in the colonial takeover of Pacific islands, but ultimately lost them all along with its other colonies after World War I. Western Samoa was mandated to New Zealand and became independent except for foreign policy on January 1, 1962.

Partitioning the Western Pacific

Western New Guinea, where the Dutch had been creeping along the coasts from their base in Indonesia since the seventeenth century, was the part of Melanesia nailed down earliest by a European power. The Dutch made no formal claims, however, until 1714, and they did not annex the western half of New Guinea until 1828. Not until 1895 was the southern section of their eastern boundary established along the 141st meridian and the Fly River by a treaty with Britain. There was never any formal treaty with Germany for a boundary in the north but the 141° line was never disputed. Dutch activity was always confined to the coasts and they made almost no attempt to penetrate the interior. The Dutch half of New Guinea became the Indonesian province of West Irian on May 1, 1963.

Except for an occasional trader, blackbirder, or explorer white men avoided the fever-ridden mangrove swamp coasts of the eastern half of New Guinea. But by the mid-seventies some interest in the area began to appear in

Queensland Colony, whose bêche-de-mer and pearl-shell fishers had been exploiting islands in Torres Strait for a decade. Nevertheless, unfriendly natives and prevalent malaria discouraged approaches to the main island.

In the 1870s agents of the Godeffroy company, operating from Apia, appeared to trade in Micronesia and the islands north of New Guinea. A decade later the Germans were recruiting labor for their Samoan plantations in New Britain (the largest of the Bismarcks) and nearby islands. Here Germans and Queenslanders met on the same errands. The Australian colonies' suspicions of Germany in the 1870s developed into an incessant pleading with the home government to annex New Guinea and the other Melanesian islands for the security of Australia. In 1883 Queensland attempted to force the issue by taking possession of New Guinea at Port Moresby in the name of Queen Victoria, but the action was declared unconstitutional by the Colonial Office, which claimed that only the imperial, not a colonial government could take such a step.

A change in Chancellor Bismarck's imperial policy—which had previously protected German traders, but refrained from outright annexation of islands except for naval coaling stations—took place in 1883. In April 1884 Germany proclaimed a protectorate over northeastern New Guinea, the Bismarck Archipelago, the Admiralty Islands, and all nearby smaller islands. Having repudiated the Queensland attempt the previous year, the British government reversed itself in November 1884 and took possession of southeastern New Guinea. Germany annexed its portion of the island in 1885 and the British followed suit in 1888. In 1901 British New Guinea became a territory of Australia under the name of Papua. Following World War I Australia also acquired German New Guinea under a League of Nations mandate. After World War II, in 1949, Papua and New Guinea were combined into a single administrative unit. On December 1, 1973, the Territory of Papua New Guinea became self-governing internally and fully independent in 1975.

The Northern Solomon Islands had been included in the German protectorate over northeastern New Guinea, which was relinquished after World War I to Australia. In 1893 the British had declared a protectorate over the Southern Solomons, largely because of the disruption caused by blackbirding and retaliatory massacres by the natives, frequently of innocent parties. At the end of this decade the Santa Cruz group and various smaller islands were added to the protectorate and in 1900, as part of the deal whereby Britain gave up all claim to Western Samoa, the islands of Santa Isabel and Choiseul, with various small islands, were transferred by treaty from Germany to Britain. Thus only the large islands of Bougainville and Buka remained part of the German territory.

The many years of devoted hard work by the missionaries of the Melanesian Mission smoothed the way for British administration in the Solomons as well as the trading activities of, at first, Burns Philp Company and later W. R. Carpenter and Company after World War I. The Solomons were one of the principal combat areas in World War II and suffered accordingly. After the Japanese withdrawal, the capital was shifted from the town of Tulagi, which had been destroyed, to Honiara on Guadalcanal, and the long task of restoring plantations and reestablishing government began. In 1953 the headquarters of the British High Commissioner for the Western Pacific, who until the previous year was also governor of Fiji with offices at Suva, was moved to Honiara. The British interest in the New Hebrides also came under his jurisdiction, as did the Gilbert and Ellice Islands Colony up until 1971.

The curious and unique government that developed in the New Hebrides group was the result of British and French rivalries and was not the clear-cut solution arrived at by the British and Germans in New Guinea. For many years the New Hebrides were the center of the labor traffic. Anglican and Presbyterian missionaries as well as British and French plantation owners were also settled in the islands. But while both missionaries and planters were becoming established throughout the group, as late as 1885 there was no government of any kind. John Higginson, an Irish-born French planter and largest landowner in the islands, had unsuccessfully asked the French governor of New Caledonia to annex the New Hebrides as early as 1871. Both Britain and France pursued gunboat diplomacy. The Australian colonies, always jittery about the French presence in New Caledonia, became increasingly alarmed that the French might take over the islands entirely and strongly urged British annexation.

Suggestions and counter proposals went back and forth between the French and British governments for years until, finally, in 1886 the two countries agreed to establish a joint naval commission to maintain order in the New Hebrides. The formal convention was signed on November 16, 1887, and final details settled early the following year. Two French and two British warships, commanded alternately by officers of the two countries, were charged with protecting the lives and property of their nationals. Unfortunately, the commission arrangement did not work, for there was no civil law or government.

In 1906, when German traders attempted to get a toehold in the group, Britain and France agreed to establish a condominium and this arrangement was set up by a convention on October 20, 1906. The Banks and Torres islands were included with the New Hebrides and a capital was established at Vila on Efate for the two resident commissioners who were to govern under the respective Pacific high commissioners of the two countries. The two powers were to have equal rights and residents were given six months to choose whether they would live under French or British law. A police force, courts, taxes, and all the paraphernalia of European government were set up. As some arrangements proved unworkable, various changes and modifications have been made from time to time. To obtain this standoff with the French, the British agreed to abrogate the London agreement of 1847 giving France complete and undisputed sovereignty in the Leeward Islands of the Society group. The cumbersome condominium government, while it has worked, is probably the most expensive administration ever fostered on a small territory. Nevertheless, the agreement reached in the New Hebrides completed the European partitioning of Melanesia among the great powers.

North of Melanesia the tiny Micronesian islands constituting the Caroline, Mariana, and Marshall groups stretch across more than forty degrees of longitude. Although many of the islands were discovered by the Spanish in the sixteenth century, except for Guam and some of the other islands of the Mariana group, Spain did little to either colonize or annex them. As German traders began penetrating to the most remote atolls, Spain reiterated her claim to both the Carolines and Marshalls in the 1870s. But Spain was too weak to do anything about it when Germany declared a protectorate over the Marshalls in 1885. In August of the same year the Germans tried the same thing at Yap in the Carolines, but strong Spanish objections brought on agreement to leave the decision to the pope. Not unexpectedly, the pontiff decided in favor of Spain, with Germany retaining trading rights.

Those trading rights gave the energetic Germans increasing influence throughout the islands. Following the Spanish-American War, Guam was ceded to the United States in 1898 for use as a naval station. The following year Spain and Germany arranged by treaty for the remaining Mariana Islands and all of the Carolines and Marshalls to be turned over to Germany for four million dollars.

German possession of the islands was of short duration, for no sooner was that country enmeshed in World War I than the Japanese moved in. Following the war Japan was given the League of Nations mandate over the islands. In the mid-thirties Japan withdrew from the league, fortified the islands, and closed them off to the outside world. World War II destroyed the industries and plantations which the Japanese had developed, and after that conflict the entire area became the United States Trust Territory of Micronesia.

The only other Micronesian group, the Gilbert Islands, had been proclaimed a British protectorate by Captain E. H. N. Davies of the H.M.S. *Royalist* in 1892. It was not until 1915, however, that these islands, together with the nearby Polynesian Ellice group, were annexed by Great Britain at the request of the native governments. At various times other small islands, mostly uninhabited, were added to the colony. Until 1971, when he became responsible directly to London, the resident commissioner of the Gilbert and Ellice Islands Colony, with headquarters on Tarawa, came under the high commissioner for the Western Pacific at Honiara in the Solomons.

The Annexation of Hawaii

The Hawaiian Islands, from the time they were united by Kamehameha I about 1810, had a long history as an independent island kingdom in the Pacific. Eight monarchs reigned over the "Paradise of the Pacific" until Queen Liliuokalani was deposed on January 17, 1893.

Almost from the beginning two nations, England and the United States, took more interest in the Hawaiian Islands than did any others, although France and Russia sometimes looked on enviously from the sidelines. Discovery and earliest contacts were British, but within a few years of the islands' discovery, the majority of foreign residents were American and increasingly so were the ships calling at Hawaiian ports.

As early as 1794, however, Captain George Vancouver was ceded the Hawaiian Islands by Kamehameha I and accepted them in the name of King George III. This cession, however, was never confirmed and the British made no attempt to annex the islands. Although their governments were increasingly staffed by American advisers, Hawaiian monarchs always greatly admired their British royal colleagues and to a certain extent looked upon them as their friendly protectors. When a flag was chosen for the country the Union Jack flew in the canton on a field of red, white, and blue stripes.

A dispute concerning British nationals resulted in another attempt to cede the islands to the crown by Kamehameha III in 1843, but again the policy of nonintervention prevailed and Britain insisted on Hawaiian independence with guaranteed fair treatment for British subjects.

But while Hawaiian royal sentiment may have been British-oriented, American missionaries and traders were becoming more numerous and influential, and the economy of the islands came ever more completely under American control and domination as the nineteenth century moved into its second half.

A step toward closer Hawaiian-American association came in 1884 with the signing of a reciprocity treaty by which the United States acquired the future naval base of Pearl Harbor. Both France and Britain formally protested the cession of Pearl Harbor in 1887 and suggested that the three powers guarantee Hawaiian independence and neutrality. The United States, which had urged a similar arrangement for Samoa with England and Germany, was not interested in the suggestion.

The rather shaky Hawaiian monarchy, bolstered by a succession of strong missionary advisers, provided a government under which the growing economic power of the sugar planters flourished, but there was increasing agitation for annexation to the United States. When the last king, Kalakaua, a consistent friend of the Americans, died, he was succeeded in 1891 by his sister Queen Liliuokalani. A latent "Hawaii for the Hawaiians" movement received impetus and strength at her accession, for her policy was to break away from foreign domination of her government and revive the power of the native chiefs. At the same time the McKinley Tariff of 1890 destroyed the advantage that Hawaiian sugar shipped to the mainland had held through the reciprocity treaty of 1875. The sugar industry was depressed and Americans in the islands became alarmed.

In January 1893 the queen, an ardent Hawaiian patriot but an imprudent politician, decided to proclaim a new constitution greatly reducing the power of the legislature and restoring many of the crown's former prerogatives. The strong opposition of Americans forced her to announce postponement, but this did not prevent a rapid series of events—a mass meeting of foreign residents in Honolulu and the landing of marines from the U.S.S. *Boston* to keep order. On January 17, 1893, Queen Liliuokalani was deposed and the Hawaiian monarchy came to an inglorious end. A provisional government drew up a treaty for American annexation which was ready for signature on February 14. Proponents of the treaty were optimistic but it was not ratified by Congress before the anti-imperialist President Cleveland returned to office for his second term on March 4, 1893. Nor was it ever.

A Republic of Hawaii was set up with Judge Sanford Ballard Dole as president and in 1895 Queen Liliuokalani, accepting the inevitable, relinquished all rights to the throne. The road to annexation was a long and tortuous one but the inevitable took place at a dignified ceremony on August 12, 1898, in President McKinley's administration. Hawaii became a territory of the United States and President Dole became U.S. Governor Dole. It took even longer for the final political step, for although statehood was first advocated for the territory in 1919 it was not until 1959 that the necessary bill passed Congress and was ratified by a Hawaiian plebiscite. In June 1959 Hawaii became the fiftieth state.

Of all the Pacific island groups only Tonga has retained any semblance of independence throughout its history. The group was united by King George I Tupou in 1845 and the kingdom continued into the twentieth century, with King Taufa'ahau as reigning monarch in the 1970s. In 1900, however, Basil Thomson, acting for the United Kingdom, concluded a treaty with King George II Tupou, and a British protectorate over the islands was proclaimed on May 18, 1900.

Thus, as we have seen, the last half of the nineteenth century almost exactly coincided with the partitioning of all the islands of the Pacific among the world powers. The progressive and continuing European impact, beginning with exploration and followed by missionaries, traders, and exploiters, culminated in some form or degree of European or American political control of every piece of Pacific real estate, no matter how desolate or impoverished. By 1900 it was all part of a completely European-oriented economic and political world.

CHAPTER 13

Exploitation

The spread of colonialism, as the great powers took over the various islands during a period of about fifty years, brought political stability. This in turn encouraged financial investments that in some islands completely transformed the economy. Traders enlarged their holdings; big companies with substantial financial resources risked investment. World conditions helped to increase markets for island exports, especially coconut products and phosphate, and encouraged experimentation with agricultural crops that could flourish in island soil and climate.

Nevertheless the economic road was strewn with experiments that failed commercially. We have already seen how the introduction of cotton to Queensland, Fiji, and other islands during the American Civil War lasted only until that conflict was over, although the indentured labor traffic which it introduced continued for more than forty years. Soybeans, various spices, indigo, and palm nuts proved not successful as export crops. Rubber, grown to some extent in New Guinea, was tried without success in Samoa. Copra, sugarcane, pineapples, phosphate, and some of the mineral resources of Melanesia became valuable exports in the world's markets. But a number of lesser, mostly agricultural, products—often extremely localized—have also contributed to the island economies. Their local value and importance is considerable; their economic contribution beyond the Pacific rarely significant.

The South Seas produces fruit in variety and abundance. Only the pineapple industry of Hawaii, however, is a major cash crop and important export. It began about 125 years ago (1850) but remained insignificant until a process for canning pineapple was developed near the turn of the century. Pre-

184

viously the spoilage on the three-thousand-mile voyage to the West Coast was so high that it made shipping fresh fruit a risky business, and heavy production was not required for peddling pineapples to ships in Honolulu Harbor. Once canning proved successful, the industry increased rapidly. The labor, more seasonal than that of the sugar plantations, was drawn from the same sources. Pineapple farming, at first, caused some misgivings among the sugar planters until it became evident that pineapples, unlike sugar, grew best at a higher altitude, creating no competition for the lower-lying cane producing acres. Today the Hawaiian pineapple industry is one of the four great economic staples (sugarcane, the military, and tourists being the other three) of the islands. Over 80 percent of the world's canned pineapple and pineapple juice is produced in Hawaii and nearly the entire production goes to the Mainland (as island dwellers call the continental states). Pineapple growing has also begun in Tahiti and Fiji. Regrettably, the delicious large grapefruit called *pamplemousse* in Tahiti is not yet found in the world's markets.

Some bananas are exported from Hawaii to the West Coast and from Fiji to Canada and New Zealand. The Cook Islands (where excellent citrus fruits are grown), Western Samoa, Tonga, and Niue ship bananas, oranges, and grapefruit to the New Zealand market. With the increase of commercial air freight, other tropical fruits, especially papayas, are becoming available in the urban markets of Europe and America.

A few vegetables have been found profitable for export. Notable among them are white potatoes, introduced at an early date into Tahiti and New Zealand to supply whalers and other ships and now exported as young new potatoes from Hawaii to California and from the New Guinea highlands to Australia. American corn or maize, which once seemed an encouraging cash crop in New Caledonia, New Hebrides, and the Solomons, turned out to be unsuccessful. Fiji and other Central Pacific British islands export sweet potatoes, tomatoes, and other vegetables to New Zealand. In Hawaii the native taro is manufactured into a rather dreadful canned poi. Where orientals have settled in Hawaii and Indians in Fiji, rice has become an important crop for local consumption.

The production of vanilla is confined to the Society Islands. Over the peaceful lagoons of Moorea, Raiatea, and the other islands of the Leeward group the smell of vanilla often hangs heavy on the tropical air. The crop, first introduced in 1846, saw prosperous periods in the 1920s and 1960s. It is usually grown by Polynesians, pollinated by specialists, and the beans sold to Chinese stores. The Chinese tediously prepare it for market and send two-thirds of the crop to France. Vanilla production is small, but locally important. The market price fluctuates greatly and in recent years synthetic products have created an adverse competition.

Coffee and cocoa both form important small tropical crops. Hawaii exports dark fragrant beans from the Kona coast of the Big Island. Kona coffee is also popular locally. New Caledonia and the New Hebrides produce small crops of coffee, and insignificant amounts are grown commercially in New Guinea and Tahiti. Cocoa, an important crop in Western Samoa, is shipped to Great Britain. The New Hebrides cocoa crop goes largely to France. Both the coffee and the cocoa exported from the islands are used principally for blending.

Beef is raised on a commercial scale only in Hawaii, which has the distinction of having the world's largest ranch. Even here, however, not enough is produced to fill local demands. Herds have increased in New Caledonia, and in the New Hebrides local beef is as good as any that can be found. The few cattle in most islands provide only a small proportion of the beef for local consumption, which depends on the importation of tinned or frozen meats.

Fishing, which once supplied much of the protein needs of the South Seas, has declined and canned fish is a staple stacked on the shelves of traders' stores. Commercial fishing is undertaken almost solely by the Japanese in western Micronesia and out of Honolulu. Pearl shell, one of the products sought by the earliest traders, has been depleted to a point where it is no longer a lucrative export from the Tuamotus or Palaus. Commercially, Pacific pearl shell comes almost entirely from the islands of Torres Strait where its collection is strictly controlled. While mother-of-pearl and trochus shell are still used for buttons, the demand has decreased with the manufacture of plastic products.

Of the four significant cash products exported from Oceania, phosphate, pineapples, and sugar affect very limited areas. Only coconut products, especially copra, are nearly universal.

Copra

If there is a single plant that symbolizes the Pacific islands above all others it is the coconut palm. Its green tops are the first signal of an atoll just under the horizon. Groves of coconut palms cover the coastal lowlands of the high islands. To the South Sea islander it was a plant of many purposes. The nuts provided a refreshing drink, meat to eat, and oil to anoint the body. The shell made useful containers or musical instruments. The trunk provided timber for building houses. The houses so constructed were thatched with the leaves, which were also used for mats and baskets. Sennit, the all-purpose cord used throughout the islands, was made from the husks. The coconut palm thus provided most of the essentials of life in the South Seas and yet, after the first four years of growth, it required a minimum of care. Today the coconut palm flourishes as the single most important economic plant from one end of the Pacific to the other. From east to west and north to south, its usefulness is unparalleled in indigenous island cultures and its contribution to the post-white economy is paramount in its ubiquitousness.

Coconut oil was extracted from the dried meat by most South Sea islanders and used both as an ingredient for cooking and as a cosmetic to rub on their bodies. However, traders shopping around the islands for sandalwood, bêche-de-mer, and pearl or tortoise shell did not for some time consider coconut oil a viable export, although an unsuccessful attempt was made with a commercial shipment from the Society Islands in 1818. It was the whalers, experienced in transporting whale oil, who first successfully bought surplus coconut oil with cheap tobacco and found it profitable enough to place on order between island visits. By mid-century coconut oil was being used extensively in the manufacture of candles and soap. Today it is still an important ingredient in many fine soaps, in cooking oils, and in margarine. As the demand for coconut oil on world markets increased, it was soon found to be more economical and efficient to transport the raw copra rather than to extract the oil in the islands.

Copra is coconut meat removed from the shell and dried, either in the sun or artificially. Bagged and piled at a wharf, its rancid smell, familiar to every South Sea traveler, pervades the air as it awaits shipment. The drying method among native growers varies somewhat, depending on an island's climate, from natural drying, where the broken nuts are spread out on flat ground or hung in strings exposed to sun and wind, to smoke-drying processes. Plantation-grown copra is usually more thoroughly dried in big hot-air ovens. The quality, and therefore the usefulness and the price, varies with the curing method. Occasional diseases devastate the groves, and the coconut beetle and other pests must constantly be kept under control.

In some islands, notably the Cooks, Gilberts, Ellice, American Samoa, and all of Micronesia, copra is produced entirely from native groves. On other islands plantations grow a high grade of copra, although native production is seldom less than 60 percent of an island's output. White or Chinese traders are commonly middlemen who buy from native producers and sell to large companies for shipment.

Copra is the leading export product on more islands than any other item. It dominates the economy of all French Polynesia, the Gilbert and Ellice Islands, and most Melanesian and Micronesian groups. The French government not only provides price supports but subsidizes shipping companies to ensure its transportation. Lever Brothers, Burns Philp, and other giant companies gather in the production of the British-oriented islands. In the Hawaiian Islands there is no copra production and in fact very few coconut trees. Copra production fluctuates with market conditions. While Pacific production is only about 8 percent of the world's total, it is the most widespread and important industry providing cash income—in some cases the only income—and thereby economic stability for thousands of islanders scattered across thousands of Oceanic miles. To maintain copra production in the future, the aging trees of Oceania must be replaced with new plantings and the governmental programs to do this are few.

Sugarcane

Sugarcane is indigenous (probably brought by the first Polynesian voyagers) to both the Hawaiian and Fiji islands. Captain Cook, on his discovery of the Hawaiian Islands, noted sugarcane under cultivation on Kauai. The Hawaiians did not refine sugar but chewed cane for its sweet taste and admired the plant as a hedge around their gardens.

The first attempt at a cane plantation, in the Manoa Valley in 1825, was a failure. The American missionaries recognized the importance sugarcane might have for the Hawaiian economy and even experimented with a crude mill that produced some coarse dark brown sugar. Another attempt was made in 1835 on Kauai by three Yankees who founded Ladd and Company and leased nearly a thousand acres of land from the king, but they also went bankrupt. Native Hawaiians, like all Polynesians, were poor laborers and there were no others available.

The development of the Hawaiian sugar industry was painfully slow and exports never exceeded a thousand tons annually until after the Civil War. But today its value is half the economy of the islands.

Before Hawaiian sugar became big business two severe difficulties had to be solved: the scarcity of water on the dry and leeward sides of the islands and the critical labor problem. In 1895 the Hawaiian Sugar Planters' Associa-

tion was formed to find ways of irrigating the land, solving the labor problems, and making scientific experiments to improve production—all things too
expensive for individual producers. The industry received a stimulus in 1875
when the United States admitted Hawaiian sugar free of duty under a reciprocity treaty. But even after annexation of the islands by the United States
in 1898, other inequities developed that put Hawaiian sugar at a disadvantage
in the American market with sugar produced in Cuba, Puerto Rico, and the
Philippines—disadvantages not completely resolved until after statehood when
the Hawaiian economy became more completely integrated with that of the
Mainland.

Attempts were made to solve the labor problem by importing Micronesians
and Polynesians from other islands. This experiment was unsuccessful. Following the establishment of a Bureau of Immigration for the kingdom in
1864, the importation of Chinese labor was put on an organized basis and
nearly 50,000 Chinese had migrated to the islands by 1900. The first trickle
of Japanese laborers began in 1868, became a flood after 1885, and totaled
some 180,000 by 1908, when it ceased. Many Chinese and Japanese returned
to their homelands at the end of their indentured periods; others migrated to
the Mainland; but tens of thousands remained to settle in the islands. In the
late 1870s arrangements were made for Portuguese, mostly from Madeira and
the Azores, to emigrate to Hawaii and about 20,000 did so from then until
1913. Two years before the importation of Japanese laborers ceased, the
plantations began bringing in Filipinos through an arrangement made between
the Sugar Planters' Association and the government in Manila. Over 65,000
Filipinos were in Hawaii by 1931, but more of these have been repatriated to
their homes than any other group. Small numbers of individuals of other
nationalities, imported at various times, have been absorbed into the cosmopolitan population of the islands.

The irrigation problem was solved as efficiently as the labor problem.
Sugarcane requires enormous quantities of water and sunshine to flourish.
The sun was there everywhere, but water was abundant only in the mountains
and on the wet, windward sides of the islands. Great tracts of land on the leeward sides were nearly deserts.

The problem was first solved on Maui in 1876 by two sons of missionaries,
S. T. Alexander and H. P. Baldwin, who built the great Hamakua ditch that
tapped the enormous water resources on the windward side of Haleakala, the
third highest mountain in the Hawaiian Islands, and brought forty million gallons of water a day to Maui's dry central plain. Similar projects followed on

Oahu, Kauai, and Hawaii, and today the mountains of the islands are riddled with tunnels and ditches that are essential to growing some of the most productive sugarcane in the world. Later the system was supplemented by hundreds of wells pumping water from infinite underground sources into the irrigation ditches of the surrounding sugar fields. Some 250,000 acres, all the land suitable for the purpose in the islands, is now growing cane—the single most important industry contributing to the economic prosperity of Hawaii.

Sugarcane appears to have been indigenous to the Fiji Islands, although improved varieties were long ago imported for the plantations by David Whippey, the Nantucket adviser to cannibal chiefs, who erected a small mill producing sugar for local use in 1862. Ten years later there was a large mill at Suva and shortly thereafter flourishing sugar plantations along the Rewa River. Production increased until the late 1880s when world sugar prices fell. While sugarcane growing began on the wet side of the two principal islands, it is now confined to the irrigated leeward sides where the crops are much better. Various companies were formed, merged, or went out of business, with the Colonial Sugar Refining Company the only manufacturer since 1926.

As in Hawaii there was a labor problem, for the cultivation and cutting of sugarcane requires large forces of manpower. It is hard, monotonous, dreary work to which the Fijian, like the Hawaiian, is temperamentally totally unsuited. We have already seen that labor was supplied during the earlier period by the importation of indentured men from the New Hebrides and other Melanesian islands to the westward. In the late nineteenth century the first Indian indentured labor was imported and gradually replaced the Melanesians, who were all repatriated when Fiji became a crown colony. The indentured labor traffic was abolished in 1916, but during the time it was in force over half of the sixty thousand Indians who had been brought to the islands decided to remain in Fiji. The descendants of these Indians, who now outnumber the native Fijians, have been the source of Fiji's most critical racial, social, and political problems.

In 1905 the government passed an ordinance which allowed the Colonial Sugar Refining Company to build a railroad for hauling cane to its mills. Free passenger service on the railroad has been traditional ever since.

Indians still provide most of the labor in the sugar industry. These efficient people can produce more cane than the company is able to buy, for the amount of sugar that can be exported from Fiji is now limited by international agreement. This situation causes discontent among the farmers. Sugar became, and indeed remains, the principal Fijian export and also the primary source of employment in the country. Fijian sugar is sold largely to Britain, Canada, and New Zealand. Over 200,000 tons of sugar valued at nearly £8,700,000 were exported from Fiji in 1960—two-thirds of the value of all exports. Some 160,000 acres are planted with sugarcane, mostly on land which is owned communally by Fijians and leased to Indians.

Before World War II, during the Japanese mandate of Micronesia, sugarcane was raised on Saipan, Tinian, and Rota in the Marianas. Production was small in comparison with Hawaii and Fiji, but large considering the very limited acreage available for growing cane. In addition to exporting refined sugar and molasses, over a million gallons of alcoholic beverages were produced from sugar in the late 1930s. The labor force here was mostly indentured Japanese and local Chamorros.

Because of limited acreage, the quota system, and the usual oversupply of sugar in the world markets, production of this crop has probably reached its maximum in the Pacific islands. Nevertheless, the changes it has already wrought in population and economy in Hawaii and Fiji are very great and irreversible.

In both Hawaii and Fiji sugarcane farming has been responsible for the greatest importation of labor, the elements of which have changed the population forever. In both island groups it employs more people than any other enterprise. The native Hawaiians have long been overwhelmed by hundreds of thousands of Japanese, Chinese, Portuguese, and other peoples that are molding a new Hawaiian. The Indians in Fiji now outnumber the Fijians and the proportion will doubtless continue to increase although the Fijians, unlike the Hawaiians, will be a numerically powerful element in their own islands for a long time to come.

Phosphate and Mining

Phosphate is the principal ingredient of commercial fertilizers, which were first manufactured in England by J. B. Lawes in 1842. Some soils, notably those of Australia, New Zealand, and Japan, are so deficient in phosphates that without the application of fertilizers continued cropping would be impossible. Clovers will not grow, cattle will not fatten, until the land is laced with phosphate. Relatively small amounts of this essential chemical not only increase the productivity of the soil, but give grasses and vegetables a better dietary balance for both man and beast. (Sheep, however, thrive on a low-phosphate land.)

The earliest phosphate harvests were taken by American and British ships from the vast guano accumulations of the Chincha Islands off Peru, to which, as we have seen, Polynesian laborers were taken. Lesser deposits were found on some of the uninhabited islands of the Pacific, notably Baker, Howland, Jarvis, and others and on some of the Phoenix group. On August 18, 1856, Congress passed the Guano Act, allowing Americans to claim unoccupied islands in the name of the United States for the purposes of removing guano. Some forty-eight Pacific islands were eventually so claimed; others were developed by the British, espcially the John T. Arundel Company of Sydney. Except for the use of Hawaiian and other island laborers, native peoples were not affected by these operations.

By 1876 the guano deposits of Howland, Baker, and other islands were nearly depleted. It remained for Albert F. Ellis of the Pacific Islands Company (which in 1902 became the Pacific Phosphate Company with headquarters in London) to recognize that a stone doorstop in the Sydney office of the company was phosphate-bearing rock. Chemical tests on the sample, which came from Nauru, indicated a rich phosphate content. Nauru was German territory, but it was well known that Ocean Island, 170 miles to the east, was of similar formation. Both islands are just south of the equator, with Ocean Island lying 250 miles west of the Gilberts.

Ellis made a prospecting trip to Ocean and Nauru in 1900 and confirmed the rich and enormous deposits on both islands—by far the most extensive in Oceania. The British flag was hoisted over Ocean on September 28, 1901, and the island was annexed to the Gilbert and Ellice protectorate. Thus the Pacific Islands Company had no problem beginning work on Ocean, but to do so on Nauru required obtaining rights from the Germans. This was successfully accomplished in 1906 and work began on that island.

These islands are upthrust coral atolls, with their jagged old coral tops now high in the air and their shores dropping precipitously to enormous depths just outside the fringing reefs. Wharves are impossible and normal sheltered anchorages for ships nonexistent. On the tablelands of the islands the phosphate rock fills in between the limestone coral pinnacles in depths varying up to sixty-five feet on Nauru. Remarkable variety in density, color, hardness, and texture distinguishes the deposits. In some cases the phosphoric acid has impregnated the coral. But whether it is compact or gravelly, hard or spongy, brown or gray or creamy, it is singularly consistent in a tricalcium phosphate content averaging well over 80 percent. Marine fossils in great numbers and variety are scattered through the phosphate formations.

The deposits on both islands turned out to be unbelievably rich. At first the phosphate rock was dug out by hand from between the limestone pinnacles. Later mechanical shovels were brought in, but hand labor was still needed to work the narrow crevices. Loading was the most difficult problem to solve because of the lack of harbors and the depths of the offshore waters made anchoring impossible. An elaborate system of enormous, permanently moored buoys where the ships could tie up unraveled this dilemma. In the beginning, boats manned by skilled islanders lightered the phosphate through the surf to the moored ships. Later long jetties were built at Ocean Island from which the boats were loaded directly as they lay outside the reef. At Nauru an enormous cantilever was built that took the product directly from shore and poured it into the vessels' holds.

A large labor force was necessary to run these extensive operations. Ocean and Nauru were both populated, but the royalities and rents paid to the local people, who were few in number in any case, soon put them in a financial position where they had no desire to earn more. The problem was first solved by bringing in several hundred Gilbert and Ellice Islanders. Later, experiments were made with indentured Japanese laborers, and finally Caroline Islanders and Chinese recruited through an agent in Hong Kong were successfully employed.

Phosphate deposits similar to those on Ocean and Nauru were discovered on Makatéa in the Tuamotus in 1906 and were developed in a similar manner by the Anglo-French Compagnie Française des Phosphates de l'Océanie in which the Pacific Phosphate Company held a one-third interest. Here the labor force was made up of local men, Tahitians, and other Polynesians. Later Japanese, Chinese, and Indonesians were also employed for a time. In 1909 the Germans began mining phosphate deposits on Angaur in the Palaus.

After World War I, Nauru was mandated to Australia and the Pacific Phosphate Company was taken over by the British Phosphate Commission set up by the governments of the United Kingdom, Australia, and New Zealand. Costs and production were shared by the three governments, on a 42 percent basis each for Britain and Australia and 16 percent for New Zealand. After the phosphate requirements of each country were met, any surplus was sold on the open market. The production on Makatéa, where a cantilever similar to that operating on Nauru was set up, was sold largely—and the Angaur production entirely—to Japan.

Although phosphate is the largest single cash export of the Pacific, the effects of its production are confined to only four islands and to fewer people than any other major industry. The few hundred inhabitants of Ocean and Nauru are comparatively well off from royalties and many fringe benefits—so much so that they have no desire to work. No longer do the women have to crawl down in caves to secure water from Ocean Island's only natural supply, for it now comes from the company distillery or catchments. The men of the two islands have more time to train their tame frigate birds. The native cultures, transformed so quickly by the phosphate workings, were never known in detail. The young Gilbert Islanders enjoyed their terms of labor at the phosphate diggings, and the money they earned provided them with various luxuries to take home. The Chinese indentured laborers served out their monotonous terms in segregated villages with little effect on the small local population. European supervisors watched over all.

Aside from phosphate, the geological nature of the islands precludes commercial mining except in the southwestern Pacific, although the Japanese found and developed bauxite during their mandate in Micronesia. New Caledonia and the large, almost continental, island of New Guinea contain the most extensive mineral resources. Intermittent prospecting for gold, which was first discovered in the Louisiades in 1888, culminated during the 1920s in a gold rush in New Guinea, where the metal is still being exploited, as indeed it is in Fiji, where it was first discovered in 1929.

Traces of gold have been found in New Caledonia, which is rich in minerals. At one time this island led the world in the production of nickel, first mined in the late nineteenth century, and in chromium, discovered a few years later. Most of the important nickel production goes to France and elsewhere in western Europe and to Japan. Chrome production, which began in the early twentieth century, is mostly taken by the United States. Reserve resources of both metals are still substantial. At one time both cobalt and manganese were exported, and iron and coal are produced in small quantities. Originally the labor for mining was indentured from Japan, but for many years it has been imported almost entirely from Java and Indochina. All mineral resources in Oceania are finite and the day will come when mining will be but a memory, though its effect may linger on.

Certainly tourism, a leading industry for many islands, will not give out but will increase as population grows and travel becomes easier. For many years it has been one of the most important economic assets of Hawaii and Tahiti, nor is it inconsiderable in Fiji and New Caledonia. Tourism will continue to become more important to other island paradises. As camera-clicking travelers arrive at decreasingly remote islands, the accompanying souvenir trade follows. Wherever the cruise ships stop or the air-cruise director guides his complacent little herd, the hawkers set up their sleazy stands. And the ripples spread far, for today in islands that tourists never see natives are making souvenirs: wood and pearl-shell carvings, canoe models, baskets, mats, and some tapa to sell at Waikiki, Papeete, Suva, and Nouméa. Tourists and natives alike are decked in imported cotton prints made in Birmingham for the South Sea trade. The mumu and the aloha shirt, the pareau and the lavalava brighten the perspiring bodies of one and all.

More than by whalers, more than by traders, it is by big business that island life has been most changed. Population modifications alone in Hawaii, Tahiti, Fiji, and New Caledonia have been enormous. The effects of large numbers of whites, Chinese, Japanese, Javanese, Indochinese, and Indians on native peoples have gone beyond the impact stage, and these elements have become integral parts of the local populations. For the native Pacific islander life has changed traumatically since Captain Cook's day. The diet has changed, society has changed, technology has changed, luxuries have become necessities. The economy of the most remote inhabited island is in some way tied to the European-American economic world.

CHAPTER 14

Change and Life

How have the islanders of the principal archipelagoes fared? The result of two hundred years of intensive white impact varies widely from group to group. Estimates of indigenous populations made shortly after discovery are probably not very reliable, but they are all there is to go on. Some peoples have been more resilient than others. Some islands have a larger native population than the day they were discovered; others are still only beginning to return from the mere remnants they were reduced to. Certain it is that none are unchanged and none can ever again be as they were on that day when the first white topsails rose above the horizon. Nor would it be desirable even if possible. The clock cannot be turned back.

It would be tedious and repetitive and there is no need nor space here to trace in detail the results of European contact on all the islands of the Pacific. Statistically, most of this information can be found in the *Pacific Islands Year Book*. Numerous historical and anthropological studies as well as governmental surveys also provide this information. Rather we shall quickly scan the principal island groups to examine the extremes and variety of situations which have arisen—the curious legacies resulting from the unplanned, haphazard, largely uncontrolled meeting of cultures so different as to have originally been almost mutually incomprehensible.

Three places exhibit impact so massive that indigenous peoples, where they exist at all, are reduced to remnants in the general European or Asiatic populations. Native cultural integrity, if it exists, is minimal—though some of its more dramatic aspects are exhibited as tourist attractions—and political clout is almost nonexistent.

Australia and New Zealand are modern, independent European, English-speaking countries, in which the large exotic populations have completely overwhelmed the indigenous inhabitants. At the time of discovery it is estimated that Australia had a population of approximately 300,000. By about 1950 the aborigines were reduced to slightly over 40,000 full bloods and 30,000 mixed bloods. Most of these survivors are concentrated in Western Australia, the Northern Territory, and Queensland. Until the last decade few still lived in tribal groups, roaming the desolate, remote interior regions. Some tribes have been concentrated on reserves. Detribalized natives supply labor for cattle stations and farms, and mixed bloods hang around outback towns seeking employment. For the federal and state governments the aborigines are a necessary but minor concern, and the detribalized natives and mixed bloods a social and economic problem.

The New Zealand story is different. After reaching a low of about 42,000 in 1896, the Maori population has risen steadily and indeed continues to rise. The present birthrate increase is almost double that of the white population. Numbering now about a quarter of a million, almost entirely confined to the North Island, the Maoris have become an increasingly influential element. With the growth in numbers there has been a movement during the past thirty years from rural to urban areas. This has brought the two races into greater competition for employment and housing. The average education and living standards of the Maoris are still below those of the whites, but they are improving. The Maori race has contributed notable men to modern New Zealand, and in increasing numbers Maoris are entering professional, literary, and political fields. The former government policy of assimilation has become one of integration, with many aspects of Maori art, literature, and learning recognized as an important part of a distinctive New Zealand culture. While there is some discrimination, there is also increasing intermarriage, and in general the two groups live together amicably and all regard themselves as New Zealanders.

Like Australia in the west and New Zealand in the south, the Hawaiian Islands in the north have made the complete transformation from a native island community to a Western political, cultural, and economic world. Here the influx of foreign peoples has been so overpowering that the native Hawaiian is entirely submerged. Busy, heady, American, moneymaking Honolulu is the only city in the Pacific islands that can be called a metropolis. But the exotic elements, far from being entirely European as in the two English countries, are predominently Asiatic, with the Japanese being by far the largest group.

At the time of Cook's discovery the population of the Hawaiian Islands was estimated at 330,000. This is probably an exaggeration, but in any case whatever the number may have been it had shrunk to some 20,000 by 1929. In 1970 there were probably less than 10,000 pure-blooded Hawaiians but 127,000 so-called part Hawaiians. In the meantime, as the native numbers declined, foreign immigration soared. By 1970 the total population of the islands numbered over 713,000 people of various origins; in addition to the part Hawaiians, there were more than 217,800 of Japanese ancestry, 181,000 of Caucasian, 58,000 of Filipino, 38,000 of Chinese, and 81,400 of other derivations. The blending and assimilation of this heterogeneous racial potpourri is creating a new Hawaiian—a Hawaiian predominently Asiatic, with Polynesian overtones, but culturally straight American.

Besides New Zealand and Hawaii, it was the islands of central and eastern Polynesia that bore the brunt of the European impact—in terms of culture, economics, religion, and, above all, disease—during the first half of the nineteenth century. The effect in Easter Island and the Marquesas was disastrous and in Tahiti nearly so. And yet it is interesting to see what has happened since these people passed the nadir of their misery.

It is estimated that 3,000 to 4,000 inhabitants were squeezed within Easter Island's triangular perimeter of thirty-four miles at the time of its discovery in 1722. Already thinned by disease, the population was decimated by blackbirders from South America during the middle decades of the nineteenth century. The repatriation of the miserable survivors of the grueling physical labor in the silver mines and guano beds, which took place after massive international protest, resulted in the return of 15 wretched smallpox-infected individuals, whose coming quickly reduced the population to 111 in 1877. From this nearly fatal low, the number began to increase slowly, mostly after the island was annexed by Chile in 1888, and by 1971 stood at approximately 1,400. This was up from 577 in 1942, when it was estimated that about 200 were pure bloods and the remainder various mixtures with other Polynesians, Chinese, and Europeans.

Next to Easter the islands that suffered the most and have made the least recovery are the Marquesas. In the late eighteenth century these spectacular mountainous islands, whose people were acclaimed by the early explorers and traders as the handsomest in the Pacific, probably had a population of 50,000 to 60,000. This number decreased by over 50 percent in fifty years; in 1842 the French naval commander Dupetit-Thouars rather carefully calculated that there were about 20,000. Later the decline became even more spectacular, intensified not only by diseases, firearms, alcohol, and opium, but apparently by a loss of the will to live. By 1872 there were but 6,200 inhabitants, reduced sixty-nine years later to a mere 2,870. The toboggan slide continued until 1926, when the population reached a low of 2,094. During the next twenty years it crept back to 2,800 and by 1967 had nearly doubled to 5,174. As there has never been a large European or Chinese population in the Marquesas (usually under 150) the proportion of pure bloods, or of those nearly so, is high and racial mixture surprisingly small for a group so long exposed to white contact. The French were slow in bringing modern medical practices and care to the Marquesas, but the eventual establishment of hospital facilities and the control of leprosy promoted the upward trend. With the control of disease and an increase in numbers, the Marquesans have become psychologically more optimistic, and the will to survive has returned.

Population declines in the remainder of French Oceania never approached that in the Marquesas, with the exception of Tahiti, where, however, the drop was not nearly so severe. Cook's estimate of 240,000 Tahitians in 1769 is almost certainly enormously exaggerated. Even the London missionaries, who were living on the island and had a much better opportunity for accurate observations, were probably on the high side in their estimate of 50,000 inhabitants in 1797. Certain it is, however, that by 1848 the Tahitian population was down to 8,082 natives and 475 foreigners. In 1967 all of French Polynesia had a population of about 107,000, of which 61,000 were on Tahiti. In the small isolated atolls of the Tuamotus and remote Australs little miscegenation has taken place. In Tahiti, the most popular island in the South Seas for over two hundred years, it is a different story. There are probably very few pure-blooded Tahitians; in 1967 it was estimated that 65 percent of them had Polynesian blood, 25 percent white blood, and 10 percent Chinese blood. The several thousand Chinese in the Society Islands own the island stores, run most of the shops in Papeete, act as bankers, and control the bulk of the importing and small industries. In general, however, they keep themselves aloof from the rest of the population, although mixed Tahitian-Chinese girls are among the loveliest in the islands. Tahiti is today a Polynesian island with heavy French overtones.

In the islands to the west of Tahiti, the Polynesian population, while usually declining for a few years, has never been at a danger point. In the Cooks, for example, after a low of about 8,500 in 1906, the inhabitants increased to over 18,500 in sixty years. Lumping eastern and western Samoa together, Commodore Wilkes in 1839 estimated the combined population at 56,000. This was reduced to 45,000 by 1881. From 1900 on, except for the influenza outbreak of 1918, from which some 5,600 people died, there has been a steady rise and, with a birthrate of over 40 per thousand, this trend will con-tinue. There were approximately 173,000 people in the two Samoas in 1971 and population pressure in American Samoa has created a steady flow of emi-grants to Hawaii. Today about a quarter of all Polynesians are Samoans.

The Tongans, like the Samoans, are a proud people who have apparently never suffered the devastating reduction in numbers characteristic of some other Polynesian islands. The little kingdom, which probably had no more than 25,000 people at the time of discovery, was estimated to have 18,500 in-habitants by Commodore Wilkes in 1840. In the 1970s the population was over 90,000 and, as in Samoa, the birthrate was up and the death rate down.

The demographic situation in Fiji is unique in Oceania because of the im-portation of Indian labor. The Fiji Islands were reckoned to have about 200,000 people in 1859, a number which in a dozen years dropped by 30,000. An epidemic of measles wiped out more than a quarter of the people in 1875 and the devastating influenza epidemic of 1919 brought the native Fijian population to a low figure of 84,475 in 1921—a year when the number of Indian inhabitants reached over 60,000. From then on both races increased, but the Indians increased faster, and in 1944 the two peoples were almost ex-actly equal at 113,000 each. With a higher birthrate, the Indians outstripped the Fijians and by 1970 in a total population of over 524,000 outnumbered them by more than 40,000. Thus, while not as overwhelmed as the Hawaiians by Asiatics and whites, or the New Zealand Maoris by the English, the Fijians find themselves a minority in their own country.

The same situation applies to the great island of New Caledonia, where in the 1970s the native Melanesians formed less than half the population of 100,000. They had, however, increased from a low figure of a little over 27,000 in 1921 to over 47,000 in 1969. In the latter year there were about 36,000 Europeans, mostly French, nearly 10,000 Polynesians and Wallis Is-landers, and some 6,000 Indonesians and Vietnamese. After 1969 the number of Vietnamese decreased sharply due to repatriation.

The Solomon Islands, including both Bougainville and the British Solomon Islands protectorate, undoubtedly suffered a population decline due to the usual disruptive factors and the labor traffic. It is impossible to know, how-ever, how many inhabitants there were in, say, the mid-nineteenth century. In

1940 the number was estimated at about 145,000. Thirty years later a census for the protectorate alone showed a population for all races of 160,998, of which nearly 150,000 were Melanesians, over 6,000 Polynesians, and a mere 1,200 Caucasians. There has been a decided geographic shift in population in recent years as bush natives of the interior have moved to the coast, where most of the people now live.

The New Hebrides exhibit a situation rather similar to the Solomons, but the population decline—due to the labor traffic—was probably more severe, and the southern islands of the group continued to decline as late as 1936. In that year the native population was estimated to be a little over 47,000, but the first census ever taken in the group showed in 1967 a total of 77,983 individuals, of which all but about 5,000 (French, British, and miscellaneous) were Melanesians.

New Guinea is so large, so recently opened up to development (except for some coastal regions), and so comparatively heavily populated that it is in a class by itself. Because of the huge size of the island and the inaccessibility of the interior, not even plausible population estimates existed until recent years. In 1970 the eastern half of the island was probably supporting more than 2,500,000 natives, with another 900,000 in West Irian. There were besides 48,960 Europeans in Papua New Guinea and probably about 15,000 Indonesians and Asiatics in West Irian.

The last major Pacific area, Micronesia, is easily looked at. Population was never large on those tiny, widely scattered, islands; it is not now. In the areas now administered by the United States as a trust territory—that is, the Marianas (except for Guam), the Carolines, and the Marshalls—the native population more than doubled, from 50,740 in 1937 to 102,250 in 1970. Between 1945 and 1947 the United States repatriated 70,000 Japanese who had settled in the islands. The figure of almost 87,000 for Guam in 1971 is deceptive, for a large number of servicemen and their dependents is included.

The British-controlled Gilberts and Ellice Islands Colony has shown a marked upward trend. In the five years between 1963 and 1968 the population rose by nearly 5,000, from over 48,700 to 53,516. Most of this increase was in the Gilberts. The 1968 figure included 44,897 Micronesians, 7,465 Polynesians, 458 Europeans, and the remainder mixed bloods.

If one disregards Australia and New Zealand, the picture that emerges is one of a young, rapidly increasing, predominantly native population throughout the Pacific islands. Only in the Hawaiian Islands, Fiji, New Caledonia, and the Marianas do foreign races outnumber the indigenous inhabitants. Everywhere the white population is numerically small but economically and politically of enormous power and influence. But only in New Caledonia, where whites form over a third, and in Hawaii, where they number about a quarter, are they more than a fragment of the population. Asiatics have become numerically dominant in Fiji, where the Indians outnumber the Fijians, and in Hawaii, where the enormous Japanese population is augmented by large numbers of Chinese, Filipinos, and some Koreans. Indonesians are a significant element in the New Caledonia total. Besides those in Hawaii, there are also several thousand Chinese scattered throughout the islands, with concentrations in French Oceania and New Guinea. Originally imported as laborers, they are now mostly skilled artisans and businessmen whose economic clout is far greater than their tiny fraction of the population would indicate. An increasingly important and rapidly growing element throughout the islands are the mixed bloods. They are a group difficult to separate, as they may be classified with either parent stock and, indeed, they may be so mixed with native, white, and Asiatic strains as to defy classification. And no one knows how many apparently pure-blooded islanders are carrying the results of white miscegenation of a century or more ago.

Thus, except for Hawaii and the Marianas, Polynesians and Micronesians are numerically heavily dominant in their islands and are becoming increasingly so. In the islands of the Southwest Pacific, except for New Caledonia, the Melanesians are overwhelming and make up at least 85 percent of the total population of the Pacific islands, with the bulk of them living in New Guinea.

Despite the concern of fifty to seventy-five years ago that the South Sea islanders might become an extinct race, it is more likely that many of the islands will soon be suffering from overpopulation, if indeed they are not already. In fact, crowded conditions on some of the smaller islands are in part responsible for the drift toward the urban centers of the islands. Cook Islanders go to Auckland, Samoans to Honolulu; others are trying to find a living in Papeete, Apia, Suva, or Nouméa. This trend will almost certainly continue as food consumption begins to outstrip food production. Where once the smallness of their numbers was a cause for lament, it is now the magnitude which is a matter of concern as, in spiraling increase, they contribute one more element to the worldwide population explosion.

Ironically, while it was the introduction of Western diseases that was primarily responsible for sharp population decline, it was the ultimate introduction of Western medicine, sanitary measures, and health services that were the principal factors in increasing life expectancy and establishing a climate in which the population has flourished in all but a handful of places in recent years.

The western frontier of contact, civilization, and impact, moving like a wave from east to west across the Pacific, with a backwash occurring from Australia into Melanesia, has long since reached the shores of Asia. And other smaller waves, but some more than mere ripples, have come out of that continent into the islands. The frontier was one of technological revolution caused by the introduction of iron: nails, fishhooks, trade tomahawks, axes, saws, and other edged tools and utensils. With the availability of iron, stone tools quickly disappeared. Immediately, this meant that infinitely fewer hours were required to build houses and canoes, to clear land, to till garden plots. Fishing was more efficient. The introduction of clothing, especially calicoes and other cotton prints, eliminated the long hours over the tapa anvils. Reducing the required productive hours affected social structures. The coordination of traditional ceremonies became upset; there was more time for bickering, politics, and listening to missionary appeals. There was even time to become literate.

Slowly in some islands, swiftly in others, irreversible changes have taken place. Cannibalism and infanticide are no longer practiced. Christianity, in one form or anther is universal. Galvanized roofs have replaced thatch. Sewing machines and bicycles abound. Tinned meat and fish are favorite foods. The list could be multiplied many times. While the change is ubiquitous, it has varied widely from one group to another. Some people are more resistant than others. Samoans are conservative; Tahitians readily accept new ideas. The overlay of Western culture varies from very deep to pie-crust thin.

But the moving frontier has been more than one of technology and disease affecting native peoples directly. There has also been an impact on the islands themselves: a frontier of introduced plants and animals, of extinction of native birds and plants, of exploitation of resources. The prevalence of introduced plants, the cultivation of plantation crops—coconuts, sugarcane, cotton, pineapples—the grazing flocks of sheep and herds of cattle have in some places so altered the appearance of the islands that their discoverers would scarcely recognize them. Not only the resources of the land, but the equally important resources of the sea have been depleted. No longer do great pods of whales surge north and south on their seasonal migrations. There is not as much life in the waters as there once was, even though there is more on most of the land.

With the entire Pacific now closely tied into the worldwide economic and political community, the trend is largely toward nationalism. Samoa, Nauru (which became a republic in 1968), and Fiji and Papua New Guinea are already independent. The Cook Islands have internal self-government but are tied to New Zealand for foreign policy. Even in French Oceania, linked so intimately to France, there are occasional murmurings about independence, as indeed there are throughout most of the islands.

Certain it is that the old Pacific paradise of Captains Cook and Bougainville is gone. So is the tumultuous Pacific of the traders, whalers, missionaries, and blackbirders. A new Pacific is emerging; an Oceania of blended races, of modern medicine, of a new economy; of an aggressive, heady, political emancipation; of air travel that shrinks the miles—a livelier Pacific and a more coherent one in many ways. Only the look of the blue ocean itself, the coconut-topped atolls, the green lagoons, the precipitous mountains of the high islands, and the laughing personality of the South Sea islanders is unchanged.

Part II

East Asia

CHAPTER 15

The Road to Cathay

European civilization made its earliest contacts with China, as we know the area today, by seeping into the Far East through the back door—first by the long land routes across Asia, next by eastern Mediterranean seafarers sailing from the Red Sea to India, and then by Arab dhows from the Persian Gulf running the Indian Ocean with the monsoons. Although Portuguese ships were in Macao by the early 1500s and there was some continuous limited trade from then on, only in the late eighteenth century did the European seaborne trade begin its great contact with China at the far end of the Pacific.

From time immemorial caravan trails, starting at the eastern end of the Mediterranean, wound their way through mountain passes and across plains and deserts into the vast interior land mass of Asia. And back over them to the shores of the Levant came the dusty camel caravans laden with exotic products dear to European hearts. Silks and spices, gold and precious stones, incense and myrrh, as well as more prosaic articles, trickled into western Europe at high prices.

As far back as the first century B.C. two great empires dangled at either end of a silken thread. Their economies were linked but their knowledge of each other was of the haziest. China (known to the Romans as Serica), the producer, exported both raw and manufactured silk to the West, while Rome, the great consumer, dressed its fashionable women in gauze made from the unraveled silk and even sent some of this flimsy "woven wind" back eastward. The contact was from tribe to tribe, merchant exchanging goods with merchant, along the Central Asian trail. The Chinese (or Seres) did not directly visit Rome; nor Romans, China. Roman citizens occasionally ventured as far as Parthia, the westernmost depot on the route, to exchange their goods, before the caravan trail terminated at Antioch, the great western entrepôt in Syria.

Seaborne commerce with the East was opened up during the reign of Emperor Augustus by Greeks, Levantines, and other traders of the Roman Near East who sent ships down the Red Sea to India. Chinese silk was transported via caravan trails from the interior, then down the Indus or the Ganges to the coast, from where cargoes were shipped through the Red Sea and thence overland to Alexandria. The sailing directions for the Indian Ocean at this time are known from that anonymous work, the *Periplus of the Erythrian Sea*, which describes the coast of India, the trade, and the goods exchanged. The cargoes included not only silk but also Indian cotton, pepper, cloves, nutmegs, cinnamon, ginger and other spices; as well as perfume and gums, ivory and gems, dyes and ornamental woods. The oriental market for wool and linen cloth, glass, coral, and amber was never large enough to offset the cost of Roman imports, which had to be paid for in hard cash. The insatiable Roman demand for luxuries created an adverse trade balance and for years was a serious financial drain on the empire.

In 166 A.D., during the Han dynasty, an embassy arrived at the Chinese court from one "Antun, king of Tathsin," bringing presents of ivory, tortoise shell, and rhinoceros horn. These travelers, who arrived by sea, are believed to have come from Emperor Marcus Aurelius Antoninus. Roman seaborne commerce with the East declined after about 200 A.D. and merchant shipping in the Indian Ocean became a monopoly of the Abyssinians and later the Arabs. Further diminution of the silk trade occurred during the reign of Justinian (circa 550), when silkworm eggs were smuggled in a length of bamboo into Constantinople by two Nestorian monks. Justinian made the silk industry a state monopoly which enriched the Byzantine Empire and thenceforth the Mediterranean world produced most of its own silk. European knowledge of India and to a lesser extent of China was more factual during the period of Roman contact than it would be again for a millennium.

At about the same time that the silkworm was introduced to the Mediterranean, Cosmas, a Greek monk from Alexandria who had once been a merchant and sailed to India, wrote about China. He probably never got beyond Ceylon himself, but he knew that after sailing east a long way a ship must be steered north to reach "Tzinista," as he called China, from whence came silk and cloves and scented woods. Theophylactus, a Byzantine Greek, writing in the early seventh century, mentions a country called Tagas, beyond the Turkish tribes, that can only be China.

During the T'ang dynasty (618-906 A.D.) Nestorian Christianity, which had missionary centers in India and Central Asia, flourished moderately in China for some two hundred years. Alopen, a Nestorian monk from Syria, arrived at the T'ang capital of Changan during the reign of the enlightened Emperor T'ai Tsung. Converts were made, a monastery built, churches arose in several cities, and a metropolitan for China was appointed, all before 823. Throughout this period the leadership of the Nestorian church in China apparently remained in the hands of Western foreigners. The church seems to have vanished under persecution about the middle of the ninth century, although, as we shall see, it was to reappear under the Mongols.

Medieval Travelers

The Romans' scanty knowledge of China deteriorated during medieval times into myths of strange people and beasts, of the legendary Prester John who was believed to rule a Christian kingdom beyond the Muslim countries, and other hazy tales. But in the thirteenth century Europe awoke to the thundering hooves of the Mongol hordes. Having consolidated their power in Central Asia, the Mongols devastated half of eastern Europe in 1238. In April 1241 a Mongol army under the great general Batu overran Moravia and Hungary and reached the Adriatic.

At this point there was nothing to prevent the Tartars, as they were called, from overrunning all of western Europe. The feeble armies mustered by European rulers to hold them off would surely have been ineffective, but fortuitously the human tide receded into Asia from whence it came. Christendom, unknowingly, was saved by the death of the great khan, for it then became necessary for the Mongol chiefs to return to their capital in Karakorum, Mongolia, for the election of his successor.

Pope Innocent IV, anticipating another invasion, dispatched two missions to the Mongols to seek information about the Nestorian Christian kingdom of Prester John, to preach Christianity among the Mongols, and, if possible, to persuade them to cease their attacks on Europe.

Nothing is known of the mission led by one Friar Lawrence of Portugal. The other group was headed by John of Piano Carpini and included a Polish friar named Benedict who served as Carpini's interpreter for the first part of the journey. Sixty-five years old and corpulent, Carpini was neither young nor in the best physical condition for such a rigorous journey. Nevertheless he did not dally and set out from Lyons in April 1245. He reached the camp of Batu on the Volga by February 1246 and, after stopping to recuperate, pushed on to the headquarters of the great khan near Karakorum, where he arrived on July 22. Here Carpini delivered the pope's message to Kuyuk Khan, who dismissed him on November 13 with a brief and arrogant reply in which the khan opined that God only knew whether or not he was a Christian and if the pope wanted to find out he had better come and see. By the autumn of 1247 Carpini was back in Lyons, delivering Kuyuk Khan's reply to the pope. He also reported that another Mongol invasion was being planned and advised submission to it. One suspects that he was less overweight after the fatiguing journey and meager diet of deplorable food. Carpini's *History of the Mongols* and his reports give the fullest contemporary account of Mongol customs, for he was an observant man.

Missions sent from Europe to the East at this time seem to have specialized in corpulent friars, for William of Rubruck, the next traveler, was, by his own account, a heavy man. He probably met John of Piano Carpini and Benedict the Pole in Paris on their return and learned from them as much as possible about the Mongols. In 1248 William accompanied Louis IX to Cyprus. There, oblivious of the danger of the possible return of the Golden Horde, the impetuous Louis was planning the Seventh Crusade. While still in Cyprus preparing for a campaign against Egypt, Louis met a Mongol envoy who informed him that the khan and his chiefs were Christians. Louis forthwith dispatched a Friar Andrew to the Mongol court and then began his ill-fated invasion of Egypt. In the spring of 1250 he took the remnants of his defeated army to Palestine, where he received bad news from his returning envoy, who arrived with a message from the Mongol ruler, saying rudely that unless Louis sent annual tributes of gold and silver both he and his envoys would be destroyed. Hopes that the Mongols might become allies in fighting the Saracen infidels diminished. The good news from Father Andrew was that Sartach, son of Batu the great conqueror, was indeed a Christian.

Discouraged by the letter but heartened by the news that Nestorian Christianity had apparently made some headway among the Mongol chiefs, Louis decided to send his Franciscan friend William of Rubruck to the great kahn as a missionary rather than as a diplomat.

After spending a year at Constantinople collecting information about inner Asia and the Mongols, William sailed with four companions on May 7, 1253, crossed the Black Sea to the Crimea, and after three days' journey on horseback met his first Mongols on June 3. For over a year William and his companions were shunted from one Mongol camp to another, penetrating ever deeper into the heart of Asia, sleeping in the open, marveling at the yurts (those enormous tents on wheels drawn by oxen), drinking mare's milk, observing and recording the customs and lives of their uncouth hosts.

William at last reached the camp of Sartach and found that he was no Christian after all, although he evinced considerable curiosity about the good friar's holy objects and examined them closely. Leaving the son, William crossed the Volga and pushed on to the camp of the father, Batu. The great general was not impressed. His followers derided the Europeans and Batu dismissed them to stew for five weeks (during which time they nearly starved). In mid-September William was given permission to visit Mangu, the great khan.

After a difficult winter journey, William arrived at Mangu's camp outside Karakorum on December 27, 1253, where he was questioned by a Nestorian member of the Mongol government. A week later he had his first interview with Mangu. Standing in the doorway of the khan's tent, he and his companion Bartholomew sang a hymn of the Nativity while they were being searched for knives. They were then ushered into the great golden-walled tent and before the khan himself. Seated behind a dung fire and surrounded by women and sycophants, the little man dressed in a spotted skin offered them wine, mead, or clarified mare's milk. William's interpreter made sure he got the most intoxicating liquor available and soon drank himself into uselessness. Mangu, too, was not entirely sober and became somewhat irritable. Friar William left the audience frustrated by his lack of accomplishment.

In April 1254 William went on to Karakorum, where Mangu Khan was then in residence. The capital of the great Mongol Empire, founded by Mangu's grandfather Genghis Khan, was a small but cosmopolitan city. Living there were ambassadors from the numerous nations under the khan's control who had their own temples and mosques for religious worship. There were also many European captives practicing various trades or acting as servants, including an Englishman named Basil; William Boucher, a Parisian goldsmith; and other Frenchmen and Hungarians. These people formed a European community and worshiped in their own Christian church. William settled into this circle and soon assumed its spiritual leadership. To clarify his position he asked Mangu if he and Bartholomew could remain in Karakorum and preach the faith. The khan was tolerant of religions, but, suspecting that William might be a political spy, ordered him to return to Europe. Bartholomew, too weak to undertake the long journey, was allowed to remain.

It was a disappointed William who left Karakorum and for a year retraced his steps across Asia, arriving in Italy in August 1255. Later on in Paris he met Roger Bacon who, in his *Opus Majus*, made use of parts of William's narrative. Not only had the sturdy friar reached Karakorum (describing that city for Western readers for the first time) and returned, but while there he had heard of Korea and of the Chinese (whom he identified with the Seres of the Romans). He elaborated upon the writings of the Chinese, hitherto unknown in Europe, and also reported that the best silks came from China, that their artisans were superior, and that they used paper money. We are indebted to Rubruck for the first accurate description of Nestorian Christian communities among the Mongols, the earliest account of lamaist monks, and many other historical and ethnological facts, as well as for original observations on natural history. In 1264 the capital would be moved to Peking by Mangu's successor, Kublai Khan, who extended the Mongolian domains into China south of the Great Wall. And to this new capital, called by them Cambaluc, came the greatest of medieval travelers, the Polos.

Unlike Carpini and William of Rubruck, the Polos were not Franciscan friars but merchants. Although trade along the caravan route between the Mediterranean and the China coast goes back into unknown antiquity, nothing is recorded about individuals who traveled the length of that route, if indeed any existed, until the time of the Polos. Fortunately because a businessman became a prisoner of war, and had time on his hands, we have another window on that old connection—one giving a view of the entire route.

The late thirteenth century was an age of feuding princes and petty wars and rival city-states; but the pope, after long, incessant warfare, had emerged triumphant over the Holy Roman Emperor and Europe was about to become a single, great international Christian civilization for the first and only time. The domains of the great khan stretched from the eastern border of Poland to the Yellow Sea, from the inhospitable northern tundras to Mesopotamia and the steaming jungles of Southeast Asia. For all its savagery, this was also, in many ways, a cosmopolitan time; no passports or visas were required to take one throughout the known world; no constricting boundaries fragmented the world into tiny nationalistic bits.

The two Polo brothers, Nicolo and Maffeo, while on a trading journey to Constantinople in 1253-60, were prevented by a local war from returning to their home in Venice. Instead, in an extraordinary journey, they continued eastward until they reached Kublai Khan's new eastern capital at Cambaluc in 1266. Three years later they returned to Venice as the khan's emissaries. The khan requested that the pope send a hundred learned men to serve as teachers and to debate savants from other lands at his court. However, there was no pope to whom the khan's message could be delivered. Clement IV was dead and no successor had yet been elected. The interregnum was a long one. The Polos had left again for the East when word of the election of Pope Gregory X overtook them. Returning as far as Acre, they forwarded the khan's request to the new pope, but His Holiness supplied only a brace of Dominican friars.

Starting off again from Acre in the late fall of 1271, the Polos were accompanied not by the hundred savants but only by Nicolo's son Marco and the two missionaries (who gave up the journey early, getting only as far as Armenia). The party took ship to Trebizond on the Black Sea and thence journeyed overland, through Isfahan, to the flourishing port of Hormuz on the Persian Gulf. Here they may have planned to sail eastward, but instead, perhaps attracted by the rich products arriving at the port from the interior, they turned inland, crossed Afghanistan and the Pamir Mountains to the caravan route skirting the southern edge of the desert, and followed it eastward. As they entered the eastern domains of the great khan, Kublai sent out riders on a forty days' journey to meet and escort them to Shang-tu—the Xanadu of Coleridge—surrounded by sixteen miles of walls. Here the khan was in residence in his magnificent marble summer palace—the English poet's "stately pleasure-dome." Kublai graciously received the Polos, who like William of Rubruck did not hesitate to perform the kowtow, that prostration before the emperor which was to cause so much anguish among later European envoys to the Chinese court. As the khan listened to an account of their journey, he probably wondered about the absence of the hundred scholars he had requested, not really to discuss the superiority of the Christian religion, but to fill offices in his government; for the khans, lacking administrative capability and not trusting the conquered Chinese, depended on foreigners to administer their domains.

Marco described in detail and with enthusiasm the life of the court, but there is little in his book that shows he had any understanding of the common Chinese people. He admired Kublai's game preserve, his hunts with cheetahs and hawks, his ten thousand mares. Marco did not mention Kublai's move from Shang-tu to Peking, but he described the newly completed palace and imperial city in precise detail. With lavish pride Kublai developed Cambaluc into a city worthy of being the capital of the greatest empire the world had ever known.

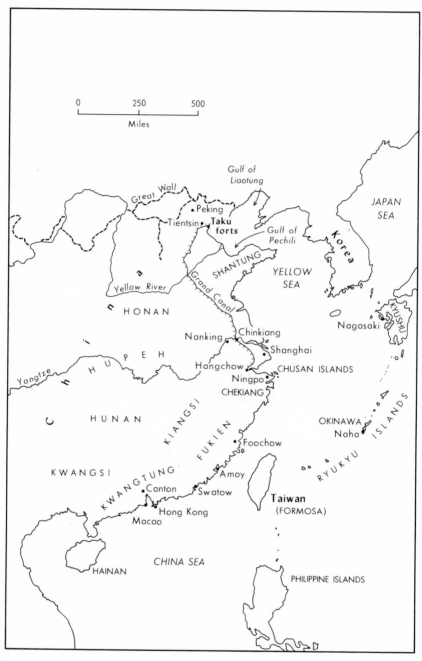

China

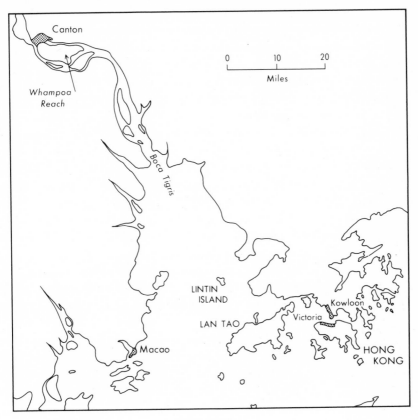

The Pearl River

During the seventeen years the Polos remained in China, Marco became a trusted administrator for the khan. In carrying out his duties he traveled throughout the country. Administrative errands took him to the wild tribes of the western provinces, to southwest Asia, and to the lovely old Sung dynasty capital of Hangchow—a city he particularly admired for its many canals and bridges, suggesting to him a larger and more splendid Venice. He was astonished by the amount of water traffic on the Yellow and Yangtze rivers and by the great extent of those waterways. He noted that the Chinese used "black stones" for fuel, and indeed they had burned coal at least since the fourth century. He also described paper currency and asbestos and many other things unknown in Europe. He not only learned about China at firsthand but he heard for the first time of Japan (or Cipangu, to use the medieval name). He had an eye for the ladies, remarking on the beauty of the Hangchow women and mentioning the twenty thousand prostitutes of Peking—a number barely sufficient to satisfy the throngs of merchants and others who came from afar and swarmed about the city's vast market place.

After seventeen years both the senior Polos and the khan were getting old, and the Venetians decided to return home. Kublai gave them one last mission —to escort a Mongol princess who was to become the bride of Arghun, Kublai's great-nephew, the khan of Persia. Leaving Kublai Khan's court in 1291, the Polos sailed early the next year from the bustling port of Zayton (near Amoy) in a fleet of thirteen four-masted ships. They spent five months in northwestern Sumatra, and Marco identified the islands of Indonesia as the source of many desirable spices. Not until after the Portuguese established their factories on the Malabar Coast of India in the early sixteenth century did Europeans know what parts of the East produced spices. The Polos reached Persia in two years' time to find that Arghun was dead. His son took on the princess, and the Polos resumed their way to Venice, arriving there in 1295. During their journey a message reached them that the great Kublai Khan was dead.

The following year, while commanding a Venetian galley at the battle of Curzola, Marco, along with seven thousand of his compatriots, was taken prisoner by the Genoese. During his captivity he dictated the story of his travels.

Marco Polo gave Europe its first factual information on China. Traveler, merchant, servant of Kublai Khan, writer, influencer of Columbus, inspirer of Coleridge, Polo wrote an account which is still enlightening after nearly seven centuries. Yet curiously enough, the things he did not mention but must have seen are as strange as the tales he did tell. He certainly passed through the Great Wall, drank tea, and saw sulphur matches, though we would not know it from his book. He tells us he is describing only half of what he learned, but even then many of his contemporaries did not believe the things he wrote.

The men we know about who succeeded the Polos as travelers to China, like those who had preceded them to Central Asia, were missionaries. In 1291, the same year that the Polos left Peking to begin their return journey, John of Montecorvino, a Franciscan who had spent fourteen years in the Near East, set out to attempt the conversion of Arghun Khan. Thus Europeans were converging on the Persian ruler from both east and west, one party bringing him a wife, the other a religion. John managed to visit Arghun who, as we have seen, died soon after without meeting his bride.

After John delivered his report on the Middle East, the pope decided that he was the right person to send to attempt the conversion of the great khan himself. Montecorvino was a man of saintly attributes, ascetic, pious, tenacious, hardworking, and diligent. Turning eastward again, he was joined at Tabuz by Peter of Lucolongo, a merchant who was to remain his companion and settle into the business world at Peking. Going overland to Hormuz, they sailed from that busy port to India, landing near Madras. During a year's stay at the Shrine of Saint Thomas (the Doubter) John made a hundred converts and then sailed for China. The exact route is unknown, but John of Montecorvino arrived at Peking in 1295, the first Roman Catholic priest recorded as reaching that city. Most of what is known about him comes from three letters: one written from Persia and two from the Mongol capital, the first dated January 8, 1305, and the other sometime in 1306. In them we learn that during a period of eleven years, up to the time of writing, he built two churches in Cambaluc, located two and a half miles apart. To provide helpers and a choir he bought a hundred and fifty boys, whom he instructed in Latin and the Catholic liturgy and baptized. Not the least of his problems were the Nestorian Christians, who did everything in their power to prevent the building of his first church and his proselytizing activities. Yet he says he baptized six thousand people, including one powerful prince of great distinction.

The pope, Clement V at Avignon, upon receiving John's last letter, expressed his delight by dispatching seven more Franciscans as reinforcements, three of whom arrived safely. Carrying out the pontiff's order, they installed John of Montecorvino as the first Archbishop of Cambaluc, acting themselves as his suffragan bishops. Montecorvino administered his diocese until his death in 1328 at the age of eighty-one. Five years later, when that news reached the pope, a group of friars and laymen was dispatched to take over the diocese, but it is doubtful if they ever arrived. The mission petered out, and it is certain that with the advent of the Ming dynasty in 1368, Christianity was eliminated in China as completely as were its friends, the Mongols of the Yüan dynasty.

One of the three Franciscans who joined John in Peking was Andrew of Perugia, who in 1318 wrote a letter from Zayton, the flourishing port near the present Amoy, where he became bishop in 1323. This letter contains some later information about John and almost all that we know of the church at Zayton, founded by a wealthy Armenian lady.

The last Franciscan friar who went to China during this period and whose tale has come down to us is Odoric of Pordenone. Exactly why he went to

China is not known. Possibly he was on a mission but he sounds more like a tourist enjoying himself. He turned up in India about 1321, where he collect-ed the bones of four recently martyred Franciscans, but did not linger. He then voyaged through Indonesia to Canton, a city that astounded him, and went on to the larger port of Zayton, leaving the bones of the martyrs at the Franciscan church there. Surprisingly, neither he nor Andrew of Perugia, who was there at the time, mention each other. Like Marco Polo, he was impressed with Hangchow, and he confirms his predecessor's description of that city—perhaps the largest in the world at the time. Both at Hangchow and at Yang-chow, his next stop, he found fellow Franciscans. Curiously enough, when Odoric reached Peking, John of Montecorvino was still alive and yet he does not mention him, although he certainly lodged at a Franciscan house.

Odoric was the first of the several travelers to describe the Chinese cus-toms of wearing long fingernails and binding women's feet. He also men-tioned the ivory tablet held by court officials to cover the lower face. He was not alone, however, in his admiration of the marvelous Mongol postal system —far better than anything of the kind in Europe.

Odoric returned to Europe a year or two before his death in 1331 and was later beatified. Thus by a whim of fate Odoric, an earthy friar and traveler, be-came a saint, while the saintly John of Montecorvino, who had labored a life-time to establish Catholicism in China, came to an obscure death in a foreign land. Odoric's book is the last and one of the best written about far Cathay in the Yüan dynasty.

Only one more formal delegation was sent to Peking during this period by the papacy in response to an embassy from the khan. A party of thirty-two, led by John of Marignolli, brought with them a war horse so huge, in compar-ison with Mongol horses, that it was a marvel to the khan. The journey lasted from 1338, when the party left Europe, to 1353, when they returned. The delegation had no authority, and made no attempt, to reactivate the bishop-ric in Peking.

The journeys of medieval European travelers underscore one fact about China from the time of Marco Polo to the end of the Yüan dynasty. Although Europe remembers the Mongols for their earlier invasions, it forgets that their empire stabilized the entire breadth of Asia from the Black to the Yellow Sea. People could travel—and did—the entire width of the continent. Although the Nestorians for many years held powerful offices in the Mongol governments, from the beginning of Kublai's reign in 1239, popes sent emissaries to the khan in perfect safety and Mongol emperors sent return embassies to Europe.

Numbers of European priests and merchants traveled to China and other Europeans served in the Tartar government. With the expulsion of the Mongols
from China by the Ming dynasty in the mid-fourteenth century, the land
routes were closed and only the Arabs met Cathay by sea. China would not
again be as well known, or in anything approaching as close touch with western Europe, for over one hundred and fifty years.

But while Western contact with the East had existed through merchants
and Nestorians in the seventh and eighth centuries and become much closer,
with a steady flow of Europeans into China, during the thirteenth and four-
teenth centuries, there was no lasting impact of one culture on the other. To
be sure a few minor foreign adoptions may have persisted in China, but no
important Western ideas or techniques influenced the flow of future Chinese
culture. The Mongols encouraged foreigners and lifted for a hundred years
that impenetrable curtain that hung between East and West. During this century many European myths about Cathay were dispelled. Tales of one-legged
monsters and men with Cyclopean eyes were discredited, the kingdom of
Prester John evaporated to reappear in Ethiopia; it became clear that no earth-
ly paradise existed, at least in China. The Ming emperors now drew the silken
curtain closed again. More than a century and a half would pass before a European peeped through it from the sea, and it would not be substantially penetrated, except by a few courageous missionaries and envoys, until the nineteenth century.

CHAPTER 16

To Cathay by Sea

While China withdrew into its hermetically sealed borders to preserve a great culture intact for half a millennium, Europe was undergoing one of those explosive awakenings that sometimes stir a civilization to its very foundations. The great intellectual revival called the Italian Renaissance was probing with critical eyes and scientific zeal into every sacred cupboard of inherited Western knowledge. Art and literature flourished. And in the bleaker north the surging religious undercurrents broke into the full surf of the Reformation, shattering forever the unity of Christendom.

Meanwhile the European demand for spices, especially to cure meat for the winter and to make spoiled meat palatable, was increasing, for so was the population. With the fall of the Mongol dynasty those trade routes which had been open both by land and by sea closed. Spices still came in but only by Arab dhows through the Red Sea, where the trade was controlled by the Turkish Mamelukes in Egypt who sold almost entirely to Italian merchants. In those pre-refrigeration days spices, like salt, were as essential for meat preservation as oil is today for energy. And even then it was the Near East that put the economic squeeze upon the West. The Turks kept raising their prices and the merchants of the wealthy Italian city-states passed on the increases to the rest of Europe. These spiraling prices were one goad that forced Europeans to circumvent the middlemen and find a sea passage to the Far East.

Foremost among the European maritime powers were the Iberian countries, particularly Portugal, where Prince Henry the Navigator had turned fishermen into deep-water sailors, founded a school of navigation, developed new ship designs, and built up a merchant marine and navy second to none.

While Portuguese voyagers were creeping down the African coast trying to find the end of the continent and open water to "run their easting down," Christopher Columbus sailed west to reach Cathay. At first he thought he had, but the discovery turned out to be a troublesome new continent across his way. Rivalry between the two great Catholic powers of Spain and Portugal became so keen that the pope, at the Treaty of Tordesillas in 1494, drew a line 370 leagues west of the Cape Verde Islands to separate their territorial claims. Spain got the New World and Portugal eventually acquired the East Indies, as well as a bonus in Brazil where, although unknown at the time, the bulge of South America lay east of the line. This treaty was intolerable to the northern maritime countries, and as soon as the English, Dutch, and French became powerful enough they ignored it. In fact Henry VII and John Cabot did not give it much thought when that Genoese seaman, who had been in the Levant in the spice trade, sailed in 1497 from Bristol for Cathay via the North Atlantic and discovered, like his fellow Genoese Columbus, that his way was blocked by a New Found Land.

Because of the sea power of Spain and Portugal, as long as they were dominant and even long after, the English and Dutch continued their efforts to reach the rich East—the long-sought countries of Cathay, Cipangu, and the Spice Islands—by way of the Arctic. One expedition after another attempted to find a Northwest Passage through North America, or the even longer and more hopeless Northeast Passage across Europe and Asia, but found their way completely and totally blocked by limitless ice.

But while the English and Dutch, with courage exceeded only by their obtuseness, got chilblains, continued to die of scurvy, or were eaten by polar bears, the Portuguese reached the economic Holy Grail. During the late fifteenth century Portugal was slowly making the African coast her own. Ivory, gold dust, coarse black Guinea pepper, and slaves were profitable exports. In 1488 Bartholomeu Dias, helped by a gale which blew him out to sea and away from the difficult coastal currents, reached the tip of Africa and set up a stone pillar at the Cape of Good Hope. He then rounded Cape Agulhas, the actual southernmost point of the continent, and continued on for thirteen days before landing at Mossel Bay. To the northeast stretched the Indian Ocean, the wide, open highway to the East. That ocean is a tricky one, however, and seeing it was not the same as navigating and sailing it.

Preparation for the final push was long and thorough. Eventually, in July 1497, a decade after Dias had sailed and in the same year that John Cabot crossed the North Atlantic, Vasco da Gama put to sea with two ships, the

São Gabriel and *São Raphael*, specially built for the voyage, a larger store ship, and a small caravel. Using the experience of Dias and thereby avoiding the contrary inshore currents and the doldrums, he sailed out into the Atlantic for three months. Then, turning to "run his easting down," he fetched the African coast north of modern Cape Town. It was a course which Portuguese and other East Indiamen would follow throughout the days of sail. The difficult doubling of the Cape of Good Hope was followed by an attempted mutiny, which was promptly quelled. At Mossel Bay, where Dias had anchored, da Gama burned one of his ships and refitted the others.

With a good southerly wind the little fleet sailed past eight hundred miles of unknown African coast and at the end of March arrived at Mozambique. Four richly laden Arab vessels lay in the harbor and their captains were less than cordial on discovering that their visitors were Christians. Nevertheless, da Gama managed to hire two Arab pilots and went on his way to Mombasa, where the Muslims were even more hostile and attempted to wreck his ships by cutting their cables. At Malindi, where the ships lay for sixteen days, the king was friendly and here da Gama engaged Ibn Majid, one of the finest celestial navigators of his day, to pilot the fleet for the last leg of the voyage to India. Sailing from this port in April 1498, they were carried by a fair monsoon across the Indian Ocean and in a month's time arrived off Calicut on the Malabar Coast of southwest India. Here they were greeted by two Spanish-speaking Tunisian Muslims. The ocean route to the East had been discovered.

While the voyage was successful, the reception was hostile. When asked why he had come, da Gama simply said, "Christians and spices." Neither the Hindu zamorin (as the unfriendly ruler of Calicut was called) nor the Arab traders who controlled the commerce took kindly to the Portuguese intruders. Under unpleasant difficulties and with great determination, da Gama managed to collect a cargo of pepper and cinnamon and hurriedly quit the port before violence developed. His long return voyage terminated when he arrived in the *São Gabriel* off Lisbon on August 29, 1499. Only one other of his four ships returned. Not only half of his ships but a third of his men, who probably died of scurvy, never came back.

King Manuel of Portugal was delighted with the news that da Gama brought back. India had been reached, and while no treaty was made with the zamorin it was confirmed, as suspected, that spices and other products desirable in the marts of Europe could be purchased in India for a fraction of their European prices. Enormous possibilities for trade were foreseen in Eastern waters, much was learned about navigation along the route, and it was ascertained that ports for refitting and refuge could be established along the east African coast. There were, indeed, "St. Thomas Christians" in southern India, as elsewhere in the East, but they were Nestorians, a sect that the Jesuits would soon be hounding as at least as heretical, if not more so, than the various non-Christians.

The king decided to take immediate advantage of the successful reconnaissance and prepared Lisbon for a commercial boom. Not for nothing did Francis I refer to his royal colleague Manuel as the "Grocer King." New wharves and warehouses were built and plans made to move the *Casa da India*, the headquarters of the Portuguese East India merchants, down to the waterfront. No time was lost in building new ships and assembling a fleet. On March 8, 1500, Pedro Alvárez Cabral, a navigator and a nobleman, sailed with thirteen ships laden with cargo for trade and a party of Franciscan missionaries. As always with the Portuguese, where Mammon went, God must go also.

Cabral, following da Gama's track across the Atlantic, discovered Brazil and dispatched one of the ships back to Portugal with the good news. His passage across the South Atlantic and around the Cape was a rough one, and five ships were lost before Cabral arrived at Calicut with the seven survivors. Here again, the Portuguese quarreled with both Hindu officials and Muslim merchants and ended up bombarding the town. Sailing south along the Indian coast to Cochin, he established a factory there and was happily loading spices when an avenging Muslim fleet from Calicut appeared and Cabral fled. Stopping at friendly Cannanore, he topped off his cargoes and sailed for Portugal, where the first ship arrived in June 1501. Despite the loss of ships the voyage was profitable and, besides, Cabral evidently heard of China and the fine porcelains produced there.

Several weeks before the return of Cabral's fleet, four more ships were sent to India under the command of João da Nova. Nova avoided Calicut, having heard about Cabral's difficulties there through a letter left on the African coast by the returning fleet, and loaded his ships with pepper and other spices at Cochin and Cannanore and then captured a Muslim vessel from Calicut. This act of piracy netted him a fortune in pearls as well as an excellent pilot and useful navigation instruments. Between trading and looting, the voyage was a remunerative one.

Cabral's experience with the continued intractability of the Muslims prompted King Manuel to send a combination trading fleet and naval force to ensure Portuguese control of the trade in India. Vasco da Gama, who had shown the way, was selected to command the huge fleet of twenty-five heavily armed vessels—twelve of the king's thirteen belonging to private merchants —that sailed from Lisbon to secure the eastern seas for God and Portugal. An ambassador from the raja of Cannanore who had been brought by Cabral to King Manuel was sent back with da Gama.

With his large and powerful fleet da Gama impressed and intimidated the rulers at the east African ports and made piratical attacks on every Arab vessel that he could approach. The large fleet enabled da Gama to carry out several goals simultaneously. While some ships loaded spices at Cochin and Cannanore, others subjected Calicut to a heavy bombardment for its incivility. The Portuguese won a clear-cut victory in a vicious naval battle with a large but disorganized Malabar Arab fleet. Treaties were made at cannon point and factories established. Leaving over half his fleet on the Malabar Coast to consolidate the Portuguese position, da Gama sailed for Lisbon in December 1502 with ten heavily and richly laden ships. Seven of them arrived the following autumn. What they could not accomplish on the Malabar Coast by peaceful means the Portuguese established by superior force.

This outline of the first Western penetration of Eastern waters, with the help of Muslim pilots and the Chinese compass, is essential to approaching the European sixteenth-century rediscovery of China by the Portuguese. With their superior ships and armament, the Portuguese consolidated their position in the East Indies, at the end of a long line of communication, with remarkable swiftness. Their first toehold, consisting of a precarious line of scattered warehouses and factories, was consolidated very largely by Affonso de Albuquerque, who went to India with da Gama in 1503. He became governor general of the Indies in 1509 and the next year captured the large city of Goa. With this bold stroke Albuquerque obtained a base with an excellent harbor and shipbuilding facilities for maintaining a permanent Portuguese fleet in the eastern seas. A fleet was essential if Portugal was to control an Eastern maritime empire and carry on unceasing war with the Muslims in an area where the flame of bitter trade rivalry was fanned by mutual racial and religious hatred. Albuquerque further solidified Portuguese domination of the spice trade by capturing Hormuz, the rich port on the Persian Gulf in 1515.

Early in the fifteenth century, under the Ming dynasty, the Chinese had embarked on an extensive exploration by sea under the talented eunuch Cheng Ho. In a series of voyages in great fleets of huge ships, Admiral Cheng Ho explored the coasts of Southeast Asia and India and the Indian Ocean as far as the African coast. Various rulers were persuaded to send tribute to the emperor in Peking and trading stations were established. The expeditions ended well before the Portuguese arrived in those seas, but the Chinese trading stations remained. The most important of them was Malacca, on the west coast of the Malay Peninsula, which controlled the strait through which all commerce between the Bay of Bengal and the Far East had to pass.

At Malacca Chinese merchants coming from the East exchanged goods with Arab vessels arriving from the West. Albuquerque, by capturing this important port in 1511, brought the Bay of Bengal commerce under Portuguese control and opened the way to the Far East. Furthermore, he could, and did, wreak havoc on the Muslim trade. It was another swift, brilliant stroke by the aggressive strategist who, in a few brief years, made his country dominant in Eastern waters. The possession of Malacca, added to that of Mozambique (fortified in 1507), Hormuz, and Goa, gave the Portuguese four strong, well-dispersed bases for their powerful navy. Albuquerque's contacts with Chinese ships and merchant captains, with whom he had cordial relations, prompted him to consider the possibility of opening a trade route to China. A roaming Portuguese trader, Rafael Perestrello, arrived in the Pearl River and proceeded to Canton in 1513-14, the first recorded European to visit China since the Polos had sailed from Zayton in 1292. Perestrello was not allowed to land, but he sold his cargo at an excellent profit and reported on his return to Malacca that there was as much money to be made taking spices to China as to Europe.

Albuquerque's desire to open direct trade with China led him to send an official emissary to the Chinese court. An expedition of four ships commanded by Fernão Peres de Andrade sailed up the river to Canton in 1517, carrying as envoy Tomaso Pirès, a supposedly tactful man of scientific interests. Because the Chinese were deeply influenced by Albuquerque's fair treatment of their merchant vessels at Malacca, Andrade received a friendly reception, although he unknowingly broke every rule in the Chinese book when he took his ships up the Pearl River to Canton. Leaving the ambassador at Canton in the midst of negotiations for permission to travel to Peking, Andrade sold his cargoes of pepper, loaded on Chinese goods, and then, apparently because illness had broken out among his crews, sailed away. So far, so good.

Pirès cooled his heels in Canton until January 1520 before he was able to begin his journey to Peking. Meanwhile his situation had seriously deteriorated. The Chinese government received warnings from Malaysia that the Portuguese were up to no good, that they were spies planning how to take over the country. Furthermore the Portuguese ruined their own chances when four more ships commanded by Simão de Andrade, brother of Fernão, arrived in the Pearl River in 1519. Simão behaved as badly as his brother had behaved well. He was arrogant to the Chinese officials, built a fort without permission on Tamão Island in the Pearl River delta, made piratical attacks on Chinese shipping, beat up a Chinese official, and allegedly kidnapped some children, whom the Chinese believed the Portuguese first molested and then steamed and ate. Luckily, a Chinese fleet about to attack the Portuguese ships was dispersed by a storm and the Portuguese escaped with a rich cargo of ill-gotten loot. Another Portuguese ship, arriving at Tamão in 1521, was forcefully detained after refusing to obey an order to leave.

The inexusable behavior of the Portuguese, combined with the ill-chosen language of the letters which Pirès presented to the celestial emperor, supplemented by a warning from the Malay sultan of Bintan, persuaded the Chinese that Pirès was indeed up to no good. He was sent back to Canton in disgrace to await an investigation of the whole series of Portuguese activities. In 1523 twenty-three of the insolent "barbarians" were executed and several other Portuguese died from their treatment in jail at Canton. Pirès himself died in prison in 1524 after suffering torture and humiliation. It was an inauspicious beginning for the renewal of relations between East and West. The incredible and outrageous action of Simão de Andrade not only spelled the death sentence for Pirès and his countrymen, but also ruined every attempt by the Portuguese to renew good relations at Canton for over thirty years. It also set the tone for Sino-European relations during the next three and a half centuries. The Portuguese, who considered all Eastern peoples legitimate prey, established trading settlements at Ningpo and in Fukien, but both were wiped out by massacres in 1545 and 1549. For some years the Portuguese were second only to the Japanese pirates in the extent to which they ravaged the China coast. Then their policy changed, and with their protection of Chinese shipping tentative trade with the Chinese began again.

Some time around 1555 the Portuguese succeeded in making an agreement with Chinese authorities to settle on the peninsula of Macao below Canton at the mouth of the Pearl River. The first Portuguese settlers arrived in 1557. Their descendants are still there. Once a prosperous entrepôt for all China trade, Macao today presents the anachronism of a Portuguese city populated and controlled by the Chinese, existing for its gold market, organized gambling, and tourism. At about the same time the Portuguese settled Macao, they also reached the Moluccas, the fabled Spice Islands where cloves were produced in abundance. No time was lost in negotiating a treaty with the sultan of Ternate and warehousing cloves.

Macao was not only the Portuguese trading port for China; it also became a center on the China coast for the new missionary zeal of the Roman Catholic Church in the sixteenth century.

The Jesuit Mission

The Society of Jesus, a new and vigorous order founded in 1540, added its own enthusiasm to the missionary effort and stimulated the older orders to fresh activity. The first Catholic missionary since the Mongol regime to attempt to penetrate the interior of China was the great Jesuit, Saint Francis Xavier, who had established the eastern headquarters of his society at Goa and had gone to Japan in 1549. In 1552 he arrived at the island of Shang-ch'uan below Canton, where the Portuguese traders were established, hoping to enter mainland China. He never did. Xavier died at Shang-ch'uan the same year, after making several unsuccessful attempts to reach the mainland, and his body was later returned to Goa.

It was not until 1582 and the arrival of the remarkable Italian Father Matteo Ricci at the head of a group of Jesuits that a successful mission was established outside of Macao. By the time Ricci died in Peking, twenty-eight years later, he had won the unqualified admiration and respect of the Chinese as a scholar. Ricci was a brilliant intellectual with a wide knowledge of mathematics and astronomy. His mastery of the Chinese language and literature also proved him a brilliant linguist, and his maps of China, the first to be seen in Europe, showed him an expert cartographer for his time.

Ricci was preceded to Macao by two other Jesuits, Michele Ruggiero, who had arrived there three years before, and Alessandro Valignano, who was now laying the plans for the China mission. Father Valignano, whose ideas for converting the East by cultural penetration were very different from those of his colleagues in India, instructed Ruggiero to learn the Chinese language so that he could converse, write, and read in that tongue. It was a frustrating experience, for Ruggiero had some difficulty finding a teacher. He was fortunate, however, in studying Mandarin, the language in which all official business was conducted, rather than the local Cantonese dialect.

Ruggiero went to Canton in November 1580 and by bribing Chinese officials managed to get as far as Chao-ch'ing, the viceregal capital of Kwangtung and Kwangsi provinces, but was then sent back to Macao. Surprisingly, in the summer of 1583 he received a letter from the governor at Chao-ch'ing inviting him to come and reside there—the first time a missionary was given permission to live among the mainland Chinese. With financial backing from a friendly Macao merchant, Ruggiero and Ricci moved to Chao-ch'ing in September 1583. Ricci spent the next seventeen years of his life learning the language and customs of China and absorbing an appreciation of its arts, literature, and history.

In order to live at Chao-ch'ing unmolested, the two priests were required by law to adopt Chinese dress and become in every way subjects of the emperor. A mission house was built there despite some local opposition, but Ricci's most significant achievement during his residence was the making of a world map showing China in something approaching its true proportion to the rest of the world. (Chinese maps of the period showed China occupying almost the entire area, with all the other countries known to them scattered insignificantly around the edges.) Ricci's map of the world with Chinese characters was printed over and over again and distributed throughout the Middle Kingdom. The increasingly high regard of Chinese scholars for Ricci enabled the priest, who was a consummate politician, to gain many ends, and at this time he prudently did not attempt to make converts.

Ruggiero went back to Macao to raise money in 1588; he was sent on to Rome, with the hope of bringing an embassy to China, but never returned. After he had been absent for some time, the people of Chao-ch'ing became suspicious that he would return with armed Portuguese—always a basic Chinese apprehension and with good reason. Father Ricci survived this brouhaha, but was nevertheless forced to leave the city and return to Canton (after seven years' work) when a new and less friendly viceroy was appointed. He was then sent to Shao-chou, over a hundred miles away though in the same province, where he remained six years and made seventy-five converts.

Ricci was not above bigotry, however, for both at Shao-chou and later at Peking, after converting learned Chinese to Christianity, he shockingly persuaded them to burn their libraries, including books, manuscripts, and printing plates that were in the slightest degree objectionable to Catholic doctrine.

Ricci's ambition to reach Peking was helped by an opportunity in 1595 to travel with a high-ranking official as far north as Nanking, the old capital. He was not allowed to stay there, however, and retired to Nan-ch'ang, a town a hundred miles away. Ricci and Father Cattaneo, his companion at the time, were now getting on better by exchanging their Chinese priests' garments for the robes of Chinese scholars, which immediately gave them higher status.

The long-awaited opportunity finally arrived in 1598 and Ricci embarked for Peking via the Grand Canal. After failing to get an interview with Emperor Wan-li, he returned to Nanking, but left again for Peking on May 18, 1600. He was detained for several months on the journey by a powerful eunuch named Ma T'ang, eventually arriving on January 28, 1601; and there he lived for the rest of his life.

After sending presents to the emperor and waiting some days, Ricci was summoned to the Forbidden City, but only, as it turned out, to keep the clocks which were part of his gift from running down. Ricci made powerful friends with the eunuchs and other high officials who ran the Chinese government, although he never laid eyes on the emperor; he kowtowed to an empty throne. Nevertheless, he was given property for a mission house at imperial expense. He made converts, but temporized on the question of ancestor worship, a point that would cause difficulties later on. Ricci constantly stressed in his letters to Rome the importance of sending to China priests who were learned and intelligent. When Ricci died on May 11, 1610, he was one of the most respected men in Peking. His burial plot was a gift from the emperor.

Rome heeded the advice of Ricci and sent to Peking many learned and outstanding individuals who served both the Jesuit mission and the emperor. One of them was Adam Schall von Bell, an astronomer, who arrived in 1622, twelve years after Ricci's death, and died there in 1666. Schall published the first description of a Galilean telescope in Chinese. As a member of the imperial bureau of astronomy he reformed and corrected the Chinese calendar (one of the very few Western contributions to Chinese life); and he wrote an important history of the China mission. Two of his colleagues constructed the first Chinese terrestrial globe.

Schall was also thrown into prison. The Jesuits, while founding several mission centers during the late Ming dynasty, also suffered occasional persecutions, notably in 1616 and 1622, some of which were quite severe.

In 1580, when the crowns of Spain and Portugal were combined under the Spanish monarchy, missionaries of other orders immediately flocked from Manila to Macao. Franciscans and Dominicans from the Spanish Philippine missions attempted unsuccessfully to establish themselves on the mainland China coast. Both Portugal and the Jesuits objected, and until 1633 Rome forbade other orders to work in Portuguese territory. By 1665, however, the Franciscans and Dominicans had become firmly established.

Although in general the Jesuits ingratiated themselves with the emperors and were often pampered by them, they never converted one. High officials occasionally, and the wretched poor. But the mission was eventually to break on one fundamental Chinese impediment. In order to make converts Ricci and his successors winked at the orthodox Confucian rites of ancestor worship. Prayers and offerings to one's ancestors were such an ingrained and normal part of every Chinese individual's existence that it was unthinkable not to conform. The Jesuits regarded this as a purely secular matter, perfectly compatible with Christianity. Not so some of the other Catholic orders, and the "Rites Controversy" divided the Catholic missions in China for about a century.

In 1644 the Manchus took over Peking and the Ming dynasty came to an end. The second emperor of the new dynasty, K'ang-hsi, came to the throne in 1661, before he was seven years old, and reigned for nearly sixty-two years. The length of his rule was exceeded only by its wisdom, for he was one of the strongest and ablest rulers China ever had.

Fortunately for the Jesuits, one of their most capable members, Ferdinand Verbiest, arrived in 1660 at the age of thirty-seven and remained in the capital until his death in 1688. The friendship established between Verbiest and the young emperor lasted and benefited the Jesuits throughout that enlightened monarch's life. The prospect for Christianity in China had never looked brighter.

During the disruptive early Manchu years, while the new dynasty was still occupied in chasing out the Mings, the Jesuits flourished. Estimates regarding the number of actual converts vary widely. Latourette, in *A History of Christian Missions*, quotes sources giving the total number of converts as 13,000 in 1627; 150,000 in 1650; 109,900 in 1663; and 254,980 in 1664. Almost certainly this last figure is too high.

In 1715 the papacy, at the instigation of Dominicans and Franciscans and after years of hearings, decided that the Chinese rites were idolatrous and incompatible with Catholic teaching, and furthermore that priests who did not insist that their converts give up the rites would be excommunicated. No longer could Chinese converts happily make offerings to their ancestors, kowtow before their shrines, and simultaneously be good Catholics.

The emperor took an opposite view from the pope. K'ang-hsi, sympathetic to the Christians, declared the rites were a purely secular matter and regarded the pope's decree as interference with the internal affairs of the kingdom. In 1717 the emperor became exasperated, confirmed his previously uninforced decrees by which missionaries who did not have an imperial permit were to be banished, churches destroyed, and Christianity forbidden to Chinese people, but they were not acted on until after K'ang-hsi's death in 1722.

Jesuits were allowed to continue to live in Peking and practice their religion themselves, but they were forbidden to attempt making any converts. This they quietly did, nevertheless, finding surreptitious ways to circumvent both papal bull and imperial decree. They were still employed by the emperors as scientists, astronomers, artists, and artisans. For example, they completed mapping the kingdom between 1708 and 1715. One of them, Guiseppe Castiglione, the talented Italian Jesuit artist (who arrived in Peking in 1715, the year of the pope's fatal decision on the rites), served several emperors (notably Ch'ien-lung) as court painter, decorator, and architect.

Christianity in China received its final disastrous blow when the Society of Jesus was dissolved by Pope Clement XIV in 1774, and over a century and a half of calculated, peaceful Jesuit penetration of China came to an end. No other Christians ever gained the privileged position which the Jesuits had held at the imperial court, though many tried. Christianity never wholly died out in China, but neither did it ever become the great awakening that Catholic orders, especially the Jesuits, and later Protestant groups hoped for.

Portuguese maritime power in the East flowered quickly at the beginning of the sixteenth century, dominated the Indian Ocean for most of it, and declined sharply at its end. The little country was overextended, its fleets too widely dispersed. Portugal broke Muslim domination of the Indian Ocean by force and, under Albuquerque, secured strategic ports. But, as the strain began to tell, Portuguese maritime efficiency and governmental administration both deteriorated. The unhealthy climate took a fearful toll. Disease decreased their numbers and miscegenation eroded their efficiency. There were no longer enough white sailors to man the ships, and with a high percentage of Lascar crews seamanship declined. Fewer ships came from Portugal and fewer ships remained in Eastern waters. Of ships making the passage, an increasingly high percentage was lost. No improvements were made in large-ship design. As navigators the Portuguese were getting worse, not better.

While the number of sailors declined, the number of clergy increased. After the founding of the Society of Jesus, the headquarters at Goa became second only to that in Rome as the vigorous order concentrated much of its missionary effort on the Far East. (We shall examine Japan in a later chapter.) The effort was largely wasted. In India and China, except for the very poor, the people were too civilized and sophisticated to be whipped into a fever for mass conversions and the indigenous religions were too powerful. Muslims have never taken kindly to Christian preaching and Hindus and Buddhists were both mainly content with their spiritual philosophies. Chinese scholars, who never professed any religion, were constantly amazed that learned men should also be priests. Furthermore Chinese of all classes, from the emperor down, would never eliminate the Confucian ancestor rites.

As the Portuguese influence became more church-controlled and less trade-inspired, hard-driving, ably navigating Dutch and English competitors began to appear in Eastern waters at the beginning of the seventeenth century, and Portuguese domination of the sea soon disappeared forever. The competition was intensified by the union of the Iberian crowns. Portugal, which had enjoyed reasonably friendly relations with the Protestant countries, now found herself as intensely hated as Spain. Nor did the Portuguese endear themselves to Eastern peoples. Their ruthlessness, cannon-ball bargaining, flagrant piracy, their lack of any understanding of native religions and customs, all ensured them a weaker position than they might have obtained by more enlightened and humane policies.

CHAPTER 17

Competitors of Portugal

Lusitanian power, although waning in the early seventeenth century, was not to be scorned and trade was still lucrative. Portuguese success in the rich Eastern spice and silk trades was a source of irritation to their Spanish rivals. The Spanish rulers, at first thinking Columbus had reached Cathay and the East Indies, soon discovered the truth: an unknown continent, inhabited by a new race, blocked the way. Furthermore there appeared to be no transcontinental passage on its long and winding coast. To be sure, the land was narrow at the Isthmus of Panama, where Balboa saw the Great South Sea from his peak in Darien, but no waterway connected the eastern and western oceans nor penetrated the long cordillera. Thus while the tall carracks poured Eastern wealth into the coffers of Lisbon merchants, the frustrated Spaniards, prevented from rounding the Cape of Good Hope into Eastern waters by the Treaty of Tordesillas, fought Indians of the Americas and brought back their golden idols. And they continued everlastingly to probe harbors and inlets along the American seaboard for a water route that would set their galleons free to cross the Pacific to the Spice Islands.

Success crowned the Spanish efforts when Magellan, who had suggested to the Spanish court that it might discomfit Portugal by sailing west, discovered the strait that bears his name and crossed the Pacific. Although, as we have seen, Magellan was killed in the Philippines, man's first circumnavigation of the world was completed when his solitary surviving ship, *Victoria*, returned to Seville in 1522 with a cargo of spices, obtained in the Moluccan islands of Indonesia, more than sufficient to pay for the cost of the entire expedition.

When the *Victoria* took on its cargo of spices in the Indies, the Portuguese

had already been in the Moluccas for a decade and had founded a trading station on the island of Ternate in 1512. They did not take kindly to the appearance of their commercial rivals in the eastern seas and this posed a cartographical problem. The Treaty of Tordesillas established a line 370 leagues west of
the Cape Verdes, but where did it fall when projected around the world? Actually both the Philippines and Moluccas were well on the Portuguese side of
it, but Spain not only maintained they were on its side of the line, along with
China and the Malayan entrepôt of Malacca, but also claimed them by virtue
of discovery. Magellan's voyage at last brought a confrontation of the Iberian
powers in the East that was no longer theoretical.

Regardless of the dilemma posed by the line of demarcation, differences
were to a large extent pragmatically resolved. The passage across the Pacific
is a long and lonely one. By the time Spain's scurvy-ridden crews arrived at
the Moluccas, their galleons slowed by weed-bearded bottoms, they were no
match for the powerfully entrenched Portuguese. After several years of
wrangling, interspersed with transpacific expeditions—all disastrous failures—
Charles V renounced all claim to the Spice Islands in 1529. He saved face at
the Treaty of Zaragoza when he both "sold and made a gift" to the crown of
Portugal of all rights in the Moluccas for 350,000 ducats. A new line of demar-
kation for the eastern hemisphere was established seventeen degrees east of
the Moluccas.

Spain now diverted its interest to the Philippines, a large and more savage
archipelago ignored by the Portuguese for the simple reason that there were
no spices of any consequence there. An expedition from Mexico in 1542,
commanded by Ruy López de Villalobos, renamed the islands, which had
been called San Lazaro by Magellan after the saint's day on which he had discovered them, for the *infante* Felipe—the future Philip II. Spain would bide
her time in cracking the Portuguese spice monopoly. Moreover, the Spaniards
knew that silk and metal-laden Chinese junks came yearly to the Philippines
to trade for gold and pearls. Beginning in 1545-48, Spain lost interest in the
Spice Islands for some twenty years while attention was focused on the exploitation of the enormously rich silver mines of Mexico and Peru.

In November 1564, a fleet of five ships sailed from Mexico for the Philippines under the command of Miguel López de Legazpe and piloted by Andrés
de Urdaneta (then an Augustinian friar but formerly a naval officer who had
sailed to the Moluccas twenty-two years before). Although Legazpe was ordered by Philip II to bring back as much spice and other treasure as possible,
the primary purpose of the expedition was to find a practical return route

eastward across the Pacific to Mexico. Legazpe reached the island of Cebu in April 1565 and founded a settlement there. But spices were few, for cloves did not grow in the Philippines (only cinnamon, which was confined to Mindanao); and the small amount of undoubted gold could not begin to rival the rich sources of that metal in the New World.

Legazpe sent one of his ships, the *San Pablo*, commanded by his nephew Felipe de Salcedo, back to Mexico, where she arrived in June 1565. Piloted by the venerable Urdaneta, she accomplished the principal purpose of the expedition by pioneering a northern route where favorable winds and currents bore her steadily eastward. It was a track the Manila galleons followed annually for the next two hundred and fifty years.

Legazpe remained in the Philippines until his death in 1572. During that time he completed Spanish domination of the islands rather easily. Trading Moros, who appeared at his base in Cebu, produced Chinese silks, porcelains, and other desirable goods, thus confirming earlier rumors. It was soon learned that Chinese junks from Fukien, as well as Japanese vessels, made yearly visits to the coast of Luzon, where they traded peacefully with the Muslim Moros. With the Spanish in solid control of the archipelago, Legazpe in 1571 moved his capital from Cebu to Manila Bay. Manila, on the threshold of the great Asiatic kingdoms and with the best harbor in the East, soon became a busy entrepôt for the exchange of trade goods between China and New Spain. In the course of its growth Manila survived Moro raids and, in 1574, the unsuccessful but violent attack of the famous Chinese pirate Limahon (as he was known to the Spanish), who assaulted the city with a huge fleet and four thousand men.

Manila was geographically more favorably situated than any other city as a center for oriental trade; tons of Chinese silk and fine porcelains came to its warehouses, and spices were unloaded from Malay ships running from the southern Indonesian islands. Thus Spanish Manila became the commercial rival of Portuguese Macao and Malacca, although the Portuguese were shipping to Europe while Spanish cargoes went eastward to Acapulco and other New World ports. Silks of all kinds, from flimsy gauzes to heavy brocades, made up the bulk of the earlier cargoes. But the galleons also carried cottons from India and China, Persian and Chinese rugs, spices from all the islands, and jewelry. Trade trivia—combs, fans, bric-a-brac, inlaid and lacquer work, porcelains, and articles manufactured of various materials such as ivory, jade, paper, and metal—filled up the space remaining in the holds.

After the pirate Limahon was repulsed from Manila, he retreated north

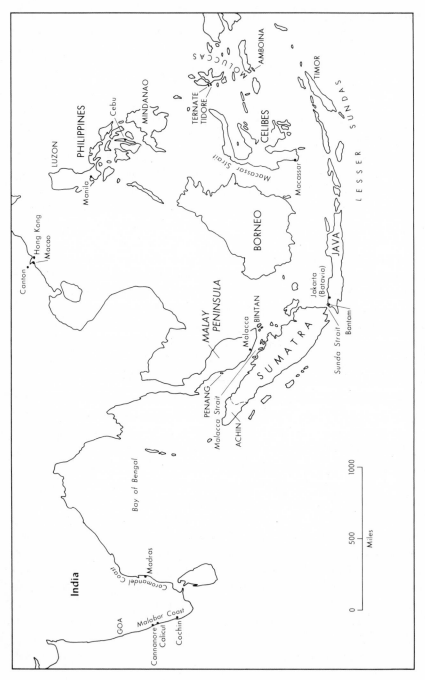

The Eastern Seas

and fortified himself on the west coast of Luzon. Juan de Salcedo, who had relieved Manila with forty-five harquebusiers, burned Limahon's junks, besieged him in March 1575, and settled down to wait him out. But the wily pirate secretly built a fleet of thirty-three small craft and early in August escaped to sea. Limahon was also wanted by the Chinese authorities, who sent a force of ten war junks to help the Spaniards. The Chinese were exasperated and annoyed when, on their arrival, they learned of his escape. Had the Spaniards been able to destroy or capture Limahon the Chinese were prepared to offer them land for a settlement on the Bay of Amoy, as they had the Portuguese at Macao. Nothing came of the project, however, and the Spaniards lost their opportunity to establish a base on the mainland. Nor, although they made several diplomatic attempts, did the Spanish ever get a toehold in mainland China. The hot-headed Francisco de Sande, Manila's third governor, recommended that he be allowed to solve the problem by sending an expeditionary force to conquer China; this impractical scheme was quickly vetoed by Philip II.

In 1580, after the death of the Portuguese's senile cardinal-king Henry, Philip II of Spain claimed the throne of Portugal. For the next sixty years the crowns of the two Iberian kingdoms remained united. The combined empires girdled the globe. But aggressive Spanish plans to make the Philippines the center of a consolidated oriental empire devoted to both military and spiritual conquest, and controlling trade from Malacca to Japan, as well as from China, Indochina, Java, and the other Malay islands, were never realized. The ambitious schemes were interrupted by the arrival of fleets of Dutch and English merchantmen in the East during the last decade of the sixteenth century.

Nor, in spite of the union of the two crowns, were the Portuguese about to give up their spheres of influence. The two countries were not formally united, and it was specifically agreed that the two colonial empires should remain administratively separate. The position of Portugal in the Spice Islands was already weakened but it clung tenaciously to the trade with Goa, Macao, and Japan. With the union, Spanish Franciscan, Dominican, and Augustinian friars looked forward to establishing Chinese missions through Macao and other points on the China coast, but the Portuguese resisted their ambitions and steadfastly supported the Jesuits. Thus the Spaniards were never able to gain any real military or religious foothold in either China or Japan, and their extensive commercial relationships with those peoples continued to be by way of the trade funneled through Manila, where silks and other products were exchanged for Mexican silver.

Arrival of the Dutch

In 1581, the year following the union of the Iberian crowns, the seven states of Holland threw off the yoke of Philip II and formally renounced their allegiance to the Spanish monarch. A long struggle ensued, but after the defeat of the Spanish Armada in 1588, there was an enormous expansion of seaborne trade, and the determined Dutch decided to counter Philip's repeated efforts to suppress revolt in the Netherlands by taking the war to his overseas empires. In the carrying out of this plan the Portuguese colonial possessions, which were far more vulnerable than the Spanish, suffered the most.

The rise of Dutch sea power during the early 1600s was as rapid and extraordinary an achievement as that of the Iberian powers a century earlier. For some years Dutch seamen had served in Portuguese ships on voyages to the East. Gossip which they brought back received expert confirmation from Jan Huyghen van Linschoten, a young Dutchman whose family had been in business in Seville and Lisbon. Linschoten lived in Lisbon and in 1583 joined the retinue of Vicente de Fonseca, the new Portuguese archbishop of Goa. He remained in India until 1589 when he returned to Holland, arriving there in 1592. In 1596 he published his great work on the East which was translated into English and German two years later. Actually the sections on sailing directions to India were printed a year earlier. Using Linschoten's directions, the first Dutch fleet commanded by Cornelis de Houtman, who had also resided in Lisbon, sailed for the East in 1595. Houtman signed a treaty with the sultan of Bantam, who controlled the crucial Sunda Strait between Sumatra and Java. In 1598 twenty-two ships sailed for the East Indies in several fleets. Of the nine that went by the Strait of Magellan only one arrived, but of the thirteen that rounded the Cape of Good Hope only one was lost. Houtman was again in command of two of the ships, with John Davis, who had tried to reach the East by the Arctic and discovered Davis Strait, as his chief pilot. The ships that got there traded in the Moluccas and negotiated several commercial treaties with island rulers. The first pitched battle with the Portuguese ended in a Dutch victory over a superior fleet in Bantam Roads in 1601.

The Dutch had begun their overseas aggression against their enemies with attacks on Portuguese bases off West Africa during the last years of the sixteenth century (1598-99) and soon were threatening Philip's Portuguese possessions in American and African as well as Asian waters.

In 1605 the Dutch took over the rich clove-producing Moluccan islands of Amboina, without a struggle, and Tidore, after bitter fighting. The following year they attacked the strategic port of Malacca, but were beaten off by the

Portuguese after a bitter four-month siege. In the same year (1606) the Dutch were surprised by a Spanish counterattack from the Philippines which recaptured Tidore and part of Ternate, where Spain maintained forts until 1662. But the tenacious Dutch continued systematically to pick off Portuguese trading stations one by one. Occasionally they suffered other setbacks: they were repulsed from Mozambique in 1607 and sustained the worst defeat in their colonial history when they tried to take Macao in 1622. Except for those two cities, as well as Goa, Timor, and some of the other Lesser Sunda Islands, the Dutch took over the entire Portuguese Indonesian spice empire. After the Portuguese were forced out of the Moluccas, they established a post at Macassar in the southern Celebes, from which the Dutch finally expelled them in 1667.

Unable to capture Macao, the Dutch effectively bypassed it, replacing the Portuguese in the monopoly of European trade with Japan in 1640. In the same year they also began an encroachment on Ceylon and by 1658 the last of the Portuguese were expelled from that island. On July 14, 1641, the Dutch dealt the Portuguese another devastating blow by capturing Malacca after a five months' attack against a stubborn and valiant defense. The Dutch now controlled both the Sunda and Malacca straits—the only two practical passages through to the islands—and were supreme in their domination of the eastern seas. Finally by founding a settlement at Cape Town in 1652, as a way station for their ships, they no longer needed to attempt the capture of Mozambique.

Complete Dutch domination over Portugal in the eastern seas, despite the two countries' relatively equal population of some one and a half million inhabitants each, was due to the great superiority of Dutch resources and planning over the impoverished and incompetent Portuguese. The Dutch had many more large ships, a big reservoir of seamen from surrounding countries, better training and discipline, and more competent leaders. Furthermore Portugal had been especially obtuse in dealing with native peoples and potentates. For over a hundred years the Portuguese were able to keep the eastern empire they had seized, but the effort required almost continuous fighting. Even though native attacks on their forts were repulsed, the constant drain on Portuguese manpower was exhausting. Until 1640 this drain was exacerbated by the need to supply troops for the armies of Spain.

One great source of Dutch strength lay in the efficiency of the Dutch East India Company, where professional competence and experience were rewarded with promotion; by contrast Portuguese trade remained the prerogative of aristocratic *fidalgos* whose promotions were determined primarily by social standing. This great national company, created in 1602 by combining various private Dutch firms, received a monopoly of the Eastern trade. The company gave the Dutch a stronger hand in dealing with native rulers and fighting the Portuguese. Without consulting the home government, it could wage defensive war, build forts, establish colonies, capture foreign shipping, coin its own money, and make treaties or alliances with native princes. Control rested with a board of seventeen directors, known as the Heeren XVII, although any Dutchman could invest in the company and general supervision was retained by the States-General, which collected custom duties.

The Dutch established the capital of their Indonesian empire at Batavia, on Java, from where they monopolized the spice and Japanese trades and subsequently established a factory at Canton. The late seventeenth century saw local potentates coerced, conquered, or befriended. To ensure high prices, the control of spice crops was tightened by destroying trees. The whole Dutch world was geared to making money. By the eighteenth century trade had paved the way for, and indeed required, the political annexation of a great geographical empire. Dutch commercial and political domination of Indonesia was complete.

The English Come East

The English had failed to find a northern passage to Cathay but, having destroyed Spanish and Portuguese supremacy on the sea by the defeat of the Armada, they began, even before the Dutch, to plan for a voyage to the East around Africa. Francis Drake's voyage was to show that the Portuguese in the Far East were badly overextended. Drake, sailing from Plymouth with five vessels in 1577 and returning with only the *Golden Hind* in September 1580, made the second circumnavigation of the world and captured the fabulous great Spanish galleon *Cacafuego*, laden with Peruvian silver. He topped off his cargo with valuable cloves in the Moluccas, where he made a treaty with the sultan of Ternate.

At the instigation of Queen Elizabeth London merchants planned a reconnaissance voyage around Africa. Three ships, commanded by George Raymond, with James Lancaster, who had lived in Portugal and was fluent in the language, as second in charge, sailed from Plymouth on April 10, 1591. A quick passage of three months brought them to the Cape. However, scurvy had afflicted the crews so severely that after a month's stay at Table Bay one of the ships, the *Merchant Royal*, was sent back to England. Raymond in the *Penelope* and Lancaster in the *Edward Bonaventure* then sailed into a wild storm in the Mozambique Channel; here the *Penelope* went down with all hands.

Lancaster limped on to the Comoro Islands, where he lost several men in a native attack. He found better shelter at Zanzibar and recuperated there for three months, at one point beating off an attack by a Portuguese ship. He made a rough, difficult passage of the Indian Ocean, skirted Ceylon, and arrived at Penang off the Malay Peninsula in June 1592. After another three months' rest, with his crew reduced to a mere thirty-four men, he went on a plundering cruise through Malacca Strait, capturing every native and Portuguese vessel in sight. Then, fearing reprisals, he started for home in November. After a difficult passage around the Cape he ended up in the West Indies, where part of his discouraged and destitute crew made off with the ship, leaving Lancaster and nineteen men stranded. He and twelve others were rescued about a month later by a French ship and brought back to England. Lancaster was the first Englishman to explore the way to the East, a way particularly difficult for the English because it involved thousands of miles of ocean sailing without the conveniently spaced stations along the African coast which the Portuguese had established and enjoyed for a century.

The second English expedition to the East was even more disastrous than the first, for of the three ships commanded by Captain Benjamin Wood that sailed from England in 1596, all were lost and only one surviving crew member, a Frenchman, returned in 1601 in a Dutch vessel.

These failures did not dampen the enthusiasm of the English for the Eastern trade, pressured as they were by the Dutch monopoly of pepper which increased the price exorbitantly. On the last day of the year 1600, a joint stock company formed by a group of merchants and adventurers under the leadership of the famous London entrepreneur, Thomas Smythe, received its charter as the East India Company with Sir Thomas as its first governor.

The company lost no time going into action. Four ships already fitted out and commanded by Captain John Lancaster in the *Red Dragon*, with the durable John Davis as chief pilot, sailed from Woolwich on February 13, 1600. The expedition was well equipped and the sailors were given two months' pay in advance. Letters from Queen Elizabeth and presents for the princes of India were provided. There were ample supplies of muskets, swords, and ammunition on the *Red Dragon*, but only one "pease pot" (piss pot), presumably for the sick and indicating that the head was a busy place. Lancaster kept scurvy under control by dosing his men with lemon juice, although the crews of the other ships suffered. The voyage was a profitable one. Lancaster cast anchor at Achin in Sumatra in June 1602, where he was enthusiastically received by the local sultan. He was met at the shore by two gorgeously caparisoned elephants. Mounting one and placing a letter from Queen Elizabeth on the other, he delivered his sovereign's message in an appropriately impressive manner. Subsequently, Lancaster captured a great Portuguese carrack crammed with merchandise in the Strait of Malacca and a profitable voyage was ensured. Going on to Bantam in Java, he loaded pepper, established a company factory, and set sail for home. The coffers of the company were filled when he arrived in the Thames in September 1603 with the Portuguese loot and 515 tons of pepper.

In 1604, the year James I made peace with Spain, the same four ships sailed again under the command of Captain Henry Middleton. Loading two of his ships with pepper in Java, Middleton sent them home (one was lost on the passage) and took the other two to the Moluccas for cloves and nutmegs. On his return in May 1606, in spite of the loss of one ship, the voyage netted nearly a hundred percent profit.

During the voyage, however, Middleton began to run into opposition from the Dutch. While they allowed their English allies to trade side by side with them in the islands, where they were rapidly establishing a spice monopoly, the Dutch were not happy about the competition and in general were anything but helpful. Rather discouraged by the uncooperative Dutch attitude, the East India Company directed their third fleet commander, William Keeling, to explore other possibilities in 1607. Keeling went to Java in the *Red Dragon* for pepper, but sent William Hawkins in the *Hector* to the mainland, where he established successful contact with the Mogul emperor Jahangir. From this time on, although the English continued to trade throughout Indonesia for some twenty years until they were finally driven out by the Dutch, the company began to concentrate more and more on India. This third voyage netted a whopping two hundred and thirty percent return on the company's investment.

The original charter of the East India Company had granted a monopoly for fifteen years, but after five mostly very profitable voyages, they applied for and got a new charter in 1609 granting them a far more stringent monopoly in perpetuity. From 1610 on the company sent ships to the East annually.

Meanwhile the Dutch further consolidated their position in the islands. In 1618 Jan Pieterszoon Coen became governor general of their East Indian empire. He was a hard-driving empire builder, cut out of the same bolt of cloth as the great Portuguese Albuqerque or the later British Clive. Over the strong objections of the sultan of Bantam, he seized the small Javanese port of Jakarta and built it into the strong fortified city of Batavia. His ambition was to go beyond the islands and build a great Asiatic commercial empire ruled from his new capital. The Dutch became solely dominant in the coastal areas of Indonesia, while local sultans ruled the interiors. After 1623 the English, as we have seen, opted for competing with the weak Portuguese in India and concentrated most of their activities on the subcontinent.

In 1616 Sir Thomas Roe, an attractive and able man, came out to India as ambassador from James I to the Mogul emperor Jahangir, to whom he presented a coach and four, complete with coachman, and from whom he obtained permission to establish an English trading post at Surat, in western India, where a successful factory was maintained for many years. But the real importance of Roe's embassy was that it established the East India Company's basis for self-government in India and began a tradition of mostly good relations which continued until about the end of the reign of Aurangzeb, the last great Mogul emperor, in 1707.

Rivalry between the English and Dutch in the Spice Islands was intense and naval battles were not unusual, although the countries were ostensibly at peace. The Dutch East India Company was far larger and richer than its English counterpart—its ships were better designed and more numerous, its employees better established and more widely dispersed. A treaty signed in 1619 gave the British one-third of the trade on condition that they contributed the same proportion to the upkeep of forts, which were to be Dutch-manned. It was an unstable compromise, and the Dutch settled the matter once and for all at the important Spice Island of Amboina in 1623. They systematically seized the ten English traders, tortured them with water and fire until they confessed, between mighty oaths it was reported, to plotting against the Dutch, and beheaded them along with their nine Japanese servants. Their justification may have been slender but the action was opportune.

This incident was one of several that, while not immediately leading to Anglo-Dutch war, irritated and strained relations between the two Protestant countries. The Dutch, pursuing an aggressive policy, had secured Cape Town as a strategic way station to the East, and the English East India Company never recovered its position in the Malay Archipelago. Only their little factory at Bantam lingered on until 1684, when they were finally expelled by the sultan who closed his ports to all but the Dutch.

European powers in the East were now fairly well established for the last half of the seventeenth century. As the eighteenth century dawned, Portugal's waning empire had dwindled to Goa and Macao. Spain sat complacently in the Philippines, enjoying trade with China through Manila and skirmishing with the always troublesome Moros. The Dutch, through a combination of force, diplomacy, and business acumen, grew ever more secure in their Indonesian empire. And the English, who were quite successful at Indian politics, were becoming established in India, especially at Surat and on the Coromandel coast, where, despite formidable Dutch competition, they had founded a factory at Madras in 1639. Less than twenty years later Madras became the company's headquarters for eastern India.

All were intensely jealous of each other; all sat on the fringes of the trade with China which (except possibly for the Dutch) they most desired. But the Son of Heaven sat content upon his Peking throne, his dim view of the barbarians brightened only by the few pet Jesuits who hung around his court.

Spices, confined to certain islands, and pepper, widely distributed, continued to be the principal products. But indigo, gold from Sumatra, tin from Malaya, and other merchandise were becoming increasingly important. In the late seventeenth and early eighteenth centuries fine India cottons were in great demand. The Dutch developed the cultivation of coffee in Java in the eighteenth century after the English and French began growing spices in territories they controlled and the Hollanders could no longer manipulate production of the crops. Tea drinking became enormously popular, especially in England, and the Chinese tea trade grew in importance. But except for the trickle of trade that came through Portuguese hands at Macao, and the Chinese junks that traded in large numbers at Manila and to a lesser extent at Batavia, China remained commercially isolated.

The Manchus, who replaced the Ming dynasty in 1644, were as isolationist as their predecessors, if not at first more so. Except for the traditional tribute system (whereby foreigners were regarded as subject peoples rather than as independent traders), they considered any kind of commerce either with Europeans or Japanese as undesirable, unnecessary, and dangerous. The Portuguese in Macao were completely under Chinese control and forbidden to allow any ships but their own in that port. The Dutch had trading stations on Formosa (Taiwan) for a time, but in 1661 they were expelled by Koxinga, the piratical warlord who established his kingdom of the sea in Fukien and Formosa for a couple of decades.

In 1676 the English obtained a license to trade at Formosa and Amoy from Koxinga's son and successor, Cheng Ching. But this privilege came to an end when the forces of Emperor K'ang-hsi defeated Cheng Ching in 1680 and overran Formosa three years later. However, while English trade goods at

Amoy were seized, K'ang-hsi drew back the silken curtain ever so slightly in 1685 by proclaiming the South China ports and the China Sea open to limited foreign commerce under the old tribute system. The English pounced on this new opportunity for European trade and in 1685 sent the *China Merchant* to Amoy—the first of hundreds of vessels in the tea trade.

The Dutch, who funneled all their Eastern trade through Batavia and specifically forbade ships to enter into direct trade anywhere else in the East, were late arrivals in the China field. But other nations were soon there. The first French ship arrived in 1698. In 1715 ships of the Ostend Company, flying the flag of Austria, appeared in the East in numbers. Danish and Swedish East India Companies, small but active, were soon sending their ships for tea. The Dutch finally entered the direct trade with Canton in 1729.

To carry on this trade, which was almost entirely in tea, the European nations had to maintain the fiction of accommodating it to the official foreign tribute system of the Chinese. The conduct of the traders, their heavy armament, and the activities of Christian missionaries were all of deep concern to Chinese authorities, who increasingly began to isolate the traders. By the 1720s the trade was confined to Canton, where all business had to be conducted with the guild of Chinese merchants known as the Cohong, who fixed prices and were responsible to the government for the Europeans' good behavior. There on the narrow strip of waterfront called Thirteen Factory Street, the European factors were confined in bored isolation, broken only by trips downriver to Macao in the off season. They were even prohibited from studying the Chinese language and culture, for the Chinese were forbidden to teach them. Infinite boredom, booze, disease, and humidity debilitated the body and demoralized the soul. Bedeviled by petty restrictions on their conduct and frustrated by oriental officialdom and protocol, the European factors accommodated themselves to difficult jobs with surprising resilience.

The Chinese silk curtain was now slightly open. But before following the pioneering European developments and impact of the Canton trade, let us turn back to see how the nations had fared with that other enigma of the East —Japan.

CHAPTER 18

Barbarians All

Unlike China, which by and large had enjoyed a centralized imperial government over many centuries, sixteenth-century Japan was fragmented into warring feudal fiefs. Swarms of Japanese pirates, called *Wakō*, raided shipping along the China coast and occasionally, as traders, went as far as the Malay Peninsula and to Luzon in the Philippines. The raids of the "robber dwarfs," as the Chinese called them, were a constant source of harassment to the Middle Kingdom and Chinese traders were forbidden to have any business dealings with them whatsoever. This was a situation made to order for astute middlemen, and the Portuguese, purely by accident, discovered it.

In 1542 or 1543 three Portuguese sailors, on a smuggling voyage in a Chinese junk from Siam to Chincheu, were driven off their course by a typhoon. After a fortnight they landed at an unknown island, which was in fact Tanegashima, off the southern end of Kyushu, where they were greeted by short friendly men who were excited by their harquebuses. Their battered junk was repaired by the Japanese, who also bought their cargo of skins for silver, and the Portuguese, well pleased, returned to Malacca. So far as is known this was the first landing of any Europeans in Japan. Soon after word of the discovery of Japan got back to Goa, the possibility of new markets attracted the independent traders, and the probability of new thousands of heathen souls beckoned the Jesuits. Within eight years, however, the Portuguese government made the Japanese trade a monopoly and granted the privilege each year to a deserving servant of the realm. Not unexpectedly, rewarding a *fidalgo* (noble) with the franchise soon deteriorated into selling it to the highest bidder. The voyage from Goa was a long one, with Malacca the only port of call

246

before Macao and Japan. These voyages became extraordinarily lucrative, not only for the government but also for the grantee, and continued almost annually for ninety years.

As we have seen, the Portuguese were first allowed by the Chinese authorities to trade annually at islands in the mouth of the Pearl River. By 1557, with Chinese permission—in return, it is said, for ridding the place of pirates—they were settling at Macao—the "City of the Name of God" in China. Because of the Chinese ban on trading with Japan, the Portuguese were soon, to their great advantage, active middlemen between the two empires. European and Indian goods sold well in Japan, but the most profitable trade was in Chinese silk, which was much superior to the Japanese product at that period and for which there was an inordinate demand. Furthermore, the Japanese paid for merchandise in silver. Silver was almost essential for dealing with the Chinese then, as it was for the next 250 years. Gold, which the Portuguese also received in Japan in the early days, later changed from an export to an import commodity in the Japanese economy. The Japanese trade kept Macao prosperous, even after competition with the Dutch and English had weakened the Portuguese island empire, until complete Dutch domination of Malaysia in 1639.

When one considers the imperious closed-door policy of Japan, ended by Commodore Perry in 1854, and the historically inflexible attitude of Chinese emperors towards foreigners, the welcoming of outsiders by the Japanese in the sixteenth century comes as a surprise. The Japanese then as now, however, were receptive to new ideas and had an insatiable curiosity about foreign things. For centuries they had been drawing on the much older Chinese civilization. Chinese characters were adopted to write the language, Chinese learning was admired and emulated, and Chinese teachers, craftsmen, religious leaders, and other professional men were welcomed in Japan and treated with distinction. The Chinese governmental system was copied and Buddhism, which became the single earliest civilizing influence in the country, was imported from China. Philosophy, arts, and letters were all imported and admired. In short, in many ways China was to Japan what the classical city-states were to Western Europe. And even after Japan developed its own national culture it never cut off her admiration for the mainland civilization.

The Southern Barbarians

At the time when the Portuguese arrived in the mid-sixteenth century there was somewhat of a hiatus in the Sino-Japanese relationship because of unsettled conditions in both countries. The Japanese emperor at this time exerted no authority from his capital at Miyako, as Kyoto was then called. Regional feudal barons controlled large parts of the country and pursued their incessant wars for domination. The Japanese attitude toward foreigners had not changed, however, and the Portuguese arrived at an opportune time. Feudal lords vied with each other in making friends with these strangers, with their superior firearms and towering ships carrying great cargoes of desirable goods. Nor did the Japanese fail to notice the deference with which the Portuguese treated the Jesuit priests, whom they consequently assumed must be the most powerful and authoritative individuals among the newcomers. In this atmosphere Europeans could play off one baron against another to make trade bargains of a most advantageous sort.

The great ships used by the Portuguese in the East Indies trade, called *naos* by the Portuguese and carracks by the English, were the largest in the world at the time, ranging in size from vessels of three hundred tons to monsters of two thousand tons. An effort was made during the reign of King Sebastian (1568-1578) to keep the size below 450 tons, since the smaller ships were more seaworthy, but after his death the tonnage increased again. The best carracks were built of teak in the yards at Goa and elsewhere in the East, where the timber was infinitely superior to Portuguese pine. They were big, clumsy, slow-sailing, lightly armed vessels. It was these great carracks or occasional large galleons that were used for many years on the nearly annual voyages to Japan which began in 1550 and lasted until 1640.[1]

A regular system was worked out for the voyages, which usually took two and sometimes three years. The great ship, laden with European woolens, wines, and manufactured goods and Indian cotton and calicoes, sailed in the spring for Malacca, where part of the cargo was exchanged for hides, spices, and aromatic woods. Passage was then made to Macao, where it was often necessary to wait nearly a year for an Eastern monsoon or for the biannual Canton silk sale which the Portuguese were permitted to attend. Tons of both raw and manufactured silk were lightered down the Pearl River to fill the carrack's capacious hold. The following summer the "black ship," as the vessel was known in Japan, after a passage of less than thirty days through the Formosa Strait and across the East China Sea, reached one of the southern Kyushu ports. Hirado was the usual port of arrival until 1571, after which the city of Nagasaki was established as the official entrepôt for the Macao trade. The silver-to-China, silk-to-Japan combination remained an amazingly stable one throughout the ninety-year period.

Japan

On the return voyage the principal cargo was silver bullion, although before 1563 gold was also carried in quantity. The only other cargo was lacquered boxes and furniture, eventually sold in Europe. The silver was discharged at Macao to purchase the cargo of silk for the following year, and more silks, porcelains, and other goods were loaded for Goa. In this trade the Portuguese had the best of all possible worlds, for silver was much more valuable in China than in Japan, and the reverse was true for silks, while porcelains, lacquer work, and other products of both countries brought high prices in Europe. As presents for the Japanese shogun (military dictator) the "southern barbarians"—as the Portuguese were called—also brought in their "black ships" Arabian horses, cages of tigers, peacocks, and other birds and animals from the Indian jungles. The single "great ship from Amacon," as the annual carrack from Macao was called, was discontined in 1618 in favor of smaller vessels called galliots, which made Dutch and English depredations more difficult. Apparently, too, at times large Chinese seagoing junks were used by the Portuguese, but little is known about them.

The Jesuits

Francis Xavier, who had been sent out to Goa about 1640, was also the pioneer of a remarkably successful Jesuit mission to Japan. A hard-working, energetic, zealous but bigoted priest, he did irreparable harm to the Portuguese cause when he persuaded the home authorities to send the Inquisition to hunt down heretics at Goa.

After meeting in Malacca a young Japanese named Anjiro who went to the seminary in Goa and was baptized as Paul, Xavier was inspired to visit Japan. He went from Goa to Malacca, where he took passage with seven companions, among them Anjiro and two other Japanese, in a Chinese piratical junk. They landed at Kagoshima in August 1549. The party received a friendly reaction from the powerful local daimyo (baron) of Satsuma, from whom Xavier learned that the emperor lived in Kyoto. He hoped to visit the emperor, not realizing that the mikado exercised no secular authority whatsoever, but the local daimyo made sure there was no opportunity. Xavier also went out of his way to make friends with the Zen Buddhist monks, who later would prove to be among the Jesuits' most formidable opponents. In the meantime, however, with the help of their Japanese companions the priests baptized about one hundred and fifty people, although Xavier was unsuccessful in his attempt to convert the abbot of the Buddhist monastery. Getting no help from the daimyo in seeing the mikado and finding that he was irritating the monks by his zealousness and verbal intemperance, Xavier, after ten months, took his party to the island of Hirado, where a Portuguese ship had arrived. From here he visited another daimyo at Yamaguchi, on Honshu Island, who supposed that he was preaching some new kind of Buddhism until the missionary began to disparage homosexuality, a practice rather enjoyed by monks and soldiers in Japan at that time. After coming close to losing his head and being hooted at when he preached in the streets of Yamaguchi, he again tried to visit the emperor, making a long and difficult journey to Kyoto which netted him nothing. On his return to Yamaguchi there were angry disputes with the Buddhist monks. One of Xavier's few converts, all of whom were poor at this time, was a blind musician baptized as Lourenzo. This man became the first Japanese Jesuit and made thousands of converts during his long life.

Xavier departed for Goa in a Portuguese ship in November 1551, accompanied by a Japanese envoy bearing letters from the local provincial ruler to the Portuguese viceroy. It is doubtful if very many real converts were made on this two year visit. The Jesuits' almost violent intolerance of Buddhism, which they did not understand, and, as in China, their misunderstanding of the Japanese regard for ancestors and accompanying household rites showed a severe lack of sensitivity to Japanese life and customs.

On his reutrn to Goa, and before leaving for Shang-ch'uan Island in the Pearl River, where he died in 1552, Xavier wrote to Ignatius Loyola asking him to send more Jesuits for the mission to Japan. Only a few were provided. By 1561 there were just six missionaries in Japan, spreading their efforts from the western to the central provinces. This number doubled by 1570. It is extraordinary that so few men could have been so abundantly successful, for Father Vilela, one of the most active missionaries, could report from Kyoto in 1564 that five hundred converts had been made and churches were already built in the capital. The hard-working Jesuits slowly improved their position, especially by interesting the rulers, some of whom were not at all unsympathetic to their efforts and most of whom wanted their friendship, to help establish trade with the Portuguese.

The missionaries' greatest good fortune, however, came when Oda Nobunaga succeeded in defeating many of his rivals and uniting large parts of the country in 1568. Once established as the most powerful man in Japan, he went on a campaign against the Buddhist monasteries (except the Zen sect), which had sided with his enemies. Ruthlessly he destroyed their buildings and slaughtered most of the monks. They were never entirely defeated but Nobunaga's opposition to the Buddhists, who had made things very difficult for the Jesuits, was associated with his patronage of the priests. Word of his protection spread rapidly and Christianity began to flourish. By 1571, the year that Nagasaki was given over to Jesuit governmental control, there were 30,000 Christians (a number that increased to about 500,000 in another decade) with two hundred churches and two seminaries. This was a remarkable achievement in thirty years, especially considering the small number of Jesuits in the country —only about twenty priests and thirty-four brothers in 1579.

When Nobunaga, on his death in 1582, was succeeded by his leading general, Hideyoshi, as military dictator of Japan, there were several high-ranking Christians in his government. The new shogun encouraged and entertained the Jesuits and was as hostile to the Buddhists as his predecessor. He gave the missionaries land for churches and, in fact, they seemed completely secure and on the threshold of enormous new successes.

Then, on July 25, 1587, Hideyoshi, in a completely unanticipated edict, reversed himself. He condemned the Jesuits and their teachings and ordered them out of the country within twenty days, but decreed that trade with the Portuguese should continue. No one really knows what caused this violent reaction. Hideyoshi protested that he did not object to Christianity but only to foreigners who were attacking the foundations of Japanese culture by preaching against their gods—i.e., condemning ancestor worship.

The Jesuits were unable to leave Japan within the prescribed time, since there was no ship due for six months. They behaved with greater discretion, celebrated mass privately, and hoped they might be able to remain. Hideyoshi relaxed and no severe persecutions followed his edict for the time being. The missionaries were allowed to stay on condition that they performed no baptisms and opened no churches. Surreptitiously and quietly, nevertheless, they carried on their work, rather relishing the thought that they might be martyrs. After a decade they began to believe Hideyoshi would not enforce his edict.

Unfortunately for them the matter was brought to another crisis with the arrival in 1593 of a group of Spanish Franciscan missionaries from the Philippines. Ignoring an agreement that Japan was to be left to the Jesuits, the Franciscans began to operate with unprincipled fervor in defiance of the edict. Hideyoshi tolerated them for three years until 1596, when the loud-mouthed Spanish pilot of a wrecked galleon proclaimed that both priests and traders were but a prelude to a foreign takeover of the country. This had been one of Hideyoshi's principal concerns and he acted swiftly. He made quick arrests of Franciscan converts and condemned twenty-six Christians, including six Franciscans, to death. In February 1597 they were all crucified at Nagasaki.

Hideyoshi did not concern himself further with the Christians, but from this time on Japanese Christians were subject to persecutions, sometimes killings, and the burning of their churches, while the missionaries, if they acted at all, did so carefully. Hideyoshi died in September 1598 to be succeeded by another strong man, Tokugawa Iyeyasu.

Although some Christian Japanese continued to be persecuted and others died as martyrs—102 in one family were beheaded in 1605—the Jesuits themselves enjoyed a respite. By 1600 most of the churches had been rebuilt and by 1615 there may have been half a million Christians in a population of about twenty-five million, a larger proportion than exists today. For some reason Christianity appealed to the Japanese much more than to other Asiatics, and the remarkable successes of Jesuit missionaries there were in sharp contrast to the frustration they experienced in China.

But the situation took another turn for the worse in 1614 when Iyeyasu banned Christianity. Two years later he was succeeded as shogun by Hidetada and the following year (1617) Japanese Christians were intensely persecuted. Hundreds were tortured, crucified, burned at the stake, or decapitated. Thousands more were imprisoned or exiled and had their property confiscated. Astonishingly, in the face of this treatment, new converts were still being made. The culmination came about 1625, when all remaining Christians had been driven underground. In 1638 there was a peasant revolt known as the Shimabara rebellion, in which Christians took the lead; it was put down with the slaughter of about 37,000 people.

Under Iyeyasu the Tokugawa shogunate had established its rule over Japan. There were, however, several powerful noble families who chafed under the Tokugawa authority. They were not powerful enough to rebel openly, but Iyeyasu and his successors were constantly afraid that they might be aided by one of the foreign trading elements. With Portuguese, Spanish, or Dutch assistance, a strong discontented vassal might successfully rise against the Tokugawas. Increasingly the shoguns moved to restrict the influence of Europeans and of Christianity. In 1625 the Spanish, both priests and laymen, were evacuated from the country. Growing restrictions on trade made the Portuguese position at Nagasaki more difficult each year. (By this time both the Dutch and the Chinese were doing more business than the Portuguese.) Inspections by Japanese officials became very severe. Macao was notified not to allow any more religious to enter Japan from the Philippines, and since both Spaniards and Portuguese had the same king the Japanese assumed that Macao officials had the necessary authority to prevent the entry of Spanish priests. Nevertheless missionaries continued to slip into the country, where priests and other Christians were tortured in increasing numbers.

The bloody Shimabara revolt of 1638 seemed proof of the continuing threat of Christianity to the regime, and it was suspected that the Portuguese had instigated it. In the spring of 1639 the shogun made the final decision to evict all the Portuguese and to prohibit them from ever again trading with Japan. Fear of rising Christian influence and power provoked the action, but, not unsurprisingly, the shogun was also strongly urged by the Dutch to expel the Portuguese. Following the arrival of two galliots from Macao in August action was taken. The cargoes were not allowed to be discharged and the Portuguese were held incommunicado at De-shima Island. On August 31 a decree arrived from Edo (now Tokyo) accusing the Portuguese of illegally continuing to bring in and aid missionaries and causing many Japanese to neglect their duties. The emperor mercifully agreed to spare the lives of the Portuguese on condition that they leave the country immediately. At the same time both Chinese and Dutch traders were warned that if they ever brought Christian missionaries to the country their vessels would be burned with all on board. The Portuguese embarked in their galliots in mid-October and departed for Macao.

The dismayed Portuguese in Macao could not believe that an appeal to continue the trade would be unsuccessful. After all, they owed considerable sums to their Japanese creditors and it seemed unthinkable that they would not want to recoup these potential losses. In 1640 an embassy headed by four of Macao's leading citizens was dispatched to Nagasaki with a special appeal to the shogun.

Iyemitsu, the shogun who had succeeded Hidetada, did not take a day to settle their fate. An edict condemning all but the thirteen lowest servants was sent to Nagasaki. The Portuguese, expecting a favorable reply, came when summoned, dressed in their gaudiest finery. They were aghast to hear the Japanese official say: "You villains! You have been forbidden ever to return to Japan on pain of death and have disobeyed that command. Last year you were guilty of death, but mercifully were granted your lives. Hence you have earned this time nothing but the most painful death; but since you have come without merchandise, and only beg for something, this sentence is commuted into an easy death."[2]

Tied up and thrown into jail for the night, they were taken next day to Martyrs' Mount outside Nagasaki. There, while the fortunate thirteen looked on, the sixty-one other members of the embassy were simultaneously decapitated. The Portuguese galliot was burned and the thirteen messengers sent back to Macao in a Chinese junk. There was no need of another warning. The Portuguese took the hint and never tried to open the trade again. The Dutch were overjoyed and held a Thanksgiving service at Batavia to celebrate the expulsion of the Portuguese.

The Tokugawa shoguns took other strict measures to seal off Japan, which had been the most open of Asiatic countries, from the outside world. Many Japanese had emigrated and established colonies in other parts of the East. These emigrants were forbidden to return and the death penalty was decreed for any others who attempted to leave the country. A prohibition was placed on building seagoing ships—henceforth only small coastal craft were to be constructed. Chinese merchants were restricted to the port of Nagasaki. The Dutch were forced to move their station from Hirado to Nagasaki, where they were allowed to trade only on De-shima Island in a prison-like atmosphere.

The withdrawal of the Japanese within their own islands was followed by intensified elimination of the Christians. It is estimated that by 1650 between two and three hundred thousand Christians had perished. Every missionary who attempted to enter the country was caught and executed, usually in some appropriate and peculiarly painful way.

The Red-Haired Barbarians

The Portuguese had enjoyed fifty years of exclusive monopoly in the Japan trade before the Dutch arrived in April 1600. Curiously, the first Dutch ship, the storm-buffeted *Liefde*, arriving with only 24 of its 110 crew members alive, came not from the East Indian headquarters at Batavia but from across the Pacific. Among the survivors was her sailing master, the Englishman William Adams, who was to remain in Japan for the rest of his life. Not until 1609, however, when two Dutch ships arrived at Hirado in late July, did the Portuguese have to worry about direct competition in Japan from their Protestant rivals. By that time Japanese trade with the Spaniards at Manila and the attempt of the Tokugawa shogun Iyeyasu to develop a Japanese overseas merchant marine were already giving deep concern to the Lusitanians. Now there were two European commercial rivals, even though the Spaniards were supposed to be allies. Iyeyasu, thinking that the rivalry might reduce silk prices, welcomed the Hollanders and gave them permission to set up a trading station at Hirado.

The Dutch, by preying on their shipping, had forced the Portuguese to give up their great ship in favor of a fleet of smaller galliots, which were designed for evasion rather than fighting although they occasionally gave a good account of themselves. By this means the Portuguese successfully eluded the Hollanders in the China Sea but were less fortunate in narrow Malacca Strait, where the Dutch intercepted and captured many vessels on their way back to Goa. The Dutch maintained an increasingly close blockade of the strait, which forecast the end of the commercial importance of Golden Goa, for the ships from Macao could no longer reach there without a running fight. Dutch command of the eastern seas was secure.

After the establishment of the Dutch at Hirado in 1609, competition with the Portuguese was even more intense. The Dutch trade slowly increased and by the 1630s was about equal to that of their rivals. Throughout this period the Dutch never lost an opportunity to warn the Japanese that unless the Portuguese trade was cut off the Lusitanians would continue to smuggle missionaries into the country who would carry on subversive activities detrimental to the Japanese government.

The Dutch carefully abstained from carrying out any Protestant missionary activities and persisted in their mealy-mouthed dealing with the Japanese, with whom they mostly got on very well. Both races were heavy drinkers and enjoyed convivial parties.

In 1613 a new variety of "red-haired barbarian" arrived. William Adams, the English sailing master of the *Liefde*, had made himself useful to Iyeyasu, married a Japanese woman, and settled down. He taught the Japanese to build Western-style ships and instructed them in geometry and other mathematics. He sent letters home urging the English to explore trading possibilities with Japan. Probably inspired at least in part by Adams, the East India Company dispatched the first English ship to Japan. Captain John Saris in the *Clove* sailed from Bantam on January 15, 1613, and, after shopping around the islands for spices, arrived at Hirado in June. He was commissioned to set up a factory there and had brought Richard Cocks to be installed as its first factor. Adams guided Saris to Edo where, after an exchange of gifts, the English were granted commercial privileges allowing them to live and trade in Japan. Cocks remained in charge of the East India Company's factory for the entire decade of its existence.

Hirado did not turn out to be a profitable trading station for the English. Although the two Protestant countries of England and Holland were supposedly allied against the Iberian nations, the Dutch never lost an opportunity to undercut their neighbors. At one point, when the Dutch seized an English ship on the high seas and brought her into Hirado, feelings became so intense that the local daimyo had to knock heads together to prevent open fighting. Cocks was a weak factor, the morale of the English staff was low, and drunkenness prevailed much of the time. One of Cocks's subordinates got away with calling him an "old drunken ass." Besides this, trade goods were in poor demand, few English ships called, and the interpreters were inadequate. Expensive presents to the Japanese, who took advantage of English ignorance, accomplished nothing. William Adams, the only Englishman in Japan who knew what was going on, died in 1620 and the factory staff was more in the dark than ever. In 1623 the company sent out Joseph Cockram in the *Bull* with orders to close up the station. Leaving the Dutch factor to collect any outstanding debts owed the company, the English traders embarked on the *Bull* and left Hirado on December 23, 1623. Cocks, whose accounts were in utter confusion, died at sea on the voyage home.

The expulsion of the Portuguese in 1639 left Japan with one thin thread of European contact through the Dutch, confined to the artificial island of De-shima in Nagasaki Harbor. Until 1640 Portuguese, which was learned by Japanese interpreters, remained the lingua franca of commerce for the East and was used by Dutch, English, and Japanese. It continued to hang on until the end of the century. Increasingly, however, Dutch replaced it as the trade language. A few Dutch also learned enough colloquial Japanese to converse, but this was forbidden after 1636 as the Japanese began their xenophobic retirement into self-imposed isolation.

Considering the small amount of actual contact each year between Japanese and Hollanders at the Nagasaki trading post during the more than two hundred years that this arrangement persisted, Dutch and European influences in Japan were more pronounced than might be expected. Japanese scholars studied Dutch and were eventually allowed to import Dutch books, provided they did not treat of Christianity. In the early eighteenth century the Japanese group called Rangakusha, or Dutch Scholars, became active. Some knowledge of European medicine was introduced. Dutch influence on the cartographical and geographical conceptions of the Japanese was considerable. Dutchmen and their ships and factory were popular subjects among printmakers. By the end of the century there was considerable knowledge in the country of other European sciences, especially astronomy, mathematics, and botany, as well as medicine. This knowledge of Western science and ways continued to increase moderately throughout the Dutch connection until the door opened again in 1854.

From being the most open and rapidly advancing country in Asia in the seventeenth century, Japan by its self-imposed isolation fell far behind during the two centuries when Europe was making rapid technological, economic, and political advances. Elimination of Christianity and the banishment of Europeans from the country where the impact had been so strong for a century not only excluded Western influence, but intensified the development of the distinctive Japanese culture, art, and literature during the two-hundred-year period of peaceful isolation.

CHAPTER 19

The China Trade

While the Chinese allowed the Portuguese their tenuous toehold at Macao from about 1555 on, that trading port, after the ending of the trade with Japan in 1640, deteriorated into a sleepy, impoverished outpost. Aside from Macao and the Portuguese's Jesuit mission at Peking and a few other stations, Europeans were not tolerated in the Middle Kingdom.

The Spanish attempted unsuccessfully to open relations with the Chinese in 1575 and from time to time thereafter, but their only substantial contact was with the Fukien traders who came to Manila. The Dutch fared no better. In 1604 and 1607 when they sent ships to Canton their requests to be allowed to trade were rejected. When they attempted to force the issue militarily by attacking Macao in 1622, they were repulsed with heavy losses. Retreating to Formosa, the Dutch then established Fort Zelandia, which Koxinga captured less than forty years later. Dutch embassies were allowed to visit Peking in 1655 and 1665 but, although they conformed in every detail of protocol, from bringing presents to performing the kowtow, no trading privileges were forthcoming. Even their provision of a naval force to help the emperor defeat Koxinga got them nothing. As far as the emperor was concerned, they were just another tributary kingdom, doing what was expected of them. The Dutch could not repeat their Japanese success and contented themselves with a little coastal smuggling.

While assorted barbarians were vainly probing at the sea frontier of China, Muscovites were trudging across thousands of miles of tundra. In 1618 two envoys from the West, military officers sent by the Russian provincial governor of Siberia, arrived at Peking and returned to Moscow to tell their tale.

Coming from a tsar as stiff-necked if not as secretive as the Chinese emperor and arriving without the absolutely essential gifts, they accomplished nothing and returned to Siberia. This was the first of many Russian efforts to establish relations with the celestial empire.

The Russian advance across Siberia was slow and methodical. They pushed on, building forts and establishing fur-trading posts on their advancing frontier, until they reached the Pacific by 1637. The migration was the plodding progress of settlers in an inhospitable environment—not the swift advance of a conqueror, for there was nothing to conquer.

Repeated Russian envoys to Peking were failures. The first in 1618 brought no tribute and therefore was not received. Another embassy in 1654 refused to perform the kowtow, although the Dutch did it the same year. After all, what were three kneelings and nine prostrations when there was a florin to be made. Baikov, the Russian envoy of 1654, refused to deliver the tsar's letter to anyone but the emperor and since he would not perform the ceremonials proper to an envoy from a tribute prince he was sent away. The same thing happened again in 1660 and was repeated in 1676. All Russian attempts at establishing commercial treaties and diplomatic relations were frustrated, but they continued to build their little forts along the Amur River.

Once the Manchus had firmly established their rule in China in 1680, they began to look to their frontiers. Military forces, moving into the Amur region, eliminated Russian posts along the lower river and attacked Albasin, one of the principal Russian forts. This pressure on the Russians, and a Mongol uprising against the Chinese, brought ambassadors of the two countries together for a peace conference at Nerchinsk, where the treaty of that name was signed in 1689. The Chinese negotiators arrived backed by a large and intimidating show of force. The Russian envoy, Fedor Alexovich Golovin, tried to offset the Chinese display of ninety armed river boats and ranks of foot, horse, camels, and cannon with pomp, rich uniforms, and martial music. The resulting treaty, the first international agreement in which the Chinese ever took part, established the eastern end of the boundary between China and Russia, stopped the Russians from settling south of the Amur River, made a trade agreement, razed the fort at Albasin, and established an extraterritorial agreement whereby criminals would be extradited for punishment by their own governments. K'ang-hsi was so pleased that he rewarded the Jesuits, who acted as interpreters for his ambassador, with land for a church within the city of Peking and an edict of toleration for Christians.

A very serious problem for K'ang-hsi in the late seventeenth and early eighteenth centuries was the rising power of the Dzungar, one of the western Mongol tribes. He feared an alliance between them and the Russians as much as he mistrusted the latter's increasing influence among the eastern Mongols. To bring these disturbing situations under control, it was essential that the boundary between the two empires be further defined. K'ang-hsi died in 1722, but his successor was equally determined to put a limit to Russian encroachment. A Russian delegation, led by Count Sava Vladislavich as ambassador, spent six months in Peking negotiating with their Chinese counterparts. The meetings were then transferred to Kiakhta on the Siberian border where the "Treaty of the Frontier," signed in 1727, established the boundary between Mongolia and Siberia. The Treaty of Kiakhta also excluded the Russians from Mongolia, but they acquired rights to trade regularly at Kiakhta under the same terms as the seagoing foreigners who traded at Canton. Thus each country achieved what it wanted most—the Russians a regular and dependable trade contact and the Chinese a secure boundary further increasing their isolation.

Sino-Russian trade through Kiakhta continued without serious interruption for as long as the celestial empire lasted. It is interesting that the Russians accommodated themselves to the strange Chinese ways much better than other Europeans on the coast. The result of their infinite patience and adaptability ensured an uninterrupted flow of both government and private trade through Kiakhta. Siberian and New World furs, leather goods, and woolen, linen, and cotton fabrics entered China, while cotton cloth, silks, tea, porcelains, lacquer ware, tobacco, and rhubarb were exported to Russia.

Canton

Direct English trade with China was slow in developing, but it was inevitable. Portuguese and Chinese authorities alike were more than a little concerned on June 27, 1637, when four English ships, commanded by Captain John Weddell, dropped anchor off Macao. The Portuguese, though polite, had no intention of giving the English any assistance, for one of the reasons they were allowed in Macao was to keep other foreigners out of the Pearl River and away from Canton. The Chinese for their part associated these new "red barbarians" with the Dutch, whom they particularly disliked and distrusted.

Weddell's heavily armed fleet was sent out by an independent merchant group, headed by Sir William Courteen, which was trespassing on the East India Company monopoly. The hot-tempered captain succeeded in annoying the Portuguese and making the Chinese more suspicious of foreigners than ever. After waiting a month off Macao, Weddell sailed up the Pearl River and entered the Boca Tigris. After the Chinese directed an ineffectual fire on his ships from an old fort, he took the stronghold. Interminable negotiations got him nowhere. Following on some small illicit trade, three of his merchants were held by the Chinese, who also attempted to burn his ships with a fleet of fire junks and almost succeeded. Weddell retaliated by destroying a village, burning junks, and seizing livestock and provisions. He succeeded in rescuing his three men only by going hat in hand to the Portuguese governor of Macao and finally departed on December 27. The fleet dispersed off Sumatra, and Weddell and his ship were lost with all hands on the voyage home. The expedition was a disaster.

A handful of English ships made equally unsuccessful attempts to trade in China during the remainder of the century. As we have seen, Koxinga's son, Cheng Chin (called by the English Cotsang), allowed the English to establish a factory at Amoy in 1676, but when the Manchus reconquered the area in 1681 the English were forced to withdraw. A real breakthrough came in 1685 when the enlightened Emperor K'ang-hsi, in an edict, opened all the ports of China to foreign shipping.

In 1698 the old East India Company received serious competition when William III granted the right to trade in the East to a New East India Company and for nearly a decade the bitter competition was detrimental to them both. The ruinous rivalry came to an end in 1709 when the Old and New Companies combined to form the United East India Company, which monopolized Eastern trade for many years.

In 1699 the New Company ship *Macclesfield* (made the first successful, though difficult, voyage to Canton. Following this venture the company sent one or more ships every year to trade at Canton, as well as at Amoy, Foochow, and Chusan (the port of Ningpo). The first English warship the Chinese had ever seen appeared before their disbelieving eyes in 1742, when Captain George Anson arrived at Canton in his battered *Centurion* on his round-the-world voyage. Her ominous presence gave them no assurance. Anson got his repairs and supplies with difficulty and left, returning a few months later with a rich Spanish Manila galleon worth over four hundred thousand pounds. The Chinese regarded its seizure as a shocking piratical act typical of these worst-of-all red barbarians. Anson, however, redeemed himself somewhat in Chinese eyes by helping extinguish a serious fire which threatened the city. In gratitude supplies were provided and the Chinese got rid of him as quickly as possible.

As both Chinese merchants and officials became increasingly aware of profits to be made from the spiraling popularity of tea drinking in Europe, the trade barrier began to crumble. Imperial concern about and recognition of this commerce resulted in an edict by Emperor Chi'en-lung in 1757, reversing K'ang-hsi's 1685 proclamation and restricting all foreign trade to Canton, where most of it had gravitated anyway and where it could be better controlled.

Following this ruling, the method of trade that was to last well into the nineteenth century developed at Canton. Overseeing the system was the Hoppo, as he was called by the foreigners. Since 1685 this official had been collector of customs for Kwangtung Province. He was appointed directly by the emperor and was usually a relative. Theoretically he ranked below the provincial governor and he did not meddle in the internal affairs of the province, but his power was great and his position enormously lucrative. The Hoppo squeezed as much out of the merchants as possible for the emperor and also made himself an enormously rich man, usually in about four years.

All trade with the Fan Kwae, or "foreign devils," was transacted through a licensed guild of merchants called the Cohong. The trade was strictly codified by Eight Regulations, but indifferently regulated. Foreign warships, for instance, could not enter the Boca Tigris, or The Bogue as it was called. Neither European women nor firearms could be brought into Canton. The foreign merchants were confined to the factories and grounds along Thirteen Factory Street and were forbidden to ride in sedan chairs, employ Chinese servants, or enter any other part of the city. They could remain at the factories only during the winter trading season. Some of the Eight Regulations were more strictly enforced than others, but even those often relaxed were always held as a threat by the hong merchants (Chinese firms in the European trade), who were responsible and accountable for the foreigners' behavior. Factories were leased to the Europeans by the hong merchants. Since the factors could not remain in Canton during the off season, they retreated downriver to Macao for lodgings and the companies also leased buildings there for the transaction of their business. Chinese were forbidden to teach Europeans the language and all trade negotiations were conducted in pidgin English, which became the lingua franca.

The English were the largest foreign group and dominated the Canton trade. At various times factories were also leased to the French, Danish, Swedes, Spanish, and Americans, Oftentimes British subjects were trading independently under other flags and acting as consuls for other countries to avoid the monopoly of the John Company (as the East India Company was jokingly called). The row of factories in European-style architecture, each with a tall flagpole in front flying the national colors, and the river before them crowded with junks and sampans were a colorful and impressive sight. They were by far the most popular subject of the Chinese oil paintings done in European style so desirable in Europe and America. Ships anchored in Whampoa Reach, thirteen miles below the city, and cargoes were lightered between them and the factories. Here too lay the hulks used as receiving ships for the transfer of opium.

At first the trade was in the usual variety of Chinese goods—silks, of course, but also rhubarb, porcelain, lacquer boxes and furniture, bric-a-brac, and fans. As European, particularly English, consumption of tea increased, it became the principal cargo and produced enormous profits. But the old difficulty of finding anything to exchange in China, a self-sufficient country, was not easy to solve. At first the English tried unsuccessfully to sell their woolens to the Chinese. Some India cotton and pepper could be disposed of, but it soon became evident that silver was the one item desired by China without limit. Therefore a constant search went on for a product that was not such a severe monetary drain.

By the late eighteenth century the number of British ships arriving at Canton each year was more than double the number for all other nationalities combined. These, however, were not all East India Company ships nor did they all come from England. More than half were private merchants in the so-called Country trade. At the same time that the East India Company, with its trading monopoly, gradually became dominant in India—and its employees served as both governmental administrators and commercial agents—a parallel local coastwise shipping developed for the entire Indian Ocean area. The Country ships, built in India and owned by independent British merchants, carried all this coastal commerce and became an important element in the China trade.

The Country trade was dominated by British captains and entrepreneurs, who were licensed by the John Company. Operating out of India, Country ships largely replaced native shipping in coastal commerce. Gradually this trade expanded eastward to China, carrying silver bullion and Bombay raw cotton (for manufacturing into "nankeens" for export), and returning with silk and tea. Later Bengal opium became the principal product going eastward.

Through the Country trade, the East India Company was able to recoup some of the drainage of silver that went into China. Country ships sold India

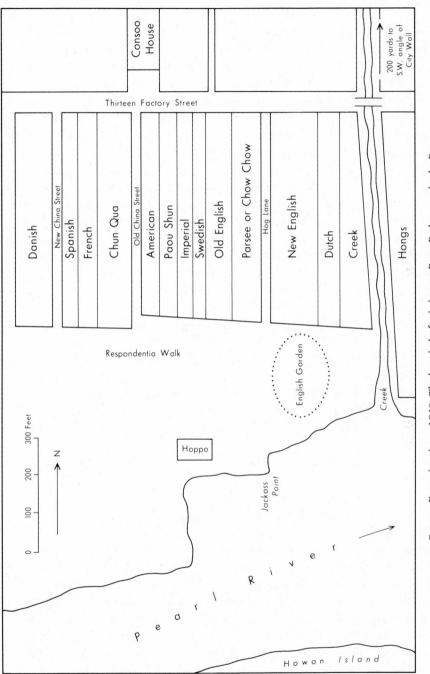

Canton Factories about 1840. The hospital of missionary Peter Parker was in the Parsee, or Chow Chow, Factory. Adapted from Maurice Collis, *Foreign Mud* (London: Faber & Faber, 1946; New York: W. W. Norton, 1968). Reproduced by permission.

cottons and, in increasing amounts, opium to Canton for silver, which could not be taken out of China. The East India Company therefore gave the Country merchants bills payable in London in return for their silver, which was then used in China to buy the company's tea. By the end of the eighteenth century opium became by far the most important of the company's exports to China and provided the only way to obtain tea in sufficient quantity to supply the enormous English demand.

Opium smoking in China arose from the contact of Chinese traders with the Dutch in Java, who had the habit of mixing a little opium with their tobacco. This practice had an enormous and inexplicable appeal to the local Chinese, who were soon smoking opium straight and who introduced the custom to the mainland in the mid-seventeenth century. By 1729 the effects of the drug were so obvious to Chinese authorities that there was an edict prohibiting its importation. But the edict was never really enforced. The mandarins simply used it as another way of squeezing more "kumshaw" from the Fan Kwae, and the foreign devils continued to import it. Most of the opium came from Bengal where company officers owned a monopoly of the supply. They sold the opium to Country traders to carry to Canton, and thus the company was not directly breaking Chinese law. At the Canton end officials regularly cleared ships carrying opium and the trade went on. Thus as tea drinking rose in England, opium smoking rose in China. Nor was this all. The sale of the Bengal crop became so valuable that the East India Company, with its increasing administrative problems in the subcontinent of India, soon came to depend on its sale for financing the government of India.

The Cohong merchants were squeezed for large sums of money not only by the Hoppo but also by lesser mandarins, the governor, and other provincial officials, and after 1760 this practice became so burdensome that many of the hong merchants were forced into bankruptcy. This in turn caused justifiable consternation among their creditors, especially the Country traders, to whom the Cohong owed large sums of money. With the situation becoming more serious, the European trading companies jointly notified the Hoppo in 1771 that they would no longer do business with the Cohong. In the face of this display of unity the Hoppo abolished the Cohong. It was reorganized by the Hoppo in 1783 with a limit of twelve (later increased to thirteen) merchants, who continued the trade with foreigners until the guild monopoly was ended by the Opium War in 1839.

After the American Revolution the Canton trade was predominantly English and American, for the latter were no longer bound to recognize the John Company's monopoly. The Danish and Swedish companies went out of business about this time and the French and Dutch continued the trade through private merchants, for their companies had been dissolved earlier. Whereas other nationalities might have up to half a dozen ships at Canton during a season, the British might have sixty to seventy, about evenly divided between the big East Indiamen and smaller Country ships.

By the last decade of the eighteenth century the Canton trade was enormous and affected all of India and English-speaking lands everywhere, as well as many others. But the Chinese still regarded it as part of the tribute system. Any political or diplomatic relations conducted by the Son of Heaven were oriented toward Central Asia, not toward the seafaring barbarians. At the same time the industrial revolution had increased British manufactures to a point where larger markets were sought and free trade became desirable. Another source of frustration and an irritant to company and Country merchants alike was the Chinese judicial system of demanding an English culprit for execution, whether guilty or not, if a Chinaman was even accidentally killed by an Englishman. The British increasingly came to the conclusion that an extraterritorial base on the China coast was a necessity.

Foreign embassies from Western powers to the emperor at Peking had been notably unsuccessful. Nevertheless, since the British company had been unable to achieve any relationship with China on an appropriate and dignified great-power basis, it was decided by Henry Dundas, head of the company's board of control, to send an embassy to China. Although the company footed the bill, the embassy was an official ambassadorial delegation from George III to Emperor Ch'ien-lung to request that some northern ports be opened to British vessels and that regular tariff fees be paid rather than the highly variable and usually exorbitant squeeze. Lord Macartney, an experienced diplomat, was selected to lead this important embassy.

The Macartney delegation left for China in H.M.S. *Lion* and after stopping at Macao for consultation with company officials, sailed north to as near Peking as possible. Loaded with an enormous quantity of presents, which were regarded by the Chinese as tribute, Macartney met Ch'ien-lung on September 14, 1793, at one of the most resplendent spectacles ever witnessed. The ambassador refused to perform the kowtow, but the emperor was cordial. The pomp and politeness were misleading, however. Requests to cede the island of Chusan for a British base and to open the ports of Ningpo and Tientsin were later utterly rejected by letter, and it was pointed out that Europeans were fortunate even to be able to trade at Canton. The embassy was a complete failure.

A similar embassy from the Dutch in 1795 had a more ignoble reception and no better luck. Another British attempt, the ill-conceived and (until it reached China) unadvised embassy led by Lord Amherst in 1816, arrived at Peking after a night of rough travel, refused to kowtow to the waiting emperor, and was dismissed without ever having an audience.

As we have seen, the years immediately following the American Revolution brought a new flag to China. The first American ship, appropriately named the *Empress of China*, arrived at Canton on August 30, 1784. The number of American vessels, all from northeastern Atlantic ports between Salem and Baltimore, increased rapidly and, while never rivaling the English in numbers, were second only to them. After 1807 the trade was almost entirely English and American. There were probably over a thousand American voyages to China between 1784 and 1844.

Compared with the East Indiamen, American vessels were small, seldom exceeding three hundred tons, and more suitable for the American type of trade. Voyages almost never went directly to Canton after the supply of ginseng (the only North American product viable in the China market) gave out, which it did very quickly. Americans had little silver and were forced to shop around for products salable at Canton. These they found in sea otter and other furs from the Northwest Coast, sandalwood from Hawaii and Fiji, bêche-de-mer from Fiji and a few other islands, sealskins from the islands of the extreme Southern Hemisphere near Antarctica, and lesser products of the Pacific such as tortoise shell, pearl shell, and edible birds' nests. Soon American traders were competing with the British, matching India raw cotton with their own cotton from the Southern states and Bengal opium with Turkish opium from Smyrna. Return cargoes, like those of the English, were largely black and green teas, sets of chinaware, silks, nankeens, and minor products such as cassia (cinnamon) and bric-a-brac. The American trade, unlike that of England and some other European countries, was not dominated by a single company, but carried on by independent merchants in Salem, Boston, Providence, New York, Philadelphia, and Baltimore. From it came much of the capital that was to later finance New England's industrial revolution.

Opium

The great tragedy of the early nineteenth century China trade was the increase in the importation of opium from India. By 1800 the amount had multiplied over four times from the preceeding decades to some 4,500 piculs (one picul equals 133 1/3 pounds) a year. In the next quarter century this had risen to about 40,000 piculs. As opium smoking spread, the social evil permeated every part of Chinese society from criminals to imperial officials. People were demoralized and reduced to poverty by its use. As we have seen, an edict of 1729 forbade opium importation, but corruption completely vitiated the ban's intent and the trade flourished. Chinese smugglers vied with foreign traders, who brought their cargoes to the floating hulks for warehousing in Whampoa Reach, for the enormous profits. The opium habit spread and so did the degree of official corruption. All condoned the trade; all shared in its profits. And as the number of addicts rose into the millions in China, the British commercial dependence on the receipts of the trade in India increased in proportion.

The Canton trade continued to increase but became less regulated and more demoralized. The most stabilizing influence was the East India Company, whose monopoly for trade in China ended in 1834, as it had been abolished twenty-one years earlier in India. Problems that had been troublesome for years became intensified. Hong merchants, continuously squeezed by government officials, were almost always in financial straits and bankruptcies became more frequent. The unending conflict between English and Chinese legal systems and punishments was often tacitly but never entirely resolved. Opium, woolens, and cotton were the big three imports to China and, as the trade mushroomed, the traditional flow of silver into the country was reversed and the silver drain became a matter of concern to Chinese officials. At the same time Chinese made destitute by the opium habit began to emigrate in large numbers to work in many countries as foreign laborers in a system often very close to slavery.

A Chinese attempt to enforce opium regulations in 1821 forced the withdrawal of the warehouse hulks and the opium fleet from Whampoa downriver to Lintin Island. It was more obvious than ever that Britain needed an extraterritorial base on the China coast. That same year the foreign factories burned in the great Canton fire that wiped out two-thirds of the city.

Two years before the end of the East India Company's monopoly, a new firm consisting of two enterprising young men, William Jardine and James Matheson, who were doing well as independent traders, became prominent. Jardine, Matheson and Company developed fast opium clippers and vastly improved drug distributing along the coast.

With the end of the East India Company's monopoly in 1834, the British government sent Lord Napier to Canton as superintendant of trade to continue the control long held by the company. He was an ill-chosen, Scottish sheep farmer and retired naval officer with no experience in the Far East or diplomacy. His inexperience immediately brought him into an impasse with the Chinese officials. When they stopped trade with the British—the usual Chinese way of dealing with troublesome foreigners—he attempted to force his way upriver with two frigates and was stopped. The concerted efforts of hong and British merchants, who were the losers in the trade stoppage, brought about an ineffective compromise. One of the Chinese conditions was the appointment of a taipan or English head trader responsible for all British trade and merchants. Napier retreated to Macao where he died in October 1834. In another two years the Canton situation was hopeless. An attempt by one element of Chinese officialdom, which had the backing of many foreigners but only lip service from the British merchants most closely involved, to legalize the importation of opium in order to stop the silver drain from the country was not approved by the emperor. He instead ordered suppression of the trade in 1837. The order had some success in the Canton area and in 1839 the death penalty was ordered for almost anyone—distributors, consumers, or foreigners—who had anything to do with opium. But smuggling by armed opium clippers along the coast increased. While the Chinese authorities attempted to suppress the trade, Captain Charles Elliot, the superintendant of British trade, was still trying to get trade agreements but was unable to communicate with the Chinese governor except through the hong merchants. Messages still had to go through the Petition Gate (the one place in Canton where foreigners could communicate with go-betweens) and not directly to the Yamen, or official establishment. Palmerston, the foreign secretary, wrote Elliot that this procedure was unsuitable and that officers of the king must communicate directly with their equals in the Chinese government. It was a standoff.

The First Opium War

The situation was rapidly deteriorating. While American and British opium clippers fought their way upriver, Elliot retired to Macao. In 1838 the governor of Kwangtung, Têng Ting-chan, ordered a series of executions which shocked the foreign community; an attempted strangulation in the foreign recreation area resulted in a Canton riot between British sailors and Chinese—the most serious incident that had so far occurred. The grave event brought Elliot hurrying back to Canton in a fruitless attempt to smooth the troubled waters. In January 1839 while he was so engaged, the emperor's order abolishing the use of opium arrived. Its immediate effect was to cause the bottom to drop out of the opium market. Trade stopped along the Pearl River.

The reason for the sudden halt in trade was the anticipated arrival of the imperial high commissioner, Lin Tse-hsü, assigned by the emperor to wipe out the opium trade at Canton. Lin, today one of the great Chinese national heroes, arrived in the lead of a splendid fleet of mandarin boats on March 10, 1839. He was a corpulent, experienced administrator, energetic and intelligent, but poorly informed about the Canton trade and ignorant of Westerners and their institutions.

Commissioner Lin did not wait to acquaint himself with these subjects. He went into action immediately to eliminate the opium trade by crushing the Chinese importers and distributors. His next step was to force 350 foreigners to surrender their opium stocks by confining them, along with Elliot, in the Thirteen Factories for six weeks, with no supplies, water, or Chinese servants. When they gave in and handed over twenty thousand chests of opium the stock was publicly destroyed. Elliot, as the British government's representative, took full responsibility for surrender of the opium. In July the situation was further aggravated by the death of a Chinese at the hands of drunken English sailors. The old problem of judicial jurisdiction could not have recurred at a more sensitive time.

Lin forced the entire British community with their ships to retreat to Macao; in August they withdrew under further pressure to sparsely inhabited Hong Kong Island, with its magnificent deep-water harbor. Meanwhile Russell and Company and other American firms who stayed on at Canton took care of the British tea trade through the successful hong merchant Howqua. Emperor Tao-kuang congratulated Commissioner Lin on his able handling of the situation.

Lin's glory was short-lived. He believed that he had now suppressed the opium traffic and set about restoring the normal legitimate Canton trade, but it could not be done. The British in Macao and Hong Kong Harbour had no intention of returning to Canton except on their own terms. Since the Americans conformed to every regulation Lin imposed, he thought that the British would soon come back and trade on his terms. In an attempt to force the

British to do this, Lin occupied and fortified the base of Kowloon peninsula opposite Hong Kong and organized impressive naval displays in the waters of the river mouth. He visited Macao, evacuated by the British, in triumph. The unhappy British merchants, angry with Elliot for giving up the opium stocks, sweated it out on shipboard in sweltering Hong Kong Harbour and gradually began drifting back to Macao.

Lin, believing that the British were beginning to crack, which indeed some of them were, demanded that each individual sign a bond placing himself under Chinese law before resuming normal trade at Canton. Elliot refused to allow this. When a British Indiaman arrived and submitted to Lin's demand, Elliot decided to act. Fortunately two British frigates had arrived shortly before, and with them he sailed into the Boca Tigris, where a fleet of twenty-nine war junks was anchored.

Attempts at communication with Lin failed and on November 3, 1839, Elliot decided to attack the Chinese fleet to prevent it from eluding him and assaulting the British merchant ships at Hong Kong. The two frigates had no difficulty defeating the war junks.

Meanwhile, Palmerston in London, listening to William Jardine's account of the siege of the Canton factories and the disgraceful treatment of the queen's representative by Commissioner Lin, decided to send an expeditionary force to China to back up demands on Peking, obtain indemnity for the destroyed opium and other merchant losses, and establish a proper respect for further plenipotentiaries of the queen. The force, under Rear Admiral George Elliot (cousin of Captain Charles Elliot), as plenipotentiary, consisting of four thousand British and Indian troops in twenty-seven transports, escorted by three line-of-battle ships, fourteen frigates and sloops of war, and four armed steamers of the East India Company, arrived in Hong Kong Harbour in late June 1840.

The British force had no difficulty in establishing complete superiority over China's antiquated military and naval forces. By September Commissioner Lin was demoted but, along with Governor Têng, stayed on as adviser to Ch'i-shan, who became governor of Kwangtung and took over negotiations. Lin eventually left Canton May 3, 1841, under a sentence of exile to Turkestan. Not only was China now at war with Britain; the opium trade was still going on.

Admiral Elliot was forced to return home because of illness and negotiations reverted to Captain Charles Elliot. The English still insisted on getting an island off the China coast and the Chinese were equally adamant in refusing. On January 7, 1841, in frustration, the British seized the Boca Tigris forts and destroyed eighteen war junks with heavy Chinese losses. This brought about the Chinese offer of Hong Kong and an indemnity of six million dollars for seized opium; in return the British evacuated the part of Chusan Island which they had occupied. Furthermore, future negotiations between the two countries would no longer be on the wholly unrealistic tribute system but as equals. Possession of Hong Kong took place on January 25.

Emperor Tao-kuang in Peking, however, issued orders to Governor Ch'i-shan to drive the British out entirely, and in exactly a month's time Chinese attacks on British shipping resulted in the reoccupation of the Boca Tigris forts. The British then captured Whampoa, pushed on to Canton, and took over the factories. A concerted Chinese attack by troops, batteries, and fire ships on the night of May 21 was repulsed and Elliot threatened to take Canton.

He did not have to. The Treaty of Canton was concluded, restoring trade which began immediately since the opium clippers had followed the men-of-war upriver. The Chinese paid another six million dollars in ransom for Canton plus additional indemnities, their troops pulled back sixty miles from the city, the forts between Whampoa and the sea were disarmed, and the British fleet returned to Hong Kong. Even though the occupation of Hong Kong was provisional upon final execution of a treaty, Elliot declared the place a free port and began putting parcels of land up for sale. But settlement was slow in coming as rampant fever, probably malaria, kept the death rate fearfully high and tornadoes whipped apart new wooden houses shortly after they were built.

In August Captain Charles Elliot was recalled and succeeded by Sir Henry Pottinger, who arrived at Macao on the tenth. Elliot's abandonment of Chusan and addition of Hong Kong to the British crown were not appreciated; both the opium merchants and the government felt that he had not carried out his orders and had accepted too little indemnity for the confiscated opium. He was nearly as discredited as his opposite number, Commissioner Lin, and henceforth he served as consul general in minor posts.

Pottinger proceeded to carry out the instructions of Palmerston which Elliot had thought ill-considered. He sent the fleet northward before the end of August, reoccupied Chusan, and took several other ports. For a year the intermittent fighting went on. A counterattack by the Chinese in March 1842 failed. The British, defeating the ill-trained, undisciplined, opium-smoking troops of the emperor, took Shanghai, Chinkiang, where the Yangtze River intersects the Grand Canal leading to Peking, and threatened Nanking. The emperor yielded and agreed to negotiate.

By the Treaty of Nanking, signed August 29, 1842, Hong Kong was ceded to the queen forever, the ports of Canton, Amoy, Foochow, Ningpo, and Shanghai were opened to foreign trade, and the British who resided in those places were granted rights of extraterritoriality under their own laws. The monopoly of the hong merchants was abolished, commercial tariffs were to be regulated at all treaty ports, and the Chinese paid an additional twenty-one million Mexican dollars for confiscated opium, hong merchants' debts, and war costs to the Indian government.

With the opening of the treaty ports came the beginning of the end of Chinese isolation and, not only a new Anglo-Chinese relationship, but a new relationship with all Western powers. No longer would the barbarians, red or otherwise, negotiate from an inferior position to the representatives of the Son of Heaven. The British, by the Treaty of Nanking, established a pattern for the Western world. But they were indefensibly wrong in using opium as the catalyst, and the Chinese official position was unquestionably right.

Three other treaties followed that of Nanking—the British Supplementary Treaty of the Bogue in 1843, the Wanghia Treaty with the Americans, negotiated by Caleb Cushing and signed July 3, 1844, and the French Treaty of Whampoa signed October 24 the same year. Cushing, drawing on the British experience, made a somewhat better treaty, fairer to the Chinese, in which the consul was not held liable for the payment of duties. Cushing secured all the rights and privileges won by the British, with the exception of the cession of an island. The Americans' treaty left the responsibility of protecting American citizens to Chinese authorities, provided for the payment of customs duties in cash, defined contraband goods, and assured the Chinese that the United States would not protect smugglers. None of these treaties, however, legalized the opium trade. Peking would not consent to sanction importation of the drug, but gave no more than lip service to suppressing it. The British did not officially recognize the trade, but British, American, Chinese, and others made enormous fortunes, and use of opium in China doubled between 1830 and 1850. The signing of the treaties which had been forced on China brought an end to an era. Chinese isolation at long last crumbled and international equality of individuals in negotiation prevailed.

Legal trade rose dramatically after the opening of the treaty ports and with an accompanying increase of piracy along the coast. Much of the legal trade in teas, silks, and porcelain was still paid for by the illegal opium trade.

As the tea and silk exports rose, more foreign firms, especially British and American ones, established offices, consulates, and their own settlements. The growth of Hong Kong and the treaty ports, particularly Shanghai, mushroomed. China was opened up to a new flood of missionary activity. New classes of Chinese grew up associated with the foreign merchant houses. These were mainly Cantonese. A new kind of Chinese merchant, the comprador, handled the business that was once the monopoly of the hong merchants and these entrepreneurs eventually developed into a new and influential business class. The Chinese coolie trade shipped thousands of male workers to the phosphate islands, Hawaiian plantations, California and Australian gold fields, and nearly everywhere that labor was required. Besides this trade, at its worst closely akin to slavery, other thousands of Chinese emigrated freely to Southeast Asia, Malaya, Indonesia, and elsewhere.

Thus the opening of the treaty ports dramatically intensified Western influence on the celestrial empire, began the penetration of the vast interior, and influenced the beginnings of great social changes in Chinese life. Business grew and flourished; new religious, medical, and academic ideas became dispersed. However, the imperial government showed signs of disintegration and, after 1850, unrest grew into revolution.

CHAPTER 20

Eastern Impact on the West

There is no resemblance whatsoever between European impact in the Pacific islands and the collision between the great Eastern and Western civilizations that took place in the Far East from about 1500 to 1850. Except for such aspects as the fashion of entertaining assorted South Sea travelers described in Chapter 3, the dilettante effect on Rousseau's philosophy, the insatiable consumption by readers of books on Pacific voyages, and a flurry of theatrical productions, imaginary paintings, and wall paper, the South Seas had little effect on the mainstream of European culture. Perhaps the most lasting was the fashionable, transitory, imaginatively appealing, literary fiction of the Pacific paradise on earth which persisted well into the twentieth century. In sum White Western contact with the islands of the Pacific was traumatic and often devastating. The reverse impact was momentarily voguish but, with the literary exception, superficial.

On the contrary when West met East in Asia the eyes of European man were opened wide, while those of East Asia were very often deliberately closed. To some extent this was due to the times. Europe, from the late fifteenth century on, was in a period of increasing intellectual activity and curiosity. The Renaissance triggered the spirit that produced two hundred and fifty years of discovery and exploration, merging into another century and a half of exploration and trade the profits of which financed the industrial revolution.

Not only strange new cultures but exotic flora and fauna impinged upon an already awakened European mind. Animals, sometimes barely heard of, were brought to Western cities from the earliest days of oriental trade. Gawk-

276

ing crowds flocked to see strange jungle beasts which had hitherto been only names to them. In 1515 the first live rhinoceros to be seen in Europe since Roman times arrived at Lisbon from Goa as a gift to King Manuel I and, in a test of behemoths, outfaced a young elephant. The creature also served as the model for Dürer's famous engraving of a rhinoceros, completed the same year. Having gazed his fill of the huge beast, King Manuel, probably following the custom of European monarchs of sending extraordinary gifts to the pope—he had already sent an elephant the year before—but possibly in desperation or a weak moment of altruism, shipped the animal on as a present to Pope Leo X. The Good Father was spared the care but enjoyed the spectacle of the rhinoceros, as it was drowned in a shipwreck on the Riviera and arrived in Rome, stuffed, the following February. Captain Jacob Crowninshield, of the famous Salem shipping family, brought the first live elephant ever seen in America from India to New York in 1816. The creature was walked through Connecticut and Massachusetts to the White Mountains and exhibited in the villages at twenty-five cents a head for the edification of the astounded inhabitants.

In India the Mogul empire was about to disintegrate and in Indonesia small states and warring rulers fragmentized native resistance to the Portuguese, the Dutch and, later, the English, who were soon well established there. East Asia presented a far different facade. China was a vast populous country, mostly well governed for centuries, with elaborate, deep-seated, traditional social customs, legal system, and attitudes. Isolationism, by desire and policy, was extreme. The country was self-sufficient. The emperor, seated on his dragon throne, was the benevolent Son of Heaven from whom all blessings flowed and in whose service princes and peasants toiled. Many Chinese institutions were far superior to anything of the kind in Europe at the time. The postal service and the civil service with its training and examinations were well-organized models that the West could profitably emulate. The traditions of pacifism, politeness, Confucian morality, the high social standing of the scholar (rather than the soldier) all embodied virtues little regarded in Europe. So satisfied were the Chinese with their culture, government, and life that only the Jesuits (whom they respected as learned men) were allowed within the country's borders. All other "barbarians," unless they came bearing tribute, in itself a privilege, and prepared to acknowledge their subjugation to the emperor, were kept clinging precariously to the few points of trade allowed them by the government of the celestial kingdom. Japan, as we have seen, at first welcomed foreign trade, Western ideas, and Christianity, but then withdrew into an isolation even more impervious than China's.

Consequently the impact of East Asia on Europe was far greater for three hundred and fifty years than was any permanent Western effect on China and Japan. Technologically, however, Western civilization was superior to the unchanging and antiquated Eastern technologies. Europeans arrived with better ships, far better guns with much greater fire power, superior military organization and discipline, and an inherent aggressiveness that ultimately prevailed and changed the East. But until the mid-nineteenth century it was Europe which drew intellectual stimulation from the older and, in many ways, more sophisticated countries.

European admiration, especially for things Chinese, reached its zenith in the last half of the eighteenth century. By that time second thoughts were developing about Chinese philosophies and systems. Trade, both legal and illegal, was beginning to reveal the built-in corruption and bureaucratic muddiness that permeated the mandarinate and rubbed off on the Cohong. But artistic furnishings made for export from China continued in high favor and decorated, indeed still decorate, the mansions of Europe and America. They also inspired a powerful aesthetic influence which became manifest in chinoiserie.

Chinoiserie

Chinoiserie in Western art and architecture was a mode inspired by China—a vision of being Chinese without being Chinese. It was the expression of what Europe thought the East to be. This extraordinary vogue derived from the descriptions of medieval travelers and the importation of porcelains, silks, bamboo furniture, cloisonné, cottons, and lacquers, and from the accounts of those who accompanied various embassies. From the very beginning of the Eastern trade Chinese artistic and household goods, often made exclusively for the European market, arrived in the West in increasing quantities.

The European mind of the seventeenth century was hopelessly confused about these imports from the East. Only the few Jesuits and traders who had been in the orient had the faintest idea where any specific thing came from. Whether the products were Indian, Chinese, or Japanese was unknown. Frequently wares took on the name or region of the East from which they were shipped to Europe and that could be a long way from their place of origin. Names became attached to products to which they bore no relation. Even India, China, and Japan became confused. Malabar, Coromandel, Malacca, Bantam, and many other names were associated with the Eastern imports as they became popular, but the geographical location of such places was vague in the popular mind, and still is. The names brought visions of exotic lands but few facts. No matter. Furniture, lacquer, porcelain, bamboo work, calicoes, silks, ivory and tortoise-shell carvings, and bric-a-brac of all sorts were avidly collected and enormously admired. The vogue increased with the rise in popularity of tea drinking. But there was not enough to go around and the imports were expensive. To supply the demand furniture was "japanned," and porcelain, fabrics, and wallpaper were all manufactured in Europe in the Chinese manner. Chinoiserie, the European interpretation of presumed Chinese aesthetic styles, became the rage. Not only were various Eastern elements incongruously mixed, they were mixed with European styles as well. And while the result was a European and not a Chinese art form, nevertheless it could not have originated without the oriental, and especially Chinese, influence. Many of the details were Chinese, but the spirit they expressed was European.

In England, where tea drinking flourished more than in any other country, the taste for oriental products and chinoiserie was second to none. The fad was common among the upper classes and intelligentsia but also had its critics and was satirized in both literature and cartoons. Established in the early seventeenth century, the taste declined during the Commonwealth. But after the dull, colorless Puritanical rule of Cromwell, Restoration England was ready for color, richness, and flamboyance. An already established enthusiasm for things Eastern received an additional impetus with the rich dowry of Catharine of Braganza, when that Portuguese infanta became the bride of Charles II, providing free trading rights to English ships in the Portuguese-dominated East and the cession of the port of Bombay to England.

Chinoiserie, beginning about 1600, took many forms and penetrated all the European arts of the late seventeenth and eighteenth centuries. Style-books of designs and patterns for decoration in the Chinese manner appeared. Manuals and treatises on the art of japanning guided the maker of screens and cabinets. The walls of mansions were graced by Chinese-style wallpaper, the textile factories of England and France produced imitations of Indian and Chinese fabrics, potteries in Germany and Holland manufactured blue-and-white porcelain in the oriental manner, and cabinetmakers could hardly produce enough lacquered furniture to keep the market supplied. Everywhere were long-tailed birds and dragons, little bridges and pigtailed figures, blossoms of Asia, flowering trees and pagodas, exotic golden figures moving through ethereal landscapes against black or colored lacquer surfaces. Some were direct copies of Chinese or Japanese originals, others were the products of inventive imaginations.

The Belgian town of Spa (near Aix-la-Chapelle), produced famous lacquer work that was widely esteemed throughout Europe. In England japanning was applied in a variety of colors besides black. Red and green were popular, and yellow, blue, vermilion, and tortoise shell were also used. These finishes were backgrounds for golden mountains, trees, flowers, animals, gardens, and buildings derived from oriental designs but very European in appearance. Dragons, camels, and especially monkeys and birds frolicked over the lacquer fields among bamboos and blossoms and flowering trees. The kilns of Delft poured forth thousands of blue-and-white tiles and dishes with Chinese patterns. During the nearly two centuries of its popularity chinoiserie followed changes in European tastes, embellishing both baroque and rococo styles.

Rococo chinoiserie, even farther removed from its Chinese inspiration, began in France during the reign of Louis XV and spread throughout Europe. The oriental figures and ubiquitous monkeys took on a Gallic gaiety, romping among latticed pavilions and across little bridges. Entire rooms of chinoiserie with lacquer-paneled walls, wallpapers, screens, tapestries, furniture, and lesser furnishings came into vogue. In England Thomas Chippendale designed handsome furniture in the Chinese style. Perhaps the most elaborate single example of chinoiserie was the entire porcelain room created in Naples in the late 1750s and moved to Capodimonte. The style was as enthusiastically received in Germany as in France and Italy, and even spread to Russia and Scandinavia.

Throughout the last half of the eighteenth century, European parks and gardens blossomed with pagodas, teahouses, and Chinese pavilions, with bridges, fishing houses, garden houses, and kiosks, all in bright paint beside little lakes or streams and shaded by weeping willow trees. But nowhere, except in France in some ways, did chinoiserie enter the landscaping of parks and gardens as it did in England. The Anglo-Chinese garden was a wonder of the eighteenth century. The first English chinoiserie garden building, the House of Confucius at Kew Gardens, was erected about 1745 and by the 1750s these whimsical, flimsy, highly ornamented, and gaily painted buildings and bridges were celebrated in books on garden decoration and appeared as bright spots in the gardens and parks of the kingdom.

Culmination of this mode came with the publication of William Chambers's large folio of *Designs of Chinese Buildings, Furniture, Dresses, etc.* in

1757. Chambers had gone to China on an East Indiaman and sketched pagodas and other buildings at Canton. He incorporated his designs, more severe than those of others, in the famous series of exotic and classical buildings which he designed for Kew Gardens, where his great ten-story pagoda, the most famous of all eighteenth-century garden buildings built in the Chinese manner, still stands. Chambers's book served as an inspiration for architects of garden buildings both in Europe and America. In France the *jardin anglais-chinois* was enthusiastically adopted and was frequently more elaborate than in England. By the late eighteenth century the English-Chinese garden fad had run its course. Few examples of this frivolity survive, and it is known largely from literature and engravings in books on garden architecture.

Chinoiserie in general declined in popularity after 1760, crowded out by the Gothic revival and neoclassicism, but did not die out entirely for another half century. In France the designs became extreme and rich, featuring opulent furniture with Japanese lacquer panels framed and ornamented by ormolu. During the same period in Germany chinoiserie developed a somewhat simpler aspect under neoclassical influence and imitation bamboo furniture was carved out of mahogany. In England there was a brief, but not popular, revival during the Regency, when one of the great lavish drawing rooms of the kind was built at Carlton House. Both the room at Carlton House and the Royal Pavilion at Brighton in the same style excited amused derision rather than wonderment. Special rich and ornate furniture was made for both. Bright Chinese wallpapers covered the walls.

Perhaps the most lasting form of chinoiserie is the still popular willowware pattern designed in 1780 and manufactured in large quantities by various porcelain factories, especially Spode. Now (made in Japan), it can be bought in every variety store and is even reproduced on paper plates. But in general the ugliness of the Opium War dispelled the romantic never-never land of Cathay from European thought. With the opening of the treaty ports travelers in numbers saw mainland China for the first time. Their books describing the barren land and teeming poor brought home the reality of the East. The vision of the flowering kingdom of Cathay—a land of azaleas and chrysanthemums, of willows and acacias, of dragons and peacocks, of monkeys and little bridges, pagodas, and eternal tea drinking from handleless blue-and-white cups gave way to the China of reality. But even today in wishful thinking the European mind still loves to conjure up this picture of a land that never existed, even as the late eighteenth century romantic vision of the South Seas has never entirely vanished from the backs of our minds.

Chinese Exports

From the earliest days of the China trade export household goods were brought to Europe, and later to America. With the establishment of the English East India Company at Canton the quantity and variety increased. Tons of porcelain; quantities of lacquered, bamboo, caned, and carved furniture; hundreds of paintings; silver and pewter; tortoise-shell and ivory carving; fans and bric-a-brac graced the homes of western Europe and the Eastern seaboard of America. Most of these things were made not only specifically for the export market, but often to suit the taste of a particular country. Furniture, sets of dinnerware, and silver were ordered individually, with the buyer specifying the style or design he desired. Portraits of merchants and captains were painted from life by Chinese artists who also limned their wives and children from daguerreotypes.

All the "trade" or export porcelain was made at the great Chinese porcelain manufacturing center at Ching-te-chen, some four hundred miles from Canton. It was imported into Europe from the very earliest days of the China trade, especially by the Dutch who received quantities of it from Chinese traders at Batavia.

With the establishment of the East India companies and the rapid rise in the popularity of tea drinking at the beginning of the eighteenth century, the importation of tea sets and other china increased. Chinese soft-paste porcelains were superior to any produced in Europe until about the mid 1700s. Besides finished blue-and-white and other decorated pieces, blank china was imported in large quantities, especially in Holland and England, where it was painted and refired for the home market.

The earliest porcelain imported in Europe was the same as that made for Chinese use. For the Western household it was ornamental but hardly useful. Soon European merchants began ordering china in shapes and sizes suitable for tableware and with the increase in usefulness came an enormous increase in popularity. The fragile porcelain made for Chinese domestic use did not ship well, and to overcome the high breakage export china became thicker and heavier. From the early eighteenth century until the mid-nineteenth chests containing hundreds of thousands of pieces of porcelain provided ballast and flooring in ships' holds, above which were stowed chests of teas, and finally the silks and nankeens which topped off the cargoes. The quantity of export ware sent to Europe and America over a hundred-and-fifty-year period is almost unbelievable.

Export porcelain varied somewhat depending on its destination. Certain forms and decorations sold more readily in Scandinavia than in England, or in France than in Holland. Complete dinner services, tea, coffee, and chocolate sets, punch bowls and decorative plates, and flagons were the most popular. But there were also many odd and individual pieces—porcelain animals, birds, and fruit, for instance. Vases and garnitures, candlesticks, flowerpots, and wall sconces were not unusual. Candlesticks, "monteith" bowls, and other European silver pieces were copied in porcelain. Nor were the furnishings of bedrooms unknown, as export-ware chamber pots, bidets, and even bathtubs brightened domestic chambers. By the late eighteenth century the forms, borders, and placing of decorative elements all conformed to European usage. Decoration, which was painted on at both Ching-te-chen and Canton, varied widely, depending on the country, the buyer, the use, and the changing styles and fashions.

Dinner sets of the ordinary stock patterns of blue-and-white or other monochrome decorations were most common and exported in vast quantities. But it is those superb sets specially painted for a customer that are most interesting. Oldest, and popular throughout the export trade, is the blue and white, for those were the common colors made for Chinese use. Famille verte and famille rose, painted in Canton, were also popular in eighteenth-century China. The blue-and-white patterns known as Nanking, Canton, and Fitzhugh became enormously popular in America. The first two, with their familiar river-temple scene, provided the inspiration for English willowware. Fitzhugh, with its diapered border and central medallion "wheel" motif appeared most commonly in blue, but also in superb varieties of sepia, orange, yellow, gold, bright green, mulberry, and black. France and southern Europe favored bright Chinese floral ornaments (although they occur everywhere). Earlier floral patterns were rather simple, usually monochrome. Some of the more elaborate patterns combined Chinese scenes, birds, animals, butterflies, and floral swags. Floral china reached its most elaborate development in the nineteenth century, with five-color decoration in the rose medallion, rose Canton, and mandarin patterns.

From about 1725 to 1800 armorial sets of tableware were among the most popular. Colored sketches of the correct crests and emblazonments were sent out from Europe to embellish the family china. In London merchants, appropriately called "chinamen," who specialized in oriental goods, presumably took orders for custom-made porcelains and gave them to ships' officers or supercargos to execute. On the Continent religious subjects, reproduced from

Biblical engravings, had a vogue. Closely related and equally well executed are scenes from classical mythology, with Paris offering the golden apple to Aphrodite leading all the rest. Genre subjects occur in wide variety, derived from European scenes and views of the trade itself. A number of punch bowls are known encircled by pictures of the Canton factories. Reproductions of sporting and hunting prints were popular with the shooting and racing gentry, and masonic emblems decorate the punch bowls and mugs of many lodges. Occasionally a cockfight, political cartoon, or memorial scene was reproduced. Punch bowls, flagons, and plates decorated with ships or other marine ornaments were exported to all the European nations participating in the China trade, but were especially favored by the Americans, whose flag flew from most of the vessels. The eagle was also a favorite ornament in the United States. In both Europe and America there are still many famous dinner sets, punch bowls, and flagons of unusually fine workmanship and decoration that bestow emphatic punctuation to the story of Chinese porcelain in the West. To facilitate selecting a pattern from the multiplicity available, "pottery chests" were sent to Europe in the late eighteenth century containing sample plates quartered to show four different borders on one plate.

As fashions for the stock sets changed in popularity, Nanking to be succeeded in turn by Canton, Fitzhugh, rose medallion, mandarin, and celadon, the quality of export china declined in general throughout the nineteenth century. Chinese porcelain remained popular in America for some time after it had been succeeded by European porcelains in the Old World. And in the United States conservative New England women often continued to prefer Canton china long after European porcelains had become fashionable in New York and elsewhere.

The late eighteenth and early nineteenth centuries saw a flowering of oil paintings done in the Western manner by Chinese artists for the export market. Thousands of port scenes were taken to Europe and America. At first the common views were of Macao, the Boca Tigris, Whampoa Reach, and the Canton hongs or factories. After the Opium War paintings of Hong Kong and the treaty ports, especially Shanghai, appeared in the market. Hundreds of these paintings have survived and record the history of Western occupation of the factories and the foreign merchants' houses and offices in other ports.

Factors, ships' officers, and supercargos frequently employed Chinese artists to paint their portraits. The earlier portraits are in a European neoclassical style while the later ones are similar to English Romantic portraiture. Near the mid-nineteenth century, when many were copied from daguerreotypes or photographs, the quality of the work deteriorated badly. Ship portraits, commissioned for merchants or captains, were in large demand and generally well executed. Other, more exotic portraits of hong merchants with whom Westerners transacted business were also brought back. Only a few of the more famous Chinese artists such as Lamqua, Tingqua, Youqua, and Sunqua, for example, are known by name, for the paintings were seldom signed. Genre scenes of Chinese landscapes, gardens, or other oriental subjects were painted on canvas or, in a reverse painting technique, on glass, as were copies of numerous Western engravings. There are, for instance, several known Chinese portraits of George Washington, after engravings of the Gilbert Stuart portrait.

Exquisite watercolors were exported in enormous quantities. The best were painted on English paper and the most popular came in sets of twelve to twenty scenes and showed the processing of tea, the making of silk or cotton, or the manufacture of export porcelain, though there were many other subjects. Innumerable albums of less well-done watercolors on pith or "rice" paper were turned out by the thousands and formed the picture postcards of the period. These, too, usually came in sets showing Chinese trades, costumes, punishments, flowers, birds, butterflies, and boats as well as landscapes and port scenes.

Quantities of furniture, made in both European and Chinese styles, were turned out in the cabinet shops for the Western market. Chinese bamboo furniture, as we have seen, was much in vogue in England during the Regency. The heavy Chinese carved furniture of rosewood or teak, often with marble table tops or chair seats, became popular for "Chinese" rooms during the Victorian period.

Lacquer furniture made after 1785 generally followed Western designs. It included bonnet-top secretaries, kneehole desks, sewing tables, small occasional tables, and other items, although dragon heads often replaced the traditional ball-and-claw feet. Nineteenth-century bills of lading list countless lacquer objects for export and resale. Smaller items included tea caddies, trays, stationery holders, gaming boxes, and sewing boxes. Silk shawls were often packed in lacquered boxes with painted liners. It was not unusual for a ship of the 1820s and after to bring back thousands of lacquer pieces of every size and description, from fans to desks. The lacquer decoration was usually in fine-quality gold but the furniture frequently of flimsy construction.

Curiously enough, the Japanese were also manufacturing lacquer furniture

in Hepplewhite style, at least toward the end of the eighteenth and the beginning of the nineteenth centuries, for some of it came back to the United States
in American vessels chartered by the Dutch for their annual voyages to Nagasaki. Card tables, tilt-top tables, knife boxes, and trays of black or bronze lacquer were decorated with gold or silver birds and flowers and sometimes inlaid with the same ornaments in pearl shell.

Unlacquered Western-style furniture followed Chippendale, Sheraton, Hepplewhite, and early Empire designs. Some is so well made that it is difficult to
distinguish from Western products. Rosewood sofas and chairs, often caned,
were especially popular, as were brass-fitted camphorwood chests, sometimes
covered with leather.

Of all the luxury items Chinese silver is the least known. The subject is interesting and complex. Chinese silver is similar to the English and American
prototypes from which it was copied, but is almost impossible to identify
without a checklist of the initials, hallmarks, pseudo hallmarks, and other de-
vices that were used by the China trade silversmiths. Much of it is document-
ed, however, on bills of lading, and several important sets have been identified
in Salem and Boston, and some of the makers are now known by name.

Lesser decorative objects and knickknacks were popular throughout the
trade. Fans of all kinds—lacquer, ivory, sandalwood, paper—painted with
scenes, flowers, birds, and whatnot were imported by the tens of thousands.
Inexpensive carvings of low-grade jade, soapstone, ivory, and sandalwood
graced Western vitrines. Carved ivory boat models, card cases, balls one inside
another, and puzzles were imported in quantity. So too were boxes and cases
made of sandalwood, silver, tortoise shell, and nacre.

Chinese export porcelains, paintings, furniture, and household goods,
while nearly always readily distinguishable, were, like chinoiserie, more European than Chinese except in their place of manufacture. And yet, like chinoiserie, the unmistakable oriental flavor gave an exotic touch to Western homes
for decades. (No similar Western touch ever penetrated the Chinese household
during the eighteenth and early nineteenth centuries.) Nor has it entirely yet
died away. Modern plumbing has banished porcelain bidets and chamber pots
to the attic. But there are still English and American living rooms and parlors
where the scent of sandalwood lingers and where, across black-lacquered furniture, golden figures walk beneath weeping willows through oriental landscapes. Red cinnabar boxes, tortoise-shell fans, and carved ivory card cases

still grace the tables and vitrines. Rows of Chinese port scenes vie for space with ancestral portraits on living room walls. From the tall cupboards orange Fitzhugh china brightens the dining rooms and reflects from the Chinese silver service of the place settings.

The West, which early adopted the Chinese compass, was not only influenced to a degree by Confucian morality and philosophy, and certain aspects of the civil service, but, more visually, by the avid vogue for oriental products and pseudo-Chinese styles which gave new flavor, a new subtle softening and brightness, to Western homes and fashions.

CHAPTER 21

The Revival of China Missions

The opening of the treaty ports brought a revival of Christian missionary activities which had languished in China for about one hundred years. After the papal decree of 1742 had ended the long Rites Controversy, the persecution of Christians increased and the Jesuits were restricted to Peking, where they were allowed some freedom, probably because they were directly under the watchful eye of the emperor.

The dissolution of the Society of Jesus in 1773, after prolonged infighting within the church, was a crushing blow to Chinese Christians. In 1784 a handful of Lazarist fathers took over the Catholic China mission and the Jesuits' church in Peking. But the French Revolution and Napoleonic Wars cut off the supply of money and men. There were further difficulties when a series of anti-Christian imperial edicts resulted in a succession of persecutions and renewed restrictions on the few remaining missionaries, whose influence continued to decline. Christianity was very much on the defensive in China in the late eighteenth and early nineteenth centuries. In spite of these circumstances in 1800 there were still about 150,000 Chinese Catholics with their own priests scattered through the country, and, while this was a mere drop in the bucket compared with the total population of over three million, it did give a firm base for a vigorous renewal of Catholic missions beginning about 1840.

The most massive nineteenth-century missionary effort in China was, however, Protestant rather than Catholic. Protestant evangelical missionary fervor was rising both in Britain and America. The London Missionary Society and the American Board of Commissioners for Foreign Missions were sending their purveyors of piety to convert the heathen throughout the world. They were soon joined by numerous other denominational mission groups—British, American, and Continental. China, with its rigid restrictions on foreigners, offered an exceptional challenge. And two men, Robert Morrison, an Englishman, and Peter Parker, an American, were inseparably associated with the early days of Protestant evangelical activity.

With commendable farsightedness the London Missionary Society, realizing the impossibility of dispatching any missioanries to mainland China, decided in 1805 to prepare the way by having the Bible translated into Chinese. The difficulty was that so far as they were aware just one Englishman, Sir S. T. Taunton, had any knowledge of the language. Therefore it was decided to send two men to the East to learn it. Only one man was available, but he was an individual of extraordinary virtues.

Robert Morrison was twenty-five years old when he sailed for China via New York on January 31, 1807, less than two weeks after his ordination. He had already acquired a smattering of the language through studying manuscripts in the British Museum and becoming acquainted with Yung-Sam-Tak, a Chinese living in London. Arriving at Canton in early September, he immediately began his intensive study of Chinese. Within two years he had mastered the language sufficiently to become a translator for the East India Company and secure his position at Canton.

Morrison was assiduous and indefatigable in his linguistic study and completed his translation of the New Testament in December 1813, a few months after his first missionary colleague, William C. Milne, arrived. In 1814, seven years after he reached China, he baptized Twae A-ko, his first convert. At about the same time the energetic Morrison began making plans for a seminary to train both European and Chinese missionaries for work in China. His efforts resulted in the founding of the Anglo-Chinese College at Malacca in 1818. (This institution never quite worked out as Morrison hoped it would, and it was moved to Hong Kong in 1842.) By 1819, with Milne's help, the translation of the Old Testament was completed. Morrison went on to make other translations and compiled a Chinese-English dictionary and a grammar. In 1816 he was official interpreter for Lord Amherst on his abortive embassy to Peking. His appointment with the East India Company came to an end when its monopoly was abolished, but shortly he was appointed "Chinese Secretary and Interpreter" to Lord Napier. Two weeks later, however, on August 1, 1834, he died suddenly at Canton at the age of fifty-three. During the twenty-seven years he labored in China his missions grew to five in number, but during that entire time only ten Chinese were baptized. Although the toils of Morrison and his colleagues produced little in the way of converts, his translations and linguistic work greatly facilitated the efforts of his Protestant successors.

Morrison was succeeded as linguist and Chinese secretary to British authorities by Karl Friedrich August Gütslaff, one of the most colorful characters on the China Coast, who was sent out to the East by the Netherlands Missionary Society.

Meanwhile the American Board had sent its first missionaries, who worked closely with the London Society, to China. David Abeel and Elijah C. Bridgman came with free passage on a ship belonging to the devout New York merchant D. W. C. Olyphant to Canton in 1830. Olyphant was the only China trader who would have nothing to do with running opium and his rooms in the American factory were known as "Zion's Corner." Abeel did not stay long in China, but Bridgman settled down to learn the language and, after he acquired a printing press, founded in 1832 the monthly *Chinese Repository*—one of the most useful nineteenth-century sources relating to China and its people. In 1834 another American arrived who was to exert great influence as the most active early medical missionary.

Before the opening of the treaty ports in the 1840s, Protestant missionary efforts were conducted in two ways. Obviously no resident missionary could work anywhere except at Canton and Macao, where both Chinese and Portuguese were generally far from cooperative though sometimes tolerant. The Protestants attempted to penetrate the empire by printing books in Chinese. A constant stream of literature from the missionary presses at Canton seeped inland, and a set of books on Christianity from this source later contributed to the Taiping Rebellion. (See Chapter 23.) Gütslaff, in several voyages along the coast, distributed much of this literature at the ports. The other means of missionary effort was to work with Chinese communities outside China in various cities of the East. By concentrating on these communities in Malacca, Penang, Bangkok, Singapore, Batavia, and elsewhere, missionaries not only made converts who might communicate with China, but even more important, they acquired experience in using the Chinese language.

Peter Parker, an impecunious but pious Yale divinity and medical student, born in Framingham, Massachusetts, on June 18, 1804, was to become, next to Morrison, the most influential missionary in pre-treaty port days and for long afterward. He received his M.D. from Yale medical school in March 1834 and was ordained as a Presbyterian minister in Philadelphia two months later. Equipped with this double-barreled intellectual armament, in June 1834 he embarked on a ship appropriately named the *Morrison*, owned by Olyphant. Arriving at Canton in October, Parker settled into the confined life of Thirteen Factory Street.

He was met by Bridgman, S. Wells Williams, a printer by trade and the missionary-historian who wrote the classic *Middle Kingdom*, and others who had also benefited by Olyphant's free transportation of clergymen to the Far East. Shortly after, Parker became sick and was sent to Singapore to recover and to study Chinese. There he was almost immediately overwhelmed with medical work.

Returning to Canton he opened, in rented factory rooms, the Canton Ophthalmic Hospital. He chose to specialize in eye diseases because they seemed to him the most prevalent in China and were entirely untreated. So successful was the hospital that Parker found little time for the mission side of his work. Not only did he treat over nine hundred patients in the first three months after the hospital opened, but the medical needs of the Cantonese forced him to extend his practice more generally and perform numerous operations. He was an innovative surgeon of outstanding skill and his successes brought support from Howqua and the hong merchants, who donated free factory space, and from British and American merchants who began to support his hospital financially. Success led to the establishment by Parker and his medical colleagues of the Medical Missionary Society in China in Canton and the founding of a branch hospital in Macao in 1838.

In March 1839, when Commissioner Lin confined Westerners to the factories during the Opium War Parker was trapped with all the others. But when most of his companions moved to Macao and Hong Kong, he was allowed to stay on by the Chinese authorities and practice his medical skills. He even made a truss for Commissioner Lin's hernia. As his medical and surgical work flourished, his knowledge of the Chinese language increased, but his missionary evangelism was left almost unpracticed. The Opium War severely cramped his style and, somewhat depressed, he sailed for America on July 5, 1840.

Parker put in a busy two years lobbying in Washington for the appointment of a minister to China, publicizing his hospital, getting married, and raising funds in both America and Europe. He returned to China with his wife in November 1842, two months after the signing of the Treaty of Nanking.

Canton in the aftermath of the war was a different place than when Parker left. Chinese resentment against foreigners ran high. There were riots, but the now-famous Parker clung to his post, busier than ever with his practice. His increasing skill in the language brought him other responsibilities; he became secretary and interpreter for Caleb Cushing's diplomatic shadowboxing during the successful negotiations for the Treaty of Wanghia, just as Morrison had performed similar duties for British emissaries.

Between Parker's medical work and his new duties as an interpreter he had no time for any missionary work whatsoever. The American Board, who were of course backing him financially, had long felt that he concentrated too fully on the medical aspect of his work. They felt the least he could do was to convert some of his patients and in 1845, much to his surprise and bitterness, they pulled the rug out from under him and withdrew their support.

Ever hardworking, Parker plunged more fully into his medical practice and also became more involved in diplomatic matters. He was appointed chargé d'affaires of the United States legation in 1846 and in 1854 he accompanied a U.S. diplomatic mission to Peking, where the long drawn out, unsuccessful negotiations brought Parker to the verge of complete exhaustion. Depressed and near a breakdown, he resigned from his various positions and returned home in 1855. His one last fling in China was not a successful one. Sent back to China in 1856 as United States commissioner, he was a notably unsuccessful diplomat. When he urged American annexation of Taiwan, Washington was so upset that he was hastily withdrawn in April 1857. After more than thirty years of retirement, he died at the age of eighty-four in 1888, by coincidence exactly fifty years after the founding of the Medical Missionary Society in China.

A diplomatic failure, Parker could take satisfaction in his medical achievements. He accomplished more than anyone else in introducing Western medicine, including the use of anesthesia, to China. Hundreds of thousands of patients had been treated, scores of Chinese practitioners trained. As the Jesuits had used astronomy, so he used medicine to gain the regard of the Chinese. And like them he found that esteem was not an open door to Christian conversion. The general Chinese disinterestedness in Christianity made them as resistant to Protestant as to Jesuit missionary efforts.

Mission activity was greatly accelerated during the 1840s after the opening of the five treaty ports to foreign residence and the founding of Hong Kong. The number of missionaries and denominations increased, schools and seminaries were founded, and more hospitals were established. In 1844, exactly ten years after Robert Morrison's death, the emperor issued an edict declaring that Christianity was to be tolerated throughout the empire and that no individual should be persecuted for professing the religion. The building of churches was allowed in the port cities and Chinese subjects were given permission to practice Roman Catholicism, although foreigners were not allowed to travel outside the ports' limits to propagate their faith. Protestants gained equal rights with Catholics the next year. In 1846 another edict further eased restrictions against Roman Catholics and restored some of their confiscated churches, but all foreign missionaries were still confined to the five ports.

The treaties and edicts, combined with a revival of Roman Catholic missionary interest in Europe, brought renewed activity to the China parishes in the 1840s. A solid base of some 150,000 practicing Chinese Catholics with their own hierarchy and two hundred years of tradition behind them gave the Catholics an advantage over their Protestant colleagues. Working through its native clergy the church began a vigorous growth. The Society of Jesus, restored in 1814, again entered the field and was joined by Franciscans, Dominicans, and Lazarists. The old Christian communities were a part of Chinese life and the Catholics, who had communicants in every province, far outnumbered the few hundred Portestants, who were still confined to the treaty ports in the mid-nineteenth century. Nevertheless, it was the latter who in the end made the most massive impact on China and, as the Jesuits had done two centuries before, became the interpreters of China to the Western world.

In pre-treaty port days, the American Board missionaries had found Singapore, with its large Chinese colony, an excellent station. Here tracts and other literature could be printed in the vernacular and here also they maintained a school and a dispensary. After the opening of the ports the Singapore station was closed out and the board ceased its work among Chinese colonies in Siam and Indonesia as well.

Opening of the ports also brought missionaries from a variety of American denominational groups. By 1851, when the last number appeared, *The Chinese Repository* had outlived its usefulness as the principal literary interpreter of Chinese life to resident Westerners. Baptists had been in evidence for some years, but now Methodists, Episcopalians, Presbyterians, and the Dutch Reformed Church (which dominated Protestant missionary work at Amoy) joined them and the American Board evangelists. Wesleyans, Presbyterians, Anglicans, and other English denominational mission groups also augmented the work of the London Missionary Society, and there was a scattering of

German (inspired largely by Gütslaff) and Continental Protestant organizations. Booming Shanghai, however, soon became the principal missionary center for both British and American Protestants. It was here at mid-century that representatives of the mission groups of the two nations worked intensively on a new Chinese translation of the Bible and came up with two versions using two different Chinese words for the Deity. The lack of unanimity between the versions was largely along nationalistic lines and both were published.

After the disagreement over the Bible translation and with the wider geographical dispersion of their efforts, the close cooperation between British and American missionaries, so evident while they were both cooped up in the Canton factories, deteriorated. American missions grew more rapidly than the British, until they dominated the Protestant evangelical field in the Middle Kingdom.

The American Board missionaries flirted for a time with the quasi-Christian Taipings and sympathized with their rebellion, but they were soon disillusioned by the increasing fanaticism of the rebels and mostly came to the conclusion that they were not really Christians after all. Following the experience with Parker, the board took a rather dim view of its representatives becoming involved in American diplomatic activities. Nevertheless, S. Wells Williams succeeded Parker as Chinese secretary to the United States legation and served as interpreter for various officers and diplomats, including Commodore Perry on his mission to Japan.

As the Roman Catholic missions grew rapidly at mid-century, Rome created a number of new vicarates apostolic to better administer their increasing responsibilities. The growth was accompanied by a new series of persecutions, for despite the imperial edicts of the 1840s, full toleration had not been granted, and the conservative Chinese were suspicious of some of the Catholic practices.

Generally speaking, Protestant missionaries did not suffer active persecution as did the Catholics, though they were obstructed by opposition and red tape. On the other hand the Protestants, unlike the Catholics, seldom ventured outside the treaty ports. Protestants were still mostly restricted to the ports during the Taiping rebellion and suffered very little from that syncretic, quasi-Christian uprising. Roman Catholics, scattered throughout the interior, fared badly during those unsettling days. While there were many more Catholics than Protestants at mid-century, the latter, although confined to only five cities, were increasing proportionately at a much more rapid rate.

The Anglo-French War against China in 1856-58 and the ensuing treaty agreements signed by the Chinese under the guns of an allied fleet, brought further advantages to missionary efforts. Additional ports were opened to foreign trade and residence. Foreigners were permitted to travel in the country outside the port areas. Toleration of Christianity, the right of both missionaries and Chinese Christians to exercise their faith, the right of a fixed number of missionaries to travel, preach, and teach within the empire were all agreed to. Direct help to the missions was provided when part of the indemnities exacted by the British and French governments in 1860 were turned over to their respective missionary groups.

The treaties of 1858 and 1860 provided the most important incentives for the increase of missionary work since the opening of the original treaty ports. Teaching centers and churches could be established in the newly opened treaty ports. Travel in the empire was legalized; property could be acquired. Finally Chinese Christians were given a sort of quasi-extraterritoriality under the foreign powers—a questionable procedure which brought numbers of less-than-sincere Chinese converts into the fold and partially removed them from Chinese government jurisdiction. This last provision was taken advantage of more by Catholics (especially encouraged by the French government) than by Protestants. Far beyond the stimulation given to missionary activities was the massive Western impact on China which resulted. The distinguished sinologist Latourette has summed this up well.

The treaties of 1858 and 1860, then, helped to make possible the foreign penetration of China by Occidental culture. In the treaty ports foreign communities arose, partly missionary, partly official, but usually chiefly commercial, and from them irradiated influences which within fifty years were to bring about a startling alteration in all phases of Chinese life. From 1860 to 1898 there was little rapid outward change in China or in her relations with Occidental culture. During these decades, however, the Empire was being quietly honeycombed, and under the ever accumulating pressure from without its resistance was eventually to crumble.[1]

The forty years following the second Chinese-Western war were ones of relative calm throughout the country. Western missionary penetration of the country, both Protestant and Catholic, steadily increased and undoubtedly speeded up the process of change in Chinese culture which became evident shortly before the turn of the century and which would have eventually taken place anyway without missionary activity. Missionary influence in this change, however, was important. Through the founding of schools and hospitals, with their moral and spiritual teaching, their personal self-sacrifice and devoted adherence to the well being of the Chinese people, the missionaries showed a better facet of Western culture than purely materialistic commercial interests and military and diplomatic arrogance could ever provide. While contributing to the imperialistic designs of European powers and the structural breakdown of old China, the missionaries also released new forces which were beneficial to Chinese life and which otherwise would have been absent.

By the last decade of the century the number of Roman Catholics in the country had increased to about half a million, with over six hundred missionaries and over three hundred and fifty Chinese priests. Catholics had also developed an extensive school system, orphanages, hospitals, and organized methods for distributing relief during the frequent famines. Occasional local persecutions, martyrdoms, riots, and disturbances occurred—the worst being the Tientsin massacre in 1871 when well over a score of French, Russians, and Chinese lost their lives.

Protestant activity and growth during the last half of the century was spectacular. The most influential single man in the Protestant movement was James Hudson Taylor, who went to China in 1853 when he was twenty-one years old and founded the China Inland Mission in 1866. Energetic, fanatical, frail of health, and without financial resources, Taylor was a man of exceptional administrative and organizational abilities. These qualities, along with his determination to bring the Gospel to the Chinese people in every part of the empire, created the most successful Protestant missionary organization in the country. The Inland Mission was not attached to any denomination—all good missionaries were accepted. Only those of the strongest faith were suitable, for no salaries were paid and the missionaries conformed to Chinese social customs, living conditions, and styles of dress. The primary purpose was not to make converts, but to diffuse knowledge of the Gospel throughout the country. Taylor's appeal for the first twenty-four missionaries (two for each province and Mongolia) brought twenty-two volunteers in response. By the time Taylor died in 1905 there were 828 missionaries working for the China Inland Mission.

Another outstanding missionary of this period was the Welshman Timothy Richard, a devout Baptist, who was more intellectual than Taylor. Richard believed that education and the spreading of intellectual aspects of Western civilization should go hand in hand with saving souls.

As the number of Protestant denominations, as well as the number of individuals in the missionary field, increased, cooperation became not only interdenominational but international as well. American and British groups dominated, providing about 90 percent of the personnel in the field, but there were also others from Canada and the Continent—mostly Scandinavians and Germans. Curiously, cooperation among the various Protestant groups was closer than among the different Roman Catholic orders and societies working in the field; and the two great branches of Christendom went their different ways. From Peter Parker's day on, the medical missionary became an increasingly important and useful part of the Protestant effort. By the early 1880s a score of them were working in sixteen hospitals and twenty-four dispensaries. Chinese medicine was not merely primitive; it was bizarre; the knowledge of anatomy was minimal and of surgery nonexistent. Western medicine and surgery performed miracles in this medical wasteland. By the end of the century the Christian communities in China were in general better off than the surrounding population. Opium smoking decreased among them, they were more literate, their women enjoyed a higher status, and in many small ways they were better off.

The demands of the great powers, reforms within the empire in the closing years of the nineteenth century, and the repercussions of the Boxer rebellion of 1900—all created a new climate of general unrest and unsettled conditions that brought on another violent reaction to foreigners and hardship for missionaries and their converts. Many Roman Catholics especially lost their lives, and Protestants experienced their first serious general persecution. Many churches, schools, orphanages, and other missionary buildings were looted and burned. Losses of both lives and property were particularly severe in the Peking area, but no part of the country was unaffected. The defeat of the Boxers by international forces brought indemnities for the missions, new treaties reaffirming the toleration clauses, and the beginning of a new era in which Christian missionaries were given far greater opportunities to spread their faith than they had ever enjoyed before. It was a change which, aided by other Western influences, created profound modifications in all phases of Chinese culture. The historic, centuries-old resistance to occidental culture crumbled. All aspects of life were virtually revolutionized under the massive Western impact. From the end of the Boxer uprising until World War I missions in China flourished as they never had before.

But the population of China was so vast that even flourishing and expanding missions made contact with only a small part of the population. Roman Catholics, for instance, while increasing membership enormously, numbered only about half of one percent of the population in 1914. The Protestants had a much greater influence on changing China than the Catholics, although they had far fewer parishioners. There were nearly 5,500 Protestant missionaries, teachers, and doctors in the country in 1914, a number which increased to over 8,100 by 1925. By the 1930s the Christian church in China had become more indigenous and partially self-supporting. It had also become less Gospel-oriented and more concerned with social service. Many Chinese Protestants occupied influential positions in the post-Manchu government. Indeed Sun Yat-sen himself, who had been educated by Protestants in Honolulu, was baptized a Christian in 1884 at the American Board Mission in Hong Kong.

Both Catholics and Protestants continued to make progress from 1914 until 1926, though under increasing difficulties. Through the remaining twenties and thirties, however, the country was in so much disorder that missionary work became more arduous. The rising power of the Kuomintang increased the difficulty of the missionaries, for its Communist wing was vigorously antiforeign. In the mid-twenties there were about two and a quarter million Roman Catholics in China and growth had slowed up materially since World War I. The infinitesimally small, but two-centuries-old Russian orthodox mission at Peking, with only about five thousand Chinese members, came to an end after the Russian Revolution of 1917. The total number of Protestant communicants is not clear, but it probably never went much over 800,000 in the early twenties and may have been considerably less. Not a great return for the nearly seven million Bibles, Testaments, and religious books distributed in 1921 and over nine million in 1924. But the vigorous work of the Protestant missionaries in education, medicine, and social work made a greater impact than their preaching ever did. The late twenties saw an intense anti-Christian movement, civil war, and disorder which forced most of the Protestant missionaries to leave the country. This development came simultaneously with the loss of enthusiasm in both Europe and America for missionary work and a consequent sharp reduction in funds available for it.

In the long history of Christian missions in China the two main branches, Roman Catholic and Protestant, seemed almost like two entirely different religions to the Chinese, who called them by different names. The Protestant missionaries came mostly from English-speaking countries, while the Catholics were from Portugal, Spain, France, and Italy. Rarely, except in occasional famine or other disaster relief work, was there any cooperation between them. In general they ignored each other.

The missions were certainly one of the most important influences in introducing Western civilization to China, although the number of Christians never numbered more than 1 percent of the population. Christianity raised and reinforced Chinese moral and ethical standards within its communities, aided education, ran nearly all the foreign-language schools in the country, disseminated Western learning, increased regard for the individual, and had some impact and stimulation upon non-Christian religions. The missionaries, both Catholic and Protestant, also served more than any other group of foreigners as the principal interpreters of China to the West. Their wave, cresting before World War I, slowly broke upon the Middle Empire and receded as revolution, war, and unsettled conditions wracked that ancient civilization from which modern China has emerged.

CHAPTER 22

No More the Forbidden Kingdom

When Japan excluded the Portuguese in 1639, only the Dutch, among all Western nations, were given trading privileges. Confined after 1641 to their little factory on artificial De-shima Island in Nagasaki Harbor, they continued to exercise their solitary prerogative with annual voyages from Batavia for over two centuries. Before the closing of the country, a series of savage persecutions had eliminated Christianity as a form of public worship and driven its remnants underground. Tokugawa Japan excluded occidentals and crushed their religion. There was heroism; there were martyrs; there was appalling cruelty, apostasy, and ruthless extermination. From being the most outgoing Asiatic nation, the country withdrew into over two hundred years of seclusion; allowing carefully supervised Chinese vessels to trade at Nagasaki, but with only the small Dutch window at De-shima open to the Western world.

Although that porthole to the West was a tiny one, a surprising amount of Western learning seeped in through it, along with often distorted geographical information. We have already noted the so-called Dutch scholars who translated numerous European works into Japanese. So accustomed did the Western nations, commercially occupied in exploiting other Asiatic countries, become to the Forbidden Kingdom's exclusiveness and inaccessibility that no serious thought was given to attempting to open commercial or diplomatic relations with Japan until the closing years of the eighteenth century.

The first people to make the attempt were the Russians. Ever since they had reached Kamchatka in the late seventeenth century, at the end of their long pioneering push across Siberia, the Muscovites had eyed the closed kingdom to the south with no little interest, and the opening of trade relations

with Japan was discussed in the Russian capitals. A Russian vessel commanded by Spanberg apparently touched at various places on the east coast of Japan as early as 1739, after following the Kurile Islands south from Kamchatka. The Polish adventurer Mauritius Benyowsky, escaping his Kamchatka exile in a stolen ship in 1771, found shelter from a storm on the Japanese coast
where he was well treated. A few years later Russian settlers in the Kuriles
made contact with Japanese from Hokkaido. Nothing came of any of these encounters.

An official Russian expedition led by Lieutenant Laxman landed on Hokkaido in 1792 in an attempt to open negotiations. They were politely received, heavily guarded, and expelled with the information that Japanese law
did not allow any relations with foreigners except at Nagasaki. Laxman's easy
landing, however, worried the Japanese and the *bakufu* (military administration of the shogunate) began to realize how weak their coastal defenses really
were.

In 1805 Captain A. J. von Krusenstern arrived off Nagasaki Harbor on October 8 in his ship *Nadeshda*, bearing a diplomatic mission to Japan headed
by Ambassador Rezanov. Krusenstern's primary objective, on this first Russian circumnavigation of the world, was to experiment with supplying Russia's Far Eastern provinces by sea as an alternative to the tedious and difficult
overland route, as well as to open trade with India and Southeast Asia. Weeks
passed before *Nadeshda* was towed into the inner harbor at Nagasaki three
days before Christmas. The ship's guns and powder were taken to shore with
only the ambassador's bodyguard permitted to keep their muskets, in accordance with Japanese law. The Russians were allowed a tiny, rocky spit of land,
surrounded by a bamboo fence and watchtowers, on which to exercise. They
were permitted only one meeting with the captains of two Dutch vessels
which arrived on their annual visit. For six frustrating, even humiliating,
months interminable negotiations with minor officials on minor matters went
on. In early April 1805 Rezanov was finally granted two interviews with a representative of the Japanese emperor (actually the shogun) who, out of hand,
rejected the tsar's letter and gifts and presented the ambassador with a document forbidding Russian ships ever to visit Japan. To expedite *Nadeshda*'s departure the Japanese gave Krusenstern two months' provisions without charge,
provided every assistance to hasten his sailing, and promptly got him out of
the harbor by April 17. The attempt to open negotiations with the island kingdom was a complete failure. Krusenstern's success in charting some sections
of the Japanese coast was small consolation. Rezanov, driven by frustration

to blustering and intemperate language, made a bad impression at the Japanese trading posts on Sakhalin and in the Kuriles in 1806 and in 1807 created renewed Japanese fears of planned Russian aggression.

In 1811 Captain Golovnin, while exploring the southern Kuriles in the frigate *Diana*, was captured by the Japanese, who held him for two years. Golovnin suffered severe, even cruel, treatment from his captors at first, but eventually gained their admiration. In 1813 the *Diana* was allowed to enter Hakodate and pick him up, and the involuntary guest left his hosts with mutual expressions of esteem. After his return to Russia Golovnin wrote a very interesting account of his imprisonment.

The British frigate H.M.S. *Phaeton* entered Nagasaki Harbor in 1808, during the Napoleonic Wars, searching for Dutch prizes, and was supplied with provisions after threatening bombardment. Ten years later a British merchantman entered Tokyo Bay (then called Edo) but had no luck trading, and in 1824 the inhabitants of a small island off Kyushu had a scuffle with some rowdy English sailors. But amid pressures from without and rising criticism within the country, the Japanese policy of exclusion remained completely in force during the early nineteenth century. In fact the episode involving British seamen resulted in 1825 in a new expulsion order under which no foreign ship could approach the shore and any seamen who landed were to be summarily killed or incarcerated.

Meanwhile American shipping and interests in the Pacific and Far East were increasing. Vessels in the China trade, carrying their furs, sandalwood, and bêche-de-mer to Manila and Canton, passed hard by the shores of Japan. With the opening of the Japan whaling grounds, American whalers began to look enviously at the good closed harbors nearby where refitting could be so easily done and where fresh supplies were so conveniently available. The increased American shipping created more incidents of sailors, cast away on the shores of Japan, being subjected to cruel and abusive treatment.

Apart from Captain John Kendrick's attempt to sell sea otter skins on the Kii coast in the *Lady Washington* in 1791, the earliest American visits to Japan were in ships under Dutch charter. The Dutch, fearing English men-of-war throughout the Napoleonic conflict, often took advantage of American vessels when they were available. The first American charter voyages from Batavia were made by Captain William Robert Stewart, a rascally character, in the New York ship *Eliza* in 1797 and 1798. In 1799 Captain James Devereaux made a successful voyage for the Dutch and brought back to Salem a substantial amount of Japanese lacquered furniture made in the English style.

Several other American vessels sailed the Batavia-Nagasaki run during the next few years.

An optimistic group of missionaries, including Peter Parker, S. Wells Williams, and the irrepressible Karl Gütslaff, sailed from Macao in the Olyphant company's ship *Morrison* in 1837, accompanied by the American merchant C. W. King, to return seven shipwrecked Japanese sailors to their homeland. These joint disciples of God and Mammon hoped their humane efforts would be rewarded with the opening of the country to trade and missions. But the ungrateful Japanese authorities, now apprehensive of all foreigners, refused, in the face of two American attempts, even to let their compatriots set foot on their native soil and the disappointed group returned to Macao.

When news of the crushing power of Western naval strength in the Opium War trickled through to Japanese governmental authorities in 1842, the edict of 1825 was relaxed. Three years later H.M.S. *Samarang*, on a surveying voyage, was given a reasonably courteous reception at Nagasaki, and the American whaler *Manhattan*, returning twenty-two Japanese seamen the same year to Uraga, was civilly treated and given provisions. A French man-of-war, which caused displeasure by landing a missionary in the Ryukyu Islands, was not so well received in 1846.

Meanwhile the number of American whaleships and other vessels continued to increase in the waters near Japan and there was rising sentiment in the United States toward opening the country. Growing public interest induced Washington to dispatch Commodore James Biddle with two warships in an attempt to open trade negotiations. He arrived in Tokyo Bay in 1846 and had as little success against the adamantine attitude of the *bakufu* as other foreign attempts. Like the Russians he departed with a letter warning him never again to appear on the Japanese coast. Commander Glynn in the U.S.S. *Preble* arrived at Nagasaki three years later to pick up fifteen shipwrecked American seamen. After getting a runaround for several days, thirteen emaciated survivors and a half-breed American Indian adventurer named Ranald MacDonald were delivered to him.

Glynn noted that Japanese ports would be excellent coaling stations for trans-Pacific steamships. In a visit to President Millard Fillmore in Washington in 1851 he suggested that strong diplomatic measures be taken to get the ports open. Commercial, religious, economic, and even patriotic pressures were building up to send an expedition to Japan. When seventeen shipwrecked Japanese sailors were brought into San Francisco, they were seized upon as a good excuse to send a fleet to Japan for their humane return and at the same time to begin negotiations for opening the island kingdom. The man eventually selected for the mission was Commodore Matthew Calbraith Perry.

Coming of the Black Ships

Commodore Perry was a member of one of the most distinguished naval families the United States ever produced. A pompous, dignified, experienced, and patient but firm officer, he was well suited by nature to command the East India Squadron and to lead this expedition to end Japan's isolation.

At Perry's insistence the East India Squadron was strengthened and steam men-of-war included. Perry sailed from Norfolk on November 24, 1852 in the U.S.S. *Mississippi*, a steam sidewheeler that was one of his favorites. Heading across the Atlantic, Perry called first at Funchal where he laid in a good supply of Madeira, sailed on to St. Helena for another brief stop, and arrived at Cape Town, where he took on fresh meat and vegetables. On April 6, 1853, Perry arrived at Hong Kong. Here he found three more of his East India Squadron—*Plymouth*, *Saratoga*, and the storeship *Supply*—awaiting him. S. Wells Williams was engaged as an interpreter. Leaving Hong Kong, Perry took his fleet to Shanghai where the U.S.S. *Susquehanna* had preceded him with the United States minister to China. Here he transferred his pennant to the *Susquehanna*, with her more ample living quarters. He agreed to leave the *Plymouth* at Shanghai to look out for the welfare of Americans and Europeans, uneasy in the midst of the Taiping Rebellion. Sailing from Shanghai with two steam frigates and two storeships on May 17, he crossed the East China Sea to Okinawa, where he arrived on the twenty-sixth. From Okinawa he took two ships to the Bonin Islands in June to investigate the potential of Port Lloyd, where whalers obtained fresh supplies, as a coaling station. Perry spent four days in the Bonins, wrote a report to the secretary of the navy recommending Port Lloyd as a coaling station for trans-Pacific steamships and also suggesting that the uncertain sovereignty of the islands be settled between Britain and the United States, and returned to Okinawa. On July 2 he sailed for Japan with the steam frigates *Susquehanna* and *Mississippi* towing two sailing sloops of war. On July 8, 1853, the four ships, cleared for action, entered Uraga Harbor and dropped anchor near the entrance of Tokyo (then Edo) Bay.

The sight of the black ships, as the Japanese called them, in bold line of battle, threw the Japanese into utter confusion. To them the visit was inconceivable and they mobilized their antiquated military forces to defend their shores. Perry took a determined stand from the beginning. With his ships surrounded by Japanese guard boats, he allowed no boarders. One minor official who arrived was told that the commodore came in peace with a letter from the president of the United States to the emperor. In that case, Perry was informed, he must go to Nagasaki—the only place where such a communication would be received. This he refused to do and promptly dispersed the picket boats by threatening to fire on them. Besides taking this firm attitude he also not only refused the offer of free provisions, by which the Japanese had successfully gotten rid of other foreign ships, but volunteered to share his own supplies with them. Furthermore Perry maintained face by not allowing himself to be seen by any Japanese and refusing to receive any official below what he considered cabinet rank.

The heavy mobilization of Japanese troops and the building of additional earthworks along the shore did not deter him. When he was again urged to go to Nagasaki, Perry threatened to march on Tokyo and deliver the letter to the emperor. Japanese nerves were not calmed when boats from the fleet began a survey of Tokyo Bay. An attempt by guard boats, loaded with spear-carrying soldiers, to prevent the survey was dispersed when the *Mississippi* was brought up, and the work continued under the protection of her guns.

After lengthy negotiations Japanese officials agreed to receive President Fillmore's letter at a specially prepared building. Commodore Perry emphasized that he did not expect an immediate reply but would return for further negotiations after several months. On July 14 Perry landed a force of bluejackets and marines, protected by the guns of his ships, at the agreed-on beach village of Kurihana. Perry himself then went ashore with two ships' bands playing and marines presenting arms. Japanese troops greatly outnumbered the small American contingent at this showy feudal spectacle.

The occasion was tense and dramatic. One careless step or misunderstood movement in the confrontation could have reduced it to a bloody conflict. But control and discipline on both sides were perfect.

Perry presented the letter with ceremony, was told it would be delivered to the emperor, and that he could now depart. The commodore assured the Japanese officials that he would return in the spring for an answer to his letter. Then, after boldly sailing up Tokyo Bay, where he anchored for a couple of nights, he departed on July 17 in the same manner he had arrived, with the steamships towing the sailing vessels.

Commodore Perry, by his decorum, firmness, patience, and discipline, made an enormous impression on the Japanese, who viewed these barbarians with a new respect. He was well pleased with his performance. The job was capably and expeditiously done without armed incident in a flammable situation.

Perry made a six-day stop at Okinawa and then sailed for Hong Kong, where he arrived August 7. Other components of his squadron arrived one by one until they numbered ten naval ships and two chartered vessels. During the commodore's stay around the mouth of the Pearl River, he successfully avoided being pinned down to the China coast by merchants and diplomats who wanted to keep the ships there to protect American interests during the Taiping Rebellion. When a Russian squadron, which had spent three months at Nagasaki unsuccessfully trying to get a treaty, arrived and suggested joining forces with Perry on his return to Japan, the commodore decided not to wait for spring but to sail immediately unencumbered by the Russians. He took his squadron out of Hong Kong January 14, 1854, and, again making a stop at Okinawa, anchored once more in Japanese waters on February 13.

During Perry's absence the shogun had died and a new shogun was now in power. The president's letter had been considered by the *bakufu* and a diplomatic commission appointed to negotiate with the commodore. A preliminary dispute over a site for the negotiations was settled when both sides agreed that Yokohama was a suitable place, and a new building was erected there for the purpose.

Proceedings began on March 8, when Commodore Perry with his officers made an imposing landing in full dress uniform, to a seventeen-gun salute, preceded by five hundred seamen and marines and three ships' bands. A twenty-one gun salute honored the emperor and another seventeen-gun salute was fired for the Japanese commissioners. The Japanese negotiators were prepared to give shipwrecked sailors better treatment and to open a harbor for supplying ships with provisions and fuel, but they wanted no part of a trade agreement. Perry gave them a copy of the trade agreement with China for their information. The conferences proceeded at a leisurely pace, gifts were exchanged, Japanese commissioners consulted higher authority at Tokyo, and there were reciprocal entertainments.

On March 31, the Treaty of Kanagawa, the first ever made between Japan and a foreign power, was signed. The treaty provided for permanent peace between the two countries, the opening of the ports of Shimoda and Hakodate to American ships for supplies, the humane treatment and repatriation of shipwrecked U.S. seamen, and the establishment of an American consulate, as well as the extension to the United States of any privilege given any other power. All was concluded in a friendly and peaceful manner with each side maintaining face and claiming diplomatic victories.

Before leaving Japan, Perry visited Shimoda where he stayed twenty-five days, the sailors enjoyed shore leave, and the harbor was charted. He then sailed to Hakodate, the other open port. This harbor too was charted. Hakodate was a fine, ample port and its location made it a convenient shelter for American whalers. In July he made a stop at Okinawa where he negotiated the Treaty of Naha with the local government, opening that port too for American ships.

The Japan expedition opened the Forbidden Empire for the first time in two and a half centuries. Perry had not gotten the trade agreement Americans wanted, but the toe was in the door. Japan soon signed similar treaties with the British, the Russians, and eventually the Dutch.

If Commodore Perry, backed by the guns of his fleet, was the man who successfully set the bamboo door ajar, it was another remarkable man who, in patient isolation, opened the door wide to the Western world. Rarely has a more perfect diplomatic appointment been made than President Franklin Pierce's selection of Townsend Harris, a New Yorker, as the first United States consul general to Japan. Harris had spent six years in Eastern waters as a merchant and this experience had given him a thorough and sympathetic understanding of oriental attitudes and customs. He was patient, tactful, and highly intelligent.

Consul General Harris was not exactly received with open arms when he arrived at Shimoda on August 21, 1856, as the first accredited representative of any country to Japan. One obstacle after another was put in his way. He was virtually isolated and urged to leave, but his perseverence and patience gradually overcame every obstacle. On September 4 he hoisted, on a newly erected flagpole, the first consular flag ever seen in the island empire.

Working methodically by himself and without any intimidating military presence, the skilled diplomat successfully persuaded the Japanese, who came to have a very high regard for him, to sign a commercial treaty on July 29, 1858. Additional ports were opened up, import duties were fixed, extraterritorial privileges were granted Americans, and the United States agreed to supply technological advisers and modern arms and ships to Japan. After the United States had led the way, similar commercial treaties were signed almost immediately by Japan with Britain, France, Russia, and Holland.

The signing of the treaties soon brought numbers of foreign merchants and residents, especially to the Yokohama area. Unsettled times resulted as Japan's entire economic system was shaken under Western commercial impact. A revolution was followed by the fall of the shogunate and the establishment of imperial power in 1868 under Mutsuhito, the Meiji emperor. The way had been paved for modern military and industrial Japan, and in a few years the astounding change from a feudal, static, medieval country to one of the most dynamic, industrialized, Westernized nations of our time had been completed. Equality with other nations came in the closing year of the nineteenth century when Western powers relinquished extraterritoriality. Equality also soon produced a Western style of colonial imperialism. The sleeping country had not only been awakened, it had learned its lessons well.

Manjiro

In considering Western influence on the forbidden island kingdom, brief notice must be given to the extraordinary story of Manjiro, the Japanese fisherman. The difficulties endured by Western sailors shipwrecked on Japanese shores was one of the principal causes of external pressure on Japan. Conversely, shipwrecked Japanese sailors were picked up by Western vessels from desolate oceanic islands, off the coast of Japan, or from drifting waterlogged junks as far away as the West Coast of the United States. Attempts were usually made, not always successfully, to return these unfortunate men to their own country, where they stood the risk of being beheaded for leaving.

It was such a group of five young Japanese fishermen, wrecked on the desert island rock of Torijima, southeast of Honshu, living in a cave and surviving on shellfish, seaweed, bits of edible vegetation, and an occasional seabird killed with a rock, that Captain W. H. Whitfield in the American whaler *John Howland* rescued in 1841. The youngest of the group was a fifteen-year-old boy named Manjiro. Manjiro was a bright lad and Captain Whitfield, taking a liking to him, brought the boy back to Fairhaven, Massachusetts. For three years he lived with Captain Whitfield and his bride in their new farmhouse or with a relative near the school in which he was enrolled. Manjiro, a good student, completed his work at Bartlett's Academy, learned the coopering trade, and bought himself a copy of Nathaniel Bowditch's *New American Practical Navigator*.

In 1846 Manjiro shipped on the whaleship *Franklin* for a voyage to the Pacific. During the cruise he came close to the shores of Japan and tried to talk with fishermen, but he had forgotten much of his own language. When his ship put into Honolulu he had the opportunity of seeing some of the friends with whom he was shipwrecked and he was also befriended by the Reverend Samuel C. Damon, seamen's chaplain for the port. On the *Franklin*'s next cruise to the whale grounds, the captain became ill, the first mate took command, and Manjiro, with his knowledge of navigation, became the mate. After a three-year cruise and circumnavigation of the globe, Manjiro, the first Japanese ever to navigate a ship in the Western manner, returned to Massachusetts.

Late in 1849 Manjiro was off again on a lumber ship for the California goldfields. After panning a few hundred dollars' worth of gold, he took passage for Honolulu, where he again met his friends and Chaplain Damon. And Damon it was who aided Manjiro and two of his surviving companions to make arrangements for returning to their homeland. Purchasing a whaleboat, which he named *Adventurer*, Manjiro planned to obtain passage across the Pacific on a whaleship and be launched near the Ryukyu Islands. From there he believed he could find his way home.

The three Japanese signed on the whaleship *Sarah Boyd* and in due course were put over the side in their whaleboat near the Ryukyu Islands, where they landed in January 1851. Taken to Naha, Okinawa, by Japanese guards, they were closely questioned and their boat and possessions subjected to an uncomprehending inspection which exasperated Manjiro. From Naha they were transported to Japan, where Manjiro was queried by the local daimyo or provincial governor, Shimadzu, about America and especially the foreign ships He built a model of a whaleship and then a larger vessel which he demonstrated around Kagoshima Bay. The three wanderers were then taken to Nagasaki where they endured a much longer and intensive examination, were made to trample Christian symbols to prove they had not been converted, and were imprisoned. Surprisingly, after the official investigation found all in order, they were released. Back in their native province they were subjected to a third inquisition. Manjiro then returned to his home, where he was greeted by his joyful mother and taken to see his own tomb which she had had erected when he did not return.

Upon Perry's arrival Manjiro was summoned to Tokyo to enlighten the *bakufu* about the Americans, although he was never allowed to meet any of them. He was questioned by top ministers of the government, some of whom suspected him of being educated by the Americans and sent ahead of Perry's squadron as a spy.

Manjiro continued to live in the capital and became famous as the man who had lived in the West. His whaleboat was reproduced by the hundreds, and he was made curator of the large collection of gifts which Perry had brought.

He oversaw the construction of Western-type vessels and was ordered by the *bakufu* to translate Bowditch's *New American Practical Navigator* into Japanese. He completed the work in 1857 after eighteen months. He then became a faculty member of the newly established naval training school. Following his attempt to set up an American-style whaling industry for Japan, Manjiro was selected as an interpreter and authority on American customs to accompany the first group of Japanese ambassadors to Washington. They sailed in the U.S.S. *Powhatan* while Manjiro traveled in the escorting *Kanrin Maru*, a ship purchased from the Dutch. Manjiro navigated the ship across the Pacific to San Francisco, where she received a tumultuous welcome. The ambassadors, who had been forced into Honolulu, proceeded to Panama in the *Powhatan*, crossed Panama, and boarded the U.S.S. *Roanoke* for the east coast.

The *Kanrin Maru* returned to Japan by way of Honolulu and Manjiro, his talents wasted as far as the ambassadors were concerned, went with her and revisited his old benefactor, Samuel Damon. In 1861 and 1862 he was sent on a colonizing expedition to the Bonin Islands and later took another whaling cruise.

In 1870 a group of Japanese was sent to Europe to observe the latest European military techniques, being put to the test in the Franco-Prussian War, and Manjiro accompanied them as an official interpreter. Again he visited San Francisco, crossed the continent on the newly built railroad and, while the rest of the group visited New York for five days, made a return to Fairhaven to visit the Whitfields. It was a felicitous and heartfelt reunion. When Manjiro reached Europe, he became ill and was forced to return to Japan. He suffered a stroke in 1872, from which he recovered, and lived until 1898 when he died in Tokyo at the age of seventy-one.

Manjiro, as an individual living in two disparate civilizations, symbolized more than any other person the traumatic mid-nineteenth century exchanges between East and West, exchanges which put history on a new and unalterable course that reached its climax in World War II. If this young Japanese— the product of a feudal world who through adventurous accident mastered the life of a New England village—had returned to his homeland a few years earlier he most certainly would have been beheaded. But the knowledge he acquired during his wanderings was important to a Japan beginning to awaken from a long slumber. He not only escaped what would earlier have been an inevitable fate; he was given high social status and became his country's first, and very influential, interpreter of America, of Western ships and shipbuilding, of whaling techniques, and of navigation. As the sympathetic carrier of a certain area of Western knowledge, he softened a bit some of the impact of the West, and especially the United States, on his country. He was one of those rare people—the right man, in the right place, at the right time.

Following the opening of Japan there was an unsettled political period before the establishment and reforms of the Meiji government. With political stability, the Japanese people went into an absolute frenzy about all things Western. Western military methods and industrial technology were not the only things adopted with avidity. The popular arts were transformed by Western influence, while ancient classical and traditional art was scorned and neglected. Flowing robes were replaced by trousers, sandals by leather shoes, craftsmanship by mass production, and beauty by shoddiness. Beyond the obvious and superficial changes taking place, the very essence of traditional Japanese culture was also being undermined by occidental influences. The old formal ways of life were adapted quickly to the industrial revolution. Enormous amounts of Western literature as well as technical and academic books were badly translated, mostly from English, into Japanese with an almost total lack of discrimination. Curiously, Western influence on painting and sculpture, which were greatly neglected during this period, was far less than on literature and drama. Only when appreciation for their own classical art was stimulated by foreign scholars in the late nineteenth and early twentieth centuries did Japanese sophistication in traditional painting and sculpture return.

The drive toward Westernization achieved its goal in 1894 with the revision of the unequal treaties, and Japan became a full modern nation equal to all others in the family of the Western world.

Many Western scholars were employed in Japan in specialized fields during the transformation of the country. Western medicine was introduced mostly by German doctors, and there is still a Teutonic tinge to the Japanese medical world. An impressive contingent of brilliant men went to Japan from the Boston area. Edward S. Morse, a student of Louis Agassiz and director of the Peabody Museum of Salem, went to Japan in 1877; there he founded the first oceanographic station in the country and established modern zoological, anthropological, and archaeological studies. His excavation of the Omori shell mounds was the first archaeological dig in Japan. Morse's enthusiasm for Japan and his influential position in the Boston academic world brought others. Drs. William Sturgis Bigelow and Charles G. Weld were among the noted collectors of art and Ernest Fenollosa, who stimulated the Japanese to an appreciation of their own classical heritage, became an imperial commissioner of fine arts for Japan and the outstanding authority in the world on Japanese and Chinese art.

The visits of these Bostonians created a lively and deep intellectual interest in Japan and things Japanese in the Boston area which is still evident today. They also brought the greatest collection of Japanese art in the world to the Boston Museum of Fine Arts, which through Dr. Charles G. Weld became the repository of Bigelow's and Fenollosa's incomparable holdings. An unequaled collection of the pre-Western arts and crafts of the country, accumulated by Morse, was purchased by Weld for the Peabody Museum of Salem.

All of these men are well remembered and honored in Japan today. Both Ernest Fenollosa and Sturgis Bigelow became Buddhists, and there are memorials to them in the grounds of Miidera temple, overlooking Lake Biwa. Other Bostonians interested in the arts and literature who were influenced by visits to Japan included Percival Lowell, who wrote several books on the country and later became an eminent astronomer, Henry Adams, and John La Farge. Lafcadio Hearn, the New Yorker who arrived in Japan as a journalist, married a Japanese wife, and wrote enthusiastically about the country all his life, is buried in the same cemetery as Manjiro.

Another important Japanese artistic effect on the West, especially in England and France, was inspired by the two great innovative wood-block printers Katsushika Hokusai (1760-1849) and Andō Hiroshige (1797-1858). Their new-style landscape prints hit Europe like a fresh breeze in the last half of the nineteenth century and their admiration almost amounted to a cult. These enormously popular works noticeably affected the painting of the period, especially that of James A. McNeill Whistler, who spent most of his time after the 1850s in Paris and London. The concise formal elegance of the Japanese prints and of Chinese porcelain decoration fascinated Whistler and their influence became especially evident in a group of paintings which he executed in 1864. Van Gogh and Gauguin also discovered universal values in Japanese works which helped them solve artistic problems that profoundly concerned them.

The influence (impact if you will) of Japanese art was different in nature from the widespread passion for Chinese decorative arts and export manufactures throughout the Western world earlier in the century. The appreciation of Japanese art was more esoteric, more aesthetic, and arrived full fledged in Boston through the efforts of Edward Morse and his friends and disciples, who disseminated it throughout the Western artistic world with evangelical fervor.

CHAPTER 23

The Final Impact

As foreign pressure closed in on Japan and Commodore Perry's forcible opening of the Forbidden Kingdom was succeeded by internal revolutions resulting in the dominant emergence of the emperor, occidental intrusions bored deeper into the corrupt and increasingly chaotic mainland Chinese empire. The complete military and psychological defeat administered by the British in the Opium War left the country in a state of shock. Two crises, one an internal revolt and the other an international conflict, simultaneously afflicted the ailing Middle Kingdom. Both occurred as Peking's control of the country declined. Pirates plagued the coast; groups of bandits roamed the countryside, unchecked except by local militia companies who were frequently too involved fighting each other to maintain law and order. To maintain private military organizations local leaders or secret societies developed rackets to extort contributions and illegal taxes from the people. Against this background of turmoil a young religious mystic and rebel named Hung Hsiu-ch'üan appeared in Kwangsi province in the 1840s.

The Taiping Rebellion

Hung, an unstable, fanatical, and eloquent leader, was inspired by Christian ideas picked up through some of the Chinese tracts printed at the Protestant press in Canton. In a prosperous country under stable conditions he would have been considered a madman. In the southern China of the mid-nineteenth century he became a messiah. Believing that he had seen God in a vision and that he was a younger brother of Jesus Christ, he adopted the most military

314

teachings of the Old Testament and set out to save mankind. And a good deal of mankind at this particular time and place thought it needed saving.

Several years of preaching attracted to his cause a group of young and vigorous leaders who organized his followers. Many of them were Hakkas, a partially unassimilated people who had their own communities and language in South China. The vigorous movement appealed to thousands of destitute, lawless, and otherwise economically deprived people in a confused and impoverished country. Thus in disordered Kwangsi province there was rising support for the "God Worshippers Society," as Hung's quasi-Christian organization called itself.

The group's first military uprising against the government occurred successfully late in 1850 at the village of Chin-t'ien. Following their victory, Hung and his companions announced the establishment of a new dynasty called the Taiping—or the "Heavenly Kingdom of Great Peace." The Kingdom of Peace immediately set out on a path of war. From southern Kwangsi the rebellion spread northward. Hung and his leaders organized their revolutionary army reasonably well. Religious and political movements were combined. The troops were ordered to obey the Ten Commandments and not to molest civilian populations. Men and women, who both served as soldiers, were kept separated, and all troops were disciplined to follow orders and not panic on the battlefield.

The rebellion was far from one of unimpeded victory. Hung was joined by another skillful military leader named Yang Hsiu-ch'ing. Bitter battles were fought against government troops who were so ill disciplined that they drove civilians into the ranks of the Taipings. The size of the rebel force increased dramatically as the fighting went on. As their numbers built up, and the morale of imperial troops declined, victories followed. Spreading north, the Taipings bypassed most of the strong points and, descending the Yangtze River in a large flotilla, captured Nanking in March 1853.

Along with their military campaigns, the Taipings attempted to reform the political and social systems. They introduced a new calendar, different from either the Chinese or Western, which they claimed was the calendar of the Heavenly Father. A steady stream of propaganda books and pamphlets issued from the rebel presses and were disseminated throughout the overrun countryside. The Deity himself descended to earth to bring evidence against traitors and spies. Quasi-Christian fanaticism destroyed the idols and symbols of Buddhism and other religions; gambling and opium smoking were prohibited, corrupt government officials were overthrown, new moral standards were proclaimed. In a decadent and increasingly chaotic land these straws of stability were eagerly grasped by the people.

As the rebellion gathered momentum, it swept over an enormous area of eastern China in a little more than two years from the time of the village up-rising at Chin-t'ien to the capture of Nanking. The extraordinary successes of this revolution were due to its popular base and the superior military skill of its leaders. Encouraged by the fall of Nanking, the Taipings moved on the im-perial Manchu capital itself. But they never reached Peking. Their ill-armed but always courageous forces were repulsed at Tientsin in 1853, although they might easily have captured the capital had they sent an adequate army for the purpose. After two more years of sporadic fighting, the North China military expedition ended in May 1855. Meanwhile, from their celestial capi-tal at Nanking, Hung and Yang set up an administration that dominated the rich lower Yangtze valley. Social and land reforms, not as successful as their military efforts, were attempted by the rebels in the area they controlled. Their religious beliefs, based on a scanty and corrupt knowledge of Christian-ity, were adjusted to confrom to Chinese ethics and incorporated elements of Buddhism, Confucianism, and other beliefs, even though they destroyed Con-fucian tablets and Buddhist idols.

The new society proclaimed by the Taipings was more and more domin-ated by the illiterate Yang Hsiu-ch'ing, while Hung, as the third in the heaven-ly hierarchy after God and Jesus Christ, wrote books and documents from his seclusion in the palace at Nanking. This increasing dominance of Yang, who in his trances claimed to have direct communication with God, led to eventual disaster for the rebel movement. In 1856 Hung, jealous of Yang's challenge for power, had the brilliant general assassinated. An ensuing purge resulted in the elimination of all the original leaders of the movement and their replace-ment by a group of Hung's bootlicking sycophants. From idealism and auster-ity the Taipings deteriorated into corruption and inefficiency. Only the rise of an outstanding new military leader, Li Hsiu-ch'eng, kept the Taiping regime alive until 1864, when foreign elements entered the scene.

Before that happened, however, the imperial Ch'ing government was beset by other wars and rebellions. The fact that it eventually emerged intact as the national government is a remarkable tribute to its tenacity. Nearly every prov-ince was involved in one kind of rebellion or another. Chinese Moslems, beset by floods and famines, took over a large area between the Yellow and Huai rivers in 1853. Another rebellious military group called the Nien movement developed in 1856 and often cooperated with the Taipings. Other Chinese

Moslems in Yunnan province revolted and continued to give trouble for over a decade.

Meanwhile, in addition to the revolts and uprisings throughout the country, the Ch'ing government was again faced with foreign aggression. Despite the unsettled conditions trade went on—tea and silks were being exported; opium was still pouring into the country. The trade now, however, was through Shanghai and Foochow rather than Canton, where the exclusion of foreigners from the walled city was still a serious problem for Westerners. As early as 1847 the British had tried to force the issue with a naval raid up the river which, indeed, secured assurance (though it turned out to be only lip service) that the city would be opened in the future. After Perry's treaty opened Japan in 1854, the United States, Britain, and France all tried to negotiate new treaties with Peking. The hardening resistance of the Ch'ing government to further penetration by the West and a series of minor incidents, including an insult to the British flag and the execution of a French missionary, brought on the Anglo-French War with China.

A British naval force that sailed up the Pearl River to Canton in 1856 accomplished nothing. But in June 1858 a joint Anglo-French force went to Tientsin, where the negotiators for those countries secured treaties allowing their ministers to reside at Peking. Similar treaties were almost immediately consummated with the United States and Russia. The Chinese government soon changed its mind, however, and when plenipotentiaries arrived the next year they were not allowed to go to Peking. After four British gunboats were sunk trying to force the Taku forts, which controlled the sea approach to the capital, the ministers turned back.

The impasse did not last for long. In 1860 the British and French returned with powerful naval and military forces. The imperial army was defeated, the emperor fled, Peking was captured, and the summer palace, already looted, was ordered destroyed by Lord Elgin in retaliation for Chinese murders of the advance party. The Conventions of 1860 confirmed the 1858 treaties and wrung new concessions from the defeated Ch'ing government. Britain was ceded the Kowloon Peninsula opposite Hong Kong, while France obtained permission for Catholic missionaries to own property in the interior and indemnities for destroyed property. After the conclusion of these treaties all of China was open to Western penetration. The Russians pulled off a coup when they persuaded China to cede them the eastern coastal province of Manchuria, where Vladivostock had already been founded.

Hsien-feng, the anti-foreign emperor, died in August 1861 and his brother

Prince Kung, together with Tz'u-hsi, the dowager empress, took over the power for the new boy-emperor. They immediately turned their attention to improving foreign affairs and suppressing rebellion. A strong regional army of some seventy thousand men was built up and supplied with foreign arms. At Shanghai important help was given by a Western-officered mercenary force known as the "Ever Victorious Army," financed by merchants and led by the colorful Frederick Townsend Ward of Salem, Massachusetts. Technically, the Western powers were supposed to be neutral between the Chinese government and the Taiping forces, but after the rebels reached the outskirts of Shanghai in 1862, this pretense was abandoned. Ward, who had campaigned successfully, died in 1862 and was succeeded by the even more colorful Englishman, Charles George "Chinese" Gordon. Chinese government forces captured Nanking in July 1864 and the Taiping rebellion came to an end. Hung, the founder of the movement had already died, and Li Hsiu-ch'eng was executed.

Western participation now expanded to all parts of the empire. Both traders and missionaries penetrated the interior and other ports were opened. The importation of opium was at last legalized. China itself began its long struggle towards modernization.

Open China

China's new attitude toward foreigners was welcomed by the principal powers, Britain, France, Russia, and America. The British played a leading role in foreign matters including the domination of the foreign trade, which was conducted almost entirely in English. The new tariff agreements needed an efficient customs service and this was assured when an Englishman, Horatio Nelson Lay, was made inspector general of customs by Prince Kung in 1861. The imperial Maritime Customs Service, a remarkable organization further developed by Robert Hart, the second inspector general, lasted well into the twentieth century. The service's staff, headed by foreigners, about two thirds of whom were British, trained thousands of Chinese civil servants. The duties collected from merchants were turned over to the Chinese superintendents of customs at each port. But the customs service did more than collect tariffs; it suppressed smuggling, completed the charting of the China coast, erected aids to navigation, and became the most influential and stable link between foreign merchants and Chinese officials.

China's response to the opening to the West was unlike that of Japan, where a great surge of nationalism and energetic development, together with the adoption of occidental technology, turned the country into a modern state in a generation. China, a much larger and more populous country, still infused with Confucian ideals and standards, was much slower to respond; indeed there was a revival of Confucianism in the sixties. To be sure, arsenals and shipyards were established, mechanics were trained in machine shops, technical manuals and treatises were translated into Chinese, technical schools and mission schools turned out their graduates. But there was an inertia that the country could not rid itself of, and there was also a latent resentment against all foreigners. Most scholars and governmental officials, while recognizing the superiority of Western ships and arms, still felt there was little China needed from outside her borders.

But in spite of its national foot-dragging, China was drawn reluctantly and irrevocably into closer association with the rest of the world. Growth of the treaty ports was phenomenal; the Suez Canal, opened in 1869, brought western Europe closer to China than ever before; and in the early seventies the great cities of the East were tied to the world by telegraphic cable. Where modernization in Japan came with the speed of a rocket, in China it crawled at a snail-like pace through the remainder of the nineteenth and into the twentieth centuries.

China's lethargy left it more vulnerable than Japan to the imperialistic rivalry of European powers and the colonial expansionism that intensified after 1870. The peripheral areas of the empire began to melt away. Russia had already gotten the Manchurian coast and solidified its position in Central Asia. Burma was taken over by Britain. France, with planned imperialism, had made most of Indochina a colony by the mid-eighties and in the Sino-French War of 1833-85 took over North Vietnam (then called Tonkin) as well.

In 1894 and 1895 came the disastrous Sino-Japanese War, and China saw Korea, the Ryukyu Islands, Formosa, the Pescadores, and the Liaotung Peninsula pass to the island empire. In the ensuing scramble for concessions Germany obtained a lease of Kiaochow on the Shangtung Peninsula. Russia occupied Port Arthur in December 1897 and the following March obtained a twenty-five year lease of the city along with a good part of the Liaotung Peninsula. The intense Western rivalry in China following the Sino-Japanese War nearly broke up the empire. At the same time it resulted in many internal reforms by radical leaders who were supported by Emperor Kuang-hsü. The emperor attempted to put them into effect during the so-called Hundred Days between mid-June and mid-September 1898. These reforms threatened the position of thousands of established officials and a conservative reaction brought Dowager Empress Tz'u-hsi out of retirement. Backed by the military on September 21, 1898, she seized power in a coup d'etat, imprisoned the emperor in his palace, and took over again as regent. Several of the reformers were executed and others went into exile.

The Boxer Rebellion

The conservative reaction was accompanied by rising feelings against all foreigners. Hatred of missionaries and their Christian converts grew in intensity. Resentment over the European powers' seizure of ports, shame at the defeat by Japan, opposition to the construction of railroads, and a growing fear that China would be dismembered and parceled out among the foreign powers brought a hardening attitude. All of these feelings were intensified by severe floods and famine in 1898.

The vehicle for expelling the barbarians turned out to be a secret society, with a military organization, called "Righteous and Harmonious Fists," translated as Boxers. This fanatical group, encouraged by the empress, believed they possessed supernatural powers and were impervious to bullets. Although their mission was to destroy all foreigners, the missionaries and their converts were particular targets, for anti-Christian hostility was on the rise.

Westerners began to receive serious annoyance from the Boxers in 1899 and by the following year Chinese Christians were being massacred and missionaries endangered. Foreigners were aware of the danger to their legations at Peking and in June 1900 an international body of troops attempted to go there from Tientsin but were forced back. The foreigners did, however, capture the Taku forts.

The Boxers considered this an act of warfare, attacked the foreign concessions at Tientsin, and besieged the foreign diplomatic legations and Chinese Christians in Peking. On June 13 the Boxers massacred Chinese Christians in the capital and burned foreign buildings. The German minister was killed on June 20. Throughout the country missionaries and other foreigners were killed and Chinese Christians slaughtered. The besieged members of the legations in Peking, who were facing starvation, organized themselves to resist. An international force relieved Tientsin on July 14 and fought its way into Peking exactly a month later.

The emperor and court departed, and the dowager empress fled Peking in disguise in a peasant cart. The Boxers had already pretty well looted the city and Western troops finished the job.

In 1901, after long negotiations, the foreign powers reached a settlement, considerably moderated by American influence, with China. The announced protocol included various apologies, punishments, and indemnities, destruction of the Taku forts, amendments of the existing treaties, and numerous other points. This protocol following the Boxer Rebellion put one more nail in the coffin lid of old China. The Russo-Japanese War of 1904-05, fought largely on Manchurian soil, left China weaker in that province and replaced Russian influence there with Japanese, as well as establishing virtually a common border with Japan by the latter's consolidation of power in Korea.

Both Emperor Kuang-hsü and the dowager empress died within a few hours of each other on November 15, 1908. An infant, Hsüan-t'ung, inherited the throne under a weak regency. In October 1911, a revolution broke out which overthrew the Ch'ing dynasty and on February 12, 1912, the young emperor abdicated. Thus over two thousand years of imperial rule came to an end. At this point we leave modern China as the Republic of Sun Yat-sen takes over in, at last, a rising tide of nationalism.

An Anglo-Japanese alliance, signed in January 1902, further increased Japan's international clout in the Far East. The rising military power of the island empire was encouraged by Britain, with whom an alliance was signed, to offset Russian encroachments on China in Manchuria. Japan had special interests in this province as in Korea, where she was given a free hand.

Even more emphatically than in the Sino-Japanese War of 1894-95, Japan showed the extent of the military and naval muscle it had so quickly built up by spectacularly defeating a major European power in the Russo-Japanese War of 1904-05. Following the Treaty of Portsmouth in September 1905, Russia gave up claim to sovereignty in Manchuria and Japan took over the Russian lease of the Liaotung Peninsula and acquired the southern half of Sakhalin. Japan was now the equal of any Western imperialist power. Moving swiftly, Japan made Korea a protectorate in 1905 and, after ruthlessly putting down all Korean nationalistic resistance, in 1910 annexed the country as a colonial province called Chosen. Japan successfully continued its imperialist policy until its defeat in World War II.

The remarkable difference in the effects of massive Western cultural influence on the two great empires of the Far East is interesting, for it reflects the very deep differences between the traditional attitudes of the countries and the personalities of their people. Of all the Asiatic peoples, the Japanese most eagerly welcomed Europeans in the sixteenth century. In the next century the shoguns' fear of aggressive missionary activity by the Portuguese Jesuits, and the increasing influence of their converts, brought about their expulsion and the closing of the country until Commodore Perry's day. But once again exposed to Western influence, the Japanese exhibited the same curiosity and welcomed the superior technology in military, industrial, and other fields as enthusiastically as they had greeted the Portuguese hundreds of years before. Trade, diplomacy, and Western science soon followed. That a feudal country could so quickly take on all the external manifestations of a modern Western state is one of the most extraordinary and remarkable transformations in history.

China, on the other hand, always considered itself self-sufficient. The arrogant self-esteem of the celestial empire remained impervious to occidental missionary, diplomatic, and commercial pressure. China needed nothing from the barbarians and they were never welcomed. Only by force and intimidation did the West slowly penetrate the huge and populous country. Furthermore, as China painfully absorbed many of the superficial aspects of Western culture these elements became sinicized. No other country in the world has the assimilative capacity of China. Whatever was adopted became changed. Most recently, through Communism, the Russians hoped to bring the vast resources of the most populous nation on earth into their orbit. But they opened a Pandora's box and China has made its Communism Chinese. Again this ancient civilization regards the world with an aloof exclusiveness reminiscent of the imperial dynasties. There is still an almost unbridgeable chasm between the civilizations of China and the West.

As the world moved into the last quarter of the twentieth century, European civilization had completely inundated its surface. The largest single geographical feature of the earth—the Pacific Basin—has, as we have seen, not escaped the consequences. Indeed, so massive, so traumatic, swift and so all pervading was the sweep of Western civilization that every shore lapped by its waters and every island dotting its surface was affected, engulfed, or changed in a relatively brief period of time. The full weight of the impact fell in the nineteenth century and the twentieth has inherited its legacy.

Neolithic Pacific islanders were quickly overwhelmed; older Asiatic civilizations only slowed the impetuous surge of a technology so superior that its eventual imposition was inevitable. China, Japan, the Philippines, and Southeast Asia have all been transformed. Japan, remade by Western contact and imitating its teachers impeccably, reached a peak of imperialism scarcely ever equaled in a similar length of time, and then, suffering a crushing defeat in World War II, underwent a remarkable reconstruction and recovery. China, torn for years by rebellion and political discord, suffering from flood and famine, strained by overpopulation and a stumbling economy, after two world wars and a world depression emerged once again as a nation, united by Communist revolution and assuming a place among the world's great powers.

For better or for worse the irreversible impact of the West has changed the Pacific, changed East Asia, modified the lives of diverse peoples throughout the area who would not turn back the clock if they could. But the result has been a mixed blessing. Death, destruction, disease, alcohol, opium, gunpowder, cruelty, disruption, even the atomic bomb, have followed in the wakes of Western ships. Old gods have vanished and new ones have frequently had indifferent success. Ancient arts have disappeared or become corrupt. But these things have been accompanied too by modern medicine, education, sanitation, frequently higher living standards, and increased production of both agricultural products and consumer goods. Science and Mammon have crowded ceremonies and philosophical contemplation into the background. The ubiquitous roar of the jet has forever drowned the scream of the sacrificed warrior and disturbed the peace of little silken ladies strolling with mincing steps beneath the willow trees.

Sources and Notes

Bibliography

Sources and Notes

PART I. THE PACIFIC ISLANDS

Chapter 1. The Great New Ocean

For Magellan's Pacific contacts I have relied on R. A. Skelton's translation of Antonio Pigafetta, *Magellan's Voyage: A Narrative Account of the First Circumnavigation*. *The European Discovery of America: The Southern Voyages, A.D. 1492-1616* by Samuel Eliot Morison contains the most recent and best modern account of the Magellan voyage. Information about the indigenous inhabitants of the various Pacific islands may be found in several standard references, but is perhaps best summarized in Douglas Oliver's *The Pacific Islands* and in William Howells's *The Pacific Islanders*.

    1. See Pigafetta, *Magellan's Voyage*, I, 60, for this quotation and the one in the following paragraph.
    2. *Ibid.*
    3. *Ibid.*, p. 61.
    4. Oliver, *The Pacific Islands*, p. 24.
    5. Peter H. Buck, *Vikings of the Sunrise*, pp. 10-11.

Chapter 2. The Claw of the Devil

The late sixteenth and early seventeenth century voyages of Quiros are published in the excellent Hakluyt Society volumes of Sir Clements Markham, *The Voyages of Pedro Fernandez de Quiros, 1595 to 1606*. For the best account of the voyages of Quiros and Mendaña, as well as of all voyages of Pacific exploration through Cook and Bougainville, see John C. Beaglehole's *The Exploration of the Pacific*.

    1. Markham, *The Voyages of Pedro Fernandez de Quiros, 1595 to 1606*, I, 41.
    2. *Ibid.*, p. 43.
    3. *Ibid.*, p. 75.
    4. Beaglehole, *The Exploration of the Pacific* (Stanford, 1966), p. 182.
    5. John Hawkesworth, *An Account of the Voyages . . . for Making Discoveries in the Southern Hemisphere*, I, 481.

6. *Ibid.*, p. 485.

7. Louis Antoine de Bougainville, *A Voyage Round the World*, p. 241.

Chapter 3. Paradise Found

The definitive Hakluyt Society edition of Cook's voyages, edited by John C. Beaglehole, is by far the best reference for these great expeditions. Bougainville's voyage has much to say about the young Tahitian whom he brought to Paris, and George Keate's two works listed in Part I of the Bibliography tell the story of the unfortunate Prince Lee Boo. For the hundred years of Pacific exploration from Cook's third voyage through the *Challenger* expedition see Ernest S. Dodge, *Beyond the Capes*.

1. Beaglehole, *Journals of Cook*, I, 75.

2. *Ibid.*, I, 99.

3. *Ibid.*, I, 101.

4. *Ibid.*, I, 171.

5. *Ibid.*, I, 387-388.

6. *Ibid.*, III, 263.

7. Bougainville, *Voyage*, p. 262.

8. *Ibid.*, p. 266.

9. Beaglehole, *Journals of Cook*, II, 428.

10. *Ibid.*, III, lxxxv.

11. *Ibid.*, II, 951.

12. *Ibid.*, III, lxxxvii.

13. James Boswell, *The Ominous Years*, p. 311.

14. Keate, *An Account of the Pelew Islands*, p. 342.

15. Nathaniel Portlock, *A Voyage Round the World*, pp. 361-362.

Chapter 4. Island Harvests

There are excellent references describing the details of the various trades. F. W. Howay, "An Outline Sketch of the Maritime Fur Trade" is a good summary of that commercial activity. For general histories of fur traders in the Hawaiian Islands see Harold Whitman Bradley, *The American Frontier in Hawaii* and Ralph S. Kuykendall, *The Hawaiian Kingdom, 1778-1854*. The same two authors are also good general references for the Hawaiian sandalwood trade, and their bibliographies will lead one to many other sources. For the Fijian sandalwood trade see R. A. Derrick, *A History of Fiji*. The bêche-de-mer trade is described in E. S. Dodge, *New England and the South Seas*; and by Dodge, "Fiji Trader," and R. Gerard Ward, "The Pacific Bêche-de-mer Trade with Special Reference to Fiji," both in Ward, ed., *Man in the Pacific Islands*. The accounts of such traders as Edmund Fanning, *Voyages and Discoveries in the South Seas, 1792-1832*; Amasa Delano, *Narrative of Voyages and Travels in the Northern and Southern Hemispheres*; and Benjamin Morrell, *A Narrative of Four Voyages to the South Seas* give excellent examples of traders who shopped around in the various trades to fill out their cargoes.

1. John Ledyard, *Journal of Captain Cook's Last Voyage*, p. 70.

2. James Cook and James King, *A Voyage to the Pacific Ocean*, III, pp. 434-438.

Chapter 5. Whalers Ashore

The whaling industry has had many historians. Among the most reliable are Alexander Starbuck, whose *History of the American Whale Fishery* is indispensable, and William M.

Davis, whose *Nimrod of the Sea; or, the American Whaleman* presents the best economic history. Charles Wilkes's *Narrative of the United States Exploring Expedition* and R. G. Ward and E. S. Dodge's *American Activities in the Central Pacific, 1790-1870* contain a great deal of material relating to whaling in the Pacific. *The Last of the Logan*, edited by Harold W. Thompson, is a good example of the many personal accounts of voyages and adventures relating to the whale fishery.

1. Wilkes, *Narrative of the United States Exploring Expedition During the Years 1838, 1839, 1840, 1841, 1842*, V, 485.

2. Starbuck, *History of the American Whale Fishery From its Earliest Inception to the Year 1876*, p. 97.

3. *Ibid.*, p. 98n.

4. Wilkes, *Narrative*, V, 498.

5. Ward and Dodge, *American Activities in the Central Pacific, 1790-1870*, VII, 141.

6. *Ibid.*, pp. 134-139.

7. *Ibid.*, p. 112.

8. *Ibid.*, p. 154.

9. *Ibid.*, p. 19.

10. Daniel Wheeler, *Extracts from the Letters and Journal of Daniel Wheeler . . . of the Islands of the Pacific Ocean*, pp. 65-66.

11. *Ibid.*, p. 66.

12. *Ibid.*, p. 118.

13. *Ibid.*, p. 119.

14. Robert McNab, ed., *Historical Records of New Zealand*, I, 255.

15. *Ibid.*, pp. 257-258.

16. Thompson, ed., *The Last of the Logan*, p. 57.

17. Wilkes, *Narrative*, II, 399-400.

18. *Ibid.*, p. 374.

19. Dodge, *New England and the South Seas*, p. 39.

20. Robert W. Kenny, ed., *The New Zealand Journal, 1842-1844, of John B. Williams of Salem, Massachusetts*, p. 66.

21. McNab, ed., *Historical Records*, pp. 608-609, 663-666.

22. Starbuck, *American Whale Fishery*, p. 111n.

23. Davis, *Nimrod of the Sea*, p. 322.

24. *Ibid.*, p. 253.

25. *Ibid.*, p. 301.

Chapter 6. Save Thy Brother

The literature on missions and missionaries in the Pacific, especially biographies and letters, is voluminous. Those cited have been found most helpful, but many others have been used. The Spanish effort in Tahiti is fully given in Bolton G. Corney, *The Quest and Occupation of Tahiti*. Richard Lovett's *The History of the London Missionary Society, 1795-1895* is the most important single source for that great Pacific missionary endeavor.

1. Corney, *The Quest and Occupation of Tahiti by Emissaries of Spain During the Years 1772-1776*, I, 278-279.

2. *Ibid.*, II, 94-100.

3. *Ibid.*, II, 319-349.

4. *Ibid.*, III, 213.

5. James Montgomery, ed., *Journal of Voyages and Travels by the Rev. Daniel Tyerman and George Bennet, Esq.*, II, 109.

6. *Ibid.*, II, 110-111.

7. Lovett, *The History of the London Missionary Society, 1795-1895*, I, 339.

8. Aaron Buzacott, *Mission Life in the Islands of the Pacific*, pp. 236-245.

Chapter 7. Ceremonies and Conflicts

Official or other accounts were published of nearly every naval expedition sent out by the various Western governments from Captain Cook's time on. They are summarized in E. S. Dodge, *Beyond the Capes*. Those selected for quotation in this chapter are typical and illustrate the various situations that arose with contacts between naval officers and Pacific islanders.

1. William Bligh, *The Log of the Bounty* (London: Golden Cockerel Press, 1937), I, 381.

2. Bligh, *A Voyage to the South Sea*, pp. 65-66.

3. *Ibid.*, pp. 69-70.

4. George Vancouver, *A Voyage of Discovery to the North Pacific Ocean and Round the World*, I, 92.

5. *Ibid.*, I, 99. Because of the Tahitians' custom of changing their names, the first two monarchs, father and son, were both known to various explorers as Otoo or Tu and Pomare. In addition, as Bligh noted, Pomare I also called himself Tinah. For the sake of clarity, they have generally been referred to here as Pomare I (1797-1803) and Pomare II (1803-21). The succeeding rulers were Pomare III, a child (1821-27); Queen Pomare IV (1827-77); and Pomare V (1880-d.1891), who made over the kingdom to France the same year he became king.

6. *Ibid.*, I, 100.

7. *Ibid.*, I, 110-111.

8. *Ibid.*, I, 145.

9. *Ibid.*, II, 124.

10. *Ibid.*, II, 126-127.

11. *Ibid.*, II, 159-160.

12. A. J. von Krusenstern, *Voyage Round the World, in the Years 1803, 1804, 1805, & 1806*, I, 114-115.

13. *Ibid.*, I, 118-119.

14. Olive Wright, ed., *New Zealand, 1826-1827: From the French of Dumont D'Urville*, p. 125.

15. *Ibid.*, p. 129.

16. Wilkes, *Narrative*, III, 278.

17. *Ibid.*, III, 281.

18. *Ibid.*, III, 285.

19. *Ibid.*, III, 265.

Chapter 8. They Came to Do Good

Probably few subjects relating to the Pacific islands have been written about more frequently than the American missionaries in Hawaii. Their story has been told many times and is well known. Perhaps the most basic book on the subject is the *History of the Sandwich Islands Mission* by Rufus Anderson. The *Historical Sketch of the Missions of the American Board in the Sandwich Islands, Micronesia, and Marquesas* by S. C. Bartlett is also useful. *Protestant America and the Pagan World*, by Clifton Jackson Phillips; *The Hawaiian Kingdom, 1778-1854*, by Ralph S. Kuykendall; and *The American Frontier in Hawaii*, by Harold Whitman Bradley, are good modern sources with extensive bibliographies on the subject.

Chapter 9. Botany Bay

There are many histories of Australia giving the well-known information of the country's founding. Several have been consulted but I have found A. Wyatt Tilby, *Australasia*, and C. Hartley Grattan, *The Southwest Pacific To 1900*, especially useful. The classic accounts of the establishment of the New South Wales convict colony are those of Arthur Phillip, *The Voyage of Governor Phillip to Botany Bay*, and John Hunter, *An Historical Journal of the Transactions at Port Jackson and Norfolk Island. The Convict Ships, 1787-1868* by Charles Bateson contains the most information on the vessels. For the Tahitian pork trade I have relied largely on that most comprehensive account in H. E. Maude, *Of Islands and Men*. Maude's study of beachcombers and their way of life in the same volume has also been very helpful.

1. Hunter, *An Historical Journal*, p. 134.
2. Thomas Dunbabin, *The Making of Australasia*, p. 112.
3. McNab, ed., *Historical Records of New Zealand*, I, 521-530.

Chapter 10. Pakeha and Maori

The general historical events recounted in this chapter are well known and are dwelt on, at least to some extent, in every history of New Zealand. I have found the following especially helpful: *The Cambridge History of the British Empire*, vol. VII, part II, *New Zealand*; Keith Sinclair, *A History of New Zealand*; W. P. Morrell and D. O. W. Hall, *A History of New Zealand Life*; A. W. Shrimpton and A. E. Mulgan, *Maori and Pakeha* (Auckland N.Z., London: Whitcombe & Tombs, 1921); and the works of A. J. Harrop, particularly his *England and the Maori Wars* (Freeport, N.Y.: Books for Libraries Press, 1971).

1. Marsden's journal in McNab, ed., *Historical Records of New Zealand*, I, 334-335.
2. *Ibid.,* p. 359.
3. Charles Darwin, *Narrative of the Surveying Voyages of His Majesty's Ships* Adventure *and* Beagle, III, 577.
4. Wilkes, *Narrative*, II, 382-383.
5. Sir Apirana Ngata, *The Treaty of Waitangi*.

Chapter 11. Traders and Blackbirders

Dorothy Shineberg's book, cited below, is the most complete and thorough study of the Melanesian sandalwood trade. The classic account of the labor traffic, written by a participant, is William T. Wawn's *South Sea Islanders and the Queensland Labour Trade*, first published in London, 1893, and recently reprinted. Another contemporary account, recently published, is W. E. Giles, *A Cruize in a Queensland Labour Vessel to the South Seas*, edited by Deryck Scarr. The viewpoint of one who tried to regulate the traffic will be found in *Kidnapping in the South Seas, Being a Narrative of a Three Months' Cruise of H.M. Ship Rosario*, by Captain George Palmer. *The Western Pacific and New Guinea*, by Hugh H. Romilly, contains an interesting chapter, "The Old Labour Trade." Modern studies may be found in R. A. Derrick, *A History of Fiji*; John M. Ward, *British Policy in* the *South Pacific (1786-1893)*; Owen W. Parnaby, *Britain and the Labor Trade in the Southwest Pacific*, and his "The Labour Trade" in *Man in the Pacific Islands*, edited by R. Gerard Ward; Deryck Scarr, "Recruits and Recruiters," in *Pacific Islands Portraits*, edited by J. W. Davidson and Deryck Scarr; and Peter Corris, "'Blackbirding' in New Guinea Waters, 1883-84," in *Journal of Pacific History* (1968).

1. Shineberg, *They Came for Sandalwood*.

2. E. S. Armstrong, *The History of the Melanesian Mission*, pp. 120-124.

3. Wawn, *The South Sea Islanders and the Queensland Labour Trade* (1973 ed.), p. 436.

Chapter 12. From Confusion to Colonies

There are several very good books giving in great detail the history of European and American diplomacy in the Pacific. Most useful have been: *International Rivalry in the Pacific Islands, 1800-1875*, by Jean I. Brookes; *The Southwest Pacific To 1900*, by C. Hartley Grattan; *Britain in the Pacific Islands*, by W. P. Morrell; *British Policy in the South Pacific*, by John M. Ward; and *America in the Pacific*, by Foster R. Dulles. Also helpful for this chapter have been: *The Pacific Dependencies of the United States*, by John W. Coulter; *Colonialism, Development and Independence*, by H. C. Brookfield; *Russia's Hawaiian Adventure, 1815-1817*, by Richard A. Pierce; and *The United States and the Hawaiian Kingdom*, by Merze Tate.

Chapter 13. Exploitation

The following books have been particularly useful in writing this chapter: *Ocean Island and Nauru, Their Story*, by Albert F. Ellis; *King Cane: The Story of Sugar in Hawaii*, by John W. Vandercook; *Fiji*, by Sir Alan Burns; *The French Pacific Islands*, by Virginia Thompson and Richard Adloff; and the four-volume *Pacific Islands*, published by the Royal Navy's Naval Intelligence Division.

Chapter 14. Change and Life

Some of the information in this chapter is based on personal observation and much is general knowledge gleaned from the modern literature. Particularly helpful have been: A. Grenfell Price, *The Western Invasions of the Pacific and Its Continents*; R. Gerard Ward, ed., *Man in the Pacific Islands*; Douglas L. Oliver, *The Pacific Islands*; Felix M. Keesing, *The South Seas in the Modern World*; C. Hartley Grattan, *The Southwest Pacific Since 1900*; Austin Coates, *Western Pacific Islands*; and the eleventh edition of the *Pacific Islands Year Book*, edited by Judy Tudor.

PART II. EAST ASIA

Chapter 15. The Road to Cathay

The most helpful sources for this chapter are Henry Yule's classic works *Cathay and the Way Thither* and *The Book of Ser Marco Polo, the Venetian*; and William W. Rockhill's *The Journey of William of Rubruck to the Eastern Parts of the World, 1253-55*. Nigel Cameron's *Barbarians and Mandarins* is a valuable and well-written compilation.

Chapter 16. To Cathay by Sea

A number of works were read and referred to for this chapter, but the most useful were C. R. Boxer, *The Portuguese Seaborne Empire, 1415-1825*, and Kenneth Scott Latourette, *A History of Christian Missions in China*. A delightful book on one of the later great Jesuits is *Guiseppe Castiglione: A Jesuit Painter at the Court of the Chinese Emperors* by Cécile and Michel Beurdelay. The reader might also refer to other volumes in this series, including *Foundations of the Portuguese Empire, 1415 to 1580* by Bailey Diffie and George Winius and *Rival Empires of Trade in the Orient, 1600-1800* by Holden Furber.

Chapter 17. Competitors of Portugal

The many scholarly studies of C. R. Boxer, especially *The Portuguese Seaborne Empire* and *The Dutch Seaborne Empire*, and those of J. H. Parry, particularly *The Spanish Seaborne Empire* and *Trade and Dominion*, have been most helpful. Among numerous other reference works should also be mentioned *Nusantara: A History of the East Indian Archipelago*, by Bernard H. M. Vlekke, and *Asian Trade and European Influence in the Indonesian Archipelago Between 1500 and About 1630*, by M. A. P. Meilink-Roelofsz, as well as several books on the East India Company listed in the Bibliography.

Chapter 18. Barbarians All

In addition to the reference works cited in the previous chapter, the following have been invaluable: C. R. Boxer's *Fidalgos in the Far East, 1550-1770*, *The Christian Century in Japan, 1549-1650*, *The Great Ship from Amacon, 1555-1640*, and *Jan Compagnie in Japan, 1600-1850*; G. B. Sansom, *The Western World and Japan*; and Edwin O. Reischauer and John K. Fairbank, *East Asia: The Great Tradition*. The Principal reference for the English episodes is *The Voyage of Captain John Saris to Japan, 1613*, by Ernest M. Satow.

1. Boxer, *Fidalgos in the Far East, 1550-1770*, pp. 269-271. Boxer lists fifteen years, all in the last half of this period, when no voyage was recorded.
2. Boxer, *The Great Ship From Amacon*, p. 165.

Chapter 19. The China Trade

The literature on the time and subjects covered in this chapter is enormous and many works have been referred to. Essential are the works of Hosea Ballou Morse, including *The Chronicles of the East India Company Trading to China, 1635-1834*, and *The International Relations of the Chinese Empire*. Russia's early relations with China are well covered in Clifford M. Foust, *Muscovite and Mandarin: Russia's Trade With China and Its Setting, 1727-1805*. Some of the most useful books on the late eighteenth and nineteenth century China trade include: *The "Fan Kwae" at Canton Before Treaty Days, 1825-1844*, and *Bits of Old China*, both by William C. Hunter; *Prelude to Hongkong* by Austin Coates; *Foreign Mud* by Maurice Collis; and *The Old China Trade* by Foster R. Dulles. A different perspective on the Opium War will be found in *The Opium War Through Chinese Eyes* by Arthur Waley.

Chapter 20. Eastern Impact on the West

Good general background is provided in the enormously informative *Asia in the Making of Europe*, Volume II, by Donald F. Lach. Hugh Honour's *Chinoiserie* and Gertrude Z. Thomas's *Richer Than Spices* are excellent works about the oriental influence on European fashion. Chinese export porcelain is well covered in three authoritative books: *China-Trade Porcelain* by John G. Phillips; *Chinese Export Porcelain for the American Trade, 1785-1835*, by Jean N. Mudge; and *Oriental Lowestoft* by J. A. Lloyd Hyde.

Other articles are expertly covered in Carl L. Crossman's invaluable book *The China Trade*.

Chapter 21. The Revival of China Missions

The single most important reference for this chapter is Kenneth Scott Latourette's classic *History of Christian Missions in China*. Other works of considerable usefulness include: *The History of the London Missionary Society, 1795-1895*, by Richard Lovett; *Protestant America and the Pagan World* by Clifton Jackson Phillips; and *Peter Parker and the Opening of China* by Edward V. Gulick.

1. Latourette, *A History of Christian Missions in China*, p. 281.

Chapter 22. No More the Forbidden Kingdom

G. B. Sansom's *The Western World and Japan* offers the best introductory study of Japan and the West. The basic book for Perry's opening of Japan is the official *Narrative of the Expedition of an American Squadron to the China Seas and Japan* by Francis L. Hawks. *Black Ships off Japan* by Arthur Walworth, and *"Old Bruin": Commodore Matthew C. Perry, 1794-1858*, by Samuel Eliot Morison, are excellent books in a rather extensive literature on the subject. Manjiro's story is well presented in *Voyager to Destiny* by Emily V. Warinner. Much has been written on the Boston men in Japan, and extensive references will be found in *Fenollosa: The Far East and American Culture* by Lawrence W. Chisholm. Van Wyck Brooks's essay, *Fenollosa and His Circle*, is an excellent short account on the subject. Dorothy Wayman's *Edward Sylvester Morse* provides a biography of its subject.

Chapter 23. The Final Impact

The best overall modern history of China, Japan, and other parts of the Far East, covering both domestic and international aspects of these countries, is *East Asia: The Modern Transformation* by John K. Fairbank, Edwin O. Reischauer, and Albert M. Craig. S. Y. Teng, *The Taiping Rebellion and the Western Powers*, covers that important episode admirably. *Britain, China, and the Antimissionary Riots, 1891-1900* by Edmund S. Wehrle describes this restless period in some detail. The excellent bibliographies in these works will lead the reader into the very extensive literature on China in the late nineteenth and early twentieth centuries.

Selected Bibliography

PART I. THE PACIFIC ISLANDS

Anderson, Rufus. *History of the Sandwich Islands Mission*. Boston: Congregational Publishing Society, 1870.

Armstrong, E. S. *The History of the Melanesian Mission*. London: Isbister, 1900.

Bartlett, S. C. *Historical Sketch of the Missions of the American Board in the Sandwich Islands, Micronesia, and Marquesas*. Boston: American Board, 1878.

Bateson, Charles. *The Convict Ships, 1787-1868*. Glasgow: Brown, Son & Ferguson, 1959.

Beaglehole, John C. *The Exploration of the Pacific*. 3rd ed. Stanford: Stanford University Press, 1966.

————, ed. *The Journals of Captain James Cook on His Voyages of Discovery*. Hakluyt Society Publications, extra series, vols. 34-36. Cambridge: At the University Press for the Hakluyt Society, 1955, 1961, 1967.

Beardsley, Charles. *Guam, Past and Present*. Rutland, Vt.: Charles E. Tuttle, 1964.

Bligh, William. *A Voyage to the South Sea . . .* London, 1972.

Boswell, James. *The Ominous Years*. New York: McGraw-Hill, 1963.

Bougainville, Louis Antoine de. *A Voyage Round the World, Performed by Order of His Most Christian Majesty, in the Years 1766, 1767, 1768, and 1769*. Trans. John Reinhold Forster. London: J. Nourse, 1772.

Bradley, Harold Whitman. *The American Frontier in Hawaii: The Pioneers, 1789-1843*. Stanford: Stanford University Press, 1942.

Brookes, Jean Ingram. *International Rivalry in the Pacific Islands, 1800-1875*. Berkeley: University of California Press, 1941.

Brookfield, H. C. *Colonialism, Development and Independence: The Case of the Melanesian Islands in the South Pacific*. Cambridge: Cambridge University Press, 1972.

Bryan, Edwin H., Jr. *American Polynesia and the Hawaii Chain*. Honolulu: Tongg, 1942.

Buck, Peter H. (Te Rangi Hiroa). *Vikings of the Sunrise*. New York: Stokes, 1938.

Burns, Sir Alan. *Fiji*. London: H.M.S.O., 1963.

Buzacott, Aaron. *Mission Life in the Islands of the Pacific*. London: J. Snow, 1866.

Chapman, J. K. *The Career of Arthur Hamilton Gordon, First Lord Stanmore, 1829-1912.* Toronto: University of Toronto Press, 1964.

Clark, Thomas B. *Omai, First Polynesian Ambassador to England.* Honolulu: University of Hawaii Press, 1969.

Coates, Austin. *Western Pacific Islands.* London: H.M.S.O., 1970.

Cook, Captain James, and Captain James King. *A Voyage to the Pacific Ocean. Undertaken, by the Command of His Majesty for Making Discoveries in the Northern Hemisphere . . . In the Years 1778, 1779, and 1780.* 3 vols. London, 1784.

Corney, Bolton G. *The Quest and Occupation of Tahiti by Emissaries of Spain During the Years 1772-1776.* 3 vols. London: Hakluyt Society, 1913, 1915, 1919.

Corris, Peter. "'Blackbirding' in New Guinea Waters, 1883-84," *Journal of Pacific History,* 3:85-105 (1968).

Coulter, John Wesley. *The Pacific Dependencies of the United States.* New York: Macmillan, 1957.

Darwin, Charles. *Narrative of the Surveying Voyages of His Majesty's Ships* Adventure *and* Beagle . . . , vol. III. London: H. Colburn, 1839.

Davidson, J. W., and Deryck Scarr. *Pacific Islands Portraits.* Canberra: Australia National University Press, 1970.

Davis, William M. *Nimrod of the Sea; or, The American Whaleman.* New York: Harper, 1874.

Delano, Amasa. *Narrative of Voyages and Travels, in the Northern and Southern Hemispheres* . . . Boston, 1817.

Derrick, R. A. *A History of Fiji.* Suva: Government Press, 1957.

Dodge, Ernest S. *Beyond the Capes: Pacific Exploration from Captain Cook to the Challenger, 1776-1877.* Boston: Little, Brown, 1971.

————. "Early American Contacts in Polynesia and Fiji," *Proceedings of the American Philosophical Society,* vol. 107, no. 2 (April 1963).

————. "Fiji Trader," *Proceedings of the Massachusetts Historical Society,* vol. 78 (1966).

————. *New England and the South Seas.* Cambridge, Mass.: Harvard University Press. 1965.

Dorsett, Edward Lee. "Hawaiian Whaling Days," *American Neptune,* 14:42-46 (1954).

Dulles, Foster R. *America in the Pacific.* Boston: Houghton Mifflin, 1932.

Dunbabin, Thomas. *The Making of Australasia.* London: A. & C. Black, 1922.

Dunmore, John. *French Explorers in the Pacific.* 2 vols. Oxford: Clarendon Press, 1965, 1969.

Ellis, Albert F. *Ocean Island and Nauru, Their Story.* Sydney: Angus and Robertson, 1935.

Fanning, Edmund. *Voyages and Discoveries in the South Seas, 1792-1832.* Salem: Marine Research Society, 1924.

Giles, W. E. *A Cruize in a Queensland Labour Vessel to the South Seas,* ed. Deryck Scarr. Honolulu: University of Hawaii Press, 1968.

Grattan, C. Hartley. *The Southwest Pacific To 1900.* Ann Arbor: University of Michigan Press, 1963.

————. *The Southwest Pacific Since 1900.* Ann Arbor: University of Michigan Press, 1963.

Hawkesworth, John. *An Account of the Voyages Undertaken by the Order of His Present Majesty for Making Discoveries in the Southern Hemisphere.* 3 vols. London: W. Strahan and T. Cadell, 1773.

Hohman, Elmo P. *The American Whaleman.* New York: Longmans, Green, 1928.

Howay, F. W. *A List of Trading Vessels in the Maritime Fur Trade, 1785-1825*, ed. Richard A. Pierce. Kingston, Ont.: Limestone Press, 1973.

———. "An Outline Sketch of the Maritime Fur Trade," *Canadian Historical Association, Annual Report.* 1932.

Howells, William. *The Pacific Islanders.* New York: Scribner, 1973.

Hunter, John. *An Historical Journal of the Transactions at Port Jackson and Norfolk Island . . .* London, 1793.

Keate, George. *An Account of the Pelew Islands, situated in the Western Part of the Pacific Ocean; Composed from the Journals and Communications of Captain Henry Wilson, and Some of his Officers, who, in August 1783, were there Shipwrecked, in The Antelope, a Packet Belonging to the Honourable East India Company.* 5th ed. London, 1803.

[Keate, George]. *The History of Prince Lee Boo, a Native of the Pelew Islands Brought to England, by Capt. Wilson.* Philadelphia, 1802.

Keesing, Felix M. *The South Seas in the Modern World.* New York: John Day, 1941.

Kenny, Robert W. "Yankee Whalers at the Bay of Islands," *American Neptune*, 12:22-44 (1952).

———, ed. *The New Zealand Journal, 1842-1844, of John B. Williams of Salem, Massachusetts.* Salem: Peabody Museum, 1956.

Krusenstern, A. J. von. *Voyage Round the World, in the Years 1803, 1804, 1805, & 1806 . . .* Trans. Richard Belgrave Hoppner. 2 vols. London, 1814.

Kuykendall, Ralph Simpson. *The Hawaiian Kingdom, 1778-1854.* Honolulu: University of Hawaii Press, 1947.

Ledyard, John. *Journal of Captain Cook's Last Voyage to the Pacific Ocean, and in Quest of a North-West Passage, Between Asia & America; Performed in the Years 1776, 1777, 1778, and 1779.* Hartford: N. Patten, 1783.

Lovett, Richard. *The History of the London Missionary Society, 1795-1895.* 2 vols. London: Henry Froude, 1899.

Luke, Sir Harry. *Islands of the Pacific.* London: George G. Harrap, 1962.

McNab, Robert. *The Old Whaling Days: A History of Southern New Zealand From 1830 to 1840.* Wellington: Whitcombe & Tombs, 1913.

———, ed. *Historical Records of New Zealand*, vol. I. Wellington: John McKay, 1908.

Markham, Sir Clements, ed. *The Voyages of Pedro Fernandez de Quiros, 1595 to 1606.* Hakluyt Society Publications, 2nd series, vols. 14, 15. London: Hakluyt Society, 1904.

Martin, K. L. P. *Missionaries and Annexations in the Pacific.* London: Oxford University Press, 1924.

Maude, H. E. *Of Islands and Men: Studies in Pacific History.* Melbourne: Oxford University Press, 1968.

Meares, John. *Voyage Made in the Years 1788 and 1789 From China to the North West Coast of America.* London, 1790.

Mendaña, Alvoro de. *The Discovery of the Solomon Islands by Alvoro de Mendaña in 1568*, ed. Lord Amherst of Hackney and Basil Thomson. Hakluyt Society Publications, 2nd series, vols. 7, 8. London: Hakluyt Society, 1901.

Metge, Joan. *The Maoris of New Zealand.* New York: Humanities Press, 1967.

Montgomery, James, ed. *Journal of Voyages and Travels by the Rev. Daniel Tyerman and George Bennet, Esq. . . . Between the Years 1821 and 1829.* 2 vols. London: F. Westley & A. H. Davis, 1831.

Moorehead, Alan. *The Fatal Impact: An Account of the Invasion of the South Pacific, 1767-1840*. London: Hamish Hamilton, 1966.

Morison, Samuel E. *The European Discovery of America: The Southern Voyages, A.D. 1492-1616*. New York: Oxford University Press, 1974.

Morrell, Benjamin. *A Narrative of Four Voyages to the South Seas . . .* New York, 1832.

Morrell, W. P. *Britain in the Pacific Islands*. Oxford: Clarendon Press, 1960.

————, and D. O. W. Hall. *A History of New Zealand Life*. Christchurch: Whitcomb and Tombs, 1957.

Ngata, Sir Apirana. *The Treaty of Waitangi: An Explanation*. Wellington: Published for the Maori Purposes Fund Board, 1922.

Oliver, Douglas. *The Pacific Islands*. Rev. ed. New York: Doubleday, Anchor Book, 1961 (2nd printing, corrected, 1962).

Pacific Islands. Geographical Handbook Series. Royal Navy, Naval Intelligence Division. 4 vols. 1939-45.

Pacific Islands Year Book, 11th ed. Ed. Judy Tudor. Sydney: Pacific Publications, 1972.

Palmer, Captain George. *Kidnapping in the South Seas, Being a Narrative of a Three Months' Cruise of H.M. Ship Rosario*. Edinburgh: Edmonston and Douglas, 1871.

Parnaby, Owen W. *Britain and the Labor Trade in the Southwest Pacific*. Durham, N.C.: Duke University Press, 1964.

Phillip, Arthur. *The Voyage of Governor Phillip to Botany Bay*. London: J. Stockdale, 1789.

Phillips, Clifton Jackson. *Protestant America and the Pagan World: The First Half Century of the American Board of Commissioners for Foreign Missions, 1810-1860*. Harvard East Asian Monographs, no. 32. Cambridge, Mass.: Harvard University Press, 1969.

Pierce, Richard A. *Russia's Hawaiian Adventure, 1815-1817*. Berkeley: University of California Press, 1965.

Pigafetta, Antonio. *Magellan's Voyage: A Narrative Account of the First Circumnavigation*, trans. and ed. R. A. Skelton. New Haven: Yale University Press, 1969.

Portlock, Nathaniel. *A Voyage Round the World . . . in 1785, 1786, and 1788 . . .* London, 1789.

Price, A. Grenfell. *The Western Invasions of the Pacific and Its Continents*. Oxford: Clarendon Press, 1963.

Quinby, George I. "Hawaiians in the Fur Trade of North-west America, 1789-1820," *Journal of Pacific History*, 7:92-103 (1972).

Robertson, George. *The Discovery of Tahiti*, ed. Hugh Carrington. Hakluyt Society Publications, 2nd series, vol. 98. London: Hakluyt Society, 1948.

Romilly, Hugh Hastings. *The Western Pacific and New Guinea*. London: John Murray, 1887.

Rose, J. H., A. P. Newton, and E. A. Benians. *The Cambridge History of the British Empire*, vol. VII, part II: *New Zealand*. Cambridge: At the University Press, 1933.

Shineberg, Dorothy. *They Came for Sandalwood: A Study of the Sandalwood Trade in the South-West Pacific, 1830-1865*. Carlton, Victoria: Melbourne University Press, 1967.

Sinclair, Keith. *A History of New Zealand*. London: Oxford University Press, 1961.

Smith, Bernard. *European Vision and the South Pacific, 1768-1850*. Oxford: The University Press, 1960.

Starbuck, Alexander. *History of the American Whale Fishery from its Earliest Inception to the Year 1876*. Washington: G.P.O., 1878.

Tate, Merze. *The United States and the Hawaiian Kingdom: A Political History.* New Haven: Yale University Press, 1965.

Thompson, Harold W., ed. *The Last of the Logan: The True Adventures of Robert Coffin Mariner in the Years 1854 to 1859* . . . Ithaca, N.Y.: Cornell University Press, 1941.

Thompson, Laura. *Guam and Its People.* San Francisco: American Council, Institute of Pacific Relations, 1942.

Thompson, Virginia, and Richard Adloff. *The French Pacific Islands: French Polynesia and New Caledonia.* Berkeley: University of California Press, 1971.

Tilby, A. Wyatt. *The English People Overseas,* vol. V: *Australasia.* Boston: Houghton Mifflin, 1912.

Vancouver, George. *A Voyage of Discovery to the North Pacific Ocean and Round the World* . . . 3 vols. London, 1798.

Vandercook, John W. *King Cane: The Story of Sugar in Hawaii.* New York: Harper, 1939.

Ward, John M. *British Policy in the South Pacific (1786-1893).* Sydney: Australasian Publishing, 1948.

Ward, R. Gerard, ed. *Man in the Pacific Islands.* Oxford: Clarendon Press, 1972.

————, and Ernest S. Dodge. *American Activities in the Central Pacific, 1790-1870.* 8 vols. Ridgewood, N.J.: Gregg Press, 1966-67.

Wawn, William T. *The South Sea Islanders and the Queensland Labour Trade.* London: 1893. Ed. Peter Corris, Honolulu: University of Hawaii Press, 1973.

Wheeler, Daniel. *Extracts From the Letters and Journal of Daniel Wheeler* . . . *of the Islands of the Pacific Ocean* . . . Philadelphia: Joseph Rakestraw, 1840.

Wilkes, Charles. *Narrative of the United States Exploring Expedition During the Years 1838, 1839, 1840, 1841, 1842.* 5 vols. Philadelphia: Lea & Blanchard, 1845.

Williams, John. *A Narrative of Missionary Enterprises in the South Sea Islands.* London: J. Snow, 1837.

Wilson, James. *A Missionary Voyage to the Southern Pacific Ocean, Performed in the Years 1796, 1797, 1798, in the Ship Duff.* London, 1799.

Worcester, Dean C. *The Philippine Islands and Their People.* New York: Macmillan, 1899.

Wright, Olive, ed. *New Zealand, 1826-1827: From the French of Dumont D'Urville.* Wellington: Printed by the Wingfield Press for Olive Wright, 1950.

PART II. EAST ASIA

Barr, Pat. *The Coming of the Barbarians: A Story of Western Settlement in Japan, 1883-1870.* London: Macmillan, 1967.

Beurdelay, Cécile and Michel. *Guiseppe Castiglione: A Jesuit Painter at the Court of the Chinese Emperors.* Rutland and Tokyo: Tuttle, 1971.

Boxer, C. R. *The Christian Century in Japan, 1549-1650.* Berkeley: University of California Press, 1951.

————. *The Dutch Seaborne Empire, 1600-1800.* London: Hutchinson, 1965.

————. *Fidalgos in the Far East, 1550-1770: Fact and Fancy in the History of Macao.* The Hague: Nijhoff, 1948.

————. *The Great Ship From Amacon: Annals of Macao and the Old Japan Trade, 1555-1640.* Lisbon: Centro de Estudos Historicos Ultramarinos, 1959.

————. *Jan Compagnie in Japan, 1600-1850.* The Hague: Nijhoff, 1950.

————. *The Portuguese Seaborne Empire, 1415-1825.* London: Hutchinson, 1969.

————, ed. *South China in the Sixteenth Century*. London: Hakluyt Society, 2nd Series, No. 106, 1953.

Brooks, Van Wyck. *Fenollosa and His Circle*. New York: E. P. Dutton, 1962.

Burnell, A. C., and P. A. Tiele, eds. *The Voyage of John Huyghen van Linschoten to the Indies*. 2 vols. London: 1885.

Cameron, Nigel. *Barbarians and Mandarins: Thirteen Centuries of Western Travelers in China*. New York and Tokyo: Walker/Weatherhill, 1970.

Chisholm, Lawrence W. *Fenollosa: The Far East and American Culture*. New Haven: Yale University Press, 1963.

Coates, Austin. *Prelude to Honkong*. London: Routledge & Kegan Paul, 1966.

Collis, Maurice. *Foreign Mud*. London: Faber and Faber, 1946.

————. *The Great Within*. London: Faber and Faber, 1941.

Costin, W. C. *Great Britain and China, 1833-1860*. Oxford: Clarendon Press, 1937 (reprint, 1968).

Crossman, Carl L. *The China Trade*. Princeton: Pyne Press, 1972.

Dulles, Foster R. *The Old China Trade*. Boston and New York: Houghton Mifflin, 1930.

Fairbank, John K., Edwin O. Reischauer, and Albert M. Craig. *East Asia: The Modern Transformation*. Boston: Houghton Mifflin, 1965.

Foster, William. *The Embassy of Sir Thomas Roe to the Court of the Great Mogul, 1615-1619*. 2 vols. London, 1899.

————. *England's Quest of Eastern Trade*. London: A. & C. Black, 1933.

————. *The Voyage of Sir Henry Middleton to the Moluccas 1604-1606*. London: Hakluyt Society, 1943.

————. *The Voyages of Sir James Lancaster*. London: Hakluyt Society, 1940.

Foust, Clifford M. *Muscovite and Mandarin: Russia's Trade with China and Its Setting, 1727-1805.* Chapel Hill: University of North Carolina Press, 1969.

Furber, Holden. *John Company at Work*. Cambridge, Mass.: Harvard University Press, 1948.

Glamann, Kristof. *Dutch-Asiatic Trade: 1620-1740*. Copenhagen: Danish Science Press; The Hague: Martinus Nijhoff, 1958.

Greenberg, Michael. *British Trade and the Opening of China, 1800-1892*. Cambridge: University Press, 1951 (reprint, 1969).

Gulick, Edward V. *Peter Parker and the Opening of China*. Cambridge, Mass.: Harvard University Press, 1973.

Hao, Yeh-P'ing. *The Comprador in Nineteenth Century China: Bridge Between East and West*. Cambridge: Harvard University Press, 1970.

Hawks, Francis L. *Narrative of the Expedition of an American Squadron to the China Seas and Japan, Performed in the Years 1852, 1853, and 1854, Under the Command of Commodore M. C. Perry, United States Navy*. 3 vols. Washington, 1856.

Holt, Edgar. *The Opium Wars in China*. London: Putnam, 1964.

Honour, Hugh. *Chinoiserie: The Vision of Cathay*. London: John Murray, 1961.

Hunter, W. C. *Bits of Old China*. London: Kegan Paul, Trench, 1855.

————. *The "Fan Kwae" at Canton Before Treaty Days, 1825-1844*. London: Kegan Paul, Trench, 1882.

Hurd, Douglas. *The Arrow War: An Anglo-Chinese Confusion, 1856-1860*. London: Collins, 1967.

Hyde, J. A. Lloyd. *Oriental Lowestoft, Chinese Export Porcelain, Porcelaine de al Cie des Indes*. Newport, Monmouthshire: Ceramic Book Co., 1964.

Lach, Donald F. *Asia in the Making of Europe*. 2 vols. Chicago: University of Chicago Press, 1965, 1970.

Latourette, Kenneth Scott. *The Chinese, Their History and Culture*. New York: Macmillan, 1946.

——. *A History of Christian Missions in China*. New York: Macmillan, 1932.

Lattimore, Owen and Eleanor. *Silks, Spices and Empire*. New York: Delacorte Press, 1968.

Lovett, Richard. *The History of the London Missionary Society, 1795-1895*. 2 vols. London: Henry Froude, 1899.

Meilink-Roelofsz, M. A. P. *Asian Trade and European Influence in the Indonesian Archipelago Between 1500 and About 1630*. The Hague: Nijhoff, 1962.

Morison, Samuel Eliot. *"Old Bruin": Commodore Matthew C. Perry, 1794-1858*. Boston: Little Brown, 1967.

Morse, H. B. *The Chronicles of the East India Company Trading to China, 1635-1834*. 5 vols. Oxford: Clarendon Press, 1926-29.

——. *In the Days of the Taipings*. Salem: Essex Institute, 1927.

——. *The Gilds of China*. London: Longmans, Green, 1909.

——. *The International Relations of the Chinese Empire*. 3 vols. London: Longmans, Green, 1910, 1918.

Mudge, Jean M. *Chinese Export Porcelain for the American Trade 1785-1835*. Newark, Delaware: University of Delaware Press, 1962.

Nievhoff, John. *An Embassy from the East India Company of the United Provinces to the Grand Tartar Chan, Emperor of China*. Trans. John Ogelby. London, 1669.

O'Connor, Richard. *Pacific Destiny*. Boston: Little, Brown, 1969.

Orange, James. *The Chater Collection: Pictures Relating to China, Hongkong, Macao, 1655-1860*. London: Thornton Butterworth, 1924.

Parkinson, C. Northcote. *Trade in the Eastern Seas, 1793-1813*. Cambridge: At the University Press, 1937.

Parry, John H. *The Age of Reconnaissance*. Cleveland: World, 1963.

——. *Europe and a Wider World, 1415-1715*. London: Hutchinson University Library, 1949. Republished as *The Establishment of the European Hegemony, 1415-1715*, New York: Harper and Row, Harper Torchbook, 1961.

——. *The Spanish Seaborne Empire*. New York: Knopf, 1966.

——. *Trade and Dominion: The European Oversea Empires in the Eighteenth Century*. London: Weidenfeld and Nicolson, 1971.

Penrose, Boies. *Travel and Discovery in the Renaissance, 1420-1620*. Cambridge, Mass.: Harvard University Press, 1952.

Philips, C. H. *The East India Company, 1784-1834*. Manchester: Manchester University Press, 1961.

Phillips, Clifton J. *Protestant America and the Pagan World: The First Half Century of the American Board of Commissioners For Foreign Missions, 1810-1860*. Cambridge, Mass.: Harvard University Press, 1969.

Phillips, John G. *China-Trade Porcelain*. Cambridge, Mass.: Harvard University Press, 1956.

Preble, George Henry. *The Opening of Japan*. Norman: University of Oklahoma Press, 1962.

Prestage, Edgar. *The Portuguese Pioneers*. London: A. & C. Black, 1933.

Pritchard, Earl H. *The Crucial Years of Early Anglo-Chinese Relations, 1750-1800*. Pullman, Wash.: State College of Washington, 1936.

Reischauer, Edwin O., and John K. Fairbank. *East Asia: The Great Tradition*. Boston: Houghton Mifflin, 1960.

Rockhill, William Woodville. *The Journey of William of Rubruck to the Eastern Parts of the World, 1253-55*. Hakluyt Society Publications, 2nd series, vol. 4. London: Hakluyt Society, 1900.

Rowse, A. L. *The Expansion of Elizabethan England*. London: Macmillan, 1955.

Sansom, G. B. *The Western World and Japan*. London: Crescent Press, 1950.

Satow, Ernest M. *The Voyage of Captain John Saris to Japan, 1613*. London: Hakluyt Society, 1900.

Schurz, William L. *The Manila Galleon*. New York: E. P. Dutton, 1939.

Selby, John. *The Paper Dragon: An Account of the China Wars, 1840-1900*. New York: Praeger, 1968.

Spence, Jonathan. *To Change China: Western Advisers in China, 1620-1960*. Boston: Little, Brown, 1969.

Staunton, Sir George. *An Authentic Account of an Embassy from the King of Great Britain to the Emperor of China*. London: G. Nicol, 1797.

Sykes, Sir Percy. *The Quest for Cathay*. London: A. & C. Black, 1936.

Tang, Ta-Kong. *U.S. Diplomacy in China 1844-1860*. Seattle: University of Washington Press, 1964.

Temple, R. C. *The Travels of Peter Mundy, in Europe and Asia, 1608-1667*. Vol. III, Parts I, II. London: Hakluyt Society, 1919.

Teng, S. Y. *The Taiping Rebellion and the Western Powers*. Oxford: The Clarendon Press, 1971.

Thomas, Gertrude Z. *Richer than Spices*. New York: Alfred A. Knopf, 1965.

Vlekke, Bernard H. M. *Nusantara: A History of the East Indian Archipelago*. Cambridge, Mass.: Harvard University Press, 1943.

Waley, Arthur. *The Opium War Through Chinese Eyes*. London, George Allen & Unwin, 1958.

Walworth, Arthur. *Black Ships Off Japan*. New York: Alfred A. Knopf, 1946.

Warinner, Emily V. *Voyager to Destiny*. New York-Indianapolis: Bobbs-Merrill, 1956.

Wayman, Dorothy. *Edward Sylvester Morse*. Cambridge, Mass.: Harvard University Press, 1942.

Wehrle, Edmund S. *Britain, China, and the Antimissionary Riots, 1891-1900*. Minneapolis: University of Minnesota Press, 1966.

Wilbur, Marguerite Eyer. *The East India Company and the British Empire in the Far East*. New York: Richard R. Smith, 1945.

Wright, Mary Clabaugh, ed. *China in Revolution: The First Phase, 1900-1913*. New Haven and London: Yale University Press, 1968.

Yule, Henry. *The Book of Ser Marco Polo, the Venetian*. 2 vols. London: John Murray, 1875.

——. *Cathay and the Way Thither*. Hakluyt Society Publications, 1st series, vols. 36, 37. London: Hakluyt Society, 1866.

Index

Index

345

DATE DUE

GAYLORD			PRINTED IN U.S.A.